Managing Intelligence

A Guide for Law Enforcement Professionals

Managing Intelligence

A Guide for Law Enforcement Professionals

John Buckley

CRC Press
Taylor & Francis Group
Boca Raton   London   New York

CRC Press is an imprint of the
Taylor & Francis Group, an **informa** business

CRC Press
Taylor & Francis Group
6000 Broken Sound Parkway NW, Suite 300
Boca Raton, FL 33487-2742

© 2014 by Taylor & Francis Group, LLC
CRC Press is an imprint of Taylor & Francis Group, an Informa business

No claim to original U.S. Government works

Version Date: 20130524

ISBN 13: 978-1-4665-8642-0 (pbk)

Library of Congress Cataloging-in-Publication Data

Buckley, John, 1961-
  Managing intelligence : a guide for law enforcement professionals / John Buckley.
    pages cm
  Includes bibliographical references and index.
  ISBN 978-1-4665-8642-0
  1. Knowledge management. 2. Electronic surveillance. 3. Law enforcement. I. Title.

HD30.2.B835 2013
363.2068'4--dc23   2013014923

Visit the Taylor & Francis Web site at
http://www.taylorandfrancis.com

and the CRC Press Web site at
http://www.crcpress.com

Contents

3   Understanding Intelligence   49

4   Human Rights, Legislation, and Ethics   81

Foreword

As president of the International Association of Law Enforcement Intelligence Analysts (IALEIA), I had the pleasure of meeting John at an IACP conference in Chicago a few years ago. We hit it off straight away, trading our Associations' book for his, entitled *The Human Source Management System*. Of course it didn't hurt that I needed some muscle to help move boxes, and, ever the gentleman, John was quick to assist a damsel in distress. It became apparent to me very early on that John is a brilliant and thought-provoking individual and our conversations regarding analysis, intelligence-led policing, and intelligence management are always rife with healthy debate. He always encourages me to articulate my opinions and thoughts and questions my beliefs and, despite that annoying trait, we have remained friends ever since.

When John asked me to write this foreword and sent his manuscript of *Managing Intelligence* for me to read, I felt like the book had been written for me. In my 26 years of experience in law enforcement, I have worked in some very proactive modern thinking units and some not-so-forward thinking. After reading the book, I can see that often the success of an Intelligence Unit is tightly linked to how well the Intelligence Unit is managed. It's not rocket science, but it does require knowledge, experience, proper tools, common language, and a well-executed plan.

In my travels as president of IALEIA, I have had the pleasure of meeting and speaking with analysts, intelligence officers, and intelligence managers from all over the world, from agencies at all levels of government. Through these conversations, I have come to realize several constant themes, including the misuse or under utilization of analysts, the lack of understanding the difference between analytical and intelligence products, and the need for a clear understanding of intelligence-led policing that fits with the model implemented in any agency.

In this new book, John hits on all of these topics and several other provocative themes. But more than that, he doesn't just write about the management of intelligence, rather he points out past mistakes, includes examples, and provides ideas for actual implementation of his ideas. I would encourage anyone who is working in the field of intelligence to read it. John writes in a way that is passionate and insightful. He asks hard questions, but more importantly, he provides possible answers. His use of humor and metaphors makes what can sometimes be very very dry material interesting and applicable.

Despite being compared to a pig (I won't give it away, but it's Chapter 8), I finished reading the book feeling both understood and confident that if given the opportunity, I could change the world, or at least my Intelligence Unit. At the very least, I have a guidebook to follow.

Jenny Johnstone
President
International Association of Law Enforcement Intelligence Analysts

About the Author

John Buckley served over 28 years as a police officer working mainly in the intelligence and counterterrorism arena.

John is the author of two other books: *The Human Source Management System: The Use of Psychology in the Management of Human Intelligence Sources* and *Invest Now or Pay Later: The Management of Risk in Covert Law Enforcement*. John consults and delivers training on an international basis to a wide range of agencies. Some of them even bring him back a second time!

John can be contacted at info@hsmtraining.com. Offer him a plane ticket and a case of beer and he is pretty much yours!

Acknowledgments

This book could not have been completed without the support and contribution of many people. I would like to thank all those that I have worked with over the years that have guided me toward a better understanding of what "managing intelligence" should be about. There are many in law enforcement I would love to name specifically, but such is the nature of their work that their contribution, as always, must remain in the shadows for that is the nature of the business.

Most importantly, I want to thank my dad for continually harping on at me to keep writing—we all need a bit of "harping" to keep us focused but... maybe not every day!

I am grateful to Patrick Monro of Monro Design for providing the graphics, and Chris Westphal and the staff at Visual Analytics Inc, Maryland, for use of the analytical diagrams, a few views taken from their excellent product. I want to thank all the staff at CRC Press and diacriTech for their assistance in publishing the book.

I want to thank my good friend Dawn Starling for the hours during which she was subjected to an endless stream of thoughts on intelligence management, as we wandered the roads of America. Her guidance and insight were so often a cure for my incoherent ramblings. I thank Sonia Sasseville for her help with the chapter on analysis, and Jenny Johnstone for agreeing to write the Foreword and not to forget that they prove the point I raise later about analysts—both are pretty damn cute! I cannot fail but to acknowledge the assistance of my little New Jersey friend, Erin Mirra Moloney. For all her work with a "very ugly baby," a big thank you is needed.

For everyone I have forgotten to mention—well you know me by now. It was not intentional, it is who I am!

And finally for my inspiration, who I am not supposed to mention, so I will not.

The Concept of Managing Intelligence

1

Facts do not cease to exist because they are ignored.

Aldous Huxley

1.1 Introduction

Beginning with the theme of "facts" and Huxley's quote, we will state a few more simple facts: First, if you are a member of a law enforcement agency (LEA), you are likely to have an interest in how well your agency is managing intelligence; second, if you take a long hard look, you will probably find it is not doing that well; and finally, the failings are probably being ignored. The reader may ask "On what evidence are such judgmental statements made?" To which the reply would be "Observation, experience, and the researching of stories that appear in the media on a daily basis, where law enforcement has made often serious errors in managing intelligence." Looking at their own agency, the reader may already be aware of many failings in regard to intelligence management. Alternatively, the reader may be sure that their agency is managing intelligence as effectively as any agency could do, which would then beg the question: "If one agency can do it right, then why are so many getting it wrong and often so badly wrong?" The reasons are many and include a lack of understanding, a lack of knowledge, but probably most often blindness (sometimes willful) to the fact that there may be problems. If we don't look, we won't see and if we do look, our eyes are often clouded by self-delusion. There are often powerful motivators within law enforcement to ignore what we know to be there, including a lack of sufficient power to change things for many, a reluctance to enter into the inevitable conflict that merely suggesting change brings, or quite simply a belief that there is insufficient finance to make the necessary changes. Of course, the reader may just be reading this book without any personal involvement in law enforcement and they will have the benefit of perusing the content with an unbiased eye, as getting rid of one's historic "baggage" is often a significant part in looking at anything afresh. And just in case the reader is from the military or the intelligence community seeking the opportunity to gloat over how badly their colleagues in law enforcement do things—similar problems are present in their agencies. So now that we are all suitably annoyed, depressed, or whatever, we can start to move forward.

The fact that you are reading this provides fairly strong indicators that you have some of the essential qualities for effective intelligence management: an open mind, the desire to learn "new stuff," and the fact that you aren't plagued with the affliction that affects many potentially good intelligence officers—the "I already know everything" syndrome.

So what is this book about? Working as a law enforcement officer for a long time (probably too long), the author was fortunate to work with people who knew a lot about information gathering. That knowledge had been built up over a prolonged period under very trying circumstances. These were good police officers, smart people with great dedication and some with very clever ideas. But they also made mistakes, and sometimes bad things happened as a result. As with all aspects of life, there was significant learning to be had from both successes and mistakes. And some things are harder to learn than others. Some lessons were never learned or at least the learning was never acknowledged. For the author, perhaps the most disappointing thing is that many of the lessons that were learned were never shared and have now been forgotten or, more accurately, left for the next generation to relearn, with the inevitable cost of doing so. It can be safely said that law enforcement personnel are not the most proficient at knowledge management—a matter we will discuss in greater detail later in this chapter. Hopefully, this brings us to the origins of this book and what it seeks to achieve.

Undoubtedly, within law enforcement, military, and intelligence services, in many parts of the world, there is a huge amount of good practice being used with regard to intelligence management, but there are also many people involved in the business who have an inadequate knowledge of what intelligence management is about. This is understandable as members are often limited by the nature and size of the agency they work for, limited by the training that is available to them, and limited by a shortage of literature from which to develop their skills. Unfortunately, in recent years there have been a lot of misunderstandings created about what intelligence management is. Among the more pervasive of fallacies are, first, an overreliance on what is commonly referred to as "open source" intelligence, and the belief that all one needs is a computer and access to the Internet and the bad guys will post what their intentions are. Second, the belief that as long as you have software to trawl through your own databases, miraculously you will find there what the bad guys intend to do next. Surprisingly enough, both these misguided beliefs are all too readily perpetuated by software manufacturers and other protagonists in the commercial sector. Undoubtedly, there is place for both these elements within the intelligence business area, but, as we will argue later, there is so much more to intelligence management than either of these two aspects. The readiness with which some accept these solutions at face value points to the need for a greater understanding of intelligence in all its facets.

Acknowledging that there are several good books on intelligence analysis, there is an extremely limited amount of material that starts with the basics and then discusses all aspects of the intelligence business in a "law enforcement" context, the context being of significant relevance. What this book seeks to provide is a sort of idiot's* guide, for want of a better term, for both beginners and for those who are smart enough to realize there is always more to learn, and a book that is specifically aimed at law enforcement.

1.2 Readers and Readership

The book is intended to be read from the beginning to the end, starting with more simple aspects of intelligence management and building to a more complex picture. That said, it is also meant to act as a work of reference, where readers can return at a later stage and refresh their knowledge on certain aspects. There are parts of the book that some readers may disagree with. This is not surprising given that intelligence management is not an exact science. There are many different ways of doing things, and inevitably practitioners will have different views of what is the "right" way to do things. Without delving too deeply into to a semantic argument, it is necessary to start by saying that there are many right ways and also quite a few wrong ways of managing intelligence. This book will provide the reader with ways that will work. This book will describe how and why they work. The methods described will be "right" in that they will be effective, legal, and ethical. They will also be tried and tested. The book will also touch on some of the "wrong" ways to do things. There are many opportunities in intelligence management to waste resources or to behave in an unethical or unlawful manner. Having said all that, at the end of the day, it is up to the readers to decide for themselves the methods they choose to use.

This book is primarily aimed at members of police agencies regardless of the nature of their agency. It is recognized that intelligence is managed in policing agencies of varying sizes and agencies that are carrying out diverse roles. There are also many "nonpolice" agencies that carry out law enforcement function and that require effective intelligence management structures. In addition, there are an increasing number of private sector organizations that have a need for intelligence management. Those nonpolice agencies that may find interest in the methods discussed include the following:

- Customs
- Border security
- Environmental agencies

* The sort that the idiot writing this book wishes he had had, many years ago.

- Fraud investigation units within insurance companies
- Investigators of social welfare benefit fraud
- Brand enforcement/counterfeit goods investigators, working within the commercial sector
- Local government bodies with investigative powers, such as food/health standards investigators
- Tax fraud investigators
- Retail security and loss prevention departments
- Gambling/betting commissions

This is a far from a comprehensive list and the number of agencies involved in working with intelligence is worth consideration by those involved in policing from the following two perspectives:

- There are many government agencies that may already be investigating people who are the subject of a police investigation. The tentacles of crime often stretch out in many diverse directions. If the right data sharing agreements are in place, much can be obtained from these agencies.
- While conducting covert information gathering operations, the potential to come across another agency, working the same target, is significant. This has implications for officer safety. It also has the potential for one agency to compromise the investigation of another.

The structures outlined in this book will address both these issues.

1.3 Purpose

The rationale behind the book is as follows:

- To provide law enforcement with a better understanding of intelligence management
- To add to the body of knowledge in regard to the management of intelligence
- To capture the key points of what has been written in relation to the management of intelligence, with particular regard to its application in a law enforcement environment
- To address some of the legal and ethical considerations in intelligence management
- To clarify many of the ambiguities surrounding intelligence management that have created difficulties for those directly or indirectly involved

- To dispel some of the myths that surround intelligence gathering held by the uninitiated, the misguided, and those that arguably should know better
- To provide a system for the effective management of intelligence in a law enforcement context, regardless of agency size or the jurisdiction in which they operate
- To provide an ethical and lawful framework in which information can be gathered and used effectively for intelligence purposes
- To identify to those who may be interested in those areas of intelligence management who would benefit from further research

Sherman Kent (1955), viewed by many in the United States as the father of intelligence analysis, commented on the importance of creating a body of literature regarding intelligence that would assist in developing intelligence management as a profession:

> Intelligence today is not merely a profession, but like most professions it has taken on the aspects of a discipline: it has developed a recognized methodology; it has developed a vocabulary; it has developed a body of theory and doctrine; it has elaborate and refined techniques. It now has a large professional following. What it lacks is a literature. From my point of view, this is a matter of greatest importance. As long as this discipline lacks a literature, its method, its vocabulary, its body of doctrine, and even its fundamental theory run the risk of never reaching full maturity.

It could be argued that there is little new contained in this book, but at least what is here is in one place, where practitioners can easily access key aspects of their profession. Hopefully, this first lesson won't be lost on those who want to manage intelligence effectively. How many LEAs can say *all* their intelligence is in one place?

1.4 What the Book Will Not Include

In the interests of managing expectations, it is perhaps worth taking a moment at this juncture to mention a few things that are not included in the book. First, as the book is intended for a broad readership, only the most general reference will be made to secret information gathering techniques. Intelligence practitioners are all too aware of the need to keep some techniques secret, or at least the methodology used in those techniques. For example, the fact that law enforcement uses undercover officers could hardly be regarded as secret, yet what remains, for the most part, hidden are the methods undercover officers use to gain the trust of the criminals that they seek to infiltrate. Even then, many of these methods have been played out in public, at some stage.

By comparison, for the most part, the methods used in processing information into intelligence are widely available in the public domain, and the processing of that information is largely the same, regardless of the technique used to gather the information in the first place. Discussion of these methods is not of a sensitive nature. Furthermore, the most common vulnerability for law enforcement is also not so sensitive that it is not up for discussion. This problem involves the processing of the information and the method of storing the resulting intelligence. Agencies sometimes obtain intelligence that is of such a sensitive nature that the agency's existing intelligence system cannot meet the required standards for security and/or where the agency's discovery/disclosure process for handing intelligence used in judicial proceedings is insufficient to protect the origin of the intelligence. Both these factors potentially lead to serious compromise. Unfortunately, computer hackers and defense lawyers have been all too successful in exploiting such weaknesses. Methods to combat such threats are discussed at length later.

Second, this book is not intended to be in the form of a comparative justice study of the various legislative requirements used in the intelligence management process. Nevertheless, it will draw on good practices from throughout the world. Much of the terminology used will make reference to the U.S. and U.K. legislation, policies, and procedures primarily, because both jurisdictions have invested heavily in progressing the concept of intelligence management. Having said that, no jurisdiction gets everything right all the time, and where good practice has been identified in any jurisdiction, it will be used. Of interest to the majority of readers will be the similarities in expectations that the public has, regarding the behavior of those involved in gathering information for intelligence purposes.

Third, although the book may, by way of example, examine some of the structures in place in specific jurisdictions for managing intelligence, it will not provide an in-depth critical view of each of these. This is because many are jurisdiction specific and some of those structures merely add to the general confusion that exists in managing intelligence. Where parts of these structures are useful, these parts will be included.

Fourth, the book will not address some "intelligence"-related functions, which may or may not be engaged in by intelligence agencies or the military in combat zones. In particular, there remains a significant debate in regard to actions used to obtain information from "unwilling" subjects. The debate over whether or not such activities are legal, ethical, or indeed effective will undoubtedly continue for many years to come. That said, such activities are not within the remit of law enforcement officers and are therefore excluded from this publication.*

---

* This is probably just the author ducking out of a "too difficult to do" discussion!

Fifth, the book will not provide your agency with the "perfect" solution for intelligence management. Whether such a beast exists or not is open to debate. No one solution fits every agency, and, in creating an intelligence management system, what may be desired is often constrained by internal issues and resource limitations. It is up to those within the agency to create a system, based on a solid foundation of good practice, which works for that agency, yet is capable of linking with partner agencies.

1.5 Intelligence: A Brief History with a Law Enforcement Focus

If we are to begin to understand something, then at the beginning is generally a good place to start. Therefore, it is to the origins of intelligence gathering that we first turn. Intelligence has been around for a long time. It has been described as *The Second Oldest Profession* (Knightley 1988) and at times probably gets as bad a reputation, if not a worse reputation than that as held by the "oldest" profession. It is mentioned in one form or another in many Greek fables and overquoted from a certain ancient Chinese text whose author's name seems to appear *ad infinitum* in every intelligence lecture and book on the subject since he penned it three millennia ago!* Somewhat strangely, reference to intelligence gathering is found in the Bible. Told in the Book of Joshua (Chapter 2.1), the story of how Joshua sent spies into Jericho prior to his attack on the city: "And Joshua the son of Nun sent out of Shittim two men to spy secretly, saying, 'Go view the land, even Jericho.' And they went, and came into a harlot's house, named Rahab, and lodged there." This was obviously a successful operation as Joshua went on to capture the city and in the manner of effective intelligence commanders rewarded Rahab for her services: "And the city shall be accursed, [even] it, and all that [are] therein, to the Lord: only Rahab the harlot shall live, she and all that [are] with her in the house, because she hid the messengers that we sent." All that said, it remains unclear as to how many present-day police commanders would view sending two officers to live with a "harlot" to obtain intelligence.†

As the centuries moved on, the use of intelligence in wars and in a national security context was commonplace. Queen Elizabeth I of England had her personal intelligence chief in the form of Francis Walsingham. Of interest to many will be allegations laid against Walsingham of entrapping people into situations where he could arrest them, lay charges against them,

---

* Sun Tzu: *The Art of War*—Everyone happy now? As an aside—take care with Sun Tzu quotes; there are many and varied translations and many of these become distorted to suit the circumstances under which they are quoted.

† It would probably be easy enough to find two officers who would undertake such an operation but difficult enough to find two who wouldn't mess it up!

and then have them beheaded. One such operation led to the beheading of Elizabeth's cousin Mary, Queen of Scots. This was probably not the first time that accusations of entrapment have been made against an intelligence officer and certainly will not be the last. Such allegations are commonplace to this day and should bring home, to everyone involved in the intelligence arena, the necessity for fully accountable methods of information gathering.

Information gathering has often been used by parties seeking national independence, who used spies to infiltrate the ruling nation. Both sides in the American War of Independence pitted spy against spy in the need to obtain better information about what the other side intended. One of the bloodiest confrontations from such spying activity came in Dublin in 1920 when Michael Collins, the then Chief of staff of the Irish Republican Army (IRA) (a terrorist grouping), having first infiltrated the British Intelligence system using informants, arranged for the killing of many people he had connected to British intelligence. On Sunday, November 21, 1920, the assassinations began with the IRA killing of 13 people linked to British intelligence and this action was followed by reprisals that culminated in a total number of deaths for that day being 31, including unconnected civilians killed in follow-up operation while attending a football game. Aptly named "Bloody Sunday" and while just another bad day in Ireland, there are many lessons to be learned from it for those involved in intelligence management.

It is with the advent of two world wars that intelligence management, as it is now widely recognized, came into being. Part of the advancement came about as a direct result of advances in technology and in particular the radio, which made it much easier to rapidly transmit information, often over long distances, from those gathering it on the ground to those assessing and responding to it. It is during this period and in particular the post–World War II that many of the modern-day intelligence agencies came into being. The rising tensions during the Cold War period meant that those involved on both sides of the divide invested significantly in the development of information gathering methods. It is on these agencies, and the methods they used, that much of the practice now followed by law enforcement has been based. Unfortunately, many of the methods developed by these intelligence agencies do not always translate well to either the post–cold war problems that exist now in relation to national security or the law enforcement context. James Woolsey, the former director of the Central Intelligence Agency, commenting on the fall of the Soviet Union and the changing intelligence picture articulated his thoughts on the situation:

> We have slain a large dragon, but we now live in a jungle filled with a bewildering variety of poisonous snakes. And, in many ways, the dragon was easier to keep track of.

The very nature of this "jungle" is that law enforcement officers have found themselves right in the middle of the battle with many of the "poisonous snakes." Many of the problems for law enforcement officers stem directly back to where their "knowledge" of intelligence management has originated—the military, and intelligence services. The problem with taking tactics designed in one area and using them in another is that there are many differences in the reasons for the collection of intelligence and in the function that intelligence has to perform for each of these business areas. Adding to the design discrepancies is the problem of miscommunication of concepts—ideas are not always conveyed effectively. Furthermore is the fact that relationships between intelligence agencies and law enforcement are not always as professional as the public deserve. Highlighting some of these internecine disputes between law enforcement and the "IC" (intelligence community), Mike Bayer, a branch Chief in the Diplomatic Security Service of the U.S. Department of State, remarks, "Out of undue regard for certain concerns, Law Enforcement and the IC have repeatedly stymied one another. Law enforcement invokes privacy concerns and investigative case secrecy to protect its information. The IC invokes 'sources and methods' to protect its capabilities" (Bayer 2007). Bayer's comments are hardly unique to the United States and are indicative of some of the potential causes for the apparent difficulty law enforcement has in developing intelligence management processes to meet its specific needs.

To try and add some degree of understanding as to the differences in using intelligence in a "law enforcement" context and using it in an "intelligence agency" or "military" context is like comparing apples, oranges, and pears, where the "oranges" represent law enforcement intelligence management and the "apples and pears" the other two disciplines. Table 1.1 illustrates the similarities and the differences between these three contexts.

Before continuing to address these issues with regard to law enforcement, it would be an oversight not to mention a further problem—that of the influence of the business community in relation to "intelligence." There is significant interest on the part of the private sector in relation to intelligence management. However, law enforcement should not allow its requirements or what the private sector dictates as good practice in such aspects of intelligence management as analysis. It is a different game with different rules, and to return to the fruit analogy—it's tomatoes!

Law enforcement needs oranges. It needs to create intelligence management methods, processes, and systems that are designed to meet their needs and are within law enforcement budgetary constraints. Some have made the argument that intelligence in law enforcement is "new" and while acknowledging that some countries and some LEAs have been slower to the table than others, to say intelligence management is new is an incorrect reflection of the situation with some LEAs across the world. Intelligence has been part of the U.K. policing for over a century, and in 1893 the Special Irish Branch was set up in the London Metropolitan Police to gather intelligence relating to the

Table 1.1   Apples, Pears, and Oranges and Intelligence Management

Apples, Pears, and Oranges	Intelligence Management
They are all fruits.	Intelligence management in all three disciplines is fundamentally similar.
Any fruit is good for you.	All intelligence management techniques have validity.
They are all seeded fruits.	There are some close similarities between the three disciplines.
They all taste nice! What do the differences matter?	While the taste matter is a subjective judgment, many practitioners in the other disciplines fail to make the distinction that what is right for them may not be right for law enforcement.
All three working together make a nice fruit cocktail.	There are times when it is necessary for all three disciplines to work together.
I want to make orange juice.	Law enforcement does not need many of the products that are required by military and intelligence services.
I can't afford apples and pears. Oranges are cheaper and do what I need.	Many of the resources used for military and intelligence services are way beyond the budget of law enforcement regardless of department size.
We don't have oranges—you're getting apples and pears.	In many jurisdictions, there has been insufficient investment in the creation of knowledge around intelligence management in law enforcement; therefore, law enforcement is forced to take what it can get.
We all manage with apples and pears. They work out great for us. Why would you want oranges?	Many of those involved in intelligence receive their training through academies/universities where the majority of training on intelligence relates to the objectives of military and/or intelligence agencies. This means that the standpoint of the intelligence community and the military with regard to intelligence continues to be promulgated. This problem is not helped by the lack of written work on law enforcement intelligence management.

threat from terrorism originating from Ireland. So, even when it comes to counterterrorism, intelligence is not a "new" discipline for law enforcement.

In the United Kingdom, structured intelligence management has been a common factor in policing for well over 20 years, and intelligence-led policing has been national policy for over 11 years. It could be argued that law enforcement, within the United Kingdom, was forced to adopt a more proactive attitude to intelligence because of the major threat posed to its citizens by terrorist organizations such as the IRA. Undoubtedly, the highly coordinated nature of the U.K. policing, the limited number of police agencies, and the significant central oversight also contributed to best practice being readily promulgated. Unfortunately, if truth were told, many of the problems that are discussed in this book are still prevalent in the United Kingdom. Acknowledging this does not detract from the fact that many LEAs in other countries have been very slow to adopt the tried and true methods developed in the United Kingdom that have been proven effective.

Specifically, where huge lessons can be learned from the U.K. circumstances is in the efforts of law enforcement, military, and intelligence agencies in dealing with the terrorist campaigns in Northern Ireland, continuing from the late 1960s to the present day. Much of what was learned in dealing with the terrorist organizations in that context easily translates to any law enforcement strategy to defeat terrorism and/or organized crime. Undoubtedly, many mistakes were made by law enforcement, but the success of all involved in intelligence gathering must be acknowledged. At the time that the mainstream IRA and the various "loyalist" (Protestant-based) terrorist organizations moved away from campaigns of violence to more political campaigns, law enforcement with the assistance of the military and intelligence services was thwarting four out of five intended terrorist attacks—surely proof that something was being done right. All the terrorist organizations were heavily penetrated, and with many of their more experienced members serving lengthy prison sentences the internal pressures to desist from violence became significant. To add to this, international intelligence–based strategies had significantly disrupted the supply of weapons and moves to mitigate terrorist financing had left the IRA all but bankrupt.

Ireland is not the only place where notable successes have been achieved through intelligence work. Intelligence agencies in Israel have had significant results in penetrating organizations that pose a threat to their national security, efforts that unfortunately, as with the situation in Ireland, have been somewhat overshadowed by related controversies. Canadian law enforcement has had notable success in addressing the criminality stemming from organized motorcycle gangs, and the United States can claim significant success from the intelligence that led to the identification of the hiding place of Osama bin Laden and other Al Qaeda and Taliban leaders.

Before finishing this brief summary of the history of intelligence management, it is worth drawing attention to situations where gathering intelligence on citizens by law enforcement has far exceeded any democratic remit. One only has to look at the excesses of many "policing" and intelligence agencies in the former Soviet Bloc countries, or in many countries where dictators currently hold power, to realize that the powers given to law enforcement need to be used wisely. It is essential for any agency gathering information on its citizens to have in place robust checks and balances with regard to under what circumstances the agency can gather such information. LEAs exist to protect the rights of citizens, not to disavow them of those rights.

There is learning in both the successes and the mistakes that have been made by intelligence agencies and law enforcement through the years. The most significant problem has been the failure to share with other LEAs all the knowledge that has been learned and to further develop methods as fully as possible that make intelligence management more effective.

1.6   Is There a Lack of Knowledge?

Despite the tragic events of 9/11 and other similar attacks in Mumbai, Madrid, and London, law enforcement has drawn significant criticism for its failure to develop adequate intelligence management systems. These criticisms are only compounded if one was to consider the vast sums of money that have been invested, in particular in the United States, in the hope of developing a more integrated approach to intelligence. From a U.S. perspective, perhaps one of the most valid critiques that could be made is that the events of 9/11 were not the starting point for the development of intelligence systems within law enforcement. In 1973, the National Advisory Commission on Criminal Justice Standards and Goals called on every LEA and every state to immediately establish and maintain the capability to gather and evaluate information and to disseminate intelligence in a manner that protects every individual's right to privacy while it curtails organized crime and public disorder. Many agencies are "still" not meeting these standards. Peterson (2005) in a report for the U.S. Department of Justice wrote

> … the intelligence operations of state and local LEAs often are plagued by a lack of policies, procedures, and training for gathering and assessing essential information.

Peterson continues:

> To correct this problem, fundamental changes are needed in the way information is gathered, assessed, and redistributed.

In the report from the U.S. Department of Justice, in regard to *Integrated Intelligence and Crime Analysis* (Ratcliffe and U.S. Department of Justice Office of Community Oriented Policing Services 2007), there is criticism of police leadership in relation to linking intelligence with crime data:

> The broader field of police leadership has failed to train police managers in how to understand and use intelligence. As a result, many police executives are often unaware that they are seeing only part of the picture if they receive

crime analysis that lacks an intelligence context, or an intelligence briefing that lacks the crime activity context.

Recognizing the lack of structure to many of the United Kingdom's intelligence gathering efforts, the U.K. government in its document on the implementation of the National Intelligence Model (U.K. Government Home Office 2000) commented,

> Intelligence has lagged behind investigation in the codification of best practices, professional knowledge and in the identification of selection and training requirements of staff.

Added to the corporate failings of many agencies are the failings of individual officers. Many intelligence practitioners are often so heavily committed to the work in which they are involved that they never have time to look outside their world and see what is happening elsewhere or even to take time to raise the question, "Are we doing this as well as we could?" What they are doing appears to work for them and the old adage "If it is not broken, don't fix it" comes into play. Confident in our own methods, we choose not to step outside and take a look at what others are doing, and worse, holding the mistaken belief that we are the best at what we do, which makes us reluctant to examine anyone else's ideas. These are human failings, but as we strive to become more professional in our role, we must continue to seek greater knowledge. Collectively, under scrutiny the whole law enforcement community fares no better. Commenting on the principles of best practice for agencies working with strategic intelligence, McDowell (2009:177) remarks on what he considers to be a worldwide problem:

> Despite the many agencies and Intelligence Units that demonstrate adherence to such principles, many more appear to have simply let slide any genuine attempt to think carefully through the whole genre of collection planning.

Unfortunately, the reality is that McDowell's comments ring true in relation to so many other aspects of the intelligence business. Cooper (2005) highlights some of the problems that might be encountered in changing attitudes:

> The Intelligence Community is not normally self-reflective and usually avoids deep self-examination, but recognition and acceptance of the seriousness of its problems by all levels of the community is a necessary prerequisite for true change, including significant modifications to current organizational cultures and ethos. Agreement on the basic diagnosis must, therefore, precede detailed propositions about effective remedies.

All too often inquiries into events where intelligence did play a part or should have played a part have identified shortcomings with the way both intelligence agencies and LEAs have managed gathering and processing information and sharing the subsequent intelligence. Many different agencies, in many jurisdictions, have come under significant criticism. In the United States, two notable inquiries into the events of 9/11 highlighted significant failings relating to intelligence, including failures in analysis, collection, and sharing (The House Permanent Select Committee on Intelligence and the Senate Select Committee on Intelligence's Joint Inquiry 2002; 9/11 National Commission Report 2004). In Canada, both the Ipperwash Inquiry* (2007) and the Air India Inquiry (2010) were critical of intelligence management processes. The Air India Inquiry specifically addressed the issue of the difficulties between intelligence and evidence and how such matters were handled by law enforcement. In the United Kingdom, there has been significant public speculation and criticism of how intelligence relating to the 7/7 bombers was dealt with by the Security Service (MI5) and whether or not the attacks could have been prevented. Although the coroner at the inquests into the victims and a parliamentary committee both subsequently cleared the Security Service of any failure, the amount of negative press coverage undoubtedly damaged the reputation of that service. After a not dissimilar terrorist attack in the town of Omagh in Northern Ireland, the police ombudsman for Northern Ireland (2001) issued a statement criticizing intelligence handling and made recommendations with regard to the management of intelligence. Furthermore, the response of many LEAs to problems with regard to information management identified in the Bichard[†] report has left much to be desired. The report identified the need for a much greater integration in information management systems, and while agencies may publically state their internal systems are integrated, many remain as dysfunctional as before the report or the subsequent national guidance, the Management of Police Information (MOPI), issued in 2006 and updated in 2010 (ACPO 2010).

While undoubtedly "hindsight bias" (Hoffrage and Pohl 2003) and a lack of understanding of the fallible nature of intelligence both play at least some part in this type of criticism, significant parts of it can be justified, and there is much for those involved in the business to take on board and improve on. Notwithstanding this, it is hard for anyone to be on the receiving end of such comments as are found in these reports particularly when in the vast majority of cases the individuals concerned were doing their utmost to prevent or investigate such events, only to find themselves on the wrong end of criticism. Such as the nature of the intelligence business: get it right and no one thanks you—get it wrong and everyone blames you!

---

* This was an inquiry into a fatal shooting linked to an aboriginal land rights issue.
† The "Bichard" report relates to the findings of Lord Justice Bichard in the murder of two schoolgirls, Holly Wells and Jessica Chapman in Soham, England, and the failure of police information management systems to properly process information relating to a sex offender.

Unfortunately, it is often not just a lack of foresight that negates change. Within most LEAs, there is a core of officers who refuse to develop the way in which they work to meet modern standards of behavior and to act in a way that would be considered as best practice. Reluctance to change is a well-documented and understood human condition, but the failure of a law enforcement officer (or agency) to adopt an entrenched position and refuse to change to meet new circumstances is unacceptable. Many law enforcement officers will be employed with their agency for in excess of 30 years. If, in the later years of their careers, their methods remain largely similar to those at the commencement of their careers, then the potential harm to the agency increases exponentially year after year. For a long time, dinosaurs ruled the earth. Unfortunately for them, things changed, and even if they noticed that things were changing, their inability to adapt to meet the evolving environment meant they became extinct. For those law enforcement officers who cling to the methods of the past and appear insistent on resisting every aspect of change, their metaphorical extinction can only be for the benefit of their agency and the public they serve.

All too often processes for gathering information and converting it into intelligence have been allowed to develop in what can be considered at best to be an ad hoc basis. Significant amounts of information that would have worth if they were processed into intelligence lies in cupboards, on stand-alone computers with limited readership, or in the heads of the officers receiving them. In addition, significant amounts of what could be valuable intelligence are held by specialist teams with very little sharing with the rest of the agency. While some of this failure can be laid at the door of individual officers who regard the intelligence as being for the exclusive use of their "team," the majority of the blame lies with the agency's leadership for failing to create an effective intelligence management system. Ratcliffe and U.S. Department of Justice Office of Community Oriented Policing Services (2007) are scathing in their comments with regard to law enforcement intelligence processes:

> The structure of information handling processes within policing is not set up for the new millennium and ideas about intelligence management and dissemination from the 1970s still pervade the thinking and organizational culture of police agencies in the twenty-first century.

Despite a huge amount of work being done to improve the management of intelligence, there still remain significant gaps in knowledge and application. As Walsh (2011:2) remarks, "The fragmentation of practice and lack of theory within and across different fields of intelligence, most importantly, have contributed to missed opportunities for the integration of intelligence knowledge into tactical, operational and strategic decision-making." While Walsh arguably approaches the topic from an academic, as opposed to a practitioner's, perspective, his case is easily made when one starts to look for research material with regard to intelligence management. Some would argue that academia has little to contribute to the processes of intelligence gathering and management because at least some of the material produced by academics post-9/11 has contributed little of any practical use. However, it could also be argued that those working in intelligence have made failed to identify specific research topics that would suit academic input and make a real practical contribution to the management of intelligence.

Some of the problems that are created when there is a lack of a cohesive approach to intelligence management among different agencies include the following:

- Failure to share information vital to investigations
- Failure to identify threats to life and property
- Failure to identify the extent and nature of the criminality occurring
- Failure to identify the identities of those involved

A problem found in many larger agencies is that of internal branches and units that work independently of each other, with the result being that intelligence ends up in numerous individual silos that remain unconnected in any way. Adding to this problem is that the means used to store the intelligence is often paper based and/or on different software platforms, making it all but impossible to retrieve the intelligence in a central location without huge effort. Although software to search across conflicting and separate databases is available, it is often extremely expensive as programs have to be written to match those contained in each separate computer, and such software can only be used where each of the individual computers is connected to an intranet or is "online." Too often individual branches/units may review or update their intelligence processes, but all too rarely does a LEA review how each of these processes links into an overall intelligence system, the end result being that intelligence management remains disconnected. In essence, the agency fails to join up its own dots let alone be in a position to join up to the wider law enforcement intelligence community. Where an agency is in this position, all the problems that are created with disparate LEAs not being connected are present, merely on a smaller scale. The big difference between failing to connect many agencies and a failure to connect internal units is that it is easy to lay blame on the one person who is responsible for the dysfunction—the "Chief"!

The use of particular words has had a significant effect on many practitioners involved in the management of intelligence, none more so than can be illustrated by the word "intelligence," which has caused numerous misunderstandings and a seemingly endless debate. Another such word is "analysis"; again, a word with which the ambiguous and multiple different uses confuse many who should have a better understanding. Ratcliffe and U.S. Department of Justice Office of Community Oriented Policing Services (2007) comment on the confusion surrounding terminology: "Within both the intelligence and crime analysis fields, conflicts regarding terminology hinder better cooperation. In reality, terminology confusion is also a factor within individual branches of analysis as much as between the different fields. For example, the International Association of Law Enforcement Intelligence Analysts has a separate definition for crime-pattern analysis, criminal analysis, and criminal intelligence." With such variance afoot, it is difficult, if not impossible for those involved on a daily basis, in the management of intelligence to have a clear understanding of what is meant, let alone those new to the discipline or with limited exposure to it. It is because of the ambiguity with regard to terminology that some of the commonly used aspects relating to intelligence management will require revisiting and redefining within this book.

1.7   Coming to Intelligence

The majority of people coming to intelligence will be placed in a position where the agency has already some form of mechanism for dealing with information that they wish to use as intelligence. The individual may come to the role within the intelligence management arena in a number of ways:

- As a new member to the agency, appointed to fill a new or existing post
- As an existing member of the agency to fill a new post or existing post
- As a new or existing member mandated to make changes to the way things are being done

With each of these appointments, there are issues that need to be considered.

A new member may well be expected to fit into the existing structures and get on with their work. This has a number of disadvantages for both the new member and the agency. First, the existing mechanisms within the agency are perpetuated without any regard to the fact that they may not be fit for purpose. The way it has always been done becomes the way it will always be done! Second, fresh insight that would improve how business is done, and which the new start may be in a position to impart, is not integrated into the agency's mechanisms. This will often result with the new member becoming disillusioned by the inability of the agency to change and develop. This subsequently leads to this person becoming demotivated and less productive. Third, the new member may be perceived by existing staff as a troublemaker, intent on criticizing their working methods. This is likely to lead to the new start being ostracized by colleagues.

When existing members are appointed to fulfill a post, they will bring with them all their preconceived notions of how they would like things done. These notions may well clash with how existing staff are working. Furthermore, existing staff will have preconceived notions of their colleagues, which may also lead to conflict. On the other hand, the agency members may have been selected purely because they are willing to perpetuate the existing mechanisms. In this case, it is the agency that loses as inefficient mechanisms are perpetuated.

Where the agency may have appointed a person with the intention of making changes because of some issue that has become apparent, this individual is significantly more likely to be met with hostility from the commencement of their role. Change is never easy to bring about and is often met with hostility, as people internalize events and take up defensive positions. When appointing a person to such a role, senior management must first be sure in the ability of that person; second, resolute in their support for that individual; and third, be prepared to hear things that they may not want to hear.

Failure to recognize the problems that are likely to be encountered means that the management of intelligence is likely to remain dysfunctional. Fortunately, many existing members of staff are just as likely to welcome the opportunity to have a root-and-branch examination of how things are done and welcome the opportunity if and when management presents it. It is only by regular and thorough audit of existing intelligence management structures that any agency carrying out this role can function effectively, efficiently, and safely. Any such review of intelligence processes should have the blessing of the Chief, the commitment of all the senior management team, and the intimate involvement of at least one senior management member.

Perhaps, the most specific and accurate condemnation of police intelligence systems was delivered by Sheptycki (2004) and is contained in the list that he refers to as "organisational pathologies in police intelligence systems." Many of these are all too familiar to anyone working in intelligence management. They include the following:

- The existence of a "digital divide." Police computer systems, both within and among agencies, don't talk to each other. Intelligence is not shared. Compounding this is the "duplication" of effort caused by different agencies keeping the same information on disconnected systems.
- Criminal investigations that cross agency boundaries are not linked. This "linkage blindness" is akin to failure to connect the dots.
- Too much low-quality information creates "noise," but it becomes impossible to distinguish what is important from what is not. This

problem is exacerbated by an overuse of open source material and the trawling of records management systems for information that is, in reality, of little intelligence use, while all the time creating the delusion of being productive.

- Lack of training and lack of analytical capacity creates circumstances where information is not properly processed to intelligence.
- Poor, labor-intensive systems create circumstances where information is either not reported or not recorded, resulting in the loss of valuable material.
- Intelligence gaps that occur because of the inability of LEAs to be sufficiently flexible with regard to their geographic or hierarchically areas of operation. This has been a significant problem in the United Kingdom, where the implementation of the National Intelligence Model created three arguably "false" tiers of criminality to which police directed resources only to find that many criminals were operating between the tiers with relative impunity. While poor interpretation of the model was the cause of this problem, as opposed to the model itself, the net result was the same. Geographic limitations create problems for all aspects of law enforcement.
- Friction between agencies arising from different missions, structures, and methodologies to the extent that it becomes all but institutionalized in its nature. This is in part at least driven by a lack of trust.
- "Hoarding" intelligence in silos to be used when it is most beneficial to the person controlling that intelligence. If this is occurring, it is a clear indication of a broken intelligence management system and a potential "hotbed" for corruption. Staff should not have discretion as to when and how they submit material and when and how they will act on it.

1.8   Connecting the Dots

One of the popular explanations for the failure of the various intelligence and LEAs in the United States to identify the terrorist plot prior to the 9/11 attacks was an inability to connect isolated pieces of intelligence that collectively would have provided forewarning of the attacks. Alluding to the dot-to-dot puzzle books, where a child attempts to create a complete picture by joining what outwardly appears to be random dots on a page, the term "connecting the dots" (9/11 Commission Report 2004:16) became synonymous with the failure to join up pieces of intelligence held by various different agencies. The Commission's assessment was that, prior to the attacks, there were a number of different pieces of intelligence (dots) that were held by various agencies, and had there been a system or process in place to connect these "dots," it would have been possible to foresee the attacks. While there may be a strong element of hindsight bias at play here, and whether or not, had the limited amount of dots available been successfully connected, that there would have been sufficiently clear picture to prevent the attacks will never be known. However, what was apparent was the need to have greater connectivity among the producers of intelligence in both the intelligence and law enforcement communities. Much of the drive to make changes with regard to intelligence management within the United States stems from this mind-set.

Although the desire for improved connectivity has undoubtedly significant relevance, it can be argued that there has been created a situation where many involved in intelligence gathering, particularly those with limited understanding of it, focus on the connectivity issue to the detriment of other aspects of intelligence management, including failure to understand the difficulties in collecting information of such specificity that it would prevent similar attacks and a failure to realize that merely merging the information already held will not necessarily produce more intelligence of worth. The tendency to create ever more sophisticated mechanisms for searching the many and varied databases that are out there does not of itself make it easier to find the intelligence that is desired. If we are trying to find the proverbial needle in a haystack, then the methods currently being advocated by some will create a situation where although the potential is there that more "needles" will be gathered, the concurrent collection of "haystacks" of worthless material means the needles will no easier to spot. The thought of a few more needles in a vastly greater haystack brings only false comfort.

A decision maker's desire is the ability to use intelligence to create a clearer picture of what the criminals or terrorists who are under investigation are likely to do or how they have done it. Those directing the information collection have to ensure that the various information gathering processes produce sufficient numbers of the "right" dots to be used to create a picture, and then that the intelligence system is capable of accurately joining those dots together. Illustrated in Figure 1.1 are a number of dots that if joined could form a picture. However, in box 1, there are insufficient dots to provide a clear picture. In box 2, there are so many dots, it is impossible to

Figure 1.1 Joining the dots.

see the picture, but it remains present. The dots in box 3 have been collected in a structured manner and while there are still only dots present and not a whole picture, sufficient dots exist to make a reasonable estimate as to what the picture is of.

1.9   Terrorism and the Need for Change

If somehow the need to combat crime is not a sufficient driver for law enforcement to adopt a more professional approach to managing intelligence, then surely the threat from terrorism should focus minds and provide sufficient incentive. If one was only to consider the number of terrorist attacks carried out in many different countries post 9/11 and look at law enforcement's limited development of its intelligence capability in the period since, the word "depressing" might spring to mind.

Even after all the money that has been expended, there remains limited understanding within law enforcement of the nature of terrorism and until one understands an enemy, any efforts to fight it are at best haphazard. Dealing with terrorism creates many problems for law enforcement with some officers being so hamstrung by mistaken views that much of their efforts are misdirected. Dealing with terrorism is not dissimilar to a game of chess; it is useless merely to plan one move ahead and wait to see what the other party does. To win one must not only plan one's own moves but predict the moves that the other party is likely to make. Commenting on the nature of terrorism, Treverton and Gabbard (2008) remarked the following:

> Because terrorism is the tactic of the weak, terrorists have to be flexible. They cannot be understood in isolation from what we are doing to counter them. Hijackers did not come to their tactic as a preference; they chose it because they had found seams in our defenses.

Unless law enforcement recognizes the nature of terrorism, the measures it needs to take to combat that threat will always be misguided. The structures and methods currently used by many agencies are inappropriate for use in combating terrorism.

Furthermore, investigating terrorism by its very nature carries with it substantial risks, which some in law enforcement do not have a sufficiently strong strategic outlook to deal with. The idea of short-term gain, both professional and personal (for self or the agency), is carried through the long-term detriment of counterterrorism strategies. In addition, the nature of the risks, the ambiguity involved, and the tactics necessary to deal with the risks mean that some officers simply do not have the stomach for such work. Add this to the lack of a systematic approach to intelligence management, and the chances of preventing a terrorist attack become significantly reduced.

1.10   Knowledge Management

The ever pervasive Wikipedia* in its definition states that knowledge management

> ... comprises a range of strategies and practices used in an organization to identify, create, represent, distribute, and enable adoption of insights and experiences. Such insights and experiences comprise knowledge, either embodied in individuals or embedded in organizations as processes or practices.

To paraphrase, it is about getting hold of what is known throughout an agency and putting it in a place where it can be accessed. In discussing "knowledge management" when it comes to intelligence, the origin of that knowledge is to be found within a broad range of individuals, including law enforcement members, military personnel, members of intelligence services, and practitioners who are involved on a daily basis with managing intelligence. Given the diverse nature of their backgrounds and their geographical locations, it is unsurprising that much of what could be shared is not shared. Unlike other professions, such as medicine, where theory and "hands-on" experience are often shared, those involved in intelligence have failed to gather knowledge of their profession in a structured way and then share that knowledge effectively.

The many reasons that law enforcement officers and intelligence practitioners, in particular, are not as efficient as they should be at knowledge management could be debated at length, but it is worth mentioning a few of the possible reasons to set the scene for what will follow:

- Much of the work they are involved in is of a sensitive if not secret nature. With each sharing of knowledge comes a risk, real or imagined, that the bad guys will find out something to their advantage.
- Many practitioners would argue that they are too busy with their involvement in cases to take the time required to write down what they know. Some would argue they should mentor more junior colleagues through an ad hoc apprenticeship-type approach.
- For some there will be a reluctance to share the knowledge they have worked hard to gain over many years. Debatably, knowledge equates to power and the sharing of that knowledge (without gaining something in return) diminishes the power that the individual believes the knowledge gives. This is rational and logical behavior, albeit from a very selfish standpoint.

---

* The Web site Wikipedia provides one of the best examples of the difficulties in managing intelligence. For the most part it is useful, accurate, and well intentioned, but you can't wholly trust where it gets its information from!

- There will be many practitioners who can carry out their particular function effectively but do not have the ability to articulate in a suitable format exactly what they are doing and why. The real failure here is that of the agency and not the practitioner as it is an agency responsibility to put in place knowledge capture structures.
- Many people who are attracted to intelligence gathering are often the type of people who abhor something as mundane as "writing stuff down." They are "doers," and it is often a challenge to get them to complete records that are essential for their daily functioning let alone anything else.
- Because of its very nature, the type of knowledge used in intelligence management is difficult to elicit from the experienced practitioners; the most effective method for knowledge transfer is through observation and/or practical application. Unfortunately when such methods are used, bad practice can be as readily shared as good.
- A reluctance to share mistakes. Few people are prepared to share, even with fellow professionals, the mistakes that they have made, yet it is from these very mistakes that much can be learned. This failing can only be exacerbated by the macho culture that is prevalent in law enforcement.
- Adding to the failure of practitioners to share their knowledge is the lack of significant academic research in the field. There is a limited amount of work that steps beyond a rehash of what has been oft written or that concentrates on practicalities as opposed to specific events. Cooper (2005) pulls few punches in his criticism of the intelligence community and the lack of effective research and knowledge management. Citing an overreliance on the methods used during the Cold War, he writes,

The Intelligence Community presently lacks many of the scientific community's self-correcting features. Among the most significant of these features are the creative tension between "evidence-based" experimentalists and hypothesis-based theoreticians, a strong tradition of "investigator-initiated" research, real "horizontal" peer review, and "proof" by independent replication. Moreover, neither the community as a whole nor its individual analysts usually possess the ingrained habits of systematic self-examination, including conducting "after action reviews" as part of a continual lessons-learnt process, necessary to appreciate the changes required to fix existing problems or to address new challenges.

1.11   Moving On

Now that we have identified a context for the book and have set in place the relevant historical and theoretical background, we can progress to examine the more practical aspects of intelligence management, hopefully fusing both theoretical and pragmatic perspectives. As the philosopher Immanuel Kant imparts:

> Experience without theory is blind, but theory without experience is mere intellectual play.

References

Association of Chief Police Officers (ACPO). (2010) *Guidance on the Management of Police Information*. 2nd ed. United Kingdom: National Police Improvement Agency.

Bayer, M. (2007) *Can't We All Just Get Along? Improving the Law Enforcement-Intelligence Community Relationship*. Washington, DC: National Defense Intelligence College Press.

Cooper, J.R. (2005) Curing analytical pathologies: Pathways to improved intelligence analysis. Available at: https://www.cia.gov/library/center-for-the-study-of-intelligence/csi-publications/books-and-monographs/curing-analytic-pathologies-pathways-to-improved-intelligence-analysis-1/analytic_pathologies_report.pdf (accessed September 2012).

Hoffrage, U. and Pohl, R. (2003) *Hindsight Bias: A Special Issue of Memory*. Champlain, NY: Psychology Press.

The House Permanent Select Committee on Intelligence and the Senate Select Committee on Intelligence. (2002) Report of the Joint Inquiry into the terrorist attacks of September 11, 2001. Available at: https://www.fas.org/irp/congress/2002_rpt/911rept.pdf (accessed December 2012).

Kent, S. (1955) The need for an intelligence literature. *Studies in Intelligence*. Central Intelligence Agency Library. Available at: https://www.cia.gov/library/center-for-the-study-of-intelligence/csi-publications/books-and-monographs/sherman-kent-and-the-board-of-national-estimates-collected-essays/2need .html (accessed August 2012).

Knightley, P. (1988) *The Second Oldest Profession: Spies and Spying in the 20th Century*. New York: W.W. Norton.

Honourable Commissioner Linden, S.B. (2007) Report of the Ipperwash Inquiry. Canada: Attorney General for Canada. Available at: http://www.attorneygeneral.jus.gov.on.ca/inquiries/ipperwash/index.html (accessed December 2012).

Commission of Inquiry into the Investigation of the Bombing of Air India Flight 182 (Canada) and John C. Major (Commissioner) (2010) Air India Flight 182: A Canadian tragedy. Available at: http://jnslp.wordpress.com/2010/06/18/nationalsecuritylaw-commission-of-inquiry-report-air-india-flight-182-a-canadian-tragedy/ (accessed July 2012).

McDowell, D. (2009) *Strategic Intelligence: A Handbook for Practitioners, Managers, and Users*. Lantham, MD: Scarecrow Press Inc.

National Commission on Terrorist Attacks upon the United States. (2004) The 9/11 Commission Report. Available at: http://www.911commission.gov/report/911Report.pdf (accessed August 2012).

Peterson, M. (2005) *Intelligence-Led Policing: The New Intelligence Architecture*. Washington, DC: U.S. Department of Justice, Bureau of Justice Assistance.

Police Ombudsman for Northern Ireland. (2001) Statement by the Police Ombudsman for Northern Ireland on her investigation of matters relating to the Omagh bombing on August 15, 1998. United Kingdom: Police Ombudsman for Northern Ireland. Available at: http://www.policeombudsman.org/modules/press/press.cfm/action/detail/Press_ID/41/Archive/2001/year/2001/level/page (accessed December 2012).

Ratcliffe, J.H. and U.S. Department of Justice Office of Community Oriented Policing Services. (2007) *Integrated Intelligence and Crime Analysis: Enhanced Information Management for Law Enforcement Leaders.* Washington, DC: Police Foundation.

Sheptycki, J. (2004) Organisational pathologies in police intelligence systems. *European Journal of Criminology* 1(3), P308–P332.

Treverton, G.F. and Gabbard, C.B. (2008) *Assessing the Tradecraft of Intelligence Analysis.* Washington, DC: Rand Corporation, National Security Research Division.

U.K. Government Home Office. (2000) *The National Intelligence Model: Providing a Model for Policing.* London: Home Office.

Walsh, P.F. (2011) *Intelligence and Intelligence Analysis.* New York and London: Routledge.

Intelligence in Context

2

Most ignorance is vincible ignorance. We don't know because we don't want to know.

Aldous Huxley

2.1 Introduction

Arguably, one of the biggest problems in relation to law enforcement and intelligence revolves around the ability to contextualize intelligence within that environment. Law enforcement is a subject that attracts significant interest and criticism in relation to how well it functions as a profession in general and at an individual agency level. Inevitably, there is criticism and a continuous stream of ideas as to how it can be improved. Unfortunately, the expectations of those making the suggestions are rarely met, at least in part, because they were unrealistic in the first place. In recent years, intelligence has emerged as having the potential to assist greatly in law enforcement efforts, but if the potential benefits are to be realized, it must be understood in the specific environment in which it is to be used. Furthermore, the other aspects of policing that predominate must be taken into consideration. This chapter explores a number of commonly used policing models/strategies and seeks to integrate the concept of intelligence management with the effective elements of these models/strategies.

2.2 Context

Law enforcement is, out of necessity, continually evolving, as the needs of society and the very structure of society changes. Although many crime types, such as murder and robbery, remain the same, other new types of crime evolve, such as complex frauds and Internet-related crimes. As crimes continually evolve, the law enforcement methods used to investigate these crimes must also continually evolve, as it has done with the use of techniques relating to deoxyribonucleic acid (commonly referred to as DNA), unheard of a generation ago but now having become a standard investigative tool. In a similar vein, criminals are using emerging technology to facilitate their criminality, forcing law enforcement agencies (LEAs) to use modern technology as a tool to capture the criminals at their own games. Within this ever-changing playing field, there is an increased pressure on law enforcement from citizens to prevent crimes from happening, before there are victims and if that is not possible, law enforcement is expected to catch the perpetrators and hold them accountable for their crimes, quickly and without making mistakes. And the best part is that all this is to be done with very limited resources. Although it can be argued that the public have unrealistic expectations of law enforcement, perhaps seen elsewhere only in their expectations of health care, there is an obligation on law enforcement to provide the best value in relation to discharging their obligations. And that is the rub—who decides what the policing priorities are and how is the most effective way to police? How do the public get the best value out of their police service?

A number of policing strategies have been suggested as ways to police effectively and it is appropriate to give a brief outline of these and where they sit with regard to intelligence management. Before going any further, however, it is important to note that effective intelligence management in no way conflicts with any of these policing methods and is, or should be, at the core of them all. We will consider the following three policing strategies:

1. Community-oriented policing
2. Problem-oriented policing
3. Intelligence-led policing (ILP)

It is accepted that there are many other policing strategies and that for purists, arguments could be raised as to whether any or each of these is a policing strategy, but what should be acknowledged is that when it comes to modern policing, all three of the strategies mentioned here are frequently discussed at a strategic level and often linked to or purportedly based in intelligence. An understanding of these concepts is necessary in order that intelligence professionals can meet the demands of those working at the strategic level. Similarly, it is essential that those working at the strategic level and using these policing methods have a real understanding of what intelligence can provide to them.

2.3 Community-Oriented Policing

"Community-oriented policing," or "community policing" as it is also known, has become a very popular model for policing both in the United States and in the United Kingdom. Community policing envisages the police and the community as partners in problem solving, and makes officers responsible for responding to a broad range of problems that the community brings to them, some of which are, arguably, not strictly the mandate of law enforcement. The idea of a fatherly type figure, dressed in blue, standing on the street corner and ready to see the child safely across the road or to escort an elderly resident home while carrying her grocery bags epitomizes the image of the community officer for most citizens. The descriptions by academics and policy makers create a much less appealing but supposedly more accurate interpretation of community policing. For example, in the United States, the Office of Community Oriented Policing Services (COPS) defines community-oriented policing as follows:

> Community policing is a philosophy that promotes organizational strategies, which support the systematic use of partnerships and problem-solving techniques, to proactively address the immediate conditions that give rise to public safety issues such as crime, social disorder, and fear of crime.

Community policing has the primary aim of regaining the legitimacy of the police in the eyes of the public, even though some would argue that it also extends to the community the right to determine police priorities. It has its origins in attempts by law enforcement to bridge the gaps between themselves and the communities they serve and in particular what can be described as "hard to reach" or "minority" communities. Many communities, for a variety of different reasons, have an implicit distrust of law enforcement in all guises. Law enforcement is often perceived to be oppressive, biased, and altogether untrustworthy. Even where police could be of benefit to these people, the distrust is so deeply seated it cannot be overcome. The problem is further exacerbated by what these people may view as incompetence on the part of the police. The philosophy behind community-oriented policing is that if police make the effort to reach out to those communities, get to know them and get to understand their everyday problems, then a bridge will be built between the police and the community to the benefit of both.

Much of the implementation of community-oriented policing focuses on placing a uniformed presence on the streets within communities, specifically those ones where the problems exist. The officers involved are expected to build relationships, engage with community concerns, and address their problems with regard to crime. It is very much based on the idea of the pleasant and approachable officer, known and liked by everyone in the community. Many proponents would argue that the officers should be from the community in which they are operating. People are more apt to trust one of their own, but this is a belief that brings with it huge problems including officer safety issues and corrupt behavior. There are a number of problems with community-oriented policing, both from a theoretical perspective and from the practical implementation, which are as follows:

- There are doubts with regard to its effectiveness in achieving its objectives. In the United States, the National Research Council (Skogan and Frydl 2003) in discussing the approach remarked that it

"...demonstrated little or no evidence of effectiveness and only weak to moderate in relation to community relationships."

- The assumption is often made that all it takes for officers to be accepted is for them to be out there in the community. It fails to recognize the many deep-seated problems that exist within such communities where the police have always been viewed as the "enemy" and any citizen seen talking to them is likely to be viewed with hostility. It is extremely difficult for an officer to appear friendly if they are continually seen as a threat and they must stay focused on staying safe.
- Communities can place significant demands on officers that officers may not be able to meet (Weisburd and Eck 2004).
- Many law enforcement officers lack a sincere belief in the model and show what could only be described as tacit commitment to it.
- In some jurisdictions grants play a major role in community-oriented policing initiatives and a lack of funding leads to the termination of related schemes. This inevitably raises questions as to whether or not police Chiefs really see value for money in the model or merely use it as an additional funding mechanism.
- With limited resources available to law enforcement, many agencies simply cannot afford to have an officer performing these duties, as there are too many response type calls that need urgent attention.
- The agency becomes focused on what the community believes to be the problems as opposed to what the real problems are. There are many crimes that do not attract much notice from the public, yet can yield huge returns for criminals. Often mistakenly perceived as victimless crimes, these include many types of fraud, shoplifting and the sale of counterfeit goods. As these are unlikely to grab headlines, there is little pressure to devote any resources to them, yet ultimately they cause significant harm to the wider community. This problem is exacerbated by the fact that criminality is likely to be spread over a wider area with no community representative clamoring for the Chief's attention.

Community policing has its good points. It is a very attractive model to communities in that it can provide them with a sense of empowerment. Good community officers can do great work within communities and earn the respect of citizens within those areas.

One way a Chief may look at the potential dilemma in relation to community policing is to ask the question, Is it essential or just desirable? There is no doubt that from a "policing by consent perspective," community policing is very desirable, but unfortunately it can be one of the first things cut when budgets are cut. However, another option exists and that is to make it more effective as a model. Integrating community policing with a specific intelligence-based focus can add significant benefits to law enforcement. How this can be done is discussed later in the chapter.

As can be seen from the COPS definition mentioned previously, there are close parallels between community-oriented policing and problem-oriented policing and it is this policing model we discuss next.

2.4   Problem-Oriented Policing

Problem-oriented policing is a concept developed by Herman Goldstein (1990) in which he advocates a broader approach to addressing policing issues than that of the more traditional enforcement approach. Recognizing that the police do not have it within their power to resolve many of the issues that lead to crime problems, Goldstein proposed that with each crime problem, an investment should be made to resolve the causes of that problem, as opposed to merely enforcing the law and bringing offenders to justice.

A problem-oriented approach in policing can be applied to many different aspects encountered by police, including dealing with impaired driving, crime problems relating to truancy, and addiction-related crimes. Central to the problem-oriented approach is studying the nature of the crime problem and identifying its cause. This is followed through with a comprehensive approach to control the problem that is specifically tailored to the actual cause. A fundamental part of the problem-oriented approach is the engagement with other statutory and nonstatutory bodies to assist law enforcement in tackling the problem. In this model, the responsibility for action and change does not lie only with law enforcement, but instead it is shared within the community itself.

Although much of the theory of problem-oriented policing is readily accepted, the practical benefits are not so obvious. Weisburd, Cody, Hinkle, and Eck (2008) in a systematic review of problem-oriented policing concluded that

> "...problem-oriented policing is effective in reducing crime and disorder, although the effect is fairly modest."

The main problem with the concept of problem-oriented policing, from a policing perspective, is the simple fact that there are limited resources available for police to adopt problem-oriented strategies to address many of the problems they meet. They are too busy dealing with the problems they already have. Furthermore, it can be argued that although the problem-oriented approach is likely to be helpful in addressing the everyday issues encountered by policing—such as road traffic collisions, antisocial behavior, and petty crime—it is of little use when attempting to address serious and organized crime. The somewhat utopian belief that there is a solution to all criminality, if only one takes the time to solve the wider social issues, leaves many in law enforcement deeply skeptical of the whole philosophy.

Nevertheless, problem-oriented policing has much in common with an intelligence-based approach to crime control. Seeking a longer term solution to problems by gaining an accurate understanding of the nature of the problem is fundamental to successful problem solving. It is here that effective information gathering and intelligence management can assist both law enforcement and their partners in developing effective crime control solutions. This creates a need to delve deeper into the nature of the problem to gain the maximum amount of information needed to correct the root cause of the problem, and this can be accomplished only by using the information-gathering techniques that form part of any intelligence management system. The connection between problem-oriented policing and an intelligence-based approach is clear enough for anyone with simple logic to see, yet these two policing strategies are rarely mentioned in the same breath, let alone viewed as synergistic.

2.5 Intelligence-Led Policing

There are many different perspectives in relation to interpreting the meaning of ILP. The International Association of Law Enforcement Intelligence Analysts (2011) defines ILP as

> The collection and analysis of information to produce an intelligence end product, designed to inform police decision makers at both the tactical and strategic levels.

The United Kingdom's Association of Police Officers provides significant guidance on ILP in its document entitled *Introduction to Intelligence-Led Policing* (ACPO 2007). Highlighting that

> The concept of intelligence-led policing underpins all aspects of policing, from neighbourhood policing and partnership work to the investigation of serious and organised crime and terrorism

it stresses the need for

> the effective and efficient collection, recording, dissemination and retention of information allows for the identification of material which can be assessed for intelligence value and enables decision-making about priorities and tactical options

Ratcliffe (2008), one of the main advocates of ILP, describes it as

> a business model and managerial philosophy where data analysis and crime intelligence are pivotal to an objective, decision-making framework that facilitates crime and problem reduction, disruption and presentation through both strategic management and effective enforcement strategies that target prolific and serious offenders.

Discussing the purpose of ILP, the United States Department of Justice (2009:5) highlights that

> At its core ILP helps leaders make informed decisions to address agency priorities.

and continues that

> The end goal of ILP is to enhance proactive policing efforts and further the positive outcomes of law enforcement actions towards reducing crime and protecting the community against a variety of threats.

Although these give us insight into some of the theory behind ILP to gain a better perspective, we will take a much deeper look at two different policing models, both of which are often articulated as being examples of intelligence-led approaches. The first model incorporates much broader policing concepts than its name would apply, and the second, it can be argued, actually bears little connection to intelligence. The two concepts are as follows:

- The National Intelligence Model (NIM)—A model used throughout the United Kingdom
- CompStat—A model used extensively in the United States

2.6   National Intelligence Model

The National Intelligence Model, or NIM, (ACPO 2005) is a business model for law enforcement that is used by police and others throughout the United Kingdom. As with many aspects of life, if one understands how and where the concept of the principles of the NIM originated, then one has a better understanding of its original goals. Many aspects of the model have their origins in Northern Ireland and the conflict there. In the mid 1980s, when terrorism was ubiquitous, and the Royal Ulster Constabulary was attempting on a daily basis to thwart terrorist attacks stemming from both loyalist and republican traditions, there simply were insufficient resources to deal with all potential avenues of attack. To maximize the use of limited resources and to deploy those resources in the most effective way to prevent loss of life, "Tasking and Coordination Groups" (TCGs) were set up. Each TCG was governed by a senior police officer, who was briefed on the intelligence available and made decisions as to the most effective use of resources. This strategy became a highly effective part of the battle against terrorism and significant good practice in the use of intelligence was developed. Many of the principles tried and tested in the extreme circumstances of Northern Ireland in the 1980s were translated, adapted, and further developed in England by Kent Constabulary to meet the needs of a more mainstream policing environment.

In 2000, the Association of Chief Police Officers incorporated the concept into its policy and its role as a national model was strengthened with the introduction of the Police Reform Act in 2002. Police agencies may now be inspected to see if they have effectively implemented the model and are using it properly. The NIM may still have flaws, but its introduction across all police agencies undoubtedly raised standards and went a long way to integrating intelligence into everyday policing. NIM usage is mandatory in the United Kingdom for police services, but many of the methods used in its implementation may vary from agency to agency in different jurisdictions.

One of the fundamental parts of the NIM is that for the purpose of managerial planning, the model divides criminality into three levels, each according to the seriousness of its nature and the breadth of the geographical impact it is having. Although there has been some confusion as to where certain aspects of criminality fit within the three levels, most of this confusion comes down to inflexibility with regard to interpreting the levels and the mistaken belief that there needs to be rigid adherence to them. The three levels of criminality can be described roughly as follows, first as it is applied in the United Kingdom and second how it would translate to other jurisdictions:

1. *Level 1—Local crime and disorder.* "Local" here is intended to refer to crime and disorder affecting a relatively small geographical area, for example, in the United Kingdom, as part of a "district" command area in larger police services; in the United States, the area policed by a small police service or a number of small agencies limited to a small county; and elsewhere, policing carried out in an limited geographical area in a reasonably sized police service.
2. *Level 2—Regional crime and serious public disorder.* "Regional" here is intended in the United Kingdom to refer to a crime impacting across district command boundaries and potentially affecting neighboring LEAs. By its very nature, this type of criminality is more likely to be of a serious nature requiring significant law enforcement resources to investigate and a joint task force type approach. Level 2 criminality is likely to affect all of a major city such as Miami or Manchester, or affect whole regions in the United Kingdom or a whole state in the United States, depending on the extent of the problem.
3. *Level 3—Multijurisdictional, serious and organized crime, and terrorism.* This level of crime will affect a huge part of a country, be nationwide and may even be transnational. It will require substantial resources to investigate and is likely to require a national or international response. Such crimes are likely to include drug importations, arms sales, and human trafficking. By their very nature, most terrorist causes will fall within this level.

These levels provide a Chief with insight in regard to the likely resources that will be needed to successfully deal with the problem and where they can expect to obtain those resources from. From an intelligence management perspective, it provides guidance as to where intelligence must be obtained from and where it must be shared if the nature and extent of the problem is to be correctly identified, and when it comes to investigation, what intelligence-gathering resources will need to be deployed to further any investigation. Information gathering will be of significant assistance for all three levels of criminality, and it would be a mistake to believe that any gathering method should be ruled out purely because of the level of criminality involved. Nonetheless, the more intrusive and resource-intensive methods may prove to be unsuitable for some lower level aspects of criminality. Figure 2.1 shows the NIM and as can be seen, it is not the easiest model to understand.

There are many different components that form the model, a fact that has led some to believe it has been "over engineered" (John and Maguire 2004), an argument that has significant merit. However, as a means for prioritizing objectives both at strategic and tactical levels and for monitoring progress in pursuit of these objectives, it certainly has worth.

Although there is general acceptance of the NIM both within U.K. policing and internationally, it is not without its faults:

- The name "National Intelligence Model" is a misnomer that in itself alienates many from using it, a point showed by comments such as "I am in uniform policing; my job is nothing to do with intelligence!"

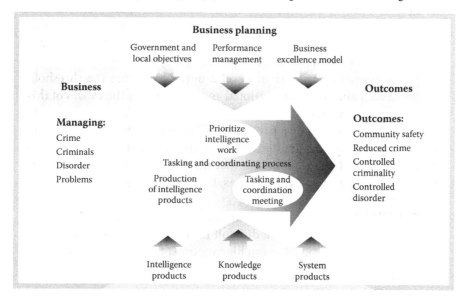

Figure 2.1 The U.K.'s National Intelligence Model. (NCIS, *National Intelligence Model*. London: NCIS, 2000.)

The fact that it is misnamed is now widely accepted and it is now more correctly viewed as a police business model that is to be used across the entire policing service.

- There is a limited understanding of how the model is intended to work properly. Although many may grasp the overarching principles, their lack of real understanding of the practical aspects of its use means that many merely pay lip service to more specific parts. For example, when it comes to setting priorities at either strategic or tactical levels, these are often left vague or stated as woolly aspirations, as opposed to specific achievable priorities that staff can work toward. The primary cause of this problem is the lack of training in the NIM and how to implement it, with officers often having to rely on their similarly informed peers to guide them or to take guidance from national manuals that, in themselves, are often confusing.

- There can be confusion about which of the three NIM levels certain types of criminality fall into. The argument is made that certain levels of criminality are ignored because of police investigative structures that clearly correlate with the NIM levels. Street crime obviously falls within Level 1, so it is the responsibility of local police commanders to deploy resources accordingly. Serious and organized crime with in a particular force area will fall in Level 2 and therefore to specialized units within that agency. But what of that criminality that isn't serious enough for the specialized units but causes problems over several police districts within a force area—more than Level 1 but not quite Level 2? Who deals with that? National and transnational crime falls within Level 3, so it is the remit of national LEAs. But here too a similar situation is created with crime that crosses between the area of one police agency and one or more other police agencies—more than Level 2 but not meeting the threshold for Level 3 and the use of national agencies. One of the causes of this particular problem is the imposition of false boundaries, based solely on the area covered by a particular police agency. Because police are constrained by the paradigm in which they normally work, they find difficulty in the new paradigm that the NIM has created. Criminals are not constrained by such areas, therefore police agencies need to adopt a more flexible approach.

- The NIM has become overcomplicated with the terminology used in many aspects of it being difficult for the layperson to grasp. Even many of those involved in intelligence don't fully understand a lot of the jargon used.

There are effective elements within the NIM, but it is not in itself the panacea for all policing.

2.7   CompStat

CompStat, which is short for "computerized statistics," is a prevalent policing concept in the United States. CompStat uses statistical data obtained from police records to identify and map crime problems and trends, intending that adequate police resources can be deployed to rapidly address issues. Essentially, what the CompStat process does is use data that the police have, analyze that data, and create statistical products such as those identifying hot spots through mapping various crime types. These products, in theory, enable management to identify where resources should be deployed and to come up with solutions to address the crimes. Some would argue that CompStat borrows from problem-oriented policing and attempts to shift policing from a system based on response to calls to one in which police use data to structure decision making, whereas others could argue that it is in direct conflict with problem-oriented responses.

Figure 2.2 shows the basic functioning of the CompStat process and how analytical products are used in the decision-making process. Proponents of CompStat argue that these analytical products constitute the "intelligence" element in an intelligence-led approach. What should be noted in the figure below is that the analytical product created relies solely on statistics, with all the inherent flaws of statistical analysis.

As a process that is often viewed as being intelligence based, there are numerous criticisms of it from both its theoretical basis and its practical

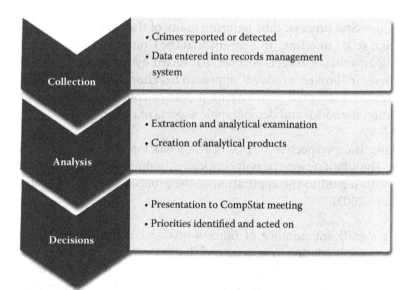

Figure 2.2 The CompStat process.

application. Judging from a theoretical perspective, the following concerns can be levied:

- The use of data and the lack of any analysis other than statistical leads to resources being deployed against incidents that could in effect be merely a crime blip. This can mean that resources are wasted while generating the delusion that the problem was solved.
- The frequency of CompStat meetings means that managers end up responding to the immediate crises and not implementing more preventive and longer term problem-solving approaches. The significant levels of pressure placed on managers to address the figures presented means that it could be argued that CompStat is merely a data-driven reactive policing model as opposed to a proactive analysis-based approach.
- CompStat relies heavily on the assumption that data are entered correctly by staff on initial inputting into the system, but haven't we all heard of human error? The lack of checking this assumption and effective analysis with regard to the data means that the very foundations of what the CompStat meeting plans are often questionable.
- Much of the CompStat process relies on visual displays of a geographic nature, based on the data available. Although such graphics can be visually impressive, they often fail to give a true representation of what is occurring. Data are not examined systematically by the product recipients to establish the underlying causes of the patterns.
- Often, only certain crime types are included for discussion in the CompStat process, thus ignoring many of the socioeconomic issues that relate to crime. This means that the CompStat process excludes other policing aspects such as that raised by Kellig and Cole (1996) in their "broken windows" approach to crime prevention. A broader approach adopted in analyzing problems could take into consideration the social and demographic aspects of crime.

From the perspective of practical application, an examination by the Police Foundation was heavily critical, highlighting a number of concerns with regard to the application of the process (Willis, Mastrofski, and Weisburd 2003):

- A significant number of officers involved in CompStat resent it, because it appears to operate and devalue other policing approaches and tasks, driving officers to a point of being solely involved in keeping senior management happy at the next CompStat meeting. The perception of the way in which CompStat exclusively focuses on crime control, whereas at the same time appearing to be in direct conflict with other policing practices such as community policing and problem-solving approaches, does little to win the confidence of many practitioners and academics.

- The oppressive way in which senior management conducted many CompStat meetings became a prominent feature of the process with the punishment of middle managers for failing to meet the standards of accountability emerging as a common trait. Needless to say, this drew significant resentment from those in middle management.
- Little or no analysis is carried out to identify whether strategies to deal with reported crime were successful or failed. All that is of concern is to get onto the next identified issue. This often leads to the crime type reemerging once resources are deployed elsewhere. Lack of evidence in regard to what works and why means that crimes are merely displaced as crime managers respond on a short-term basis with no longer term solutions being identified. In short, CompStat becomes a form of reactive policing.

Perhaps the greatest concern is the fact that many of the problems found with CompStat are inherent in the process's design. As Willis et al. conclude,

> ...many of the limitations of CompStat that we observed are built into the very principles of the program's design and are therefore inevitably replicated wherever it is faithfully attempted.

Unfortunately for the many agencies who are adopting the CompStat process, their expectations will probably not be met. CompStat, although well intentioned with regard to adopting a more proactive approach to policing, fails to meet the standards of what could truly be referred to as ILP, and arguably fails in many ways as being effective from a proactive standpoint. Perhaps these agencies may find comfort from the fact that they were correct in the assumption that a more proactive, logic-based approach to policing has real benefits and that with some adaptations they can achieve their intended goals.

2.8   Agency Size

Another factor likely to influence how intelligence within an agency is managed relates to agency size. LEAs come in many sizes from huge agencies such as the London Metropolitan Police and the New York Police Department, each with tens of thousands of staff, to the extremely small agencies that are so prevalent in the United States. We will consider agency strength from two perspectives: where and how agency size matters and where and how it doesn't.

2.8.1 Size Matters

When someone tells you that it doesn't—they are just being kind! It is diffi-cult, if not impossible, to gain the maximum benefits from intelligence if the agency does not have sufficient resources to allocate to intelligence gathering and processing.

2.8.2 Size Doesn't Matter

If a small law enforcement agency (LEA) is prepared to adopt the standards of behavior that meet international good practice and makes a concerted effort to fully integrate its intelligence function with neighboring agencies, then the intelligence can be managed effectively to the benefit of all the partners. Unfortunately, all too often such integration is not done because of petty bickering and/or a lack of understanding of what is required for effective intelligence management. In reality, agencies end up paying lip service to the concepts of effective intelligence management and delude themselves (and others) that they are doing it effectively.

Where agency size is most rapidly recognized as a problem is in the United States, which has thousands of police services, many with less than 25 members. Osborne (2006:9), writing on the changing nature of law enforcement intelligence in the United States, states,

> Developing systematic crime and intelligence analysis at the local level of law enforcement remains a challenge due to the sheer number of local law enforce-ment agencies in our nation. Each agency is separate and has a mission to protect and serve within its own boundaries. Each agency is beholden to its taxpayers to make their concern its own priority.

The actuality for many small agencies is that it is extremely difficult if not impossible to create and maintain adequate systems to gather, man-age, and exploit intelligence. Smaller agencies are unlikely to have either the financial resources or the people to carry out such work effectively. The U.S. Commission for Accreditation of LEAs (CALEA) has highlighted the diffi-culties for small agencies meeting standards for accreditation:

> This is an especially sad situation, of course, since small LEAs are precisely the ones most in need of professional benchmarks and external, objective review designed to help them make sure (and help them prove to their communi-ties and political leaders) that they are operating according to contemporary operational and administrative standards. (CALEA 2009)

Using the CALEA agency size categories as a point of reference, we can identify, as a possible guide, the threshold for the realistic expectations that an LEA should have in relation to the extent of any intelligence management function. CALEA use four categories based on the total number of agency staff (not just sworn officers), which is of particular relevance, given that many intelligence staff are often not sworn officers:

- A size: 1–24 personnel
- B size: 25–74 personnel
- C size: 75–299 personnel
- D size: 300 + personnel

Categories "A" and "B", that is, under 75 staff would have an extremely limited, if any, real intelligence capacity, with at best one or two staff being involved in intelligence management and related functions, limited to little more than recording information as it is gathered and forwarding it, if and when appropriate, to investigative units. The difficulties in properly managing intelligence for those agencies falling into Category A or B are immense, both when it comes to establishing and financing an effective system and to the intelligence contribution they can make to wider law enforcement problems.

A category "C" agency should have a functioning and structured Intelligence Unit (see Chapter 7) with analytical and response capacities. The Intelligence Unit in a category "C" agency is also likely to carry out support-ing functions for other specialized intelligence gathering roles. These roles, forming part of the agency's overall intelligence management system, relate to the processing of information received from units such as those involved in undercover and/or source management.

A category "D" agency will have at least one fully functioning Intelligence Unit, possibly more, depending on its size and the nature of its work. Furthermore, a category D agency is likely to have other specialized units demanding additional processes that feed into the agency's intelligence management system. Large law enforcement units are likely to have many Intelligence Units with one attached to each specialized investigative branch, and where the agency is responsible for a response/patrol function, there should be one in every district or region.

It should be noted that these numbers are used only as guidance and may vary depending on the nature of the LEA. It should also be borne in mind that in the majority of jurisdictions outside North America, LEAs will be significantly larger than the threshold set for Category D agencies.

The United States is not the only area where agency size is a problem for modern policing, though arguably it is at the extreme end with over 18,000 separate police agencies. Within U.K. policing, there is a concerted effort to significantly reduce the number of police services from approximately 50 to potentially nine, which would then mirror the United Kingdom investigative/intelligence structures currently in place to combat terrorism. That said, the smallest police service in the United Kingdom consists of about 500 members. The practicalities of amalgamating agencies and adopting a more conjoined approach presents a picture that is hard to find any rational objective against. The main objection to larger policing agencies is the loss of "local control," which the cynic might argue is little more than nepotism involving local elected representatives and the local police Chief. However, the need for changes in the way policing is carried out, to address such modern realities as transnational criminality and terrorism, means that greater integration is likely to be a major factor in policing over the years to come. When it comes to intelligence management, it is all but impossible for the smaller agencies to be effective, given the present and future economic realities.

Another significant problem for law enforcement when it comes to establishing effective intelligence management structures is that the geographical boundaries, often established in an arbitrary or historic manner, bear little or no correlation to the criminality that law enforcement is tasked with investigating. For example, in the United States, a Campus Police Chief will have responsibility for the behavior within the geographical boundaries of a university. Statistically, they may have only a few incidents of disorder, damage, or assaults within their area of jurisdiction. On the other hand, statistical analysis done for the Chief in the town that surrounds the campus may have significant problems with assaults, disorder, and damage. But who is committing these crimes? Probably some of the thousands of students who are living on the campus!

The limited geographical areas that small agencies work in mean that if they try to go it alone, their efforts to create effective intelligence management to serve their own community and the wider community will be all but wasted. The criminals they are operating against are not constrained by a city or county boundary, and the efforts to thwart their activities need to be pragmatic rather than dictated by a geographically limiting agenda.

Adding to these problems is the fact that implementing this system costs money, a lot of money. The training required for staff and the computerized systems to support effective intelligence management are both financially prohibitive for all but the most financially viable small agency and even then it is difficult to justify such expenditures for a few officers. The only viable effective alternative for small agencies is to pool resources with other agencies in the same geographical area, be it region, county, or state, sharing both resources and financial responsibilities. This will involve the following:

- Joint staffing
- Central purchase of a shared computer system
- Joint policies and procedures
- Joint training
- Shared strategic and tactical objectives where possible

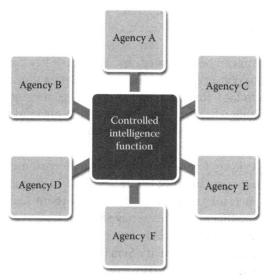

Figure 2.3 A multiagency intelligence management system.

Figure 2.3 shows a multiagency approach to intelligence management. In this model, there is only one "Intelligence Unit" and one "Intelligence Repository" (both terms are defined in Section 3.7). All the agencies involved work to the same policies and procedures for intelligence management, and they all use the same software for all functions in the intelligence management system.

Although such an approach may seem like an anathema to many, the reality is that it is the most efficient way to operate and results in significant cost savings. For those who use the "connecting the dots" analogy, this model of interagency working ensures at least that all the dots are in the one box to start with. It can be argued that, conceptually, the "Fusion" model found in the United States is similar, but from a practical perspective there are significant differences. Although implementation of the "Fusion Center" model has had problems (as discussed in Chapter 12), at this stage it is sufficient to say that the only reason that the model advocated here won't work is because those involved won't make it work—the theory is sound.

2.9   Terrorism and Law Enforcement Intelligence

Given the threat posed by terrorism and the increasing role that LEAs have to play in combatting that threat, it would be remiss not to mention the role of intelligence management in counterterrorism efforts. Few in law enforcement have real understanding of the dynamic and complex nature of terrorism or of the individuals involved, what drives their behavior, and the strategies needed to defeat them. Trying to use a computer program to identify where the next attack will be, as some have suggested, begs belief and reeks of desperation. Terrorism can be combated, and one of the key components is good intelligence, but to obtain good intelligence one must know what is required and where to go to look for it. Furthermore, an agency must have the structures in place so that when a member falls over some vital piece of information, as is wont to happen, that piece of information is captured and dealt with properly.

Generally speaking, law enforcement is not accustomed to dealing with terrorism and there can be only limited benefit in turning to intelligence services for support; for the most part, most of them have equally limited experience. Few intelligence agencies have had prolonged exposure to terrorist campaigns operating within their own boundaries, with the most notable exceptions being the U.K.'s Security Service (MI5), which has many years' experience in dealing with terrorism connected with Ireland; and Spain's Centro Nacional de Inteligencia (CNI) (The National Intelligence Centre) which was involved in dealing with terrorism in the Basque region. Even now, so many years after 9/11, experience still remains limited. Fortunately, the number of successful attacks has been limited, and other potential attacks have been thwarted, often because of effective intelligence gathering. However, there still remains a significant lack of knowledge and experience when it comes to dealing with terrorism.

Gathering intelligence on terrorism is similar to gathering intelligence on any other group, but there are some notable differences:

- It is a long-term commitment of significant resources to a problem that is likely to have low occurrence but potentially very high impact. Justifying long-term investment is difficult, particularly when there are many more pressing problems that are presently harming communities.
- There are many misunderstandings of the psyche of a terrorist. Habitually trying to demonize them or put it down to mental illness is flawed and, more important, ineffective. In short, if you understand what motivates and drives your behavior, it is the same sort of thing that motivates and drives a terrorist!
- There is a lack of background knowledge about those involved, the history of their people, their familial country of origin, their culture, and their faith (if that is relevant to the particular cause). To defeat terrorism one must start by understanding its roots; therefore, this is a good starting point for gathering intelligence when a new grouping is identified. For example, if an extremist group that links their cause to the Islamic faith is formed with members of Pakistani origin, it

is likely to be different from a group formed comprising those of Somali origin. Similarly, if a U.S. agency is investigating "sovereign" extremists, understanding the background to their views is vital to the investigators, because though both are from the same country, how each of their values have been shaped will be different.

- Intelligence with regard to terrorism is more likely to be fragmentary and sparse. Often it will come from dubious origins and be incapable of substantiation. Those receiving and dealing with the intelligence will possibly have very limited experience of the subject and find it difficult to contextualize the intelligence they have. This creates the real potential for errors to be made even when everyone is focused on the potential threat.
- The high level of secrecy involved with a terrorist investigation can lead to officers who need to know being unaware of a problem. Finding the balance is difficult but often swings one way or other for the wrong reasons.
- Penetrating a terrorist group is extremely difficult and there are huge risks. No one should be in charge of such operations if they do not have the proven ability to manage high-risk operations and make those really difficult "life and death" decisions.

Collecting intelligence on terrorism is the same as collecting intelligence on any organized crime grouping. Law enforcement needs an effective overt presence in the areas that serve as a "host" for those involved, with officers reaching out to that community and policing it in an approachable and impartial manner. Community officers need to receive training in how to spot potential human sources, and they must be briefed on who and what to look for with regard to suspicious activities. Covert operations will always be necessary, though it can be extremely difficult if not impossible to insert an undercover officer into some such groups. Hence there becomes an increased reliance on the agency's ability to proactively recruit human sources from those already within the terrorist group.

2.10   Integrated Intelligence Approach

An "integrated intelligence approach" is not a model of law enforcement but an approach that brings together many different methods using intelligence as a thread to bind them. In essence, it is about ensuring that there is a coordinated approach across all the various aspects of law enforcement and that the actions being taken are based on knowing as much as possible about what is occurring. In an integrated intelligence approach, different aspects of law enforcement complement each other and are used in a way in which all parties work toward the same goals. This approach reduces the relatively common occurrence in law enforcement, where one part of an agency or one agency not only doesn't work with other branches or agencies but also actually ends up working against them.

Intelligence is well recognized as vital to effective policing. In the United Kingdom, Her Majesty's Inspectorate of Constabulary (HMIC),* in a 1997 report on intelligence, stated,

> Good quality intelligence is the lifeblood of the modern police service. It allows for clear understanding of crime and criminality, identifies which criminals are active, which crimes are linked and where problems are likely to occur. It enables valuable resources to be targeted effectively against current challenges and emerging trends ensuring the best opportunities for positive intervention and maximum value for money.

Ratcliffe (2007), writing for the U.S. Department of Justice Community Oriented Police Services, in advice for law enforcement leaders, states,

> Nearly every modern policing strategy, from problem-oriented policing to CompStat and intelligence-led policing, requires an analysis of the criminal environment as the starting point to choosing a crime reduction strategy.

Unfortunately, because of a poor understanding of what intelligence is and how it should be used, many involved in law enforcement still view intelligence as having "nothing to do with them."

Having an effective intelligence management system in place provides service to all parts of the agency and is in turn fueled by the efforts of all within the agency. Intelligence allows leaders to have a clear picture of what the existing crime problems are and what future crime problems are likely to be. It provides them with the details to deploy resources in areas more effectively. Through being better informed, they can develop strategies to address criminality and can share their knowledge with partner agencies in order that a more holistic approach is taken to address the problems. Community policing efforts are channeled in a way that not only provide service to the community but facilitate further information being gleaned from that community to be used for intelligence purposes. The agency's priorities are clearly identified to all staff members and all staff members work to those priorities.

In an integrated intelligence approach, the expectation is that each and every member of staff understands what intelligence is, their responsibilities in collecting it, and how it can benefit them. An integrated intelligence approach assumes that the agency will be proactive in gathering intelligence,

---

* Her Majesty's Inspectorate of Constabulary is responsible for oversight of all U.K. police services on behalf of central government.

not merely relying on information that comes to them through reported crime. As Harfield and Harfield (2008:28) remark,

> The fundamental failing of an intelligence system based solely on criminal investigation is that those who successfully evade detection will not feature in it. A system informed only by police data ... will only ever reveal part of the picture.

An integrated intelligence approach ensures that where supervisors lack knowledge with regard to intelligence management, there are structures in place to guide both the collection and subsequent use of intelligence. This lessens the chances of the agency being exposed to harm through misman-agement of what can be a difficult area of business. It also substantially reduces risks to the public. An integrated intelligence approach takes aspects of law enforcement that are known to work and seeks to add value to them.

2.11   Conclusion

This chapter has sought to highlight the environment that is prevalent within law enforcement and provide understanding of the context in which intelligence is likely to be used and how intelligence can form a thread run-ning through many of the current models used in law enforcement. Some advocates of community policing and problem-oriented policing think that there is a conflict with ILP and some go as far as viewing intelligence as an anathema. Far too often, the differences between the various strategies are highlighted rather than concentrating on what each has in common. Isn't it the goal of every agency to function in the most efficient and effective manner possible? Creating integrated structures where staff understand the benefits of intelligence and where intelligence is provided to them in a timely manner means that an agency is more likely to function effectively. An integrated intelligence approach is about working smarter together.

References

Association of Chief Police Officers (ACPO). (2007) *Introduction to Intelligence-Led Policing*. U.K.: Centre for Policing Excellence (Centrex)

Carter, D.L. (2004) *A Guide for State, Local, and Tribal Law Enforcement Agencies*. U.S. Department of Justice: Office of Community Oriented Policing Services.

Commission for Accreditation of Law Enforcement Agencies (CALEA). (2009) Acc-reditation for small law enforcement agencies, *Update Magazine*, Issue 101, October 2009. Available at: http://www.calea.org/calea-update-magazine/issue-101/accreditation-small-law-enforcement-agencies (accessed September 2012).

Goldstein, H. (1990) *Problem-Oriented Policing*. New York: McGraw-Hill.

Harfield, C. and Harfield, K. (2008) *Intelligence: Investigation Community and Partnership*. Oxford: Oxford University Press.

Her Majesty's Inspectorate of Constabulary. (1997) *Policing with Intelligence: Criminal Intelligence—A Thematic Inspection on Good Practice*. London: Her Majesty's Stationary Office.

Kellig, G. and Coles, C. (1996) *Fixing Broken Windows: Restoring Order and Reducing Crime in Our Communities*. New York: Simon & Schuster.

National Criminal Intelligence Service (NCIS). (2000) *National Intelligence Model*. London: NCIS.

Skogan, W. and Frydl, K. (Eds.) (2003) *Fairness and Effectiveness in Policing: The Evidence*. National Research Council. Committee to Review Research on Police Policy and Practice. Washington, DC: The National Academies Press.

Osborne, D. (2006) *Out of Bounds: Innovation and Change in Law Enforcement Intelligence Analysis*. Washington, DC: Joint Military Intelligence College.

Ratcliffe, J.H. and U.S. Department of Justice Office of Community Oriented Policing Services. (2007) *Integrated Intelligence and Crime Analysis: Enhanced Information Management for Law Enforcement Leaders*. Washington DC: Police Foundation.

Ratcliffe, J.H. (2008) *Intelligence-Led Policing*. Cullompton, Devon: Willan Publishing.

United States Department of Justice, Office of Justice Programs Bureau of Justice Assistance. (2009) *Navigating Your Agency's Path to Intelligence Led Policing*. Global Justice Information Sharing Initiative.

Weisburd, D. and Eck, J.E. (2004) What can police do to reduce crime, disorder, and fear? *Annals of the American Academy of Political & Social Science*, 593, P42–P65.

Weisburd, D., Telep, C.W., Hinkle, J.C. and Eck, J.E. (2008) *The Effects of Problem-Oriented Policing on Crime and Disorder*. Campbell Systematic Reviews. Available at: www.campbellcollaboration.org/lib/download/228/ (accessed December 2012).

Willis, J.J., Mastrofski, S.D., and Weisburd, D. (2003) *CompStat in Practice: An In-Depth Analysis of Three Cities*. Washington, DC: The Police Foundation.

Understanding Intelligence

3

The first step in wisdom is to know the things themselves; this notion consists in having a true idea of the objects; objects are distinguished and known by classifying them methodically and giving them appropriate names. Therefore, classification and name giving will be the foundation of our science.

Carolus Linnaeus, *Systema Naturae* (1735)

3.1   Introduction

Throughout this book, we will use the term "intelligence." However, one of the greatest problems for the use of this term in a law enforcement context is the widespread lack of understanding of what the term means and the confusion that stems from this misunderstanding. In this chapter, we will seek to gain a greater understanding of the term—what it is and what it is not. We will discuss different definitions of the term and the strengths and weaknesses in each of these definitions. We will create distinctions between the meaning of intelligence as used in this book and other terms such as "data" and "information." Later in the chapter, we will look at different types of intelligence and explain each of these types. This step-by-step approach is essential if the reader is to gain a better understanding of what it is we are trying to achieve in managing intelligence and how many of the hurdles that regularly occur can be avoided.

Undoubtedly, some readers may disagree with the definitions we give for each of the terms and with the explanations as to how they were derived. As with any definition, the reader is entitled to disagree with it. However, what we seek to provide is a common understanding of terminology, so that we can progress to the important matters such as how to gather and use intelligence. A lesson from Hayakawa and Hayakawa (1990:40) in their discourse on language can assist us in becoming embroiled in a futile argument:

> … we waste energy in angrily accusing people of intellectual dishonesty or abuse of words, when their only sin is that they use words in ways unlike our own, as they can hardly help doing especially if their background has been widely different from ours

Grieve (2008:10) speaks of "labels widely employed but variously understood" and "illusionary perception of consensus." Sohi and Harfield (2008:75) discuss the nature of language used in intelligence management, suggest how ambiguities arise, and identify how the word intelligence "...may not enjoy a common meaning." Lowenthal (2006:123) in discussing the ambiguities that arise in intelligence refers to what he calls "lowest-common-denominator language" and describes these as "an attempt to paper over differences with words everyone can accept." The unfortunate aspect is that many involved in intelligence are prepared to perpetuate the ambiguity that surrounds words, adopting an attitude akin to that of Lewis Carroll's (1871) Humpty Dumpty: "When I use a word it means just what I choose it to mean—neither more nor less."

It is safe to say that there have been significant problems with regard to language in intelligence management and that the specific problem of defining the word intelligence is widely recognized. Those in law enforcement have a different reality than those who work in the military or in intelligence agencies, even though a significant amount of how law enforcement understands intelligence management originates from these two domains. The failure to translate terminology to this different reality has led to confusion. Further confusion is added when it is understood that law enforcement agencies (LEAs) receive huge amounts of information that is of little if any use from an intelligence perspective. Many law enforcement officers are uncomfortable with the term, "intelligence," because they have no real understanding of its nature. Others have taken the meaning bestowed from intelligence agencies and failed to see how the terminology and techniques need to be adapted to the law enforcement arena. Some others simply can't understand that there is a difference between intelligence and information: Walks like a duck. Talks like a duck. It's a duck! Looks like information. Sounds like information. It's information—well, actually, no. It's intelligence! And because the difference has never been properly explained to them, and because those who should know better and who are responsible for promulgating accurate knowledge continue to use the words intelligence and information interchangeably, the confusion is perpetuated and abounds.

The bottom line is that we cannot speak a language unless we know the meaning of each of the words we are using. Meanings matter, and there is enough ambiguity in intelligence work without tolerating more. Intelligence professionals should never use the words intelligence and information interchangeably. To do so is asking for confusion. If you learn nothing else from this book, remember this: information and intelligence are not the same. Let us now try and define some of the key words and concepts.

3.2 Data

The term, *data*, is used to describe statistical information contained within an LEA's records. In our context, data will be found in the form of the agency's structured records with such records likely to include the following:

- The criminal records of offenders
- Reported crime statistics, such as those demanded by government
- Facts pertaining to reported incidents; for example, nature of incident, location, time, date, and so on

For most LEAs, keeping such records as these is very much part of their daily business, with these types of records being held within the agency's record management system. There are two main problems with data. First, many LEAs place an overreliance on this type of data and exaggerate its worth. This is due in part to the fact that its "factual" nature creates the illusion that the picture it creates is accurate, and although there is a degree of accuracy, it is no more accurate than a map accurately creates a picture of a landscape. Given that there is little or no added expense in collecting the data, the ease with which it can be accessed, the lack of risk in obtaining such data (as opposed to some forms of information), and the ability to argue that any decision based on it is based in fact make such overreliance an easy path for the agency to follow consciously or subconsciously. Second, for the most part, data alone lacks meaning. As Davenport and Prusak (1998:3) remark, "Data describes only part of what happened; it provides no judgment or interpretation and no sustainable basis of action." Any decision making based purely on data is likely to be fundamentally flawed. Take for instance the Chief who looks at data pertaining to burglaries in a particular district under her command; if she sees that District Alpha has a large number of burglaries on Friday nights and decides to respond by putting all her resources into that area, the most likely results are either a geographical displacement of the problem or that the problem will desist for as long as the Chief can sustain the resources. Then the problem will resume. What the Chief needs to do is start by getting answers to questions such as the following: Why is it happening in this area? Why has it started happening? Who are the possible suspects? What do we think is happening to the stolen goods? What other possible solutions exist? Data is helpful, but it is a long way from what should be regarded as intelligence. To reiterate, the term, "data," will be used throughout the book to refer to statistical material obtained from an agency's systems.

3.3   Information to Be Considered for Intelligence Purposes

The term, *information to be considered for intelligence purposes*, is used to describe any material communicated in any medium to the agency or obtained by that agency in any way and something that the agency deems should be regarded as being of potential use for intelligence purposes. This description originates from the United Kingdom's management of police information (MoPI) and is deliberately broad in its nature. It is meant as a "catch all." The term "information for intelligence purposes" will include knowledge passed from any person to the agency, visual and auditory media, facts and records that have been acquired by whatever means, opinions expressed, and the interpretation of events by relevant parties. This list is not exclusive. Throughout the book, any use of the abbreviated form, information, will be used in the understanding that it refers exclusively to information to be considered for intelligence purposes.

The decision whether or not material should be regarded as information to be considered for intelligence purposes is made by a trained person based on an objective assessment against agreed criteria. The senior responsible officer (defined in Section 3.7) has the ultimate say with regard to how any material is to be regarded within an agency. There are a number of points that need to be acknowledged with regard to this definition, which are as follows:

- The word, information, is widely used in common parlance and within the law enforcement community. There is a need to draw a distinction between its common usage and the usage here. At present, many LEAs struggle with the whole information definition debate. No better illustration is needed than the United Kingdom's Association of Chief Police Officers (2010) policy document: MoPI,* which fudges around the words "intelligence" and "information" and leaves most of law enforcement struggling to find meaning.
- The definition of information we use here is deliberately broad. It is intended to be so in order that all involved keep an open mind. Something that may appear unimportant to the lay officer may be of vital importance to an intelligence officer. Better the information is submitted and then discounted by a trained professional than it not submitted by an untrained or uninitiated officer.
- There is an expectation that information will be the subject of further action by a trained professional. The need for a person who has the authority to dictate what is to be submitted eliminates other officers' withholding material because they decide it has no potential intelligence value or because they want to retain control of it.
- Information informs the person receiving it. Information is intended to be of further use. It is more than data that has been recorded for other reasons, such as a prosecution or as prisoner's custody record.

---

* MoPI defines police information as "...information required for a policing purpose" with policing purpose to include (1) protecting life and property, (2) preserving order, (3) preventing the commission of offenses, (4) bringing offenders to justice, and (5) any duty or responsibility of the police arising from common or statute law.

If value is added to data, it may be regarded as information for intelligence purposes. What we may have initially regarded as mere numbers can, if contextualized, categorized, and formatted, become useful information.

- Information for intelligence purposes must be processed into an intelligence product before it can be placed in an intelligence repository.
- The term, "information," should not be constrained by what is known at this present day. Technology is advancing at an incredible speed. In order for the content of this book to have a degree of longevity, it is important not to rule out types of information that may not exist or be widely available at this time.

Information will be received by an LEA from many different origins and in many different ways. Later, we will examine where information may originate and the different processes required to take the information from its origin into the agency and how it is then dealt with in the agency. The massive amount of potential material that is available means that the agency has to have in place the apparatus to decide what information has value and what information has no value. It will be a judgment call: take too much information and the agency is swamped; don't take enough, and the agency's effectiveness is limited. Once an agency accepts information into its intelligence process, from whatever origin, it must do something with it. Later, we will examine the various options.

3.4   Intelligence

One only has to look at any reputable dictionary to begin to understand why there exists much confusion over the term, "intelligence." For example, the Oxford Dictionary online includes the following definitions:

- The ability to acquire knowledge and skills
- The collection of information of military or political value

The Free Dictionary (also online) definitions include the following:

- The capacity to acquire and apply knowledge
- The faculty of thought and reason
- Superior powers of mind
- Secret information, especially about an actual or potential enemy
- An agency, staff, or office engaged in gathering such information
- Espionage agents, organizations, and activities considered as a group

The Free Dictionary continues with a different interpretation of intelligence that includes the following:

- The capacity for understanding; ability to perceive and comprehend meaning
- Good mental capacity

From such definitions, we can easily identify two strands, one of which though not unconnected can for the most part be set aside. The two strands are as follows:

1. Intelligence in a psychological context. This is to do with the functioning of the mind and is something that most people have some grasp of. It is about the power of the mind: how smart you are, how good you are at thinking, your capabilities with bookwork, your ability to function in society, and so on. This definition is without doubt the most commonly used and understood meaning of the word and arguably its original meaning.
2. Intelligence in a law enforcement or military context. This is about gathering and processing of information toward what are perceived as hostile forces, be they criminal, terrorist, or a foreign power.

Although it is the second of these strands that this book will concentrate on, what should not be ignored is the links that will become apparent between intelligence in the law enforcement context and intelligence in a psychological context. There are many threads found in the psychological context that have permeated the law enforcement context. These include matters such as the ability to acquire knowledge and the faculty of thought and reason. Such psychological processes are fundamental to the management of intelligence.

Moving away from the more general definitions, we will now mull over some of the definitions used by specialists in the field of intelligence management. Our purpose in this is twofold:

1. If we are going to spend a considerable amount of time trying to collate the best methods to use in doing something, we should have a fairly good idea of what it is we are trying to do, and these "experts" are the people best positioned to point us in the right direction.
2. One of the major problems in the management of intelligence is lack of clarity over what it is we are trying to do. For the remainder of this book, our desire is that we will be able to have an agreed understanding of the subject we are talking about; this agreed understanding being derived from a newfound commonality within the definitions that we have examined.

The lack of clarity around terminology has raised concerns about potential failings. Ratcliffe, and U.S. Department of Justice Office of Community Oriented Policing Services (2007) in their document on intelligence sharing state,

> Misunderstandings about the difference between intelligence and information—a lot of intelligence-relevant information is never transformed into actual intelligence data.

The common myth, held both publicly and by some in law enforcement, that intelligence refers to the covert tactics used to gather information, is worth debunking before we go any further. Many covert methods have become synonymous with the word intelligence. This view is perpetuated by numerous fictional stories in the movies, on television, and those in law enforcement who would like to see themselves as some type of secret agents performing high-risk stakeouts and bugging houses. The meaning of intelligence is further distorted by the perspective that everything and anything gathered by such means is automatically intelligence. Unfortunately, a similar mind-set in law enforcement leads to the erroneous belief that if a product is obtained through covert tactics, it is intelligence, whereas material obtained through traditional policing methods is information.

There exist many definitions of intelligence. The following are given as examples, followed by comment on each, with reference to the salient points contained in the definition. The reasons that so many are included is to show the complexity in attempting to tie down the concept and to identify common themes that run through each of them. In addition, it illustrates the way that some involved have attempted to take what they perceive as an easy route and to leave subsequent interpretation ambiguous. Undoubtedly, the "making do today" attitude followed by leaving it for someone else to fill in the details later is reflective of a law enforcement quick fix culture and a more generally held belief that as long as we are moving, we are making progress.

- Intelligence is "processed information" (McDowell 2009:11). This is succinct and accurate and, although this definition requires some further clarity (the devil being in the detail surrounding the process involved), if only this concept was understood by all involved, law enforcement would be on much more solid ground. Harfield and Harfield (2008:55) provide the same definition: "Intelligence is processed information." In addition, they state the purpose of intelligence as being to "inform decision making," an addition that undoubtedly has merit if one is following the principles of intelligence-led policing.
- Intelligence is "information that has been subject to a defined evaluation and risk assessment process to assist with police decision making" (Association of Chief Police Officers 2005). Although correctly

identifying that intelligence is information with something done to it, the something done to it, as suggested here, is confusing.

- "Intelligence is the combination of credible information with quality analysis—information that has been evaluated and from which conclusions have been drawn" (International Association of Chiefs of Police 2002:11). While noting that there are different definitions given at different times by this organization, a not uncommon occurrence, we again see the linking of information with a process to get a result.
- "Criminal intelligence can be said to be the end product of a process often complex, sometimes physical, and always intellectual, derived from information which has been collated, analyzed and evaluated to prevent crime or secure the apprehension of offenders" (Association of Chief Police Officers 1975 Para: 32). Here too, the word criminal has been added and a greater emphasis placed on what the intelligence gained is to be used for.
- "Information plus analysis equals intelligence" (Ratcliffe and U.S. Department of Justice Office of Community Oriented Policing Services 2007). This simple definition is accurate, save for the fact that there is a lot of confusion over the term, "analysis." The term is often taken as if it is something done by an analyst in a purist sense of the word, but what is intended in this definition is a more general interpretation of the term explained in further reading of the Department of Justice (DOJ) document. (Misunderstandings pertaining to the role of the analyst and the term, "analysis," are explored in Chapter 8.)
- "Criminal intelligence is the creation of an intelligence knowledge product that supports decision making in the areas of law enforcement, crime reduction, and crime prevention" (United States Department of Justice 2007:40). This definition, although similar to the previously mentioned DOJ definition, shifts the emphasis in the definition to meet the needs of the targeted audience—law enforcement leaders—by including the term decision making and emphasising that one aspect. Changing definition to meet the needs of one target audience or another is, at best, unhelpful, as it provides different parties with different terminology when they should be working together.
- "Intelligence is information that is capable of being understood, information with value added, information that has been evaluated in context to its source and reliability" (United Nations Office on Drugs and Crime Regional 2011). This definition, although not the most easily read, introduces the important aspect of evaluating both the origin of the material and the information supplied—an aspect overlooked by surprisingly many.
- "Intelligence is an analytic process deriving meaning from fact. It is taking information collected in the course of an investigation, or

from internal or external files, and arriving at something more than was evident before. This could be leads in a case, a more accurate view of a crime problem, a forecast of future crime levels, an hypothesis of who may have committed a crime or a strategy to prevent crime." Not unsurprisingly, given the author of this definition is the International Association of Law Enforcement Intelligence Analysts (1996:2), there is a heavy emphasis on analysis, which is not uncommon but unfortunately misleading.

- Intelligence is "the product of systematic gathering, evaluation, and synthesis of raw data on individuals or activities suspected of being, or known to be, criminal in nature. Intelligence is information that has been analysed to determine its meaning and relevance. Information is compiled, analysed, and/or disseminated in an effort to anticipate, prevent, or monitor criminal activity" (International Association of Law Enforcement Intelligence Analysts Inc. 2011:29). The change in definition from that used by the same organization in the previous definition is worth noting.

- "Intelligence is the product resulting from the collection, processing, integration, evaluation, analysis, and interpretation of available information concerning foreign nations, hostile or potentially hostile forces or elements, or areas of actual or potential operations. The term is also applied to the activity which results in the product and to the organizations engaged in such activity." This definition comes from the United States Interagency Threat Assessment and Coordination Group (2007) in their *Intelligence Guide for First Responders*. Of note in this definition is the recognition that intelligence is a product, and the word, "integration," is an arguably less ambiguous word than the more commonly used word, "collation."

- The U.S. Code of Federal Regulations: 28 CFR 23.3 (b) (3) (U.S. Bureau of Justice Assistance 1998) states that "criminal intelligence information" that can be put into a criminal intelligence sharing system is "data which has been evaluated to determine that it: (i) is relevant to the identification of and the criminal activity engaged in by an individual who or organization which is reasonably suspected of involvement in criminal activity, and (ii) meets criminal intelligence system submission criteria." As this definition has significant impact on U.S. law enforcement, it is discussed at some length in Chapter 4, although it is hard to let pass the ambiguities in a phrase like criminal intelligence information.*

---

* There is so much cause for confusion in these three words that you would need a forklift to pick it up.

On realizing that these are just some of the many definitions of "intelligence" that are in common use and reading the differences in them, one's first feeling may be one of bemusement. However, when one considers that law enforcement professionals sit down on a daily basis and have discussions that relate to intelligence and given the fact that these discussions often relate to life-and-death situations, public safety, and significant expenditure, it would perhaps be more reassuring if there was a common understanding of what the word meant. That said, one would be foolish to dwell for too long on critiquing the situation—it is what it is. A more productive approach is to draw on the expertise involved in creating such definitions, take what is important from each and then find the common threads running through them.

3.5 Intelligence Defined

For the purpose of this book, the definition of intelligence is as follows:

> Intelligence is a product, derived from the movement of information through an agreed process, which is created for the purpose of assisting in the prevention or investigation of crime and/or for the purpose of national security.

Within any agency, the process must be standardized throughout that agency and put in writing. In addition, there must be clarity around the use and meaning of the terms used consistently throughout all agency documentation. Figure 3.1 illustrates the information-to-intelligence concept.

As this is the definition that we will use throughout this book, the following statements are made to add clarity and to address the concerns some readers may have:

- Intelligence can take the form of many different products, but it is always a product.
- Information can come in any form or originate in any way. It is what is collected by the agency.

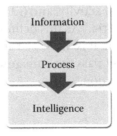

Figure 3.1 Intelligence illustrated.

- Intelligence is not what is collected; it is what is produced after the collected information is processed.
- Each agency will have its own agreed process to create products and a list of various intelligence products that may result. In an ideal world, all LEAs at least within a jurisdiction would be producing the same intelligence products.
- A number of key elements must be included in any "information-to-intelligence" process. These are collection, submission, and repositing. These terms will be explored at length in Chapter 6.
- The term, "process," is used to avoid the need for further explanation of each and every act that takes place during that process and specifically to avoid including ambiguous terms such as "analysis."
- The inclusion of the term, "national security," recognizes that many LEAs have a significant role to play in protecting the well-being of their nation.
- Intelligence is not what is collected; it is what is produced after the collected information is processed.

3.6   Intelligence: Practical Examples

To understand the production of intelligence, it may be useful to consider some examples. Each of the terms within quotation marks will be explained in depth later. For now, what is important is the ability to understand the process.

Example 1

At 2:00 a.m., Constable Malik of the Blackhill Police Department observes a person acting suspiciously in the vicinity of the Blackhill Shopping Mall, the scene of a number of burglaries. He speaks with this person and identifies him as Peter Townsend, 26 years, of 2 Hampton Court, Blackhill. When questioned, Townsend is vague on his reasons for being there. Constable Malik later completes an "information submission" and submits the details of what occurred to his "Intelligence Unit."

In the Intelligence Unit, the "intelligence officer" reviews the information submission and identifies Townsend as a well-known burglar. The intelligence officer transfers the information to an "intelligence report" and lodges it in the "intelligence repository."

An intelligence product in the form of an intelligence report has been created.

Example 2

James Golburn, an analyst at the Blackhill Police Agency, is asked to research burglaries in the Blackhill police district over the past six months.

From the "intelligence repository," he obtains details of all persons recorded there as being suspected of involvement in burglaries and any other intelligence relating to burglary, such as how the stolen goods are disposed of. From the agency's record management system, Golburn obtains details of all the burglaries that have occurred over the preidentified period. These details will include the modus operandi used and the dates, times, and locations of all the burglaries.

When Golburn analyzes all this material, he is in a position to create a number of intelligence products, including "problem profiles," "offender profiles" (which if the intelligence system is working properly will include Townsend), and "geospatial mapping" (again, if the intelligence system is working properly, it will include the Blackhill Shopping Mall). Each of these intelligence products will contain references as to where each piece of information contained within has been obtained.

Golburn files each of these intelligence products in the intelligence repository.

In this example, a number of intelligence products have been created, namely, a problem profile, an offender profile, and geospatial mapping.

Somewhat surprisingly, there are many involved in intelligence work who do not seem to realize how simple a piece of intelligence can be or the type of a thing that is worth filing in the intelligence repository. It should be remembered that what is occurring during any criminal conspiracy comprises a number of smaller parts, each of which must be identified if law enforcement is to gain a clear intelligence picture. All the items listed below are examples of things that have intelligence value:

- Descriptions of suspects including photographs
- Descriptions of vehicles including license plates and so on
- Family details of a suspect
- Associates of a suspect
- Prison history of a suspect
- Places a suspect frequents or places a gang uses
- Modus operandi of a suspect or a gang
- Telephones used and numbers contacted by a suspect
- Financial history of a suspect
- Details of a suspect's pattern of life and normal means of behaving

None of the details provided in the aforementioned list has to be confirmed as factual for it to be of intelligence value. For example, the fact that a human source reports that Tom Berry, a known drug dealer, may be driving a blue Ford van is still of intelligence value. Intelligence assessments and operations are often based on intelligence that may be incomplete, vague, or tenuous.

3.7   Definitions

Throughout the book, a number of key words and terms will be used frequently. To make what follows easier to understand, some of these terms are defined at this juncture, but they will also be the subject of further discourse later:

- *Management of intelligence.* This term will be used to embrace all aspects of an LEA's involvement in this business area including gathering, processing and exploiting material, falling within the definition of intelligence.
- *Intelligence management system.* "An intelligence management system is a complete set of interlinked processes, aimed at ensuring the provision of intelligence to assist in discharging a LEAs priorities." The term refers to the procedures, structures, and processes that an agency puts in place to collect and manage intelligence.
- *LEA.* This term is used to describe any agency whose primary function is law enforcement. For ease of use, a LEA will be referred to as an LEA, or just as an agency. Agency will not be used to describe any other agency—the one most likely to raise confusion being the Central Intelligence Agency (CIA), often colloquially referred to as "the Agency." Most often, LEAs are police services, but many other bodies are now charged with investigating aspects of criminality.
- *Member of staff.* This term is intended to include both sworn and unsworn employees of the agency. For ease of use, the abbreviated form "member" will be used. Although accepting that certain roles within the intelligence gathering arena, because of their nature, will require a sworn law enforcement officer, with the attendant powers to carry out that function, the majority of roles do not. Understandably, but unfortunately, a divide between sworn and unsworn members has developed over the years, leading to significant rancor. This attitude is counterproductive and destructive within any agency. The origins of these divisions are many and include the following:
  - Lack of long-term commitment to that agency. Traditionally, police officers sign up to policing for a lifetime career normally lasting anywhere between 25 and 35 years, whereas civilian support staff have been perceived by these officers as being less committed to the agency and more likely to shift to a role within the private sector. With commitment being equated (wrongly) with trustworthiness, some individuals are of the belief that support staff should not have access to the more sensitive information.
  - There are misconceptions that support staff would be unable to properly contextualize the information within a law enforcement context because they "weren't cops." This situation was often exacerbated by age-related prejudice, as support staff were recruited direct from university and as such had relatively little life experience, whereas the police officers held a "been there, done that" attitude gained through years of patrol experience.

- The belief that only a sworn officer could do many of the roles. This problem has its roots in how intelligence has evolved within policing over the years. In the past, many of the jobs related to intelligence were done by police officers because there was no one else to do them. Intelligence training and education was, for a long time, the exclusive domain of law enforcement, military, or the intelligence services. You had to be in one of these groups to be exposed to the methods. This has changed in more recent years, with the advent of university courses in intelligence and the adoption of intelligence practices within the commercial sector. Unfortunately, the mind-set has remained with many police officers.
- The failure of law enforcement to separate intelligence gathering from investigative functions means that much of the intelligence work that could be done more cost-effectively by support staff remains with a sworn officer to perform. This also means that the officer spends less time on duties that only a sworn officer can perform. Poor intelligence processes within an agency significantly increase this problem.
- Support staff were perceived by some police officers as being a cheaper way of getting a job done that was imposed on the agency by budget cutting managers, trying to police "on the cheap." Officers were concerned that they would be forced into unemployment or the more likely scenario that they would lose their role in the intelligence system and be forced to return to street work, leaving them with a less pleasant job and a potentially bruised ego.
- Civilian support staff were resentful over what were often significant pay differences between themselves and sworn officers, with their pay often being less than half that of what a sworn officer was getting for what was perceived to be the same job. Adding to this resentment was the fact that many of those civilians working in the intelligence arena had better educational qualifications than the police officers working with them, or indeed supervising them. The potential for bad feelings to flourish was always present. The inability for civilian support staff to advance to a higher grade within the agency, through a structured career path, often added insult to injury. The resentment in pay disparity often fails to take cognizance of the fact that the police officers' pay is not based on the role they are now performing but on the role they have previously been engaged in and may be again in the very near future. The pay differential

takes cognizance of the functions they may have to perform that the support staff will never be exposed to.

If they are allowed to persist, or grow, within an agency, these divisions between sworn officers and unsworn staff are only to the detriment of that agency. The difficulty is that many are based on human failings and emotional biases, which are not easy to stifle. In building an intelligence system, the agency needs to state clearly whether the role in question needs to be carried out by a sworn officer or can be carried out by any member. The decision maker should give careful thought to each role and in doing so put aside the notion of "it always has been this way." The rationale for making any decision should be clearly identified and documented.

- *Target.* The term, "target," refers to the subject of an investigation by an LEA. The term will include both an individual and/or an organization.
- *Commodity.* This term will be defined as "any item or substance that is inherently unlawful to possess such as contraband or materials which, if not contraband, are themselves being distributed, transacted, or marketed in an unlawful manner" (United States Department of Justice 2007:36).
- *Information provider.* The information provider is the person with whom the information originates. This term will include human sources, members of the public, surveillance operators, and undercover officers. It can also include uniform patrol officers, where they submit details of their observations or incidents in which they have direct involvement, such as the stopping of a suspect person or vehicle.
- *Information submission.* An information submission is "a stated and obligatory mechanism by which information enters the intelligence management system."
- *Submitting officer.* This term refers to the officer within a particular agency who receives any information provided and then submits that information into the intelligence system. This will include uniformed patrol officers; human source handlers; investigating officers; and, on occasion, intelligence officers. It should be noted that this refers only to the submission of information and not the repositing of intelligence in an intelligence repository.
- *Chief.* This term will be used to refer to the head of an LEA. An LEA head may also be known as "chief of police," "sheriff," "director," "commissioner," or any similar term. All these are intended to be embraced by the term, "Chief." As a mark of respect, the term will be used commencing with a capital letter.

- *Senior management team.* This refers to the members of the agency who sit at the highest levels of the agency and make command decisions. There is an expectation that the senior responsible officer for intelligence management would be part of this team.
- *Senior responsible officer.* The senior responsible officer is the officer so designated by the agency's leadership as having responsibility for all matters relating to intelligence management.
- *Organization.* This term is defined as "any group of people working together for a criminal purpose. The term embraces terrorist organizations, organized crime (such as Hells Angels and Mafia), or a group of criminals that have come together to commit a single criminal act or a number of criminal acts (e.g., five ex-prisoners get together to commit a series of bank robberies)" (Reid and Buckley 2005:18).
- *Criminal.* This term is defined as an individual who spends the vast majority of their life involved in one criminal act followed by another. These periods of criminality are often interspersed with time spent in prison, an event that the individual comes to regard as an "occupational hazard."
- *Criminality.* This term refers to any criminal act in the relevant jurisdiction regardless of its seriousness. When used in this book, the term is intended to include terrorism, unless there is a specific need to distinguish between the two. It will also include public order offending.
- *Terrorist.* This term is defined as any person involved in the commission, instigation or preparation of any act of terror for political, religious or ideological cause. This terminology is intended to be broad in scope, both with regard to the role of the person concerned and the nature of the activity. It is acknowledged that the popular concept of a terrorist is that of a bomber, gunman, hijacker, and so on. For the purposes of this book, terrorism will also include people who provide any form of logistical support to the organization or political activists who are intrinsically linked to that organization. The nature of the terrorist activity will include all actions that are designed to instill "terror" in others, including the victim of the crime. The concept of *ideology* will include causes such as animal rights, anticapitalism, and anarchy groups, that promote their cause through the use of violence.
- *Human source.* A human source is defined as "a person who has been deliberately recruited and is managed to collect information to satisfy an intelligence requirement" (Reid and Buckley 2005:18). This term is used in this book only to refer to a person who is registered

and authorized by the agency to be used as a human source and is managed in accordance with the agency's procedures for human sources.

- *Member of the public.* This term refers to any citizen who provides information to law enforcement. This information will normally be given in the expectation that it is given "in confidence" and that this person's identity as the provider of it will not be exposed. The use of the words, "member of the public," is intended to distinguish between those citizens who provide information on a one-off or occasional basis and those who are registered by the agency as human sources. This distinction is necessary to ensure that the people in each of these two categories are managed correctly and that the information they provide is managed correctly (Buckley 2009).
- *Intelligence repository.* An intelligence repository is a central storage point for all intelligence products.
- *Intelligence product.* An intelligence product is any product that is so identified by the senior responsible officer. Each agency should clearly identify in writing the types of intelligence products it produces. There should be clarity around the terminology used and clear instructions as to the purpose of each product and how it is to be used. The purpose of an intelligence product is often to influence the thinking of the recipients or to provide information of use to them in their function.
- *Intelligence agency.* This term is refers to a body whose primary function is gathering intelligence to protect national security whether this is done at home, as with agencies such as the United Kingdom's Security Service (MI5) or Australia's Australian Security Intelligence Organisation, or internationally, with agencies such as the United Kingdom's Secret Intelligence Service (MI6) or the U.S. CIA. Such a list of intelligence agencies will also include those with intercept responsibilities such as the United Kingdom's Government Communications Headquarters. It is acknowledged that some agencies carry out the functions of both an LEA and an intelligence agency—for example, An Garda Siochanna, the police service in Ireland. It is also acknowledged that many LEAs have specific units that deal almost exclusively with intelligence matters. Typical of these is the special branch units found in U.K. police services and sections within the Australian Federal Police (AFP) and the Federal Bureau of Investigation. However, these will not be considered as intelligence agencies.
- *Investigation.* An investigation refers to the inquiry into any matter. In most cases in law enforcement, an investigation will be pursued

with the intention of bringing offenders to justice. However, the term
is intended to be wide in its meaning and will encompass activities
such as the prolonged inquiries into organized crime gangs and terrorist organizations.

- *Intelligence Unit.* This is the central collection point for all information that may be of use for intelligence purposes. The unit is
responsible for processing that information into intelligence. The
term, "Intelligence Unit," will always begin with capitals to stress
the importance of this unit in the intelligence management system.
- *Intelligence manager.* This is the member in charge of the Intelligence
Unit. In larger agencies with numerous Intelligence Units, it will be
normal procedure to have a senior intelligence manager of a higher
grade.
- *Jurisdiction.* Jurisdiction refers to a particular geographic area containing a defined legal authority. Jurisdictions may refer to a whole
country or a designated part of a country such as a province, state,
or city/town area. Laws for a jurisdiction may vary from laws for
neighboring jurisdictions, and jurisdictions may be governed by
both national laws and local legislation.
- *Executive action.* Executive action refers to overt action carried out
by an LEA in pursuit of an investigation or operation.* It will include
such things as arrests, searches, or public order deployments.
- *Debrief and debriefing.* The terms "debrief" and "debriefing" are frequently used in intelligence management with their meanings used
interchangeably. To clear up any ambiguities and prevent further
confusion, both are defined here. "A debriefing is an interview with a
person in order to obtain information about a specific event or events
that have taken place." Debriefing is the noun and debrief the verb.
They can be clarified by means of examples: handlers will carry out a
debriefing (noun) with a human source to extract the details in relation to the events that the source can provide information on since
the time of their last meeting with that source—the "debriefing"
refers to the event. On the other hand, a sergeant will "debrief" (verb)
her officers following a house search to ascertain how that search
went and what was found. These terms are both intended to convey
the structured obtaining of information by adherence to a recognized process. Some agencies use the terms to describe an information submission. This should be avoided.

---

* Although the term, "executive action," has its origins in the more sinister aspects of a
certain government's foreign policy and a close association with assassinating foreign
leaders, the meaning in this publication is obviously significantly different.

3.8 Purpose

The purpose of producing intelligence within an LEA is to support the role of that agency and its partner agencies, and where relevant, to provide support to the national security function.

3.9 Types of Intelligence

Intelligence is often separated into two different "types" of intelligence, which are most commonly referred to as "strategic intelligence" and "tactical intelligence." Referring to them as strategic intelligence and tactical intelligence infers that intelligence can be separated out and put into an either/or box, but this is not correct. Intelligence is intelligence, and the separation comes primarily from how any piece of intelligence is used or is likely to be used. The division or separation focuses on "its intended purpose" (McDowell 2009:13). This can be a useful division, because one item may be of interest or use at a strategic level, but it will be of limited interest or use to those at a tactical level, and vice versa.

There are a number of points worth highlighting in relation to strategic intelligence, which are as follows:

- It tells senior management what is happening and what is likely to happen in the future in relation to criminality.
- It generally focuses on a long-term perspective.
- It enables senior management to effectively deploy resources against currently identified threats/problems and emerging problems and to develop control strategies.
- Most often, it focuses on the structure of organized crime, including terrorism, patterns in ongoing criminal activity, and the threat posed by emerging criminal trends.
- Many managers don't really understand strategic intelligence, how it is gathered, and how it should be used, yet it is at the strategic level that they are making decisions. As McDowell (2009:36) comments, "...it can be fairly said that all senior police managers have some familiarity about intelligence and its potential, few indeed have more than a superficial understanding about the specific benefits...." This problem is exacerbated by a reluctance of many to attend training in the subject.
- Those involved in gathering tactical intelligence rarely have an understanding of the nature of strategic intelligence and therefore do not gather information that may be of use in addressing strategic requirements.

- Strategic intelligence must be provided in a timely manner to allow medium- and long-term strategic decision making and to facilitate the development of suitable responses.
- Strategic intelligence is sometimes perceived as competing with tactical intelligence, possibly because of the competition for limited resources or because a strategic response may be in conflict with a desired tactical response to a problem. Both tactical and strategic intelligence should complement the other. Each needs to be understood by those involved in intelligence management.
- Strategic intelligence often addresses what could be referred to as the less tangible aspects of criminality, such as providing an understanding of why a particular crime is occurring or giving insight into the mind-set of those involved.
- When dealing with terrorism, strategic intelligence is likely to include a significant focus on the political or religious issues that are part and parcel of terrorist actions.
- Most law enforcement members are more comfortable in dealing with tactical intelligence as opposed to strategic intelligence, which sometimes tends to be woollier and less specific.
- The nature of information gathered to assist in preparing strategic level intelligence products is likely to be broader than that gathered at a tactical level. For example, the information required to address a particular crime type that is of interest will include the following:
  - What features facilitate the occurrence of this crime?
  - What modus operandi is employed to facilitate the crime? How are the crimes committed? Are there any notable features?
  - Is the crime type on the increase? Why? What external factors are driving this? Is it likely to become more widespread in the longer term?
  - How many people are involved as perpetrators? How widespread is the problem? Are particular communities involved?
  - What structures surround the perpetrators? Are they in organized gangs? Are these gangs formalized?
  - What impact are these crimes having on the community? How much money is involved? Is this criminality lowering the standard of living of the community? What level of violence is associated with this crime type? Is the crime having a greater impact on particular communities?

This is far from a definitive list but gives an indication of the nature and breadth of questions that will need to be answered. It should also be noted that the answer to one question will often lead to the emergence of further questions. Such progressive development of questions enables those analyzing the problem to seek the relevant information they need and so gain a much clearer understanding of the problem if the information is received or to clearly identify the gaps that exist in any finished product. When all this information is analyzed and combined, a strategic-type intelligence product will be the result.

Tactical intelligence can be defined as "intelligence regarding a specific criminal event that can be used by operational units to further a criminal investigation, plan tactical operations, and provide for officer safety" (Adapted from International Association of Law Enforcement Intelligence Analysts Inc. 2011). However, rather than attempting to drill down into this more formal type of definition to provide understanding, it is easier to explain what tactical intelligence is through examples, augmented by some of the related problems.

Tactical intelligence usually focuses on specific criminal groups or individuals or on specific criminal activities. It directly relates to what the cops on the ground are dealing with every day. Tactical intelligence requirements will often be concentrated on providing ways to control risk in the short term. It is often used to further both proactive and response investigations. Following a murder, the investigating officer will often put out requests for any intelligence in relation to the murder. The intelligence provided in response is tactical intelligence. One of the biggest problems with tactical intelligence is that because agencies are very much focused on getting quantifiable results, all that staff are tempted to pursue is tactical intelligence. Even though this provides short-term gain for the agency and the members involved, the fact that this type of intelligence is pursued to the exclusion of any strategic intelligence can be detrimental to the longer term objectives of the agency. Tactical intelligence often relates to rapidly evolving situations where the information received is processed and acted upon within minutes. Tactical intelligence is often a critical factor for decision makers in very volatile public order situations, with commanders having to adjust operational plans as new intelligence becomes available. Some senior officers do not like to be involved in making decisions involving tactical intelligence, because those decisions are often fraught with serious risks, for which there is limited or conflicting intelligence available.

Often with the exploitation of tactical intelligence potential, longer term, more strategic consequences are overlooked. When exploiting tactical intelligence, even though there may be the need for a rapid turnaround, decision makers must also consider any longer term consequences.

3.10 Operational Intelligence

Ratcliffe (2004) identifies another level of intelligence that he refers to as "operational intelligence." He states that operational intelligence is "the creation of an intelligence product that supports area commanders and regional operational managers in planning crime reduction activity and deploying resources to achieve operational objectives" (Ratcliffe 2004:5). Debatably, the term is intended for use in larger LEAs where there are a number of command areas (geographical or other), each of which has to develop its own enforcement strategy, and this strategy is developed using "operational intelligence." In reality, what is happening is that area management is being provided with strategic intelligence referring specifically to an area, as opposed to the area covered by the whole agency. There would appear to be little benefit in creating or using a different term for what remains strategic intelligence. The term, "operational intelligence," is discussed here only to inform the reader and is not used again.

3.11   Categorizing Intelligence

For expediency, intelligence products are often categorized by the dominant theme of their content. Although such categories of intelligence have arguably limited benefit, they will often include such headings as follows:

- *Public order.* Intelligence relating to the activities of anarchist groups. This type of intelligence causes real problems for law enforcement, as it relies on the ability to draw a distinction between what is legitimate public protest and when that legitimate public protest is used to facilitate, mask, or is hijacked by those seeking to endanger public safety or create significant criminal disorder. All too often, legitimate protest by well-meaning individuals ends with violence and extensive damage to property. It should be remembered that it is the duty of police to facilitate legitimate protest. Gathering intelligence to identify those persons intent on subverting legitimate protest to pursue their unlawful agenda is a legitimate and necessary tactic to safeguard democracy. Another problem arises in gathering intelligence on groups whose methods, although peaceful in intent, involve unlawful acts committed solely in pursuit of their protest agenda. Such activities are likely to include rooftop protests, using protestors to chain themselves to objects, and so on. The problem that this creates for police is the often fine line between facilitating legitimate protest and upholding the laws of the land. An arguably more difficult decision for policing is whether or not to use intelligence gathering to establish the likely size and nature of any legitimate protest to police such a demonstration on a more cost-effective basis. For example, a source is used within the protest movement to identify expected numbers, so the Chief has an idea of what resources are needed at the event and how much it will cost the agency.
- *Financial.* Intelligence relating to financial crimes and money-laundering activities. This category has relevance, as the intelligence

involved often requires interpretation by trained financial investigators, with lay members having a limited understanding of what needs to be collected or how to interpret that which has been collected. Furthermore, it is often only trained financial investigators who the finance and banking industries will deal with.

- *Criminal.* Intelligence relating to "ordinary decent criminals" as distinct from those individuals involved in terrorism. (It should be noted that the term, "criminal intelligence," is often misused in the context of analysis in an attempt to draw distinction between analyzing data from an agency's records management system and analyzing intelligence from the agency's intelligence repository. Furthermore, Carter (2004:9) in discussing the meaning of intelligence states, "The phrase 'law enforcement intelligence' used synonymously with 'criminal intelligence,' is frequently found in conjunction with discussions of the police role in homeland security. In most cases, the term is used improperly." The prevalence and pernicious nature of confusing language undermines the credibility of what law enforcement is seeking to achieve, and leaves many with an attitude conceptualized in the statement, "If we can't even agree on a definition, there is not much point in bothering with the rest." Criminal intelligence is a term that is often used within law enforcement. Where it is being used to distinguish intelligence relating to criminality as opposed to intelligence relating to national security (national security intelligence), its usage is correct. However, using the term, "criminal intelligence," in other contexts creates confusion. Many understand criminal intelligence to denote a distinction between those involved in analyzing crime statistics and those in analyzing just intelligence, with the product created by the statistical analysis being referred to as criminal intelligence. When used in this context, the term perpetuates the two mistaken beliefs that (1) analyzing crime statistics produces intelligence and (2) analysis based purely on intelligence provides a complete picture of what is occurring.
- *Terrorism.* Intelligence relating to all aspects of terrorism, including related political strategies. It should be noted that while of necessity LEAs will encounter what some will articulate as legitimate political activity, the activity is so integrally linked to terrorism that law enforcement must gather intelligence of this nature. The difficulty that often arises is that the line between legitimate political activity and that of terrorist-related activity is rarely clear and often fluctuating. This dichotomy is often readily exploited by terrorist groups and their political counterparts such as Euskadi Ta Askatasuna (ETA) in Spain and the Irish Republican Army (IRA) in the United Kingdom and Ireland.

- *Subversive.* Intelligence relating to activities by foreign powers to undermine the state. This type of activity is sometimes dealt with either by specialist agencies or by specialized departments within a police department.
- *Counterintelligence* (CI). Activities to counter the threat posed by criminal, terrorist, or foreign states that are gathering intelligence on the legitimate government, the state as a whole, or on an LEA and/or its members. Few LEAs are not vulnerable to this threat. Unfortunately, many give insufficient thought to counteracting such activities, believing them to be the domain of intelligence agencies.

Throughout this book, these categorizations will be used only where it is necessary to distinguish between the subject matter to which an intelligence product refers, for example, criminal, terrorism, financial, and so on.

3.12   Actionable Intelligence

As the name infers, actionable intelligence is about taking action with regard to the intelligence obtained, with little or no need for further research or investigation. Actionable intelligence is defined as "intelligence with sufficient specificity and detail to implement immediate action by a LEA." Actionable intelligence requires extremely limited, if any, further development before it is acted upon. Actionable intelligence can be acted upon either by taking overt executive action or sometimes through a covert response.

3.13   National Security

The term, "national security," refers to all matters pertaining to the protection of a nation state. It is intended to be broad in spectrum and will, but not exclusively, include terrorism, subversion, economic and industrial threats, espionage, and work carried out in support of military objectives. It is recognized that those involved in managing intelligence are from different countries and that each will view the protection of their nation as paramount. Although this is an understandable position, there are times when investigating, for example, transnational crime or terrorism that the well-being of citizens of another nation should at least be considered to be of equal importance.

3.14   National Security Paradox

If we use the term, "national security," as defined in Section 3.13, then the obvious expectation would be that the protection extends to citizens of that nation, and in the vast majority of circumstances it does. However, there exists a paradox: if the protection of the nation includes the protection of citizens of that nation, then what happens when protecting all the citizens may have to be done at the cost of not protecting one citizen? Where national security is involved and the primary role of an agency is protecting national security, then protecting the nation will take precedence over the protection of an individual or indeed a number of citizens. This paradox has particular relevance when there is joint involvement between LEAs and intelligence agencies. Intelligence agencies will be more inclined to withhold intelligence where they believe it will be of long-term benefit to their role rather than share that intelligence for the short-term gain of law enforcement. This can create significant difficulties for law enforcement, as their priorities are much more focused on the immediate and on the protection of individual lives. The debate between the two standpoints is worthy of much consideration. More importantly, for those involved in intelligence management in a law enforcement context, it is a recognition that this paradox exists and exists for genuine reasons, albeit reasons that may be hard to stomach.

3.15 Radicalization

Radicalization is a term that has become popular since 9/11. It refers to the indoctrination of people (normally young in years) into terrorist organizations. There is a significant demand for intelligence relating to how this is done, who is doing it, and to whom it has been done. Radicalization is normally used in the context where a person's faith is used to draw them into acts of terrorism. Although the use of the term may have become fashionable in recent years, the psychological process it involves has been around for a long time and was very successfully used by terrorist organizations in the terrorist campaigns in Northern Ireland. From a psychology perspective, radicalization is basically the same process used to recruit many people into gangs or, for that matter, into any group.*

3.16 Military Intelligence

Although this book is not aimed at the management of intelligence to support a military campaign, the very nature of many areas of operation in which the military are engaged is likely to bring them into significant contact with

---

* When a young man, the author's father used to warn him with regard to indoctrination and brainwashing and told him numerous times of the dangers of frequenting the local rugby club, where he would be led astray by those who attended that "den of iniquity." Radicalization is neither new nor are the measures used now really any different than have been used in the past to corrupt youth.

LEAs. This is by no means a new concept, as for over 30 years military intelligence has worked in support of law enforcement in Northern Ireland and joint military law enforcement operations are now commonplace in emerging democracies, where the rule of law requires significant military support. In addition, military police units have a requirement for intelligence gathering to combat criminality perpetrated by serving personnel.

Military intelligence has often significant assets that are of benefit in addressing their own needs, but those are often of limited benefit or are unavailable to law enforcement. The terminology used by military personnel is also often at variance with that used by law enforcement, adding to the confusion and complicating joint efforts. In the interests of clarity and completeness, it is worth mentioning the most significant forms of military intelligence techniques and their equivalence within a law enforcement context. Although the definitions used are those taken from a U.S. Department of Defense (2011) dictionary, the following terms used are widely accepted across North Atlantic Treaty Organization countries:

- *Imagery intelligence (IMINT)* is "the technical, geographic, and intelligence information derived through the interpretation or analysis of imagery and collateral materials" (U.S. Department of Defense 2011:131). In this context, the term "imagery" is defined as "a likeness or presentation of any natural or man-made feature or related object or activity, and the positional data acquired at the same time the likeness or representation was acquired, including: products produced by space-based national intelligence reconnaissance systems; and likeness and presentations produced by satellites, airborne platforms, unmanned aerial vehicles, or other similar means (except that such term does not include handheld or clandestine photography taken by or on behalf of human intelligence collection organizations)." It is rare for LEAs to have ready access to the benefits of satellite imagery; however, many LEAs are now using sophisticated technology to produce a wide variety of images obtained using aeroplanes, drones, and helicopters. Although much of this material will be used for investigative purposes, crowd control, and so on, the versatility of the technology means that it is readily adaptable for the information gathering role. Of additional interest in the definition will be the exclusion of images obtained through direct human involvement; in military parlance, such imagery falls into the human intelligence (HUMINT) category. In the law enforcement context, images taken directly through the involvement of a person are likely to fall into categories included under human source collection, surveillance collection, or undercover collection.

- *Signals intelligence (SIGINT)* is "a category of intelligence comprising either individually, or in combination, all communications intelligence, electronic intelligence, and foreign instrumentation SIGINT, however transmitted" (U.S. Department of Defense 2011:255). The type of information obtained closely relates to the interception of communications that is often carried out by larger LEAs and includes telephones, e-mails, and radio transmissions.
- *Human intelligence (HUMINT)* is "a category of intelligence derived from information collected and provided by human sources" (U.S. Department of Defense 2011:129). The military definition of HUMINT is a broad one and includes any aspect of information gathering that involves people. The term, "human source," is not used here with the same meaning as it would be in law enforcement. Law enforcement divides the HUMINT category of information gathering into numerous separate categories including undercover operations, investigative interviews, and information received directly from members of the public. Because of the many and varied processes involved in these different aspects of information gathering, categorizing them as one is totally unsuitable for law enforcement from both legal and practical perspectives. Arguably, it is confusing for many military personnel, because many consider themselves to be specialists in HUMINT, whereas they specialize in only one small area of it.
- *Open-source intelligence (OSINT)* is "information of potential intelligence value that is available to the general public" (U.S. Department of Defense 2011:206). There is a direct correlation between the military and law enforcement usages of this term. The definition correctly excludes many government records that may be available to LEAs.
- *Measurement and signature intelligence (MASINT)* is "intelligence obtained by quantitative and qualitative analysis of data (metric, angle, spatial, wavelength, time dependence, modulation, plasma, and hydromagnetic) derived from specific technical sensors for the purpose of identifying any distinctive features associated with the emitter or sender, and to facilitate subsequent identification and/or measurement of the same. The detected feature may be either reflected or emitted" (U.S. Department of Defense 2011:176). With the increasing use of technology in law enforcement contexts, the use of sensor-type devices to assist in law enforcement problems is on the increase. Such technology can provide assistance in investigating illegal border crossings, drug trafficking through isolated landings, and drug growths carried out in remote areas.
- *Geospatial intelligence (GEOINT)* is "the exploitation and analysis of imagery and geospatial information to describe, assess, and visually depict physical features and geographically referenced

activities on the earth. Geospatial intelligence consists of imagery, imagery intelligence, and geospatial information" (U.S. Department of Defense 2011:118).

- *Counter Intelligence (CI)* is "information gathered and activities conducted to identify, deceive, exploit, disrupt, or protect against espionage, other intelligence activities, sabotage, or assassinations conducted for or on behalf of foreign powers, organizations or persons or their agents, or international terrorist organizations or activities" (U.S. Department of Defense 2011:64). This subject is discussed later with regard to security and the threat of penetration that the more sophisticated criminal organizations pose to law enforcement and one that is often neglected.

3.17 Intelligence: A Practical Perspective

Having examined the meaning of intelligence from a theoretical perspective, we will now look at the question of what is intelligence from a practical perspective. There are a number of reasons for this, which are as follows:

- Sometimes in the midst of a theoretical debate, there is potential to lose what is important from a practical standpoint. Although it is important for those involved in intelligence management to be aware of both concepts and terminology, it is equally important to make sure that all involved, particularly at the collection point, are aware as to what is worth recording and submitting, because it may have an intelligence value.
- Many involved in collection have a narrow focus, seeing only what is of benefit to them and sometimes only that which is of immediate benefit. Gaining an understanding of how many different aspects of intelligence can be used to create a broader or more detailed picture can only benefit LEAs.
- Training for most of those involved in intelligence work is so limited that it is often more by accident than plan that they become aware of the worth of some information. Officers cannot be expected to know what they haven't been properly taught.*

Although the following is by no means a comprehensive list of everything that may be of intelligence value, it is intended to inform those who are new to intelligence the basics and provide for those who have been involved

* This fact may come as a huge surprise to some in management.

for some time some ideas they may not have previously come across. The list is in no particular order:

- *Person details.* Where a person is suspected of involvement in criminality, details such as family details, residences, vehicles, associates, places frequented, employment, languages spoken, and telephone details are all significant.
- *Places of interest.* Any information about places frequented on a regular basis by those involved in crime will be of interest. Details to include will be proper addresses, owner's details, and names used for the premises (many places are referred to by slang terms or colloquial names). Depending on the extent of their linkage with crime, floor plans and photographs of the premises may also prove useful, such details often being obtained during searches of the premises.
- *Aliases and nicknames of persons of interest.* All too often, law enforcement relies on a suspect's given names and, to a lesser extent, aliases. Nicknames can be extremely important to those intercepting communications or involved in undercover work.
- *Patterns of life.* A pattern of life refers to how individuals normally spend their day, where they go and at what times, who they normally meet with, their routine, and so on. This is very useful if an arrest is to be made and/or for surveillance purposes.
- *Language and slang.* Coming with many criminal groupings and crime types is a language unique to that crime group or crime type. It is important that every opportunity is taken to document the jargon that is used. This reduces the chances of other intelligence being misinterpreted and helps investigations to progress. Furthermore, it gives interviewers credibility if they can show intimate knowledge of what they speak.
- *Group structure, rules, and norms.* Many investigations will focus on organized crime groups and terrorist organizations. With all such groups, there will be a degree of structure, there will be rules, and there will be norms of behavior within that group. All opportunities should be taken to collect and document such information. If you do not understand the group and how it functions, how can you expect to destroy it?
- *Stories, rumors, and gossip about persons of interest.* All these give insight into the vulnerabilities in a person and the group dynamics within criminal organizations. They are particularly useful in the proactive recruitment of sources.
- *Methods and tricks of the trade.* Criminals are by default ingenious creatures. The way in which they operate their criminal enterprises and the complexity of their schemes can easily be overlooked in the

rush to secure a conviction. Although it is fantastic to catch the thief with his hand in a cookie jar, there is a story to tell as to why he picked that cookie jar, how he got to the jar, and what he was going to do with the cookie if he got away. Investigators concentrate on the evidential aspect of the case but sometimes overlook the massive amount of information that needs to be documented, processed as intelligence, and reposited for the benefit of others, at a later time. How many times have you sat at a conference and been enthralled as a detective recants an investigation containing so many useful facts about the group you are investigating, that you are left wishing you had known them before you started your own investigation? Criminal methods and tricks of their trade need to be committed to paper and reposited in the intelligence repository.

- *Specialized criminality.* Some aspects of criminality can be highly specialized such as money laundering, computer crime, and pedophilia. Where an agency has access to any information on such activities, it is paramount that the maximum amount of information is gathered in respect of the modus operandi of those involved. Opportunities to obtain detailed information on such activities can be rare and must be exploited to the maximum possible extent. Specialized methods used by such criminals need to be processed into intelligence and shared with as broad a law enforcement audience as possible.
- *Prison intelligence.* Intelligence relating to prisons and prisoners is often overlooked by law enforcement, possibly because of an "out of sight, out of mind" or "no longer my problem" attitude by police officers. Although this is understandable, information relating to prison and prisoners is both available and of importance outside the prison walls. (Intelligence gathering in prisons is dealt with in Chapter 9.)

Where law enforcement has been working against a criminal organization over a prolonged period, the assumption is often made that all the basic information on the group has long since been collected. This is rarely the case and is one reason why many investigations can benefit from an analytical review with any intelligence gaps being identified. Developing the theme of "lost" intelligence, the following points should be borne in mind:

- There is often a significant amount of information that has never been extracted from sources that have been managed over prolonged periods of time. Handlers assume that all the sources have to offer have been previously collected by others. This problem is only countered by structured debriefing, followed by the submission and processing to intelligence of everything gained.

- Unless there is extensive debriefing of undercover officers to extract the information they pick up through osmosis, during continuous exposure to a target, much of what they learn will never be captured. The gradual and often subconscious assimilation of information is rarely recognized by the undercover officer and therefore needs to be extracted by a trained cover officer and submitted into the intelligence management system.

3.18   Conclusion

Hopefully, having clearly identified the importance of clarity in language and defined many of the key words and phrases we will use, most readers now have a better understanding of the nature of intelligence. Language and meaning is a theme that we will revisit throughout the book—such is its importance. For now, we progress to look at some of the legal issues that are likely to be encountered in creating an intelligence management system.

References

Association of Chief Police Officers (ACPO) (1975) *Report of the Subcommittee on Criminal Intelligence* (The Baumber Report). London: Association of Chiefs of Police.

Association of Chief Police Officers (ACPO) (2005) *Guidance on the National Intelligence Mode*. U.K: Centre for Policing Excellence (Centrex).

Association of Chief Police Officers (ACPO) (2010) *Guidance on the Management of Police Information*. 2nd ed. U.K: National Police Improvement Agency.

Buckley, J. (2009) Managing information from the public. In: Billingsley, R. Ed. *Covert Human Intelligence Sources. The Unlovely Face of Police Work*, pp. 97–108. England: Waterside Press.

Carroll, L. (1871) *Through the Looking Glass*. London: Penguin Books.

Carter, D.L. (2004) *A Guide for State, Local, and Tribal LEAs*. Washington, DC: U.S. Department of Justice, Office of Community Oriented Policing Services.

Davenport, T.H. and Prusak, L. (1998) *Working Knowledge: How Organizations Manage What they Know*. Boston, MA: Harvard Business School Press.

Grieve, J.G.D. (2008) Ideas in police intelligence. In: Harfield, C., MacVean, A., Grieve, J.G.D and Philips, D. Eds. *The Handbook of Intelligent Policing: Consilience, Crime Control and Community Safety*, pp. 9–15. Oxford: Oxford University Press.

Harfield, C. and Harfield, K. (2008) *Intelligence: Investigation Community and Partnership*. Oxford: Oxford University Press.

Hayakawa, S.I. and Hayakawa, A.R. (1990) *Language and Thought in Action*. Orlando, FL: Harcourt Inc.

International Association of Chiefs of Police (IACP) (2002) *Criminal Intelligence Sharing: A National Plan for Intelligence-Led Policing at the Local, State and*

Federal Level. Available at: http://www.ncirc.gov/documents/public/supplementaries/intel_sharing_report.pdf [accessed December 2012]

International Association of Law Enforcement Intelligence Analysts (IALEIA) (1996) *Successful Law Enforcement Using Analytic Methods.* Richmond, VA: International Association of Law Enforcement Intelligence Analysts.

International Association of Law Enforcement Intelligence Analysts Inc. (2011) *Law Enforcement Analytical Standards and Global Justice Information Sharing Initiative.* Available at: http://it.ojp.gov/documents/law_enforcement_analytic_standards.pdf [accessed November 2012]

Interagency Threat Assessment and Coordination Group (ITACG) (2007) *Intelligence Guide for First Responders.* Washington, DC: Inter Agency Threat Assessment and Coordination Available at: http://www.nctc.gov/docs/itacg_guide_for_first_responders.pdf [accessed July 2012]

McDowell, D. (2009) *Strategic Intelligence: A Handbook for Practitioners, Managers, and Users.* Lantham, MD: Scarecrow Press Inc.

Lowenthal, M.M. (2006) *Intelligence: From Secrets to Policy.* Washington, DC: CQ Press.

Ratcliffe, J.H. (2004). The structure of strategic thinking. In: Ratcliffe, J. H. Ed. *Strategic Thinking in Criminal Intelligence*, pp. 1–10. Sydney, NSW: Federation Press.

Ratcliffe, J.H. and U.S. Department of Justice Office of Community Oriented Policing Services (2007) *Integrated Intelligence and Crime Analysis: Enhanced Information Management for Law Enforcement Leaders.* Washington, DC: Police Foundation.

Reid, C. and Buckley, J. (2005) *Human Source Management—A Better Approach to Managing Human Intelligence Sources.* U.K: Home Office Police Research Awards. Crown Copyright.

Sohi, K. and Harfield, C. (2008) 'Intelligence' and the division of linguistic labour. In: Harfield, C., MacVean A., Grieve J.G.D and Philips, D. Eds. *The Handbook of Intelligent Policing: Consilience, Crime Control and Community Safety*, pp. 75–89. Oxford: Oxford University Press.

United Nations Office on Drugs and Crime Regional (2011) *Criminal Intelligence Training Manual for Analysts.* Programme Office South Eastern Europe. Available at: http://www.unodc.org/documents [accessed May 2012]

United States Department of Justice (2007) *Minimum Criminal Intelligence Training Standards for Law Enforcement and Other Criminal Justice Agencies* (Version 2). Washington, DC: US Department of Justice Global Justice Information Sharing Initiative.

U.S. Department of Defense (2011) *The Dictionary of Military and Associated Terms.* Washington, DC: US Department of Defense. Available at: http://www.dtic.mil/doctrine/new_pubs/jp1_02.pdf [accessed July 2012]

U.S. Bureau of Justice Assistance (1998) 28 CFR Part 23 Criminal Intelligence Systems Operating Policies Executive Order 12291. *Policy Clarification.* Available at: https://www.iir.com/28CFR_Program/28CFR_Resources/Executive_Order/ [accessed December 2012]

Human Rights, Legislation, and Ethics 4

Never presume yours is a better morality.

Graham Greene

Everything beautiful has a dark side, and some of us must dwell there, so that others can laugh in the light.

Joe Abercrombie, *The Last Argument of Kings*

4.1 Introduction

In an anarchic world, if you are strong enough, you take what you want, and the stronger you are, the more you can take. And of course the reverse of this also holds; the weaker you are, the less you will have, and the less you will keep. If you are strong enough, you can build your own army to ensure you remain the strongest and if you can't, the weaker still you become. But many countries have evolved from this anarchic and imbalanced position. It can be argued that the essence of law in a modern democratic society is the protection of the weak. Laws are there to even out the power imbalance. Democracy is about making a pact, with one party saying to another, "Give me the power to make laws and I will make laws that ensure your safety. Give me the strength and you no longer need to be concerned about your weakness." All sounds like a great deal.... Well, that is the theory ... arguably!*

Taking this somewhat simplistic theoretical standpoint at its most basic level, and accepting that a democratic government uses its power to draw up laws to protect its citizens, then by extension, law enforcement officers are the instrument of that government's power. The primary function of law enforcement becomes to protect the weak, on behalf of the government. No longer do individuals need to be concerned about their safety and keeping what belongs to them. No longer do citizens need to fight for what is theirs; they have law enforcement to do that for them. This would be ideal from a citizen's perspective, except for two aspects. First, there are

---

* And then just for keeping you safe, they hammer you each year with a tax bill! (A realistic indicator of their strength and your weakness.)

still those out there who have not "signed up" to adhere to the laws and are still trying to take away what belongs to the citizens and with whom law enforcement is in a perpetual struggle, that is, the criminals. Second, having given law enforcement the power, the citizen is quite entitled to ask as to what safeguards are in place to ensure that the power is not abused to the detriment of the citizen. As the Roman satirist Juvenal asked, "Ed quis custodiet ipso custodes?" ["But who will guard the guards?"] Or asked in a more modern context, "Who protects citizens' rights from being abused by the state?"

At this juncture, we will make the assumption that most citizens accept the right of the police to fight the law-breakers, although the complex nature of law enforcement will necessitate a return to this assumption at a later stage. This chapter begins by exploring the second set of concerns (the potential abuse of power) and discusses the checks and balances that the citizen is entitled to expect when it comes to making sure that law enforcement does not overstep the mark and abuse its position. Given the "secretive" nature of intelligence management, it is extremely important that structures are in place that enable law enforcement to demonstrate that it is not abusing the power with which it has been entrusted. From there, we will move on to other matters where legal compliance will impact the construction of our intelligence management system. Then we will discuss the situation where laws enacted by government and methods used by law enforcement are unacceptable to some citizens, and how law enforcement can attempt to make decisions on an ethical basis as to which course to chart to get through such dilemmas. We will discuss the involvement of staff in intelligence management and the responsibility that senior management has to protect them. These discussions will fall under the woolly umbrella of ethics and morals. We will finish with a brief look at the threat of corruption.

4.2 Human Rights

A significant element of intelligence management engages what are commonly referred to as "Human Rights." These rights are "inalienable" (incapable of being alienated, transferred, or surrendered), "universal" (applicable everywhere), and "egalitarian" (the same for everyone). People are entitled to these rights purely by being human. They denote basic entitlements of everyone and are often referred to as "rights and freedoms." While many countries will have their own specific Human Rights legislation, the principles involved are very similar and all are closely linked to the 1948 "Universal Declaration of Human Rights."

4.3   Universal Declaration of Human Rights

Central to all law enforcement actions should be adherence to the principles laid down in the Universal Declaration of Human Rights, a declaration adopted by the United Nations in 1948. This declaration was created by the United Nations, following the discovery of the excesses of Nazi Germany and the way in which the government in Germany abused the rights of its citizens. At the core of the principles laid down in the declaration is the relationship between the government of a country and its citizens. The term "government" is not restricted to the elected representatives but includes any person or agency acting on their behalf. This obviously includes law enforcement agencies (LEAs) such as police, customs and immigration, and other government bodies such as the military and intelligence agencies. In short, what the declaration says is that citizens have rights that are protected from state interference.

Many of these rights have significant relevance when it comes to intelligence management, and while it is impossible here to discuss at length the relevance of each and every right, it is worth highlighting the ones that have most relevance and how those rights are likely to be engaged in intelligence management. Under the declaration, the rights are documented in numbered articles, and the most relevant ones are explained below:

- "Article 2: Everyone is entitled to all the rights and freedoms set forth in this declaration, without distinction of any kind, such as race, colour, sex, language, religion, political or other opinion, national or social origin, property, birth or other status. Furthermore, no distinction shall be made on the basis of the political, jurisdictional or international status of the country or territory to which a person belongs, whether it be independent, trust, non-self-governing or under any other limitation of sovereignty."

  This article focuses on discrimination. Law enforcement must ensure that the actions it carries out in regard to intelligence management are not carried out in a prejudicial manner. One only has to remember how minority groups in Nazi Germany were singled out and their rights removed, to understand the significance of this article. Discrimination is addressed again in articles 7 and 18, which specifically address faith-based rights. These articles have particular relevance when terrorism has links to a particular faith. It is incumbent upon the LEA to ensure that their systems are sufficiently robust to ensure that people are being investigated because of their illegal actions and not because of their faith. Human Rights courts tend to take a broad view in relation to what may constitute discrimination, and all agencies should have in place additional procedures and higher levels of authorization, where information gathering is likely to take place at places of worship or against faith-based organizations. Many agencies have had significant criticism from religious groups for such activities, and given the fact that LEAs are relying on law-abiding members of these groups to come forward with information, there is much to be lost by alienating them. Harris (2009) highlights the problem:

> ... the FBI and some police departments have placed informants in mosques and other religious institutions to gather intelligence. The problem is that, when the use of informants in a mosque becomes known in a Muslim community, people within that community, the same people that law enforcement has so assiduously courted as partners against extremism, feel betrayed. This directly and deeply undermines efforts to build partnerships, and the ability to gather intelligence that might flow from those relationships is compromised or lost entirely.

- "Article 3: Everyone has the right to life, liberty and security of person."
  This article is significant, as it places obligations on the government not only to not take the life of its citizens but also to protect the life of its citizens when there is a threat. Human Rights courts including those in Canada and in Europe have placed what they term a "positive obligation" on the state to protect a life of citizens particularly where the state has some involvement in the circumstances pertaining to the threat to their lives. For example, in intelligence management, this has particular relevance when law enforcement is managing a human source, and the LEA must take measures that are reasonably practical to safeguard the life of humans sources and to prevent them from injury. This obligation to protect the human source is also present for any other person with whom the LEA is likely to engage with during information-gathering operations, and also includes agency members. It is because of this article that the agency should have in place effective risk management structures to manage all aspects of intelligence management processes when there is a threat to a person's life. According to this article, agencies should also have secure means to protect the identities of the people who have provided law enforcement with information.
- "Article 10: Everyone is entitled in full equality to a fair and public hearing by an independent and impartial tribunal, in the determination of his rights and obligations and of any criminal charge against him."

This article addresses a citizen's rights in relation to a judicial process, and from Article 10 stem significant expectations in regard to the fairness of trials. Many of the operations carried out by law enforcement will gather both evidence and information to be used for intelligence purposes. Furthermore, many individuals will end up being in front of a court because of intelligence-related activities. Law enforcement needs to bear in mind that everything it does in gathering information and managing the subsequent intelligence products may at some stage be put under scrutiny in a judicial process. While it is acknowledged that there will also be times when information has been collected and the manner in which it was collected will not be intended for court purposes, the processes and system involved should all be developed to handle material to evidential standards. Stemming from this article is the issue of "equality of arms." Recognizing that the state has huge resources to collect evidence to prove someone guilty, Human Rights courts have attempted to balance this out to the benefit of the citizen by stressing the need for those resources equally to be deployed to prove that the citizen is innocent. It is from this principle that the processes of "discovery" and "disclosure" have their origins.

- "Article 12: No one shall be subjected to arbitrary interference with his privacy, family, home or correspondence, nor to attacks upon his honour and reputation. Everyone has the right to the protection of the law against such interference or attacks."

  This article is intended to prevent the state from interfering with the private life of any citizen. The definition of "private life" has been subject to a broad interpretation by Human Rights courts, which have held that the term private life includes home, family, correspondence, and employment. Whenever law enforcement seek to gather information on a person, it is likely that this article is engaged, and therefore there must be a lawful basis and a legitimate reason to do so.

- "Article 13: (1) Everyone has the right to freedom of movement and residence within the borders of each state. (2) Everyone has the right to leave any country, including his own, and to return to his country."

  The first part of this article has most relevance in an intelligence management context. While outwardly it may appear to address merely the interference with a person's right to move freely, interpretation of this article means that the right is engaged where the state monitors the movements of a person. This is obviously what occurs when a person is subjected to physical surveillance by a surveillance team or a tracking device is placed on a vehicle. In addition, it can be argued that when and where the state monitors the movements of a person

by examining travel documents such as airline bookings or bus tick-
ets purchased by a person, then this article is engaged.

- "Article 20: (1) Everyone has the right to freedom of peaceful assembly and association. (2) No one may be compelled to belong to an
association."

  Again, it is the first part of this article that has most relevance in
an intelligence management context. Interpretation of this article
means that the right is engaged when the state monitors who a person
associates with and or attempts to curtail people's right to assemble
together. Two aspects merit consideration here. First, care must be
taken when law enforcement is monitoring one person lawfully, and
they gather details on other individuals merely through association.
Second, law enforcement may encounter difficulties in monitoring
the activities of protest movements and anarchist groups. There is
often a fine line between lawful protest and public disorder; yet, if
law enforcement gathers information on such groups, especially
using covert methods, this article is likely to be engaged.

There are other notable human rights conventions including the European
Convention on Human Rights (1950) and the International Covenant on
Civil and Political Rights (1966). Many countries have incorporated human
rights conventions into national legislation, such as the Canadian Charter
of Rights and Freedoms (1982) and the New Zealand Bill of Rights (1990).
The close links between the United Kingdom and its European partners, the
related oversight of the European Court of Human Rights, and the linkage
in legal structures between the United Kingdom and other Commonwealth
countries means that judgments made in one jurisdiction pertaining to
human rights can have significant impact on how courts, in any of these
linked countries, are likely to interpret similar events. There are a significant
number of judgments relating to protection of life, information collection,
and judicial proceedings that officers engaged in intelligence management
need to be aware of.

The United States voted in favor of the declaration at its adoption. Many
of the principles included in the declaration are also found in the U.S. Bill
of Rights, created in 1791, and refer to the first 10 amendments of the U.S.
Constitution. It is easy to recognize the shared principles between many of the
Amendments in the Bill of Rights and the related articles in the declaration.

- *Amendment I.* Congress shall make no law respecting an establishment of religion or prohibiting the free exercise thereof; or abridg-
ing the freedom of speech or of the press; or the right of the people
peaceably to assemble and to petition the government for a redress
of grievances.

- *Amendment IV.* The right of the people to be secure in their persons, houses, papers, and effects, against unreasonable searches and seizures, shall not be violated, and no warrants shall issue, but upon probable cause, supported by oath or affirmation, and particularly describing the place to be searched, and the persons or things to be seized.
- *Amendment VI.* In all criminal prosecutions, the accused shall enjoy the right to a speedy and public trial, by an impartial jury of the state and district wherein the crime shall have been committed, which district shall have been previously ascertained by law, and to be informed of the nature and cause of the accusation; to be confronted with the witnesses against him; to have compulsory process for obtaining witnesses in his favor; and to have the assistance of counsel for his defense.

It should also be noted that the U.S. Bill of Rights is seen as a means to limit the power of government, much as the United Nations declaration is viewed as protecting the rights of citizens from government interference.

These, and similar documents found in many jurisdictions, provide law enforcement with clear guidance, and in some countries legal obligations, as to the standards of behavior that citizens expect from law enforcement. Following these guiding principles, we can identify clear steps that should be taken in the case of intelligence management. First, and what is often overlooked by those critical of law enforcement activities around intelligence management, is that law enforcement is under an obligation to take whatever measures are reasonably practical to protect the rights of citizens. There are many in society who would try and deprive citizens of these rights through criminal activities. Activities such as covert operations and intelligence management are legitimate methods that the state should, and arguably must, employ to protect the rights of citizens. Second, in all aspects of intelligence management, there is a clear obligation on the state to protect the lives of citizens who provide information to the police. Third, whenever law enforcement are gathering information on citizens, they must be able to justify why they are engaging that citizen's right to privacy. Human Rights case law dictates five guiding principles, which are as follows:

1. *Legal basis.* There should be legislation that permits the agency to carry out the activity that engages the citizen's privacy. For example, there should be legislation that mandates when and under what limitations surveillance on a citizen should be carried out. This legislation should be visible to the public definitive, clearly avoiding vagueness. In the U.S. case of Connally v. General Construction Co.,* Justice

---

* Connally v. General Construction Co., 269 U.S. 385 (1926) Available at: http://supreme .justia.com/cases/federal/us/269/385/case.html.

Sutherland provided guidance in relation to clarity of legislation with similar standards likely to be expected elsewhere:

> [T]he terms of a penal statute ... must be sufficiently explicit to inform those who are subject to it what conduct on their part will render them liable to its penalties ... and a statute which either forbids or requires the doing of an act in terms so vague that men of common intelligence must necessarily guess at its meaning and differ as to its application violates the first essential of due process of law.

Similarly, in European Human Rights Courts, reference has been regularly made to the "Quality of Law" test. This sets standards for the legislation and requires the legal regime to be clear, foreseeable, and accessible.* Law enforcement policy is not sufficient to discharge this obligation. The legislation should state what level of authority is required to allow law enforcement to "spy" on the citizen. In other words, government is giving the citizen fair warning as to when and how their expectation of privacy will be reduced.

2. *Legitimate reason.* The activity must be carried out for a legitimate reason. Although there may be legislation that allows law enforcement to place a listening device in someone's house, there must be a legitimate reason for law enforcement to do so. Such reasons should be documented and are likely to include circumstances, such as the prevention and detection of crime, to preserve public order or to protect public safety. In other words, the state cannot act in an arbitrary manner.

3. *Necessary.* The concept of necessity is one that stands or falls on a case-by-case basis. Recognizing that the greater the depth of intrusion into a person's privacy, the greater the cause the state must be able to show as to why the state needs to take this course of action. If law enforcement is going to place a listening device and tracking device in a vehicle, then the citizen's level of privacy is going to be severely compromised. Law enforcement must show why they have *no option* but to take this course of action. They must also show that they took, or at least considered, less intrusive actions to gather the information and that the less-intrusive actions had failed or were likely to fail.

4. *Proportionality.* The severity of the measures that law enforcement engage in must be proportionate to the severity of the crime being investigated. Law enforcement must recognize that while they have

---

* See relevant case law: Harman and Hewitt v. U.K [1992] 14 EHRR 657; Rotaru v. Romania, No. 28341/95, 4 May 2000, European Court of Human Rights; V and Others v. Netherlands, Commission Report of 3 Dec. 1991.

power to do something, that power should be used only where it is appropriate. For example, the bugging of a teenager's house merely because they are stealing candy from the local Seven-Eleven store is unlikely to be considered proportionate. The adage "We don't use a sledge hammer to crack a nut" captures the essence of this requirement.

5. *Accountability.* Whenever law enforcement engages an individual's rights, why they have done so and the manner in which it was done must be fully accounted. In other words, there must be a comprehensive record of all that law enforcement has done in relation to the engagement of the citizen's privacy. This is about effective record-keeping, at which, unfortunately, many LEAs are abysmal. Each step of the process must be recorded in a way such that can later be readily accessed. It should be noted that this does not mean that law enforcement has to provide such details to the citizen, but that if there is a legal requirement for the records to be shown, they are available. It is good practice for law enforcement to have clearly documented procedures as to how records will be maintained throughout the intelligence management system and who is responsible for each record.

These five steps are relatively easy to achieve and should be in place for all information-gathering activities, in particular covert activities. They are intended to be sequential. This means that if there is no legal basis, the activity ceases, at which point the subsequent steps are arguably irrelevant. However, given that some jurisdictions do not have relevant legislation for some covert activities, such as managing human sources, the subsequent four steps should still be adhered to.

4.4 Anonymity and Collateral Intrusion

Two other principles closely associated with Human Rights principles should be noted, that of the concept of "anonymity" and the meaning of "collateral intrusion." Citizens have the right to go about their business without government interference. They are entitled to shop in a town center without being spied upon by closed-circuit television cameras (CCTV). Such cameras are often installed as a crime-prevention mechanism, particularly in areas where there is significant crime or a threat from terrorism. Although a citizen may be captured on such a camera, each citizen is as *anonymous* as the one next to them and their privacy is not engaged by the state. However, where such cameras are used to monitor a specific citizen, as part of a planned operation, it is then that individual loses anonymity and the right to privacy is engaged.

Appropriate legal authority for such activity should be sought, and relevant procedures should be followed.*

If law enforcement are carrying out surveillance on an individual, that person will meet with people, both as part of his criminal activity and ordinary pattern of life. Some of the people he meets with will not be involved in any criminality, yet law enforcement will have engaged those *innocent* people's right to privacy. This is referred to as "collateral intrusion." It is something done as a side effect of what is intended. Human Rights principles dictate that such side effects be kept to a minimum and that the LEA documents how it will manage the material that is obtained on these innocent individuals. On a practical level, what should occur is that the agency has procedures in place for reviewing the material at the end of the operation and/or after a reasonable period following its conclusion, for "purging" or "weeding out" of material for which there is no legal basis to keep.

It should be stressed that while in some jurisdictions, there may not be a legal obligation to comply with the aforementioned requirements, compliance with them ensures that the LEA is adhering to the best practice with regard to Human Rights—surely what most LEAs would wish to achieve and what citizens are entitled to expect. Furthermore, officers should have no fear of such processes. Human Rights principles are there to protect all citizens, including the officers, and in many cases, they place an obligation on officers and agencies to take actions that others may find morally distasteful such as the use of human sources.

Nothing found in Human Rights instruments should prevent law enforcement from carrying out its role successfully. Where law enforcement is most likely to fall foul to such instruments is through a lack of in-depth knowledge of them and how relevant judicial bodies are likely to interpret the various articles. An agency engaged in intelligence management should have access to a legal advisor with expertise in Human Rights and the application of those rights in an intelligence management context.

4.5   Practical Application of Human Rights Obligations

From a practical perspective, it is worth demonstrating how human rights obligations should be interwoven into an application to carry out an information gathering operation. Let us consider the following scenario: Miguel

---

* Those maintaining such cameras should have mechanisms in place to prevent random unauthorized access to the content provided by the cameras. Far too often, such content is provided on an ad hoc basis to television producers, for no other reason than to provide cheap titillation to viewers, with little or no respect for the rights of citizens, while all the time masquerading under the banner of "freedom of speech."

Garcia has volunteered to be a human source and give information on two criminal associates, Luis Mendoza and Pablo Diaz, both of whom are involved in drug dealing.

- First, if the agency, or to use the legal language of Human Rights courts "The State," of which the agency is representative, is going to engage the privacy rights of Mendoza and Diaz by asking a human source (Garcia) to spy upon them, then there must be a law that allows the LEA to do this. For example: the United Kingdom's Regulation of Investigatory Powers Act (2000) is permissive legislation to allow the use of human sources. Where the agency has an authorization process for such activities, the legislation being used should be specified in the application forms used.
- Second, the question should be asked, "Is this action for a legitimate purpose?" And the answer in this case is obviously, "Yes, it is to prevent and investigate crime." The officer requesting the use of Garcia as a human source should document the severity of the drug problem in their area, the nature of the investigation, and the extent of the involvement of Mendoza and Diaz. Furthermore, they should document what other less-intrusive methods that have been tried to stop Mendoza and Diaz, and how these methods have failed or how they would be unlikely to succeed. This paragraph of the application makes it clear why the actions are "necessary" and "proportionate."
- Third, a paragraph should outline the way in which the human source, Garcia, will interact with the targets of the investigation, Mendoza and Garcia, and what results are expected.
- Fourth, a comprehensive risk document should be prepared outlining all the risks involved in the operation, and how those risks will be managed, including the risk of collateral intrusion. These third and fourth paragraphs allow the agency to fulfill its obligations in relation to the right to life of all involved and to ensure that any evidence obtained as a result of the relationship meets the requirements of a fair trial.
- Fifth, the application should be forwarded to a person of suitable rank for authorization of the operation, with particular reference to the Human Rights obligations.
- Sixth, the application process and comprehensive records of all meetings between officers and the human source, Garcia, and directions given to him by the officers, ensure that everything is done in a fully accountable way, thus meeting Human Rights' obligations in relation to accountability.

Similar processes should be in place for all such covert operations including undercover, surveillance, interception, and the use of human sources.

Such processes ensure that all evidence and intelligence are more likely to be collected in a lawful manner.

4.6   Good Faith

Another concept found in many jurisdictions is that of acting in "good faith." Derived from the Latin term "bona fide," the term may be defined as "A party's state of mind in acting or carrying out an action or transaction, evincing honesty, fairness, full communication of any hidden issues or information, and an absence of intent to harm other individuals or parties to the transaction" (Webster 2010). In essence, acting in good faith is about the actor's state of mind at the time they carry out a given act and focuses on the fairness of those actions, but more so on the *intention to be fair* in carrying out the actions. While the concept, in general, may at best be described as woolly, most people have a reasonable grasp of when, and if, a person is acting with noble intentions. There are many times during information-gathering operations and in the management of the subsequent intelligence product, when there is ambiguity about what the agency should do under the given circumstances. When an agency decides on a course of action that at a later stage is proven to be either the wrong course of action or that their actions were unlawful, the fact that they have acted in "good faith" will go a long way to justify their actions and may allow evidence to be submitted to a court that would otherwise have been ruled inadmissible.

Another consideration to acting in good faith, and pertaining to Human Rights, is the need to take into consideration the context in which law enforcement activity will take place. Care should always be taken when there are higher expectations in relation to adherence to human rights, such as in dealings with faith-based groups, education establishments, or any location where there is a higher expectation of privacy or freedom of speech. Rightly or wrongly, the expectations in relation to what could be referred to as the "sanctity" of these and similar establishments should be *considered* prior to any law enforcement action. Expectations of law enforcement behavior have often been alluded to in court judgments. For example, in the judgment in the Californian case of White v Davis,[*] which dealt with covert activity on a university campus, concluding that there had been a violation of freedom of speech and assembly, the court remarked, "Although the police unquestionably pursue a legitimate interest in gathering information to forestall future

---

[*] White v. Davis, 13 Cal.3d 757 [L.A. No. 30348. Supreme Court of California. March 24, 1975.] Hayden V. White, Plaintiff and Appellant, v. Edward M. Davis, as Chief of Police, and others, Defendant and Respondent. Available at: http://law.justia.com/cases/california/cal3d/13/757.html

criminal acts... . The inherent legitimacy of the police 'intelligence gathering' function does not grant the police the unbridled power to pursue that function by any and all means." The court continued, "In like manner, covert police surveillance and intelligence gathering may potentially impose a significant inhibiting effect on the free expression of ideas." Such judgments, regardless of the jurisdiction, give a clear indication as to the need for law enforcement to have in place structures to address the issues pertaining to citizen's rights.

4.7   Reasonableness

Closely linked to the concept of good faith is that of "reasonableness." Central to the idea reasonableness is the answer to the question, "What would a reasonable man do under these circumstances?" The answer is about the judgment of any reasonable person and is used as a benchmark in courts in many jurisdictions. It is about adopting a commonsense standpoint and viewing the circumstances of a given situation objectively. The term "The man on the Clapham omnibus."* is often used in U.K. courts and refers to a reasonably educated and intelligent but nonspecialist person, against whom the conduct of others can be measured. It can be a useful tool where it is necessary to decide whether or not a party has acted in the way that a "reasonable" person should—for example, in a civil action for negligence. In carrying out intelligence-gathering operations, those involved should seek to be able to show that their actions were reasonable under the given circumstances. Unfortunately, those involved often make biased decisions based on their world view and then cannot understand why the average man in the street thinks the actions were unreasonable. Working in law enforcement often prejudices the way we view the world.

4.8   Justifying Intelligence Collection and Retention

Law enforcement must be able to justify on a case-by-case basis its reason for collecting information on a person and for retaining intelligence on a person. For those involved in law enforcement, this would appear to be an easy and possibly pointless task. An explanation running along the following lines should be sufficient: "We are trying to prevent crime and save lives. We think we should hold on to these details about this person, because they are

---

* This term is believed to have been first coined in the United Kingdom in the 1933 case of Hall v. Brooklands Auto-Racing Club. Available at: http://www.lawteacher.net/tort-law/lecture-notes/negligence-breach-lecture.php

connected to crime or may be connected to crime, now or in the future." This explanation is all a bit tenuous.

In order to consider this problem from a defensible position, it needs to be broken down into digestible parts. The first part of the argument is to establish that law enforcement needs to collect information and store intelligence if it is to prevent and detect crime, preserve public order, and keep the community safe. The next stage is to justify why information is collected on certain people. There is a difference between collection and storage. If law enforcement is going to specifically go out and look at a person, the threshold for doing so is going to be higher than that of merely storing intelligence. It is a deliberate act on the part of the agency to engage that person's privacy that must be justified accordingly. A sustainable argument must be made that the person must be monitored to investigate an existing crime or to prevent future crimes. The difficulty for law enforcement here is evidencing why they believe a crime will take place in the future, and why it is this person that will be involved in that crime. This is more easily done if the person has a history of criminal involvement—the best predictor of future behavior being past behavior. But what if the person has no criminal past, and the information is being collected just because they might do it? From where did this belief come? Intelligence…? Sometimes in intelligence, law enforcement can drift into a chicken and egg-type scenario. The main thing to remember is always to put into writing justification for the engagement of privacy. Inherently problematic that the ideas of "future criminality" and "potential involvement" may be, the rationale for retaining intelligence on a person who has not committed a crime, but might do so, is that law enforcement is able to justify, on reasonable grounds, that a relationship exists between that person and criminality. Establishing the reasonableness of this argument will be significantly easier if it can be shown that the person has the potential to commit the crimes and has the inclination to do so. This is one reason why reporting the exact words spoken by a suspect is important. Similar arguments are also likely to withstand scrutiny where a criminal organization has been the subject of investigation and a person is found to be a member of that organization.

If information about a person comes to law enforcement from whatever origin, other than with deliberate and planned collection as discussed above, then the process to turn information into intelligence should ensure that the information is subject to objective scrutiny, before it is retained as intelligence. It can be argued that the threshold for retaining such information is significantly lower as first, there was no planning on the part of law enforcement to engage the person's privacy, and second, the decision to retain the material was made after an objective assessment, by a *trained* professional. Third and finally, the intelligence will be subjected to review, after a set period of time. The reality is that, as unfortunate as it may appear for the individual, there are few potentially negative consequences for them but law enforcement cannot afford to take the risk to other citizens of throwing away intelligence that may be of use in preventing crime or compromise of public safety.

4.9   U.S. Standards for Intelligence Management

The U.S. Bureau of Justice Assistance (1998) has issued regulations detailing how criminal intelligence should be managed. These regulations are entitled "Code of Federal Regulations." Title 28, Judicial Administration, Part 23 Criminal Intelligence Systems Operating Policies (1998) and are commonly referred to as "28 CFR 23." It is sometimes argued that these regulations do not relate to LEAs that do not have a multijurisdictional function (even if they occasionally collaborate with other agencies) or to agencies that do not receive federal grant funding. However, they do set standards of behavior, and there is no good reason that every agency should not adhere to the standards. They are designed to ensure that the rights of citizens are protected and pose no problem for the efficacy of law enforcement function. Some of the key principles are summarized below with direct quotes indicated:

- *Restriction on personal information.* There is a necessity for "reasonable suspicion" of involvement in criminal activity to collect or store "criminal intelligence" on a person, and the information must be relevant to that criminal activity.
- *Restriction on collection of types of information.* Law enforcement cannot collect "intelligence information about the political, religious or social views, associations, or activities of any individual or any group, association, corporation, business, partnership, or other organization unless such information directly relates to ..." criminal activity.
- *Defining reasonable suspicion.* "Reasonable Suspicion or Criminal Predicate is established when information exists which establishes sufficient facts to give a trained law enforcement ... employee a basis to believe that there is a reasonable possibility that an individual or organization is involved in a definable criminal activity"
- *Legal compliance.* An intelligence system "shall not include in any intelligence which has been obtained in violation of any applicable federal, state, or local law."
- *Disseminating intelligence product.* Dissemination of "criminal intelligence information" is only permitted "where there is a need to know and a right to know the information in the performance of a law enforcement activity."

- *System security.* The system must ensure that "administrative, technical, and physical safeguards (including audit trails) must be adopted to insure against unauthorized access and against intentional, or unintentional, damage. A record shall be kept indicating who has been given information, the reason for release of the information and the date of each dissemination outside the project. Information shall be labelled to indicate levels of sensitivity, levels of confidence, and the identity of submitting agencies and control officials."
- Information should be such that it cannot be "modified, destroyed, accessed, or purged without proper authorization." If material can be lifted from a cupboard, it can easily be altered or destroyed—effective software solutions should substantially mitigate this risk.

As can be seen, there are strong similarities between these regulations and the expectations relating to Human Rights compliance. It is important to note that while wording may be different from jurisdiction to jurisdiction, the general principles regarding acceptable behavior are agreed upon. Similar structures as detailed to ensure Human Rights compliance will also ensure that an agency collects information in compliance with 28 CFR 23 and that subsequent storage of the product is lawful. There has been widespread adoption of the principles detailed in 28 CFR 23, but unfortunately, as with the interpretation of Human Rights guidance, poor interpretation of 28 CFR 23 leads to the disparate application of the regulations among agencies, as Ratcliffe and U.S. Department of Justice Office of Community Oriented Policing Services (2007) illustrates with his comments in relation to perceived legal constraints:

> A lack of familiarity with 28 Code of Federal Regulations (CFR) Part 23 leads many intelligence analysts to be overly cautious in their handling of potentially sensitive information. This results in both compartmentalization and silo thinking.

In addition, culturally, within the United States, there are concerns about the abuse of civil liberties by government, particularly in regard to the combining of law enforcement functions with those of the intelligence community. Commenting on this fear, Turner (2006:51) remarks,

> A fear exists that combining the two functions [intelligence and enforcement] in one agency or a group of agencies would give rise to a "Gestapo" or "KGB" that would trample American freedoms and civil liberties.

It is easy to perceive the origin of these fears, with many being raised on stories of human rights abuses by "secret police" agencies across the world. How realistic such fears in relation to the present-day United States may be subject to some skepticism, but what has to be recognized is that many people have genuine concerns about civil liberties. The nature and extent of the threat from terrorism creates a context where extensive interaction and exchange between intelligence agencies and law enforcement is likely to be required for the foreseeable future. Putting in place structures that promote Human Rights and accountability, and placing related policies in the public domain, can go a long way to assuaging such fears.

Concerns regarding the abuse of citizen's rights are not limited to the United States; similar problems have arisen in many jurisdictions. Many of these concerns arise because LEAs are caught bending the rules to suit their agendas. Acknowledging that legislation is often ambiguous in its nature, the readiness of some officers to stretch meaning, to interpret the rules, or to suit their objectives inevitably causes damage to the relationship with the public. In many cases, this occurs because the officer has only a superficial knowledge of the legislation. In others, it is because the officer is too lazy to do the task lawfully or so arrogant as to think they know better. The best way to demonstrate adherence to the legislation and the protection of civil liberties is for the LEA to develop specific policies and procedures to cover these aspects and to ensure that staff adhere to these policies and procedures.

4.10 Legislation: Problems and Solutions

The next sections provide an overview of some of the many legislative and related concerns that surround intelligence management. It is intended to provoke thought and direct readers to where they need to go. It should not be considered as an in-depth view of any of the likely issues nor should it be a comprehensive list of all such matters. Each jurisdiction is likely to have other pieces of legislation that impact intelligence management, and nowhere here is there sufficient explanation to pick up the various nuances and interpretations that will be potentially made in any jurisdiction. To summarize:

- When reading legislation, read it all and any accompanying explanatory notes. Law is often badly written.
- Do not just read the law, but also any relevant case law, and if it is new legislation, look at the context in which it has been introduced.
- Interpreting the law to make it fit what you want to do can create risks.
- Human Rights are fundamental to law enforcement, and intelligence management engages many of the principles. Officers need training to understand these principles.
- Build an intelligence management system assuming that you will have corruption and you will reduce corruption.

- Corruption will be reduced if members are trained in the psychology of corruption.
- Many of the roles associated with intelligence bring additional stresses. Members need training to identify and manage stress.
- Staff need good training in ethics and morals. This training needs to involve open and frank discussion, so members can view the concept from different perspectives.
- Audit what is being done. Members need to know what they do will be subject to regular examination.

There are a number of areas of legislation that are likely to impact intelligence management and the covert activities used to gather information. Some of the more prevalent of these are examined in the following paragraphs.

4.11 Participation in Crime

There are times during intelligence-gathering operations and investigations when it is necessary for law enforcement to authorize the participation of an individual in an act, which under different circumstances, would be criminal. This type of activity is sometimes referred to as "participation," a somewhat euphemistic term used to describe what the person is doing. Participation in crime is most often carried out by a human source or an undercover officer. Obviously, there are significant problems with this type of activity, and too often legislatures and the courts have kept their distance from addressing the issues raised. There are a number of points worth considering:

- It is always better if the jurisdiction has clear legislation allowing this type of activity. For example: Section 25 of the Canadian Criminal Code provides for a justification of otherwise illegal acts to be committed by the police in the course of an investigation and also protects civilians from liability, who act under the authority of a police officer. Although not a perfect piece of legislation, it is a long way down the road to it!
- If there is no permissive legislation or there is doubt about the illegality of the activity, the agency may chose to continue with the actions provided they have assessed all the risks and have fully justified their actions in writing.
- Those involved need to be fully aware of offenses relating to conspiracy, assisting offenders, and other similar offenses. There are a significant number of times when authorization for participation is not obtained because those members involved do not realize an offense is occurring.

- Regardless of the legal position, the agency should have a very clear set of procedures for carrying out such activity, and it must be authorized at a very senior rank. In most small agencies, the senior rank would be either the Chief or her Deputy; in larger agencies, it may be at an equivalent rank to assistant commissioner. These procedures should include the circumstances that determine how the benefits of such activity are gauged against the risks involved, and under what circumstances the agency will authorize the activity. In all such authorizations, the nature of the offense and where possible the statute engaged should be stated.
- It should be remembered that often the involvement of a source or undercover officer constitutes only one element in the operation or the investigation; many other aspects are likely to be present and these should all be taken into consideration in authorizing the activity.
- The level of criminality authorized should correlate with the seriousness of the crime being investigated: the more serious the crime, the easier it becomes to justify the actions of law enforcement to combat that crime. Obviously, within limits!
- There must be a comprehensive risk management plan in place for all such operations.
- Accountability of the highest level must be in place for all aspects of the activity. While public reporting on the frequency and nature of the criminality would increase transparency, it carries with it additional arguably unnecessary risks.
- Participation in crime can be justified for a number of different reasons, of which the main one will be to provide law enforcement a better opportunity to thwart the crime and make amenable the "would be" offenders. A second reason often put forward is to allow an undercover officer to maintain his credibility, by appearing on the wrong side of the law. This can be justified under certain circumstances, but the extent of the criminality should be limited. Furthermore, if such behavior is justifiable to protect an undercover officer, then surely it must be justifiable to protect a human source that is operating in a criminal organization? Indeed, it can be argued that it is much more likely that a source would have to undertake such activity, yet many senior officers would not countenance allowing such activity by a source. Unfortunately, this creates circumstances that are ripe for a blind eye to be turned toward what a source is really doing.
- With any participation authorization, care must be taken that circumstances do not cause an escalation in the level of criminality being undertaken.

4.12   Health and Safety/Workplace Safety-Related Legislation

Most jurisdictions have legislation surrounding health and safety in the work place, and/or such matters are addressed through the potential for lawsuits, where risks in the workplace are not sufficiently addressed. While the safety of the public will be foremost in the mind of the Chief, "officer safety" is always, hopefully, high on the agenda too. However, when it comes to workplace safety, there are often significant failings that occur with regard to intelligence management. These include the following:

- Not knowing the specifics of legislation. In many jurisdictions, the legislation creates criminal offenses for failing to discharge responsibilities. One of the most notable of such cases relates to the London Metropolitan Police and the tragic death of Jean Charles de Menezes resulting in the successful prosecution of the Metropolitan Police Service, for an offense under health and safety legislation.[*]
- Not knowing how legislation should be applied to specific roles, and not knowing how the legislation has been, or is likely to be, interpreted in courts. With each aspect of intelligence management, there are likely to be risks, and these risks need to be identified and managed, if the expectations of the courts are to be met. There are often risks to a member's health and safety in intelligence management, particularly in regard to carrying out covert operations. All too often, these risks are regarded as being a separate issue that "someone else deals with…"—the someone else being in the human resource department and having no idea what the members are actually doing on the ground, or what risks they are exposed to. For example, placing an officer into a covert observation post to gather information will bring with it many risks to the officer's safety, yet many agencies fail to detail these risks or to adequately manage them. Things as basic as health risks generated because of lack of appropriate clothing; the risk of potential injury, even if minor in nature; or the lack of plans to deal with a medical emergency all have the potential to lead to litigation, either criminal or civil.
- Not integrating the relevant legislation into the agency's procedures for carrying out specific roles. In all the agency procedures relating to any aspect of intelligence management, the responsibilities of each member in relation to health and safety should be clearly detailed.

[*] Available at http://en.wikipedia.org/wiki/Death_of_Jean_Charles_de_Menezes (accessed September 2012).

- Not identifying and documenting risks in accordance with international standards for risk management,* and not investing sufficiently to manage those risks. In many covert operations, operational risks are documented but the safety risks for those taking part are overlooked, the assumption often being that they are being covered elsewhere, when in effect they rarely are.
- Ignoring mental health issues. Many aspects of working in intelligence take a personal toll on those involved. Unfortunately, many managers in law enforcement still have little awareness of the real cost on the mental health of staff and/or they turn a blind eye to it. Highlighting problems in undercover work, Joh (2009) comments:

> Occupational hazards are legion.... And the more time spent as an undercover agent, the greater the risk that personal problems will appear. A number of studies have documented the harms visited upon undercover officers: corruption, disciplinary problems, alcohol and drug abuse, interpersonal problems, a "loss of self," and paranoia. In extreme cases, the agents "go native" and become indistinguishable from their targets.

4.13 Data Protection

Most countries have legislation surrounding the exchange or sharing of personal data that is held by either public or private bodies. The legislation is normally referred to by terminology such as "data protection" or "computer privacy" and recognizes that while citizens voluntarily give their personal details to various bodies, there should be restrictions on what those bodies are subsequently allowed to do with it. Given that huge amounts of such personal data are stored on computer databases, and the ease that such is shared from one party to another, it is hardly surprising that there is particular concern in relation to those databases. Recognizing the potential for harm to every citizen's privacy, the unlawful sharing of such data is taken very seriously in many jurisdictions, with the legislation creating criminal offenses, relating to both unlawfully asking for such information and unlawfully sharing such information. Identifying that the data may be helpful to law enforcement, the legislation will normally provide a legal way for law enforcement to obtain the information they require. Problems arise when the lawful process is not used. Law enforcement officers often have a "trusted contact" in many businesses, who they can ask "unofficially" for the information, the argument often being that no one knows the material is being asked for, and it is a "sensitive" investigation. This is often followed up with

---

* See International Standards Organisation (2009) ISO 3100:09.

the argument that it is quicker and requires less effort. Unfortunately, it will often amount to criminal behavior. Law enforcement staff need to be aware of what information they can ask a person to supply and what the lawful process is for asking for that information. In addition, care must be taken when a citizen volunteers information they have collected through the course of their employment. The citizen may unintentionally be breaching legislation, although in many cases legislation is likely to allow them to do it, where they suspect an offense is being committed. (Thought must also be given to the risk relating to employees breaching their company policy and jeopardizing their jobs.)* The nature of intelligence work means that there is often a pressing need for secrecy around investigations and officers are reluctant to use "official" channels to obtain what they want. There is also sometimes (willful) blindness to the extent of such legislation, with arguments being made that such legislation only applies to computerized records and that paper records "don't count," and/or fudging the issue around whether or not information is "personal," for example, "It is not about him; it's about his shop." The bottom line is that staff need to know the law relating to data privacy and the agency's intelligence management procedures need to direct staff in relation to the impact of legislation in regard to intelligence management. Just because the member is asking for or receiving the information with the best intentions, does not make it lawful!

4.14   Privacy

Running closely alongside issues of data protection, and as already mentioned, a fundamental human right, a citizen's entitlement to have a private life without state interference is an issue to which those involved in managing intelligence must pay significant attention.† The perceived threat to privacy is one of the main reasons that people are concerned about law enforcement intelligence gathering. There is no doubt that should an LEA turn its full capabilities to focus on an individual, there is little of that person's life that is going to remain private. It must be borne in mind that while such efforts to collect in-depth information are reserved for the most serious of criminals, or those involved in terrorism, there will be many times when law enforcement comes across information on a person that is of a very personal nature. How such information is dealt with will say a lot about the sophistication of the agency's intelligence management systems.

---

* This is a significant problem when someone is working as a human source and passing information obtained in the course of their employment.
† Of relevance to those involved in law enforcement in the United States is the Privacy Act (1974). Available at: http://www.archives.gov/about/laws/privacy-act-1974.html

Another consideration that is often overlooked is that information does not have to contain the person's name for it to be considered as personal information. When information directly or indirectly, by reason of the content of that information, identifies an individual, it should be treated as being personally identifiable information and the attendant privacy issues dealt with accordingly. The main issues surrounding private information relate to accuracy of the information and the handling and security of it. The higher standards of information handling that result from an effective intelligence management system go a long way to addressing such privacy concerns. In an effective system, all information is checked and assessed by a trained individual, before being reposited in the agency's intelligence repository. This minimizes the risk of inaccurate information being stored or being inappropriately accessed by another party. Ensuring that controls are in place for how intelligence is stored and used in an agency will assist the agency in answering concerns about privacy abuses. LEAs must be aware that unless privacy concerns are effectively dealt with, the potential exists for intelligence management structures and intelligence sharing initiatives to be seriously undermined.

4.15 Intelligence Sharing

Intelligence should only be shared with other statutory bodies, when there is a memorandum of understanding between the parties involved, clearly stating the obligations of each party in relation to the material that is being shared. Similar arrangements should be in place when sharing with other LEAs.

4.16 Evidence

As already discussed, one of the core differences between intelligence gathering for law enforcement and intelligence gathering within the Intelligence Community has always been how an intelligence product was used. For the most part, intelligence within law enforcement is a tool that assists in furthering investigations, and as such there has always been the expectation that at some stage, regardless of how far down the line, law enforcement will take executive action based on that intelligence and bring a suspect before the courts. Such action then raises the likelihood of the intelligence gathering process and attendant legalities being raised in an open court. Save in cases of espionage, the Intelligence Community has not really had to face similar problems. In more recent years, this has changed with joint "investigations" into terrorism, becoming commonplace. Issues around the intelligence-to-evidence pathway must be considered by all agencies working in investigations, where there is the potential, however remote, for there to be a prosecution.

When intelligence and intelligence gathering techniques are used in progressing an investigation, one consideration that should be made is with regard to the legality of the intelligence gathering methods that are being used. If an intelligence gathering technique has not been used lawfully, there is the potential that anything that was gained for the benefit of the prosecution from that technique is considered as being obtained unlawfully and therefore inadmissible as evidence. Regardless of how far back in the process the illegality has occurred, everything that proceeds from that point can be excluded by a court. The evidence obtained is seen as being the "fruit of a poisoned tree"; the poison being the initial unlawful behavior. While the interpretation and judgment of courts in these matters may vary significantly from jurisdiction to jurisdiction, the risk of evidence being excluded on this basis is present in most modern countries. Courts and juries may well be suspicious of anything that involves intelligence as it is often perceived as being one of the "dark arts." As the U.S. judge Richard Posner is quoted (Elahi 2012) as saying: "Intelligence is the second oldest profession, only with fewer morals." While such comments may be unfair, the fact that such suspicion revolves around the intelligence business means that those involved must make stringent efforts to ensure that everything they do is lawful and above board. Unfortunately, the risk of a challenge to the lawfulness of intelligence collection is often not identified until it is too late, and the defense is banging on the judge's door demanding the whole case be thrown out.

The main reasons this problem occurs are as follows: first, because of a breakdown in communication between the intelligence gatherers and the senior investigator, as to what the intelligence is likely to be used for; and second, inexperience in dealing with such matters. Those law enforcement officers involved in intelligence gathering on a full time basis may be limited by their experience in investigations, while those involved in the investigation may lack the specific knowledge of intelligence gathering techniques or are not consulted prior to the intelligence being collected in regard to potential legal issues.

In joint terrorism investigations, such inexperience often originates because law enforcement is unfamiliar with working with sensitive techniques and technologies, and the Intelligence Community is unfamiliar with the nature of the relevant legislation and with working within the constraints of the judicial process. Rarely are those within the Intelligence Community forced to discuss their techniques in open court, let alone be subject to the line-by-line scrutiny of a defense lawyer, where each and every person involved in the intelligence gathering process is cross examined. The bottom line is that those involved in intelligence gathering must always ensure that the techniques they use are carried out lawfully. Failure to do so may result in significant amounts of evidence being ruled inadmissible and a prosecution folding as a result.

Having established the connection between the collection of intelligence and one of the potential challenges the subsequent evidence may face in court, we move to the matter of trying to protect "sources (of all sorts) and methods" in court, and the thorny issue of disclosure.

4.17 Disclosure

Most countries have specific legislation or case law* that deals with the issue of discovery and disclosure of material when a trial is taking place. Directly connected to the rights of a defendant to a "fair trial," the principles surrounding discovery and disclosure are more or less universally the same. In short, the prosecuting authority must make available anything that will assist the defense. Material that goes toward the defendant's innocence or casts doubt on their guilt must be put before the court. This obligation to disclose material will often need to be balanced against the public interest need to keep sensitive/secret material from the defense. In many cases, there will be a fine line between whether or not material should be disclosed. While obviously there is a desire to prevent any innocent person from being wrongly convicted, there will also be a reluctance to see someone who is obviously guilty walk free because of the need to protect sensitive material; such a set of circumstances cannot be said to serve justice either. Disclosure can often be a complex legal issue, and appropriate legal advice should always be sought. However, when it comes to dealing with intelligence matters, those involved in any specific case must take a wider perspective, as the ramifications of poor disclosure can have a much larger impact on law enforcement than may be initially recognized. In any prosecution case, where there are potential ramifications for intelligence management, the legal professional dealing with disclosure should have input from someone with sufficient expertise in intelligence management to ensure that any decision made has taken into consideration all the relevant facts.

4.18 Freedom of Information

Freedom of information legislation is prevalent in many jurisdictions; its purpose is to make public the how and why of government. Given that

---

* U.S. cases such as Brady v. Maryland, 373 U.S. 83 (1963) and Giglio v. United States, 405 U.S. 150 (1974) set disclosure standards. Under these cases, the government has a constitutional responsibility to search for and produce a criminal defendant admissible exculpatory and exculpatory and impeachment material. In the United Kingdom, disclosure is dealt with under the Criminal Procedures and Investigations Act (CPIA) (1995). Other jurisdictions have similar legislation and case law.

freedom of information is about bringing activities into the public domain, there is substantial potential for conflict with intelligence management. It is incumbent upon an agency to put in place structures to prevent access to methodology and to the contents of the intelligence repository. Freedom of information is about ensuring government is held accountable for its actions, but such accountability must be balanced against protecting methodology, and intelligence that is held on suspects. Legislation relating to freedom of information is one of the main reasons that an agency's records management system should not contain any material relating to intelligence management. Such systems are significantly more vulnerable to freedom of information requests. Releasing intelligence-related material under freedom of information requests should only be authorized by someone who is sufficiently experienced and trained to recognize the harm that such a release may cause. Cognizance must also be taken of the risk of a large number of requests seeking out access to information on a similar theme, as they may form part of a more sinister strategy. The perpetrators of these so-called "mosaic attacks" combine the various small pieces of information obtained to make a complete picture, details that would never have been released, had they been presented as a normal request. Freedom of information is about informing the public what law enforcement is doing and the standards they are working to—it is not about giving away secrets that will jeopardize their ability to carry out that function.

4.19   Public Inquiries

Many jurisdictions have legislation relating to the holding of public inquiries. Generally speaking, when law enforcement is the subject of such inquiries, it is because a very serious incident has occurred and the actions of law enforcement have been questionable. Public inquiries are not a good place for any agency to be and they rarely end well for the agency involved. One of the major problems relating to intelligence management is protecting what needs to be protected while at the same time defending law enforcement actions. Many such inquiries have extraordinary powers to demand material that could normally be protected. The risk is that material that should have remained secret is launched into the public domain to the detriment of all law enforcement. Any agency finding itself involved in such an inquiry should be willing to provide as much nonsensitive material as they can but should be robust in restricting access to sensitive material to the minimum number of people who have to see it. This should include documenting the harm that is likely to be caused by exposing sensitive techniques or the origins of intelligence to the public.

4.20   International Operations

The nature of crime and terrorism means that the activities of those involved often transcends borders. This creates many difficulties, not the least of them being the legal ones. Some of the countries involved will be friendly, some hostile, and some so riddled with corruption as to make the friendship/hostility issue redundant. There will always be questions raised with regard to the legalities of such matters as tasking a human source to operate in a foreign nation or deploying officers onto foreign soil with or without that nation's knowledge that they are there. Each operation must be examined on a case-by-case basis, with input from legal advisors and those with experience working in the environment in question. Fortunately, for law enforcement, agencies such as Interpol and Europol exist to mitigate many of the potential risks.

4.21   Ethics and Morals

Dealing with the law is easy—it is written down!! Someone has made the rules and said "This is the way it is going to be." and now all law enforcement has to do is to follow these rules. But unfortunately laws do not always cover what is "right" and what is "wrong." All laws do is formalize what a particular society has agreed to as being the number and level of constraints on their behavior they are prepared to accept in the interests of getting along. When it comes to agreeing when behavior is right and wrong, it is all up for debate even the meaning of those two words. While intending to avoid a prolonged philosophical debate with regard to right and wrong, this section of the book will address the practicalities of ethics and morals in intelligence management. Of course, there may be a slight diversion or two down the philosophy road just to make everyone aware of the complexities involved.

And just to get the reader in the mood here is a progressive scenario version commonly found in ethical discussions relating to investigations and intelligence gathering. It is in four parts; answer each, and then move on to the next one. The discussion is only about right and wrong and not the effectiveness of any technique.

1. As a police officer you have a suspect in custody and he won't admit the crime. Is it right to torture an admission out of him?
2. The prisoner is a known active terrorist?
3. The prisoner has placed a bomb on a plane over the Atlantic. Only he has the code to defuse the bomb. The plane cannot turn back in time. The only way to save the 300 people on board is to get the code. The only way to get the code is to torture him.

4. A child you love with all your heart is on board. (Make sure you have this child's name and a clear visible picture of them in your mind's eye as you answer.)

Hopefully having thought the four stages through each reader will have their own answers to the scenario* and will have an idea of the nature of discussions that follow.

4.22   Knowing the Difference

For the purpose of this book, *ethics* will be regarded as pertaining to a standpoint that has been adopted by an LEA with regard to how it as a corporate body, and the individual members of that agency should behave under given sets of circumstance. Ethics combines ideas derived from the morality of those within an agency with social utility. Ethical behavior is about acting in good conscience to accepted standards of behavior. On the other hand, *morals* will be regarded as the personal code by which a person chooses to live her life. The two terms, while often used synonymously, are to be regarded here as representing two differing sets of standards. The first thing anyone involved in law enforcement must recognize is that while he may be in agreement for a significant amount of the time, circumstances exist where the morals of a member may be at odds with the ethical standpoint of the agency. In this chapter, we will explore ethical and moral aspects pertaining to intelligence management and even this is such a large subject as to force us to be limited in our discussions.

In all things ethical and moral, the essence is about doing what is right, which would be easy if we could all agree on what is right. When it comes to managing intelligence, law enforcement is likely to be provided with a significant amount of clear guidance on what society believes to be right, and this will come in the form of legislation. In other aspects, it is up to law enforcement to adopt what they perceive as an ethical standpoint on issues that can be decided in advance and codify that standpoint in procedures. When it comes to dealing with ethical matters that cannot be decided in advance, the agency must have trained its staff in ethics and ethical decision making if it is to deal effectively with any given circumstances.

---

* Some answers that you may have had include: The fact if one says at stage 1 "It is ok," then you are probably not the best candidate to be a police officer and if in stage 4 you are not attaching the suspect's vulnerable bits to a set of electrodes and cranking up the volume until the sweat blinds you, then your suitability as a member of the human race may be up for debate! (Or maybe you are just a far better person than the author!) It is all open for discussion.

4.23   Ethical Dilemmas

There are many times when ethical dilemmas arrive in intelligence management. Having raised a hypothetical scenario at the start of this section and one in which it is highly unlikely ever to occur, except in an episode of the TV drama *24*, here are a few more down to earth examples to allow the reader to explore the concept with a few questions you might want to answer. All are real-life examples.

Example 1

An undercover officer is deployed against an organized crime gang. During the operation, the undercover officer befriends the sister of one of the gang members. The association with the sister allows the officer to gain the trust of other gang members and maximize the amount of intelligence that is produced. The relationship is a sexually intimate one. The officer continues to produce significant amounts of intelligence on the gang.

- Is the officer's behavior ethical?
- Is the officer's behavior moral?
- Are the attendant sexual acts sexual assault? (Consider the deception involved and read your law!)
- Does it matter what gender the officer is?
- How would the public view what is happening?
- How would the officer's real-life partner view what is happening?
- Is the officer vulnerable to psychological damage?
- How much detail should the officer record in debriefing notes with regard to the relationship?

Example 2

Two rival gangs are engaged in a turf war over territory and who can sell drugs in that area. A number of gang members on both sides have been shot and killed. Police receive intelligence of a sensitive origin, identifying that the member of one gang, Sanchez, is being targeted for assassination by two members from the rival gang named Bellini and Kazak.

- Do they provide Sanchez with all the intelligence they have?
- What might happen if they do?
- What might happen if they do not?
- Does Sanchez's criminality have a bearing on the decision?
- Given the sensitive nature of the intelligence, can Sanchez be trusted to keep it to himself?
- If it was you being targeted, how much of the intelligence would you want to be told?
- What rank is appropriate to make the decision on what if anything to share?

Example 3

Usaf, a young Muslim, is caught for driving offenses. The officer offers to ignore the offenses if Usaf provides information on suspected terrorists living within the community. Usaf is to watch these people and try to befriend them. The offi-cer requests that Usaf goes to a mosque that the suspects frequent and that he observes their behavior.

- Is the officer's behavior ethical?
- Should Usaf escape justice for his wrongdoing in relation to the offenses he committed?
- How would different sections of the public view this?
- Should the "religious" aspect have any bearing?
- What happens if Usaf is not used to gather information?
- Should Usaf get paid for his efforts?

If anyone is of the opinion that the decisions involved in these scenarios are easily dealt with, they are not thinking through the issues. All require balanced judgments about what law enforcement is seeking to achieve and what the possible consequences are of making the incorrect decision.

Intelligence gathering has always been fraught with ethical and moral dilemmas. In discussing ethics in relation to espionage, Andregg (2007: 53) comments:

But the world of official intelligence involves activities in many grey areas of moral thought, and generates perplexing dilemmas where agents must bal-ance the national interest in security, which they are bound to protect, against some other virtue like the ancient rules against lying, stealing, killing and so forth.

While it can be argued that intelligence gathering in a law enforcement context is unlikely to extend to some of the extremes mentioned, there are many situations that will involve decisions that are not so dissimilar when one considers all the potential options.

4.24 Ethical Theory

In order to gain a better understanding of ethical issues that are likely to be encountered in intelligence management, it is necessary to have at least some exposure to mainstream ethical models. The psychologist James Rest (1986, 1994) uses a four-component model to address the psychological process involved in behaving ethically:

1. *Moral sensitivity.* This refers to the ability to recognize that an ethical problem is present. A key part of this aspect is the ability to see ethi-cal problems, not only from our perspective, but to see that which others may perceive as an ethical issue. If we are not sufficiently sen-sitive to perceive the presence of a dilemma, then there is no hope in dealing with it. It is at this stage that options are identified as possible solutions to the ethical dilemma.

2. *Moral judgment.* At this stage, the decision maker makes a judgment having considered the various options as to what is right and wrong under the given circumstances.

3. *Moral motivation.* At this stage, the decision maker must have sufficient motivation to follow through on the course of action and recognize that competing priorities often interfere with ethical prerogatives. Doing the right thing is not always easy, especially if it involves additional expenditure. Standing up for what is right is not easy either, especially if the member's manager is threatening an individual's career advancement. Staff will be motivated to behave in a less ethical manner if the agency is perceived as rewarding unethical behavior or turning a blind eye to wrongdoing. On the other hand, if ethical behavior is perceived as having worth and is seen to be rewarded, then it is more likely to become the norm. Conversely, if an ethical culture exists within the agency, it is when things become difficult that the member can be motivated by his peers to behave ethically.

4. *Moral character.* Following through with regard to an ethical decision also depends on the character of the individual. One must recognize that there may be many opportunities to fail, despite having the most ethical intentions. An officer may set out to manage an operation in an ethical manner, but when job-related pressures kick in, concerns about doing what is right may well falter. How many times do we start out intending to do what is right and end up cutting corners? Being of sufficient moral character helps one to stay in the course. It is at this point that the officer's awareness of what value she places on personal integrity is a major influencing factor.

Kidder (1995) provided a set of principles that can be used to resolve an ethical dilemma. Once learned they are easily used and very effective in the law enforcement environment. He suggested that any ethical dilemma can be considered from three perspectives:

1. *Highest moral perspective.* This deontological position argues that one should always adopt the highest moral standpoint regardless of the consequences of adopting that position. This approach holds that some things are inherently wrong, regardless of consequences that will occur. It does not matter how morally good the consequences are, some choices are just wrong! While this position may be a very noble one, it arguably fails to recognize the real world, in which we live.

2. *Care-based perspective.* This position takes the view that you should treat others as you would like to be treated. It is sometimes referred to as a "care-based approach." While this approach is very appealing, it

fails to recognize that you cannot be "nice" all the time, to everyone, if you want to get the job done.

3. *Ends-based perspective.* This position takes a utilitarian stance, arguing that the end justifies the means, and that one should do what is best for the greater number of people. Those that adopt such an approach are sometimes referred to as "consequentialists." They believe that choices are to be judged solely by the state of affairs they bring about. This approach is essentially a cost-benefit analysis, which although attractive to many pragmatists, often fails to take cognizance of the views of others.

4.25   Applying Kidder's Principles

Kidder argued that there are a number of practical steps to decide any ethical dilemma; these are adapted here taking cognizance of the existing structures within law enforcement:

1. Recognize that there is an ethical issue. This is sometimes the biggest problem in that those involved in a set of circumstances are so certain of what they are doing they fail to recognize that there is an ethical problem. This blindness is a real issue in covert law enforcement.
2. Gather the "facts." The decision maker needs to know all there is to know about the dilemma. This will extend beyond "hard" facts and should include issues such as the potential community impact.
3. Discuss the dilemma, arguing all the right-versus-wrong views. If a law is involved, the debate will normally end there, as it becomes a legal issue and not an ethical one. Guiding such discussions should always be the consideration as to how it would play out in the press if it were to become public. Adopting a more personal perspective can also help see through the haze. If one considers that their loved ones will find out and considers how those that are personally significant would view the events it can help focus the mind on what is right and wrong.*
4. Apply the principles and find the balance. Make the decision. Always look for alternatives.
5. Keep reviewing what has been decided, especially as new information becomes available.

Andregg (2007: 55) in quoting an unidentified intelligence officer suggests three rules for ethical behavior which have, undoubtedly, a pragmatic

---

* It is never good trying to explain to your mum why you did a bad thing!

appeal, although to someone who seek the higher ground they may be harder to swallow:

- "First, do not harm, especially to innocents."
- "Second, and only if techniques under rule 1 cannot protect the people, choose the lesser evil when moral dilemmas cannot be avoided. Thus if you must lie, cheat, and steal to protect the people, this is permissible with reservations."
- "Third, remember that the law of unintended consequences is real, and that perfection is not possible....the means chosen to do a thing usually determine the actual results achieved. Intentions matter little, consequences much."

4.26   Ethical Dilemmas

Rather than shying away from ethical dilemmas, let us get some of the common ones out on the table so that they can be discussed. Far too often law enforcement members are unprepared to have open discussions about the reality of what is occurring within their agency. Unless we acknowledge what is going on, we cannot deal with the issues; we leave the agency vulnerable and expose the members to considerable risk. There is no point in blaming officers for doing something wrong if you do not put clear boundaries in place with regard to how they should behave. Furthermore, the agency is damaged because the officer is often working in the belief that their actions are condoned by management and then when it goes public, the agency not only looks as if it condones wrongdoing but is shown to be incompetent at the same time. Some dilemmas worth considering include the following:

- The collection of personal and private information by law enforcement that citizens intend to keep secret. Is it right that law enforcement pry into a citizen's private life?
- Using claims of secrecy or national security to cover up wrongdoing, mistakes, and failings. The fact that much of what goes on in intelligence management requires protection should not be used as an excuse to hide away the dirty laundry. Leigh (2007) highlighted how such an attitude of secrecy may even encourage illegality or the creation of an unethical culture: "The necessary secrecy surrounding security and intelligence runs the risk of encouraging illegal and ethically dubious practices on the part of the agencies involved." There should always be mechanisms to examine such failings safely and securely. If a job has been done as best as one could do it and in

good faith, there is no reason to hide anything from someone who has clearance and a need to see it.

- Interagency rivalry. Although highlighted here as an ethical issue, there is little debate about the conduct of some agencies who excuse their bad behavior by euphemistically calling it "professional rivalry" or putting it down to "encouraging healthy competition." Covering all manner of wrongdoing including misleading others, hiding intelligence, denying resources, and moving right up the scale to deliberately jeopardizing the investigations of other agencies, this type of behavior is all too common with some law enforcement and intelligence agencies. At the bottom of it all there may be long-term and institutionalized beliefs within an agency, usually being perpetuated by some egocentric, incompetent, and insecure individual intent on abusing her position. This type of behavior produces conflict that can affect the most serious investigations. It is wrong and doesn't have to be there. Turner (2006: 54) highlighted such interagency rivalries as being a major problem in the United States since 9/11. He highlighted the effectiveness of the joint law enforcement/intelligence agencies model of cooperation used in the United Kingdom for investigating terrorism. Having said that, the United Kingdom has 40 years of practice in developing counterterrorism strategies, and even now it is not all flowers and chocolates when it comes to joint operations. Fortunately, for the most part, it does work and there is a significant amount that can be taken from it in terms of good practice.
- "Don't tell me the truth. I don't want the truth because I can't cope with the truth." Some managers consciously create circumstances, but more often subconsciously, where those reporting to them believe that the managers do not want to hear the truth, it being too difficult for them to deal with. This encourages omissions, deceptions, and distortions. Let there be no doubt, it is unethical to deceive someone who has responsibility for making judgments based on the information you provide. Nevertheless, it is acknowledged that there are times when it is necessary and ethical to deceive other members of the agency.
- Deceiving other agencies. Deceiving those in other agencies may occasionally be necessary, but care must be taken that it does not pervert the course of justice. Such deception must only be carried out when there is a pressing need to do. There can be many unforeseen ramifications. In most cases, it will only be done to protect a long-term asset from compromise.
- Lying. Telling lies, deceiving, and being economical with the truth are all part and parcel of the intelligence business. Undercover officers lie all the time, source handlers lie on occasions, press departments give out partial truths to protect operational security, investigators mislead to protect the origins of intelligence, surveillance officers lie

every time they use their "cover stories" and so on. The complexity and sophistication of some of these lies, particularly in undercover work, can be staggering. The problem for most agencies is that while they know this is happening and can actually justify why their staff do it, they rarely formally acknowledge that it is happening in policy, procedures, decision logs, risk documents, and in other documents. No one wants to be connected with such a "dirty" business, yet failure to do so creates avoidable risks for all involved.

- Manipulation. Officers often consciously or subconsciously manipulate citizens to get information from them. Many times an officer will not even recognize that he is being manipulative, but any objective analysis of his behavior will show the manipulation that occurred. How often do officers give categorical assurances to citizens that, if the citizen provides the information, no one will know where it came from? Is this manipulative or is it just back to good old fashioned lying?

- Influencing prosecutions and dropping charges. This is a legitimate technique. Cutting deals with the bad guys to get information is justifiable provided it is done in a fully accountable way. The problem here is most often the lack of accountability, which does not sit well with many (Natapoff 2009, Brown 2007).

- Paying criminals for information. This statement in itself is value laden, as implicit in the term "criminals" is prejudice. Many believe that anyone involved in crime should not benefit from that involvement, yet many human sources achieve benefit, because their involvement in crime allows them access to the desired information. Much of the reluctance to pay human sources fairly stems from moral prejudice, rather than objective assessment.

- Blackmail. Given the fact that blackmail is a criminal offense in many jurisdictions, it would seem unlikely that any LEA would condone their officers being involved in such an act. However, there are always circumstances in which the criminal threshold is not met but the conduct is certainly ethically dubious. Consider an officer approaching someone who has just been caught for theft and saying to her something akin to "If you help me I will make sure your children don't find out you were caught stealing." Or the officer who approaches a terrorist and says "If you help me I will make sure your wife doesn't find out about your affair." Blackmail? Ethical? Does it happen? Discuss it!

- Drinking on duty ... with criminals ... and even better the alcohol is paid for by the agency ... This happens with source handlers, surveillance operators, and undercover officers. The behavior can be justified, but has the agency thought through all possible scenarios?

- Sex with citizens. Long-term undercover operations come with unique problems, and when this happens, the agency needs to work out what its position is. There may be significant benefits for the operation and there may be severe moral hazards for the officer. Unfortunately, this is one of those issues that people will just not talk about, because it is "embarrassing" or just easier to say, "No it is not allowed." This is a huge problem when managing human sources. Many officers, male and female, become involved in illicit sexual relations with sources. Because the agency thinks they are covered, by merely saying it is not allowed, does not address the reasons why it occurs. Sexual relationships with a human source are probably well on the way to corrupt behavior, if not past it. However, in an undercover operation, such a relationship may justified in an ethical and moral consideration.

- Ignoring criminality. Cooper (2005), in discussing the use of strategic intelligence, repeats a story that has significant relevance in any ethical debate. The story is disputed in many quarters and its veracity is up for debate, which is hardly surprising when one reads it, given the fact that the main protagonist Winston Churchill is a heroic figure that played a significant part in overthrowing Hitler and Nazi Germany. In Cooper's words:

  > The widely repeated—but apocryphal—story that perhaps best exemplifies this understanding of "strategic intelligence" is that of Churchill's allowing Coventry to be bombed in order to safeguard the long-term informational advantages gained from Allied code-breaking achievements against the Axis. The immeasurable importance of such intelligence in the successful Allied efforts to interdict Rommel's supply lines during the North African campaign and in winning the crucial Battle of the Atlantic testify to these other equities with possibly higher priority.

For the purposes of this discussion, let us assume that Churchill had the intelligence to prevent the bombing of a major city, but let it go ahead to protect an intelligence asset that was necessary to win the war. The ethical question this raises is: Was he wrong to do that, given the huge loss of life incurred? Fortunately, in law enforcement, the consequences are never quite so severe, nor the potential gain so high. However, there will be many times when officers will have to make similar decisions, as to whether or not to take action that they know will compromise an intelligence asset, and in doing so lose that asset forever and all future intelligence they could provide. This loss has to be balanced against protecting the asset by not taking action and the potential harm that results from this. This is a huge problem for many people that become involved in intelligence; they are just unable to get their head around countenancing any decision to knowingly let criminality continue. The belief that once intelligence is available law enforcement must take action is misguided. Every law enforcement officer knows places where criminality is ongoing and nothing is done about it. Go to any major city and the cops on the street will direct you to a corner where you can buy drugs, women, stolen goods and whatever. In effect, a tacit decision has been made to let crime go on. If law enforcement wants to get intelligence at the highest levels of terrorist organizations or organized crime gangs, then the options are limited. If you recruit a source in those gangs, they are going to be doing bad things most days. If you want to keep the asset, save lives, and destroy the gang, there is going to be a cost, just as Churchill may have realized. Sometimes you just have to let things run. Intelligence is not a business for the faint of heart.

- Violence. Some who encounter law enforcement are not very nice people. They have little or no respect for human life and are prepared to take away human life with little or no excuse. In dealing with such individuals, there is a realistic chance that, at some stage, violence is going to occur and this may end in fatalities. This is a reality, and those dealing with such people need to be comfortable with the ethical, and more importantly, the moral implications that may result. In working against these types of people, there is a real chance that someone will die. It is the job of the law enforcement officer to protect all life but more so the innocent life. That of course is an ethical debate! For some, the moral implications of such actions are too difficult to countenance, and that is totally understandable. There are some people who are all too happy to let others do what they need and then are all too ready to criticize them from the high (and safe) moral ground for doing it. Such is human nature. Perhaps George Orwell sums the reality of this type of circumstance most realistically: "We sleep safe in our beds because rough men stand ready in the night to visit violence on those who would do us harm." Sometimes intelligence work requires "rough men."

In all these situations, the line between justifiable actions and wrongdoing is grey. It may be ok for an officer to justify having two or three drinks as part of the operation, but given that the alcohol is free, why not have two or three more? It would be a shame to waste the opportunity and it is not really doing any harm! This is cognitive dissonance at work,* and

---

* For a comprehensive explanation of the power cognitive dissonance, see *Mistakes Were Made but Not by Me.* by Carol Travis and Elliot Aronson (2007).

we are on the slippery slope to corruption. But it is a warm day and the beer is cold … and I work better when I am comfortable, so it really is not for my benefit.

4.27 Other Professions—Similar Problems

Other professions face ethical difficulties that are not wholly unrelated to those faced by law enforcement officers involved in intelligence management. Those in the medical profession often encounter circumstances where their responsibility to disclose information conflicts with the patient's medical needs. For example, the obligation on the part of a doctor to disclose a gunshot wound may cause a patient not to seek proper medical treatment. Faith leaders may be told something as a result of their role and feel obligated not to disclose it. While in both these cases, the individual may feel obligated by a greater calling not to disclose the information, in neither of the cases will the wider community accept it as a reason that they should not have disclosed it. One only has to look at the difficulties the Catholic Church has gotten itself into with not disclosing instances of child abuse. The argument that it was protecting the sanctity of the confessional and similar excuses just does not cut it with the public at large. So it is with law enforcement and matters they claim that they need to keep secret. The public will not accept what they see as cover ups of wrongdoing, particularly when there is a clear advantage to the agency in keeping things hidden.

In a different vein, the involvement of psychologists in various aspects of law enforcement has caused ethical dilemmas for them. For example, quandaries revolving around their involvement in the interviewing of suspects, particularly those involved in terrorism and the use to which that a psychologist's understanding of human behavior can be put. In assessing the appropriate role for its members in interrogations, the American Psychiatric Association focuses on the principle, "do no harm," while at the same time appearing, to ignore a second principle of, "contribute to society by preventing harm" (Behnke 2006). It is easy to understand why the Association would adopt the standpoint, as they would not wish to be seen as condoning the use of psychiatric skills to manipulate or harm any person, yet at the same time, the benefit that such skills can add to an investigation are immense. To be able to understand a suspect's vulnerabilities is of huge benefit to an investigator trying to solve a crime or an intelligence collector trying to prevent crimes. Similarly, the insight a psychologist can provide in relation to the motives and vulnerabilities of a potential human source are of real significance, if undertaking a proactive recruitment (Buckley 2006). The use of psychiatrists/psychologists for such tasks as this is a very typical ethical quandary and one that is difficult to resolve to everyone's satisfaction.

The better understanding we have of ethics, the better chance we have managing the dilemmas likely to be encountered. The following observations are given in order to equip the reader with a more comprehensive understanding of the nature of ethics:

- The ability to reason ethically generally increases with age. This does not mean that the older someone is, the more likely she is to be morally right. It just means that her ability to reason through the arguments is likely to have improved.
- The more one's life experience base, the more the ability for ethical reasoning. One of the dangers of prolonged involvement in intelligence work is the risk that one tends to see the world from one particular and fixed moral standpoint.
- The greater number of ethical and moral challenges experienced helps promotes ethical and moral growth.
- The greater number of ethical discussions that the individual has been involved in, whether in training or in real-life situations, increases his ethical awareness.
- Generally speaking, there is no difference in the moral reasoning of men and women.
- Organizations are influenced by the ethics displayed by their leadership. Leaders who appear to their staff as self-centered or lacking moral courage are likely to promote such behavior with their staff. If the boss is involved in breaking rules or cutting corners, do not be surprised when staff do the same. This is a significant problem in intelligence management, with managers justifying going outside recognized good practice using such excuses as lack, or resources, or that they know better, or staff to doing the same merely using a different excuse than the manager, for their actions.
- Ethical behavior can be nurtured like any other positive trait. It is up to the agency to nurture its members.
- Moral absolutism is a viewpoint that certain actions are absolutely right or wrong, regardless of the context in which the action occurs, the consequences of the actions, or the intentions behind them. The practicalities of intelligence management mean that adopting such a view is unlikely to be sustainable.
- Morality is a universal concept found in all cultures, a fact that would appear lost on some law enforcement officers, who remain certain that theirs is the only correct viewpoint.
- Immanuel Kant, one of the most preeminent philosophers in the field of ethics, argued that it was not the consequences of actions that make them right or wrong but the motives of the person who carries out the action. However, Kant also condemned espionage as

"intrinsically despicable" because it "exploits only the dishonesty of others." The fact that Kant would appear to be arguing both sides of the one coin is a clear indicator of the complexity of ethics.

4.28 Getting Your Head Around It

The very nature of ethics means that the law enforcement officer is likely to encounter many situations that to them, may first appear to not be worthy of an extensive ethical debate. As previously stated, those involved in law enforcement are normally fairly certain that they are doing the right thing. One way of gaining a better understanding of the concept of ethics is to adopt a counter-intuitive standpoint, in regard to one's normal work position. In addition, training in ethics should be a part of any intelligence-related course. Not only should it be taught from a theoretical standpoint, but ethical issues should be intrinsic to all developmental scenarios that the students are asked to undertake. All officers involved in intelligence management should receive training in ethics and morals. Such training enables officers to recognize ethical dilemmas when they occur and to deal with them effectively. Training should include the practical application of theory to real-life situations, with students being first tasked to identify the relevant ethical aspects, and then told to deal with those situations in an ethically acceptable way. Scenarios must be role relevant and should not shy from the more sensitive issues that staff members are likely to encounter. Cognizance should always be taken of the fact that a member's role may raise moral dilemmas for that individual. Even though the agency has decided what is right (an ethical decision) may be at variance with what a member believes to be right (a moral decision). Training must be delivered in an environment that encourages full and frank discussion encompassing both ethical and moral aspects. Training in ethical decision making is a *must* for all managers involved in intelligence management. There are just too many times when there is no absolutely "right" option and the decision maker must be equipped with the skills to make the best decision possible under those given circumstances and provide a full account of the reasoning behind that decision. Open and frank discussion of all the related issues should be encouraged. It is only by examining similar matters over a period of time that one is likely to know what to do when such dilemmas occur in real life. Here are some more real-life ethical examples to mull over:

- Was it ethical to dispose of the remains of Osama bin Laden by dumping them in the sea? (The terminology used is deliberate.)
- Eight terrorists blow up a police station wounding two police officers, but before they can finish their attack, they are intercepted and

all eight are shot dead by army personnel. The military had prior knowledge of the attack. Was this ethical behavior on the part of those who planned and authorized the operation?

- A 24-year-old university student was recruited as an informant and sent out by police to purchase cocaine and a weapon from violent criminals. She had been previously caught by the police supplying cannabis and was "working off" the charge. The criminals murdered her and dumped her body by the roadside. Was this ethical behavior on the part of those who planned and authorized the operation?

4.29   Behaving Unethically

There are many ways in which unethical behavior is likely to occur in intelligence management. It is incumbent upon the agency to build processes and establish procedures where such conduct is less likely to occur. Failing prevention, processes should make it more likely that it is detected at an early stage if it is occurring. Without going too deeply into the psychology of why an unethical mindset develops, it is worth identifying some of the reasons:

- Organizational pressure. Agencies and individuals in them want results and are sometimes willing to turn a blind eye to what is unacceptable behavior.
- Attribution theory postulates that we are more inclined to blame a person for an action, than blame the circumstances under which the action occurs. In other words, where an agency looks at the possibility that circumstances contributed to the wrongdoing is difficult, as psychologically speaking it is easier to attribute blame to a person rather than the circumstances.
- Ego defense. We do not want to see ourselves as bad people, or as doing something wrong, so subconsciously we justify our actions.
- Unethical behavior and the slippery slope. But do not mention the "C" word! Police officers resent the word "corruption" and to such an extent that their baseline is that, if it is even mentioned as a possibility of being present, however remotely, in any of their activities, they become defensive and antagonistic. Internalizing what should be a professional discussion as attack on their integrity, many just refuse to countenance any discussion. Supervisors wanting to avoid dealing with the attendant conflict do not bring up the subject of corruption, and so the whole topic becomes hidden. The potential for corrupt behavior in intelligence management in particular in covert activities is significant, so the next section will address it in some depth.

4.30 Corruption

As already highlighted any mention of the word "corruption" in law enforcement circles is often met with hostility by many law enforcement officers. Why this happens, is a discussion for another day, but the reality is that there are a significant number of members of LEAs who engage in corrupt behavior. Unfortunately, many aspects of intelligence management provide an environment where corruption can breed and flourish. One of the major hurdles to jump in any discussion around the nature of corruption is defining it. The United Kingdom's Association of Chief Police Officers (ACPO) (IPCC 2011) provide a succinct definition but one that is adequate for our purposes. Corruption is defined as:

> ... the abuse of one's role or position held in the service for personal gain or gain for others.

This definition of corruption is extremely broad but recognizes that what constitutes corruption is likely to take many different forms. Corruption is most often regarded, whether formally acknowledged or not, as a continuum, with the degree of "wrongness" escalating from case to case or person to person. Such a continuum has close connections with the psychology involved in corruption. Very few people join law enforcement intending to break the rules; in fact their intention is normally the opposite. Over time and as a result of changing circumstances, a person may well start down the slippery slope to corruption.

Corruption in intelligence management is likely to occur in many different ways. Here are a few examples in what should in no way be considered a definitive list.

- False claims. If operations are secret, then maybe the number of actually hours worked are secret too? It is easier to create false claims for overtime and expenses, particularly if there is a lack of good supervision.
- Kickbacks. Using inside knowledge to help a friend or acquaintance whether actually getting anything tangible for it or not.
- Checking intelligence systems for personal benefit, or for the benefit of others. This is one of the main reasons private companies recruit ex-police officers, in the hope they will still have access to law enforcement resources.
- Warning criminals of investigations directed against them.
- Warning sources of investigations directed against them.
- Undermining prosecutions for benefit or because the member is being blackmailed.
- Fixing cases without authority or where there is no accountability.

- Using "expense" money for personal benefit. The extra drink, the more expensive meal, the pole dance, and others, all of which one can excuse away because of the role, but none of which was really necessary.
- Keeping of gifts given by sources.
- Sexual relationships with citizens involved in any way in the investigation.
- Unauthorized unlawful activity such as an undercover officer taking drugs.
- Stealing money that is set aside for sources or operational expenditure.
- Opportunistic thefts during covert operations.
- Deliberate failure to keep records as directed by the agency.
- Destroying or altering records.
- Falsifying evidence and entrapment.
- Selling material to the press.
- Unauthorized release of sensitive material. This operates on a sliding scale of making public something a person believes should be public to wholesale release of sensitive information to an organization such as "Wikileaks." This type of corruption is often facilitated by poor management structures within the intelligence system but unfortunately as in one very prominent U.S. case, it is much easier to cast the whole blame on one individual rather than on those responsible for building a wholly flawed system. Corruption was present but arguably fueled by gross negligence on the part of those who built the system that was exploited.
- Loose talk. Consider the old war time posters: "Careless talk costs lives" and "Loose lips sink ships." Telling a friend what is going on is ok? Even if they aren't entitled to know? This unfortunately is human nature at work. What is the point in knowing secret stuff if you cannot tell someone you know? Such behavior is driven by needs of ego and power and sometimes other things. It would not be the first time a law enforcement officer used details of a covert operation as a pick-up line.*
- "Noble cause corruption." Just because the motive changes arguably does not really change what is being done. If a member is doing something wrong but justifying it because it is for a noble reason does not make what they are doing right; it just makes it easier for them to swallow. Common justification for such behavior is that the justice system is allowing the bad guys to walk free and that the person is only balancing things out in favor of the

---

* Fortunately, criminals and terrorists do the same!

good people. It is very easy to justify for any good cop, but it is still wrong. The excuse of noble behavior often occurs when people see themselves as "whistle-blowers." While things within the agency may be wrong, this type of behavior is often motivated by much less honorable needs than the desire to expose wrongdoing. Petty grievances, personality clashes, vindictiveness, and ego can all contribute to excuses for behavior the person chooses to label as whistle blowing.

The United Kingdom's IPCC (2011) in its document on police corruption in England and Wales highlighted a number of managerial failings that contributed to corruption. They are quoted as follows:

- Individuals "…able to claim inappropriate expenses or act criminally because the policy within the force was not sufficiently robust to ensure that this behaviour was prevented."
- "Expectations of individuals have also not always been clear. This has enabled ambiguities within policies to be exploited."
- "Computer systems have been misused by individuals either for criminal activity or personal gain. Detection of this misbehaviour was hampered in several instances as there was no audit trail to identify who had accessed a system and for what purpose. Lack of system safeguards has, in some cases, aided the misuse."
- Wrongdoing not being detected "…owing to lack of or inappropriate supervision"
- "A failure to identify issues that lead to officers being involved in criminality."
- "Lack of action by senior managers in response to 'whistle-blowing'." This allowed further incidents of a similar nature to occur and "the perceived lack of positive and decisive action had a negative effect on others."

As can be seen, all are indicative of a poorly built system and all are issues that have the potential to cause major harm in intelligence management.

4.31 Hindsight

It is at this stage worth providing a word of caution. When things go wrong and with intelligence business being what it is, they will go wrong, the actions of law enforcement will be examined with all the benefits of hindsight. Under these circumstances, it is very easy to place criticism on an agency for what it should have known and what it should have done. Such criticism is often leveled by the uninitiated who have limited, if any, knowledge of the difficulties in dealing with intelligence and by others who have their own axe to grind. Post-incident inquiries are often flawed as a result of hindsight bias (Hoffrage and Pohl 2003) and conspiracy theories. For those on the receiving end of such criticism, there is likely to be a feeling of being treated unfairly. Having invested substantial effort and undertaken significant, often personal risk, to uphold the law and to protect life, it is hard to find justification for criticism. Nevertheless, if mistakes have been made, they should be acknowledged by all involved and the lessons learned from them. It is a time for the agency to take responsibility for what happened and not attempt to scapegoat some junior members. If a member has done wrong, then they should face the consequences, but if their actions were well intended and the harm occurred as a result of genuine mistakes, it is a time for the agency to reflect as to whether the errors could have been prevented. It is also a time for managers to be leaders and take responsibility for the actions of their staff. No one should be under any illusions how difficult working with intelligence is, and unfortunately mistakes have the potential to cost lives. Intelligence is not a place for the faint of heart.

4.32   Conclusion

Intelligence management is an essential tool for law enforcement, but gathering and managing intelligence brings with it responsibilities to ensure that intelligence is collected and managed in a lawful and ethical manner. Courts in most jurisdictions have accepted the necessity of the intelligence function. However, courts have expectations with regard to how that function is carried out and have repeatedly put in place boundaries as to the extent that a citizen's rights can be engaged. There is a necessity for law enforcement to act not only lawfully but also in good faith. For the most part, the public will tolerate law enforcement's involvement in intelligence management but it is always with reservations. When it comes to intelligence gathering and the engagement of citizen's rights, there will always be the expectation of the full accountability and the highest standards of ethical behavior. Goldman (2010), writing on ethics in intelligence work, commented that: "As in life, the intelligence profession is sometimes filled with moral and ethical dilemmas for which no law, policy or regulation can assist in developing the proper response in 'doing the right thing'." However laws, policy, and regulation combined with sound training and good supervision provide a firm foundation in which law enforcement officers can do the right thing on a daily basis.

References

Andregg, M. (2007) Intelligence ethics: Laying a foundation for the second oldest profession. In: Johnson, L.K. Ed. *Handbook of Intelligence Studies*. London and New York: Routledge.

Behnke, S. (2006) Ethics and interrogations: Comparing and contrasting the American Psychological, American Medical and American Psychiatric Association Positions. *Monitor on Psychology*. P86–87. Available at: http://apa.ba0.biz/pubs/info/reports/pens-article.pdf (accessed August 2012).

Brown, E. (2007) *Snitch: Informant, Cooperators and the Corruption of Justice*. New York: Public Affairs.

Buckley, J. (2006) *The Human Source Management System: The Use of Psychology in the Management of Human Intelligence Sources*. London: HSM Publishing.

Cooper, J.R. (2005) *Curing Analytical Pathologies: Pathways to Improved Intelligence Analysis*. Available at: https://www.cia.gov/library/center-for-the-study-of-intelligence/csi-publications/books-and-monographs/curing-analytic-pathologies-pathways-to-improved-intelligence-analysis-1/analytic_pathologies_report.pdf (accessed September 2012).

Elahi, N. (2012) *Introducing Ethics in Intelligence Work*. Available at: http://www.nation.com.pk/pakistan-news-newspaper-daily-english-online/columns/30-Mar-2012/introduing-ethics-in-intelligence-work (accessed December 2012).

Goldman, J. (Ed.) (2010) *Ethics of Spying: A Reader for Intelligence Professionals*, Vol. 2. Lanham, MD: Scarecrow Press Inc.

Harris, D.A. (2009) Law enforcement and intelligence gathering in Muslim and immigrant communities after 9/11. *Review of Law & Social Change*, Vol. 34, P123–127. New York: New York University.

Hoffrage, U. and Pohl, R. (2003) *Hindsight Bias: A Special Issue of Memory*. Champlain, NY: Psychology Press.

Independent Police Complaints Commission (IPCC). (2011) *Corruption in the Police Service in England and Wales*. London, U.K: The Stationery Office. Available at: http://www.official-documents.gov.uk/document/other/9780108510991/9780108510991.pdf (accessed November 2012).

International Standards Organisation. (2009) ISO 31000:2009. *Risk Management: Principles and Guidelines*. Geneva: International Standards Organisation.

Joh, E.E. (2009) Breaking the law to enforce it: Undercover police participation in crime. *Stanford Law Review* 62(1) P155–P199.

Kidder, R.M. (1995) *How Good People Make Tough Choices*. New York: Simon & Schuster.

Leigh, I. (2007) The accountability of security and intelligence agencies. In: Johnson, L.K. Ed. *Handbook of Intelligence Studies*. London and New York: Routledge.

Natapoff, A. (2009) *Snitching: Criminal Informants and the Erosion of American Justice*. New York: New York University Press.

Ratcliffe, J.H. and U.S. Department of Justice Office of Community Oriented Policing Services. (2007) *Integrated Intelligence and Crime Analysis: Enhanced Information Management for Law Enforcement Leaders*. Washington, DC: Police Foundation.

Rest, J.R. (1986) *Moral Development: Advances in Research and Theory*. New York: Praeger.

Rest, J.R. (1994) Background: Theory and research. In: Rest, J.R. and Narvaez, D. Eds. *Moral Development in the Professions: Psychology and Applied Ethics*, P1–25. Hillsdale, NJ: Lawrence Erlbaum.

Tavris, C. and Aronson, E. (2007) *Mistakes Were Made (But Not by Me): Why We Justify Foolish Beliefs, Bad Decisions, and Hurtful Acts*. Harcourt: Houghton Milflin.

Turner, M.A. (2006) *Why Secret Intelligence Fails*. Washington, DC: Potomac Books.

U.S. Bureau of Justice Assistance. (1998) *28 CFR Part 23 Criminal Intelligence Systems Operating Policies Executive Order 12291. Policy Clarification*. Available at: https://www.iir.com/28CFR_Program/28CFR_Resources/Executive_Order/ (accessed December 2012).

Webster. (2010) *Webster's New World Law Dictionary*. Hoboken, NJ: Wiley Publishing, Inc.

Psychology and Intelligence Management

5

There is a phrase, "the elephant in the living room," which purports to describe what it's like to live with a drug addict, an alcoholic, an abuser. People outside such relationships will sometimes ask, "How could you let such a business go on for so many years? Didn't you see the elephant in the living room?" And it's so hard for anyone living in a more normal situation to understand the answer that comes closest to the truth; "I'm sorry, but it was there when I moved in. I didn't know it was an elephant; I thought it was part of the furniture." There comes an aha-moment for some folks—the lucky ones—when they suddenly recognize the difference.

Stephen King

5.1 Introduction

In trying to grasp what it was that has kept many capable police officers from making changes to dysfunctional intelligence systems, the above quote from author Stephen King came to mind. The "elephant in the room" for many law enforcement officers is the intelligence management system that is in existence when they take up their role in this business area. They readily accept things as they are, assuming them to be the "right" way of doing them and continue to do so until they leave the role. Failings within the intelligence system that would appear obvious to the objective observer are allowed to continue. Even if the observer was screaming, "Can't you see the mess?" the officer would reply, "What mess? There is no mess. This is the way it has always been."

Unfortunately, intelligence systems are not subjected to such objective scrutiny until something goes horribly wrong, and then the scrutiny is done in a very public manner often to the detriment of the agency involved. When one starts to examine many of the failures that have occurred in intelligence management, it is often found that one of the common causes is what appears to be a complete departure from rational behavior on the part of those involved. Those looking at whatever incident has occurred will often see behavior that begs belief and they are left wondering what was in the member's head when they acted in that way.

This chapter sets out to provide some indication of the things that might be in the mind of a law enforcement member when they are managing intelligence and to identify some of the common things that can go wrong in the thinking process.

5.2 Background

People are involved at all stages of intelligence management and while human input is absolutely essential, it is far from perfect and subject to numerous internal and external influences. The "human factor" can lead to many errors, and it is important to attempt to reduce such mistakes. Errors often result from actions that the person consciously takes, but that are driven by influences that they are not consciously aware of—the why behind the action. In addition, staff will do things of which they have no conscious awareness, let alone understand why they are doing it. The intelligence management system articulated in this book is designed to minimize the risk of some of these problems occurring, but giving the reader an awareness of some of the psychology involved can only help understanding. We will begin by addressing some of the problems that may appear when the idea of changing how intelligence is managed is first presented to staff.

5.3 Change

Anyone who has set out to make any sort of changes in the way things are done within law enforcement will be all too aware of the potential difficulties they are likely to encounter. Few people like the prospect of change, and many find change a highly stressful experience. Even discussion of potential change is likely to draw hostility. As Davenport and Prusak (1998:102) articulated, "Resistance to change is powerful, even in the face of indisputable objective evidence that a particular change makes sense." For those attempting to change how intelligence is managed within a law enforcement agency (LEA), only those with previous experience (or of a deeply cynical bent) are likely to have any idea of the depth of resistance and hostility that they are likely to encounter. The more wide ranging the changes and the greater number of branches or units affected, the greater the potential for real problems. Understanding the origins of such antagonism is difficult, but to attempt to create a smoother path and to predict some of the potential pitfalls, it is necessary to try. Resistance may originate in a number of ways with the potential for the various causes to interlink and compound the overall effect.

- Police officers like to predict and control the future. The ability to predict and control the future equates with safety for them. Safety is obviously a state much sought after in the situations a law enforcement officer encounters. Law enforcement officers become conditioned to having control over any and every situation so they will be safe. If there is a threat to their control, there is a perceived threat to their safety. The mind-set, strange as it may seem, flows: "Change equates with no control; no control equates with reduced safety; reduced safety equates with a bad thing!"
- Police officers, especially those engaged in specialized roles, such as those closely associated with intelligence management, are generally experienced in those roles and sure of their ability to carry out the role effectively. They want to do the job well. They believe they are doing the job well. If someone wants change, there is likely to be a conflict with how the officer sees the job should be done. The mind-set flows: "I am doing my job as well as it can be done. There is no need to change how the job should be done. To admit the need for change means I could do the job better. That is wrong. There is no need for change."
- Following on from the previous point, an officer's ability to do the job well is closely linked to their self-image—how they see themselves and also how they believe others see them. Their role becomes intrinsically linked to their ego. If someone says there is a need to change how they are doing their job, this implies that they are not doing the job as well as they could be. As people often have limited separation between their role and who they are as a person, the situation is perceived as an attack on them, not only professionally but also personally. The mind-set develops: "You want to change how I do my job. What you are really saying is that I am not doing it well. You will make others think less of me. That is not happening. No change."

5.4   Cognitive Biases

There are a number of psychological factors or "cognitive biases" that are likely to have an impact on how intelligence is interpreted and can possibly lead to a misinterpretation of the intelligence. While space prevents either a comprehensive listing of these mental failings or a lengthy discussion of those listed, the limited information given about each is intended to equip those involved with intelligence management with an awareness of elements likely to affect their reasoning.

- *Reliability bias.* If the origin of information is normally reliable, those involved in collecting that information and those involved in working with the subsequent intelligence product will assume that all subsequent materials produced from that origin are correct without validating each subsequent piece of information on a piece-by-piece basis. The reliability attached to the origin creates a situation where it becomes difficult to identify deception or where facts are misrepresented either accidentally or intentionally. The problem is exacerbated when the first impression created was one of the credibility. First impressions are often difficult to shift despite them often being incorrectly reached.
- *Confirmation bias.* People are prone to seeing what they expect to see. It is difficult to view something one has previously considered without bringing preconceptions to the table. Unfortunately, this means that people often see only what confirms their existing beliefs and subconsciously exclude any information that conflicts with that existing belief.
- *Control bias.* People have a tendency to see patterns where none exist. The desire to be able to identify what is occurring stems from an intrinsic need to be in control of one's future. If a person can understand what is happening, then they are more likely to be able to control what happens to them in the future. Unfortunately, this creates a tendency to link things that should not be linked.
- *Bounded rationality.* Herbert Simon (1957) created the concept of "bounded rationality" in which he argued that due to limited mental capacity, our minds cannot cope with the complexity of the world. In order to compensate for the limitations, what we do is create a simplified model of the world and then make subsequent interpretations of events bounded by that model. While this concept has similarities to the limitations of memory discussed later in the chapter, it cannot be easily overcome by using a visual representation of events, because it is an inherent flaw in our processing ability.
- *Pollyanna* complex.* A Pollyanna complex is the bias that refers to a person who has positive perspective on everything. They tend to be blindly optimistic regardless of the reality of the situation. They can be extremely difficult to convince that things are going, or have the potential to go, wrong.
- *Attribution bias.* Heider (1958) postulated that: (1) People are biased toward believing something was a deliberate act even if it was not. (2) People will attribute blame to a person, rather than the prevailing circumstances, almost regardless as to how big a part those

---

* "Pollyanna" is taken from the central character in the classic novel of the same name by Eleanor H. Porter (1868–1920).

circumstances actually played. (3) People fail to recognize that there may have been unintentional consequences as a result of another person's actions. (4) People fail to realize that small errors can lead to major consequences and are reluctant to accept occurrences as merely being as a result of coincidence. Conspiracies are seen where in reality the acts that led to an event were unintended.

5.5 Group Dynamics

There are many different psychological ways in which groups can function collectively that can cause distortions in either the interpretation of intelligence or deciding the action that should be taken as a result of intelligence. Two of these that may occur are referred to as the "Abilene paradox" and "Groupthink." The cause and effects of both are not dissimilar but can have catastrophic effects when it comes to managing intelligence. Harvey (1988) coined the term, "the Abilene paradox,"* to refer to circumstances in which a group of people collectively decide on a course of action that is counter to the preferences of any of the individuals in the group. It involves a breakdown of communication in which each member mistakenly believes that their own preferences are counter to the group's and, therefore, does not raise objections. Harvey identified six symptoms that form the paradox:

1. Each member decides as an individual the nature of the situation or problem.
2. Each member decides as an individual as to the steps that are required to cope with the situation or problem.
3. All members fail to accurately communicate their desires and/or beliefs to one another and in reality do the opposite. This creates a situation where each member believes something different than the reality, and an inaccurate collective picture takes prevalence.
4. Members make collective decisions based on this inaccurate perception and take actions contrary to what they want and that are counterproductive for the agency.
5. As a result of taking the wrong actions, members experience "frustration, anger, irritation, and dissatisfaction" with other members. Then, they form subgroups and blame other subgroups or those in authority for the agency's problems.
6. If the failure of communication is not dealt with, the cycle repeats and intensifies.

---

* The Abilene paradox is so called because the starting point for the research was based on a family trip Harvey took to Abilene.

Many working in intelligence will be familiar with the occurrence of such a situation in which the most important thing in the group becomes "getting along." Goffman (1959) highlights how social norms can influence how material is received, and warns how constraints, such as tact or reluctance to speak up, can reduce the chances of inconsistencies or deceptions being unearthed. He also counsels how feelings toward an individual can lead to conclusions being drawn that are not based on the facts presented.

Similar to the Abilene paradox is the more commonly known phenomenon "groupthink." Groupthink (Janis 1982) is a way of thinking that develops within a group when the desire for harmony in a decision-making group overrides objective thinking. When groupthink occurs, members seek to minimize conflict and subsequently reach a consensus without taking cognizance of alternative ideas or views. There are number of factors that create a context in which groupthink is likely to occur, many of which are likely to be found in intelligence management:

- Insulation of the group from outside influences. The secret nature of intelligence business can lead to insulation.
- Managers who are partial, egocentric, and bullying in their nature.*
- A lack of structure, method, and procedures for carrying out tasks.
- Lack of diversity in the group. Often found in law enforcement as a matter of course, when a group has members from similar social backgrounds and with similar values, they all tend to think the same way. The problem is exacerbated by the similarities of type that are attracted to intelligence work. If the team is not representative of society, problems are more likely to occur. Where the opinions of certain types of persons are excluded because of rank, gender, or purely because they cannot be heard because of others shouting their views, groupthink is likely to appear. This problem is not countered by having a "token" female who is there to make the coffee, while the men do the real work!†
- Where highly stressful external threats are present, there is likely to be greater pressure for the group to have group cohesiveness, and the need for the group to stick together. The problem will be exacerbated if there have been recent failures that can make the group feel threatened and so come closer.
- Where there are difficult decisions or moral dilemmas, both of which are commonly found in intelligence work, this will add to the likelihood of occurrence of groupthink.

---

* This would never happen in law enforcement!
† This would never ever happen in law enforcement!

Once the environment has been created for groupthink to develop, symptoms of the phenomenon are likely to appear. These include the following:

- Internal pressure is placed upon group members to conform to the views and values of the group. Self-appointed members enforce the group views, often resorting to using ridicule and insult to make sure other members conform. The illusion is created that all in the group agree when in reality their silence is a fear of speaking out. This pressure is often exacerbated by the "conscious" presence of the rank structure found in law enforcement and the failure to create circumstances where people are encouraged to speak the truth, without a fear of personal consequences.
- Unquestioned belief in the morality of the actions the group takes and illusions that they are invulnerable. This leads to excessive risk-taking and a certainty that the course of action decided upon was the only option. Furthermore it often leads to behavior so bizarre that when viewed later by an objective observer may draw the question, "what the hell were they thinking?"
- The group will become increasingly close-minded with new information assimilated to fit existing views. The group dismisses anything that challenges the group views and alienates anyone who opposes the views of the group. Depending on who that person is, they will be labeled as having a personal agenda or as being weak or stupid.

These group mentalities can be a real problem in intelligence management and have been linked to such failures as the Bay of Pigs and more recently the reporting in relation to weapons of mass destruction prior to the invasion of Iraq.

5.6 Hindsight Bias

If an agency gets into trouble as a result of failings, this bias is likely to play a significant role in the minds of those examining what happened. The term "hindsight bias" (Hoffrage and Pohl 2003) refers to the tendency that people have to view events as being more predictable than they really are. After an event, people often think that they would have known that the event was coming before it happened, if *they* had been present before it happened, or if they'd had a reason to pay attention to what was occurring in the lead up to that event. In other words, when we look back on something, we are prejudiced in believing we would have predicted that it was going to happen. An example of hindsight bias is the belief that had people paid attention to what was occurring in the run up to 9/11, they would definitely have been able to predict the attacks! Hindsight bias stems from a number of flawed beliefs including the following:

- The world is more predictable than it really is.
- We are smarter than others. This comes about because whatever happened would have been obvious for us to see, yet they did not. Of course, we are now looking back with knowledge of what did happen, and we delude ourselves that they should have seen it!
- Others failed to see what was obvious and were negligent in their role.

Hindsight bias has the potential to impact on intelligence management in a number of ways. First, when something goes wrong, those examining the events will more than likely believe that the thing that went wrong should have been predicted based on the facts that were available at the time. They look on the event as having been predictable, because they subconsciously base that judgment on the additional information they now have. Postmortems on events that go wrong are a huge problem for those involved in intelligence and allegations that one "should have known" can only be mitigated by extensive contemporaneous record-keeping including accurate decision logs. Failure to keep such records makes it more likely that allegations can be made that "you should have known." Second, hindsight bias leads to those involved in making intelligence-based predictions to overestimate how accurate their previous predictions were. These inaccurately recalled previous predictions create a situation where the person becomes overconfident about future predictions—"If I was right in the past, then I will be right in the future"—the emphasis here being on the degree of certainty. Third, hindsight bias leads to a situation in which decision makers, having been in receipt of intelligence prior to an event, and having made decisions based on that intelligence, block out the contribution that the intelligence has made to their decision-making. They adopt the position that the decision came about through *their* good judgment, and that they would have made the same decision regardless of the intelligence—"I would have done that anyway." Fourth, where a person's opinion is ignored, and subsequently proves to be correct, they inaccurately remember the degree of their conviction prior to the event of transpiring. They believe their conviction to have been much greater than in effect it was. The "I told you so" factor kicks in, and the person becomes adamant in the belief that, had they been listened to, the negative event would not have transpired.

None of the consequences of hindsight bias are surprising, nor are its causes. The amount of information that is available after an event is obviously greater than the amount of information before the event. Hindsight is always 20/20.

5.7   Memory

Given that much of the information that ends up as intelligence originates from a memory in someone's head, it is important to understand the nature of memory and the problems with it. This includes a basic understanding of what is understood by the term memory. Essentially, memory is the ability of a person to store, retain, and recall both information and experiences. Melton (1963) identifies three steps that are necessary for any person to do this:

1. *Encoding the information or event.* The person obtains the new information or experiences an event. The information is encoded based on how the person perceives and interprets the event.
2. *Storage of the information or event.* The person creates a record of the encoded information. Many believe this to be a permanent record. It is in reality a script which can and will be overwritten, often unknowingly by the person as time progresses.
3. *Retrieval of the memory.* Memories are retrieved from storage in response to a cue that the person sends to where the memory is stored. The type of cue that is sent dictates how the memory is retrieved. Sending different cues can recall the memory in different ways.

As it can been seen, the potential at any of these stages for distortion to occur is significant.

Most often memory is referred to in three forms:

1. *Short-term memory.* This is the ability to hold a very limited amount of information at the front of one's mind for an extremely limited time (up to about a minute). For most people, this ability extends to recalling between three to seven items.
2. *Long-term memory.* The amount of information that can be stored in the long-term memory is vast and it can be stored for the duration of a person's life. It is this aspect of memory that comes into play when eliciting information from a person for intelligence purposes.
3. *Working memory.* While sometimes used interchangeably with short-term memory, there is a significant difference. Short-term memory refers only to the short-term retention of information, while working memory refers to not only the retention of that information but also simultaneous use of that information. Working memory is used when we try problem-solving in our heads without recourse to written material. In recognizing the nature of working memory and its limitations, one can easily see the benefits of visual analytical products when discussing complex cases.

However, to better understand the aspects of memory that impact on information collection, the nature of long-term memory must be further subdivided.

1. *Implicit memory* requires no conscious effort on the part of an individual to recall it. It typically occurs with motor skills, such as driving a car, where no conscious thought is required to retrieve the knowledge as to what to do next.
2. *Explicit memory* requires the person to consciously access the memory. It can be further divided into two different types of memory:
   i. *Semantic memory.* This relates to facts that are stored independent of the context in which they are received. Semantic memory includes things such as types of car and street names. Semantic memory is also the way in which people store facts as part of wider interrelated groups such as their work routine.
   ii. *Episodic memory.* This relates to information that has been stored in relation to specific events. It is often contextually embedded, relating to the circumstances under which it was obtained and/or linked to other memories such as a place or time. It is in episodic memory that a person's feelings about events and other aspects personal to them are stored.

It is important that those involved in collecting information are aware of these different types of memory. For example, if a person witnesses a shooting on their *regular* journey to their place of worship, they will have a set of semantic memories relating to how they normally behave when going to worship. However, they will also have a set of episodic memories for the shooting "event." Depending on the way in which memories are retrieved, there is potential for the semantic memory to either enhance or corrupt the retrieval of episodic memory. If information is not retrieved with care, the person's memories of the specific event drawn from episodic memory can potentially be contaminated with details of their memories of what happens every other Sunday, that is, those memories being obtained from their "semantic memory." Given the fact that much of the information obtained from people for intelligence purposes is vulnerable to this distortion, those collecting information on a full-time basis need training in understanding the nature of memory and how to create more accurate recall. Those processing information obtained from citizens into intelligence and working with the subsequent intelligence products need to take the potential for distortion caused by memory deficiencies into consideration.

The fact that the memory process is inherently flawed has been recognized since around the beginning of the twentieth century, prior to which few questions were asked about the reliability of those who testified in court, the assumption being is that if they were credible and well-meaning as individuals, then the events they would recount would be accurate (Münsterberg 1925). Since then, there has been significant research in the nature of memory with a number of findings that have relevance to obtaining information from people (Buckhout, 1977; Loftus, Greene and Doyle, 1989; Schacter, 2001). These findings include the following facts:

- Even when a person witnesses an event firsthand, not everything will enter their memory. In addition, what enters memory may vary in trace strength and so the quality of memory will vary.
- Memories will be lost over time, with initial memory loss being compounded by a slower but nevertheless further degradation, as the days/weeks following the event progress.
- Memories will become distorted over time.
- Retrieval of memory is not perfect and this means that while a memory may exist, it will not always be possible to bring that memory back in its original form, thus resulting in distorted reporting.
- Subsequent events can interfere with the original memory; what was memorized at the time can be changed by what happens later.
- The person's memory will be affected by how they comprehended the event both consciously and subconsciously.

5.8   Processing Information

As information is processed, many influences come to bear without the protagonists being conscious of what they are doing. One of the most common errors in intelligence management is the distortion of intelligence. A piece of information is received by the agency, and by the time it gets to the end user it bears little or no resemblance to the original information. Not only does this waste resources and cause erroneous decision making but it can also lead to loss of life. Many readers will be familiar with the party game, "Whisper down the lane," in which a message is whispered from one person to another around a room with the last person saying aloud what they heard with the fun coming from the distortion in the message that occurs merely because it is passed verbally and whispered. Intelligence can be distorted for similar reasons but also for many other reasons, including the following:

- *Poor listening.* An officer receives information from a source or member of the public and believes he hears everything that was said. Because the officer has not been trained in active listening skills, he hears what is said incorrectly or distorts what was said to meet his view of the world.

- *Lack of accurate note taking at point of origin.* An officer receives information from a source or member of the public and believes she can remember everything that was said. They cannot and so when she writes the information submission, it is inaccurate and incomplete.
- *Fitting an officer's world view.* Officers receiving information often have preconceived ideas about what they are going to be told, so when they write the information submission, they write it so that it fits what they expect the reality to be. Details can be added or removed, or changes can be made in emphasis to suit the member's view of what is occurring.
- *Fitting an agenda.* Officers often dig themselves into a hole. They commit so heavily to a course of action or their preconceived beliefs about some matter, that they will distort or omit anything that contradicts that view. They do not want to have to say to anyone that they have gotten something wrong. Poor management exacerbates this situation, because they blame the officer when something changes, rather than accepting it as the nature of the intelligence business. This also occurs in the management of human sources where the officer becomes blindly loyal to whatever "their" source says, and then will hear nothing to the contrary. Some things are true whether you believe them or not!
- *Too difficult to deal with.* This problem often stems with management and their reluctance or inability to deal with intelligence that is set before them. They then pressurize the reporting member to change the content of his report to make it easier to deal with. A real-life example illustrates this point. A report was submitted warning of the vulnerabilities of attack at airports. Dealing with this would have resulted in considerable expenditure and would probably have been met with a great degree of hostility. The report was withdrawn by a manager and a short time later an airport in that jurisdiction was successfully attacked.
- *Overly sanitizing information.* Sanitizing information to produce intelligence reports is a skilled job. Many involved overly sanitize documents to such an extent that they have no meaning or different meaning from when the content was submitted. This occurs because those involved do not have faith in the integrity of the intelligence repository and the ability of the agency to keep material from those who do not need to see it. It also happens because some people who have the right to see intelligence, by virtue of rank or role, have never been trained in how to deal with sensitive intelligence and therefore material has to be hidden from them so they do not mishandle it!

- *Withholding intelligence.* Often officers do not report information that could change an intelligence picture. This is often done in the belief that it is to protect "sources and methods." If this justification is valid, then the agencies intelligence management system is broken. If it has no validity, the officer is acting in a corrupt manner.
- Accepting intelligence without question, or dismissing it without question, based only on previous knowledge of where the material has originated, creates circumstances where a person omits that which contradicts their previous experience.
- Words used by the originator of the information are removed because they are impolite or contain grammatical errors, yet in doing so the meaning is lost.
- One piece of intelligence may contradict another and so it is removed. Many people struggle with the ability to hold two contradictory beliefs in their head at one time; they have to conclude one is correct and then dismiss the other. Sometimes both can be true, just from different perspectives.
- *Haste.* There can be many times that due care is not taken in submitting and processing information, with the only thought given being as to the speed with which the member can get it off his desk. Haste makes waste.
- If we reject intelligence as being incorrect, we tend to reject it all, being unable to take on board that part of it may be correct. In a similar vein, if we accept the intelligence as being correct, we tend to accept it in its entirety. In addition, once we have formed an impression, it is difficult to change it. Even if more and better intelligence becomes available later, the initial impression will linger.

5.9   Expressing Uncertainty

Preparation of assessments based on intelligence reporting are a common request from intelligence customers, and with them comes the difficulty in finding adequate ways to express the level of certainty or uncertainty of an event. Such a judgment can be expressed in terms of either a numerical value, or in terms of a rhetorical value. If the value is to be expressed numerically, clarity must be given as to what is being evaluated—the percentage chance of the event happening or not happening—and how the customer is likely to take meaning from the figures. This will depend greatly upon how that numerical value is presented. Consider the following two pieces of information and think how they could be interpreted. (Please note the numbers used are only given as an example to how the manner in which information is presented can affect how it is interpreted—they are not presented as a medical statistic.)

Ninety percent of patients survive open heart surgery.
One in every ten patients dies undergoing open heart surgery.

The figures are statistically the same, but the way in which they are presented changes interpretation.

Care must also be taken with such numerical evaluation, as it is extremely unlikely that there will be any underpinning numeric data to support such an answer. Furthermore, where a numeric answer is the preferred choice of the customer, generally speaking that person will be attracted by the precision numerical evaluations offer. In these circumstances, the person supplying the evaluation is leaving herself in a position where not only is she unable to justify her evaluation with the numerical data to support it but also she is dealing with a customer who is already less likely to be comfortable with the imprecise nature that is the essence of intelligence assessments. Where possible those involved in intelligence should avoid numerical evaluations in assessments as figures create a misleading sense of accuracy.

5.10   Being Wrong

Intelligence is not an easy business to be in. Sometimes we end up backing the wrong horse. An officer may examine a piece or pieces of intelligence, which they believe to be correct, and then articulate a viewpoint based on that intelligence, which subsequently turns out to be wrong. Logic would dictate that having made an error, the most obvious move course of action under such circumstances would be to admit the mistake and move on. However, as Tavris and Aronson (2007) point out, "Most people, when directly confronted with proof that they are wrong, do not change their point of view or course of action but justify it even more tenaciously." From a logic perspective, this may seem an unlikely option for someone to take, except when one considers the impact of admitting you have been wrong. First, being wrong once means we can be wrong again; this makes us feel less certain about our ability to remain safe in the future.

Second, many of those involved in intelligence construct a public image of themselves based on their professionalism and ability to do the job. Who they are as a person is intrinsically linked to who they are as a professional. The mistaken belief that admitting their fallibility will damage their professional image and subsequently their personal image is just too hard to take.

Third, the belief that if they admit a mistake, they damage their entire future credibility means they seek out ways to limit damage to their position. Such damage-limitation techniques include reducing the importance of the accurate interpretation and discrediting the overall credibility of the person they believe responsible for undermining them. The problem occurs because individuals do not understand the psychological processes involved. This is then exacerbated by a lack of good training. Quoting Tavris and Aronson (2007),

> Currently, the professional training of most police officers, detectives, judges, and attorneys includes almost no information about their own cognitive biases; how to correct for them, as much as possible; and how to manage the dissonance they will feel when their beliefs meet disconfirming evidence. On the contrary, much of what they learn about psychology comes from self-proclaimed experts with no training in psychological science and who … do not teach them to be more accurate in their judgments, merely more confident that they are accurate.

Unfortunately, it is often the environment within law enforcement that creates circumstances where people feel unsafe about admitting that they were wrong. The macho culture that is all too often prevalent is a blaming culture, meaning that it is often easier to try and mask a mistake than openly admit it. If mistakes cannot be openly admitted, the management should prepare for a culture of deceit.

Those involved in intelligence management need to be able to admit mistakes and move on from there. Failing to admit errors only leads to more errors, self-deception, and the deception of others. There is no shame in making a mistake, and the ability to admit being wrong is a quality that every intelligence professional should strive for. Mistakes are an opportunity to learn.

5.11 Customers

If those involved in intelligence are to be effective, having a better understanding of how intelligence customers may think increases the chances of the products being accepted and used appropriately and reduces the chances of conflict.

- Most readers will be familiar with the apocryphal story of the boy who cried wolf. One of the biggest problems in disseminating threat intelligence is that very often, for one reason or another, the threat does not materialize. Those receiving the threat then become threat-weary and mistrust the existence of any threat. This problem is hard to surmount and is easily exacerbated by intelligence managers continually putting out warnings, just to cover themselves in the event something does go wrong. Clarity with regard to the quality of the intelligence on which a threat is based enables those receiving warnings to make better judgments as to how they need to respond.

- Threats to the public. The vast majority of managers on receipt of any threat connected to a member of the public are going to warn that person regardless of how sensitive or specious the intelligence on which it is based and with limited consideration to any potential fall-out. Those managing the intelligence need to take cognizance of this. The customer should never be informed of where the intelligence has originated, because unfortunately they will often pass those details out without thinking.
- Customers will always have their own agenda. If intelligence does not fit that agenda, there is a real risk that pressure will be applied to change the intelligence.* As George Orwell writes, "People can foresee the future only when it coincides with their own wishes, and the most grossly obvious facts can be ignored when they are unwelcome."
- Many customers will push to know the origin of intelligence and then base judgments on their views of the origin. For example, a customer may view the product of intercept as being intrinsically of more worth than that of a human source, and therefore respond in a different way. The origin of intelligence should be anonymized before it is disseminated.
- Overreliance on intelligence. When customers become used to always being supplied with large quantities of high-grade intelligence, they can develop an overreliance on it. This limits their ability to work without it and can lead to blame being cast, where intelligence has been unable to prevent an undesired event. Customers need to be educated about the limitations of intelligence as well as the capabilities.

5.12   Understanding Oneself

Everyone has prejudices and faults in their character, and these have the potential to influence the objectivity that is necessary for effective intelligence management. Recognizing these faults and prejudices is the first step in counteracting them. Philip Larkin, in his poem "This Be the Verse," speaks of the origin of the nature of prejudices and the distortions in the way we think that are passed on from generation to generation.

> *They fuck you up, your mum and dad.*
> *They may not mean to, but they do.*
> *They fill you with the faults they had*
> *And add some extra, just for you.*

---

* Many would argue that this is exactly what happened with the U.S. and U.K. governments, and the alleged weapons of mass destruction in Iraq!

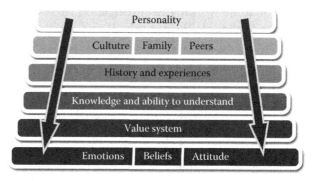

Figure 5.1 A value system.

The initial reaction to many reading these lines will be to jump to the defense of their parents citing agreement with many of the values their parents passed on to them, but that is to miss the point of the poem. It is not an attack on parents but recognition of where most of us obtain our values and the way in which we think about things. Figure 5.1 provides a model of how we develop a "value system," and how our behavior is subsequently directed by that system. While the model is a simplistic view of what takes many years to create, it illustrates the things that are most likely to shape how we view the world. Looming large is our history, and given the fact that many of our values are instilled in us from a very young age, they can be very difficult to change, particularly if one either lacks the desire or the intellectual ability to change them. For those involved in intelligence management, it should be recognized that our value system directs how we select what to attend to, and subsequently how we react to what we have taken on board. If we do not learn to manage our deficiencies, then whether we recognize it or not, the intelligence we collect or process has every potential to be distorted.

Common effects that are likely to occur in intelligence management because of a person's values include the following:

- *The inability to work with human sources.* Many officers cannot set aside their values to manage the type of people who often make the best sources. There is a direct clash between the officer's morals and the activities of the source.
- Many people cannot cope with the lack of certainty that intelligence management brings. Their need for "control" means that they are likely to put themselves under considerable stress when dealing with ambiguous or inconclusive material.
- *Personal prejudices.* Unfortunately, there are still officers working in law enforcement who are prejudiced against certain sections of the community. This affects all their dealings with that community and their ability to work professionally.

- *End goals.* For some working in intelligence, their career goals are not conducive to the intelligence role. If one has set their sights on rapid promotion and is driven by that expectation, the often long-term nature of intelligence management creates a conflict in which one looks for rapid personal gain at the cost of longer term gain for the agency as a whole.
- Ethnocentrism occurs when we perceive people from different countries and cultures as thinking and acting in the same way as we would. We then use that erroneous perception to try to understand the actions of others, without knowing that one is using flawed logic. Ultimately, this leads to poor judgments about the other party. The problem is likely to be exacerbated if a person has limited exposure to different people, cultures, and countries.
- *Looking busy.* Law enforcement can be a very results-driven culture. It is easy to fall into the trap of creating intelligence products that are of little real worth merely to show how busy one is. The end result is an intelligence repository that is full of intelligence that is of limited or no value. This problem is well illustrated by an overreliance that many agencies place on both statistical data and open-source material.
- *My source and I am right.* The Butler Report (2004, Para 599) comments on those have a vested interest in "championing their own sources." If a member is too close to the origin of information, objectivity with regard to the information's worth is likely to be lost.

5.13   Conclusion

This chapter has highlighted a few of the psychological issues that are likely to crop up on a fairly regular basis in relation to managing intelligence. Psychology is a subject that is rarely considered as having any real impact on intelligence management in a law enforcement context despite widespread evidence of psychological factors affecting what occurs in intelligence analysis (Heurer 1999). Now that we have the foundations on which to build an intelligence management system, we now move to identifying what it needs to do and how it can do that.

References

Buckhout, R. (1977) Eyewitness identification and psychology in the courtroom. *Criminal Defence* 4 P5–P19.

Butler (The Right Honourable Lord Butler of Brockwell) (2004) *Review of Intelligence on Weapons of Mass Destruction.* Report of a Committee of Privy Counsellors HC898. London: The Stationery Office.

Davenport, T.H. and Prusak, L. (1998) *Working Knowledge: How Organizations Manage What They Know.* Boston, MA: Harvard Business School Press.

Goffman, E. (1959) *The Presentation of Self in Everyday Life.* New York: Doubleday Anchor Books.

Harvey, J.B. (1988) *The Abilene Paradox and Other Meditations on Management.* Available at: http://www.rmastudies.org.nz/documents/AbileneParadoxJerry Harvey.pdf (accessed August 2012).

Heider, F. (1958) *The Psychology* of *Interpersonal Relations.* New York: Wiley.

Heurer, R. J. (1999) *Psychology of Intelligence Analysis.* Washington, DC: Center for Intelligence Study. Available at: https://www.cia.gov/library/center-for-the-study-of-intelligence/csi-publications/books-and-monographs/psychology-of-intelligence-analysis/PsychofIntelNew.pdf (accessed August 2012).

Hoffrage, U. and Pohl, R. (2003) *Hindsight Bias: A Special Issue of Memory.* Champlain, NY: Psychology Press.

Janis, I. (1982) *Groupthink: Psychological Studies of Policy Decisions and Fiascos.* Boston. MA: Houghton Miflin.

Loftus, E.F., Greene, E.L. and Doyle J.M. (1989) The psychology of eyewitness testimony. In: Raskin, D.C. Ed. *Psychological Methods in Criminal Investigation and Evidence.* New York: Springer.

Melton A. (1963) Implications of short term memory for a general theory of memory. *Journal of Verbal Learning and Verbal Behaviour* 2 P1–P21.

Münsterberg, H. (1925) The memory of the witness. In: *On the Witness Stand: Essays on Psychology and Crime.* Available at: http://psychclassics.yorku.ca/Munster/ Witness/memory.htm (accessed December 2011).

Schacter, D.L. (2001) *How the Mind Forgets and Remembers: The Seven Sins of Memory.* London: Souvenir Press.

Simon, H.A. (1957) *Models of Man, Social and Rational: Mathematical Essays on Rational Human Behavior in a Social Setting.* New York: John Wiley and Sons.

Tavris, C. and Aronson, E. (2007) *Mistakes Were Made (But Not by Me): Why We Justify Foolish Beliefs, Bad Decisions, and Hurtful Acts.* Orlando, FL: Harcourt.

The Intelligence
Cycle (Revisited)

6

We are all apprentices in a craft where no one ever becomes a master.

Ernest Hemingway

6.1   Introduction

One of the most widely promoted aspects of intelligence management is that it is a cyclical process comprising a number of separate stages, beginning and ending at the same stage. This process has become known as "the intelligence cycle." This chapter highlights both the benefits of this model and some of the criticisms about the model. It explores the suitability of the model for use by law enforcement and makes suggestions as to how to improve its applicability in a law enforcement environment. This chapter illustrates a "revisited" version of the model and gives a detailed explanation of each of the stages of the revisited model.

6.2   Models

Taking a minute before delving into the intelligence cycle, in the interests of clarity, we should share a word or two about models. A model is a visual representation of a real thing. It is not the real thing; a model of a ship may look like a ship but is not a ship. Models by their very nature are exclusive; much of what could be included is left out for simplicity's sake. Having said that, the desire to oversimplify a model can create something that is all but meaningless. The intelligence cycle is a conceptual model—it looks like the concept of intelligence management, but it has been simplified for expedience. Too many people get hung up on in-depth critique of the model as opposed to using the model to aid them in understanding and developing the concept of intelligence management.

6.3   The Intelligence Cycle

While the origins of the intelligence cycle are somewhat unclear, there is significant acknowledgment of its use in aiding understanding of intelligence management. The structure and content of the model are significantly weighted toward the role played by agencies within the intelligence community, whose primary if not sole function is the gathering of intelligence. This would suggest that it was from the intelligence community that the model originated, only to be adopted later by law enforcement, with limited adaptation to address specific differences in role and language. There are many versions of the intelligence cycle. An Australian version, illustrated in Figure 6.1, is typical of that used by many agencies and contains five elements.

A short explanation of each of these stages gives the following:

- *Direction:* Direction is given as to what is to be collected.
- *Collation:* The bringing together of the gathered information.
- *Analysis:* Analysis of the information and creation of intelligence.
- *Dissemination:* Distributing the intelligence to those who require it.
- *Review and feedback:* An assessment of the success or not of the direction given and the subsequent results achieved.

In a similar vein, but with some differences, the Federal Bureau of Investigation (2012) advocates the version illustrated in Figure 6.2.

As can be seen from Figure 6.2, there are some significant differences between this version of the cycle and the previous one. The version has six stages stressing the need for active collaboration throughout:

Figure 6.1 The intelligence cycle. (From Standing Committee on Crime and Criminal Intelligence, *Guiding Principles for Law Enforcement Intelligence*, SCOCCI, Australia, 1997.)

Figure 6.2 FBI version of intelligence cycle.

1. Requirements
2. Planning and direction
3. Collection
4. Processing and exploitation
5. Analysis and production
6. Dissemination

These stages are then followed by a return to stage 1, "requirements," thus completing the cycle.

Even within individual countries, there are often many different versions of the intelligence cycle being used by different agencies. The number of different versions of the model is a strong indicator of agreement of its worth in principle but also illustrates the number of disagreements as to how it is laid out and what it is meant to be saying. Many of the disagreements originate because of a lack of understanding of what intelligence is and from the ambiguous language used to describe intelligence as a function. The variance in both the number of stages the cycle passes through and the names placed on each of those stages is not the only problem some perceive with the model. Turner (2006:12) is scathing with regard to the model. In his commentary on intelligence failures, he writes, "...the roots of intelligence failures are embedded in the intelligence cycle... ."

Other criticisms include the iterative nature of the model, the argument being made that intelligence management is not truly a continuous cycle.

This argument, though it has some validity, fails to take into account the main purpose of the model, namely, to act as a framework.

In addition, arguments are raised that while in most versions the cycle begins with the intelligence requirements being set by the agency's leadership, the reality is that the intelligence collectors begin by providing intelligence, which then informs the leadership of what direction the agency should take. This argument has two aspects: first, the "chicken and egg" type debate and, second, how the argument impacts from a law enforcement perspective, as opposed to from an intelligence community perspective. Both aspects are discussed in Sections 6.6 and 6.35, respectively.

Recognizing that there are concerns and confusions about the intelligence cycle model, let us clearly state that the position that is adopted in this book is that, first, as an aid to understanding intelligence management, the intelligence cycle is a useful model. Second, the intelligence cycle is not intended to be a representation of an entire intelligence management system. It is in place as a guide for those with little intelligence management experience, such as most senior law enforcement managers, and helps equip them with a basic understanding of how and where intelligence management fits with ordinary law enforcement. Third, discussing the point as to where the cycle commences is in many ways academic, as such a debate takes on a "chicken and egg" scenario. There is no day zero, when nothing exists, and both intelligence requirements and existing intelligence are symbiotic. Fourth, unlike an intelligence agency, the priorities of a law enforcement agency (LEA)are not always intelligence related. For example, a police service may have major problems with road fatalities for which there is no intelligence remit. The law enforcement leader will identify what areas of law enforcement they view as a priority, a decision that should be informed by the existing intelligence picture, and then having identified priorities dictate future intelligence requirements. For example, a Chief analyzes her crime figures and identifies an escalation in the theft of high-value metals. She identifies combatting this as a policing priority. As her strategy to deal with it, she instructs the crime prevention officer to carry out visits to potential victims and also directs that intelligence be gathered to identify suspects and potential outlets for the stolen goods. These two aspects, the suspects and outlets, become the intelligence requirements to address this threat. Alternatively, the Chief may have received a problem profile from the Intelligence Unit identifying that there is intelligence to indicate that an organized crime gang is attempting to recruit new members from within the community. She identifies combatting this threat as a law enforcement priority and directs community police to begin an outreach initiative in the affected community. In addition, she directs that intelligence be gathered on the main protagonists, the methods they are using to recruit people, and details of any new recruits. These three aspects—the protagonists, the recruitment methods, and the new recruits—are the intelligence requirements to deal with this threat. Adding law enforcement priorities into the model is intended to reduce the disconnect between mainstream policing and intelligence management by illustrating where the two connect. Fifth, and running as a theme throughout the book, the term "analysis" is omitted from the model and replaced by analytical development. Acknowledging that the word "analysis" is included in the majority of versions of the intelligence cycle, it is the ambiguity and misunderstanding surrounding this word that has been a significant factor in the critique of the elements contained within the other models of the intelligence cycle.

Having outlined the background to the intelligence cycle and some of the problems with it, particularly for law enforcement, we now illustrate the revisited model used in this book and explain each stage. However, before doing so, we must address one of the main driving forces in the desire to improve law enforcement intelligence management—the issue of limited resources. LEAs are continually being asked by government, local, and national bodies "to do more with less."

6.4   Limited Resources

LEAs have limited resources, and they cannot prevent or investigate every crime. Most Chiefs realize this, although they may be reluctant to admit it in public, particularly if they are elected officials. However, that is the reality and it is best to be up-front and honest about it than to create unrealistic public expectations that will not be met. It is the Chief's job, following consultation, to decide how resources will be deployed to make the greatest impact on the most serious problems affecting the community.

Failing to understand the nature of the limited resources available is not exclusively found among Chiefs. It is much more likely to be found among more junior staff who have very limited experience of managing agency budgets or being held accountable at a public level. All too often members will blame the Chief for making cutbacks or not pursuing certain types of investigation. Comments about the public suffering, citizens being exposed to danger, and offenders "getting away with it" are all too prevalent (and if one was being jaded, complaints are most often heard after a cut in the overtime budget!). For want of a better term, the following may help form some part of a "reality check" for those having difficulty in dealing with the issues created by limited resourcing:

- All public servants work under the constraints imposed by limited resourcing. People die every day because there is not enough money in the health care budget. The public decides how much they want to spend on law enforcement. It is their choice, you work for them.

- It is the Chief's decision as to what is and what is not considered a priority. He is qualified to decide because he is the Chief. You may disagree with his decision, you may think him an idiot, and you may be right, but he is still the Chief.
- Getting upset over the lack of resources or the decisions that management are forced to make can have negative effects on the functioning of the agency and more importantly to your mental well-being. There are lots of things *within* your control to worry about. Far too many involved in intelligence work internalize every decision and then wonder why they end up on stress leave or "sucking steel"! Stress kills more cops than the bad guys do. If you want to worry about something, worry about something you can change, like the quality of your work. Intelligence professionals learn to work with limited resources by being creative in their thinking and flexible in the way they respond to circumstances.
- Working with limited resources is often a huge opportunity to learn to work more effectively. Many of the reasons that the ability of law enforcement seems constrained are purely because they work as they have always worked, failing to recognize new and better methods, or to fully implement technological advances that save resources. Just because a thing has always been done in a particular way does not mean it remains the best way of doing it. It may have been good at a time under some circumstances, but things change, and so must methods. Unfortunately, some wish to remain "walking with dinosaurs."

6.5 "Intelligence Cycle" Revisited

What an intelligence management system should be doing is well documented in many jurisdictions, and while it may not always be in the clearest of terms, the general principles have been around long enough that there really is no excuse for agencies not to have the systems in place. In the United States, the Commission on Accreditation of Law Enforcement Agencies (2002) recommends the following standards:

Certain essential activities should be accomplished by an intelligence function:

1. Include a procedure that permits the continuous flow of raw data into a central point from all sources.
2. A secure records system in which evaluated data are properly cross-referenced to reflect relationships and to ensure complete and rapid retrieval; develop a system of analysis capable of developing intelligence from both the records system and other data sources.
3. Provide a system for dissemination of information to appropriate components.

In the United Kingdom, the *Guidance on the Management of Police Information* (Association of Chief Police Officers 2010) document provides similar guidance, yet if one examines law enforcement in both countries, serious shortfalls are readily apparent in relation to meeting these recommendations. Other countries are no better. Figure 6.3 illustrates a model of the intelligence cycle that assists in understanding the principles of intelligence management, encouraged by the aforementioned documents and other similar documents, in the hope that further explanation will assist in understanding. The use of the word "revisited" is intended to emphasize the adaptation from previous models of the cycle. The charge can be leveled that this model merely adds to the plethora of other versions that are already out there, but it is for the reader to decide which model assists them with a better understanding of the concepts involved.

Revisiting the model addresses the following issues:

- Recognizes that law enforcement priorities must be established before intelligence requirements are identified
- Provides clarity as to when information becomes intelligence
- Provides clarity as to the function of an analyst in the intelligence cycle
- Links law enforcement data and nonintelligence-type records with the intelligence process

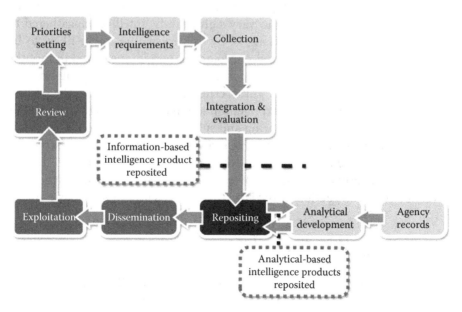

Figure 6.3 The intelligence cycle revisited for law enforcement.

While there are arguably failings with any version of the intelligence cycle, the key aspect of this model is to provide a road map for all involved in intelligence management. The model is intended to illustrate a structured approach to the management of intelligence. The key stages are as follows:

- Establishing the LEA's *priorities* that affect the agency as a whole or dictate the strategy for a particular investigation.
- Identifying *intelligence requirements* that can assist in discharging the established priorities.
- *Planning* how to gather relevant information.
- *Gathering* information.
- *Processing* that information into intelligence. This involves integration and evaluation.
- *Repositing* the intelligence.
- Providing the opportunity for *analytical input* both of existing intelligence records alone and in combination with other agency records.
- *Disseminating* the intelligence.
- *Using* the intelligence.
- *Reviewing* the success of those tactics.
- Reassessing the priorities.

The intelligence cycle is used at both strategic and tactical levels, and while the fundamentals are the same, there exist slight differences when applied at each of these levels. First, there will be one set of strategic agency priorities, which will be supplemented by tactical priorities. Second, the timescales involved are likely to vary significantly. Intelligence gathered to address strategic decision-making is, by its very nature, more likely to be gathered and exploited over a more prolonged period, measured in months or years, while tactical intelligence gathering and successful exploitation can move in hours, days, or weeks. Third, criteria used in reviewing the success of collection and subsequent exploitation are likely to vary significantly. For example, the intelligence gathering and subsequent exploitation at a tactical level may be measured in quantifiable terms such as number of arrests or the quantity of illicit goods recovered, while review at a strategic level may be much better expressed in a qualitative manner, possibly in terms such as the level of citizen satisfaction or the level that citizens fear a particular crime.

6.6   Setting Priorities

Priorities are set at strategic and tactical levels. The intelligence cycle begins at a strategic level with senior management deciding on the agency's priorities. The question may well be asked by the leadership, "How can I ask for intelligence if I don't know what I need to get intelligence on, given that the only way I will know what I need intelligence on, is to have intelligence?" In mainstream policing, the Chief starts with what they have and most often this will be their crime statistics, traffic-offending reports, and requests for police assistance. In other LEAs, such decisions will be based on similar records that the agency already has. Many may think that this pathway is an obvious one. However, what often happens, particularly where the agency leader is vulnerable with regard to future employment, is that their decision-making is influenced by those with a degree of power outside the agency pressing their personal agenda. Such behavior is likely to be based on two mind-sets: (1), where the person genuinely believes they know what policing priorities should be and advocates for them on behalf of citizens, or (2), there is personal benefit in pushing the agency in a certain direction. The term "personal benefit" is here intended to be wide in its meaning. Both these sets of circumstances are to the detriment of the public. While it is important to take on board the views of public representatives, deciding priorities should be based on sound evidence of what is occurring in the agency's domain. There should be a full audit history of how the agency's priorities were decided and on what evidence such decisions were made. This promotes integrity-based decision-making and establishes a defendable position for the leadership's decisions. There will always be people annoyed because what they deem to be a priority is at variance with what the agency has decided.*

There is significant benefit in having an analyst prepare strategic assessments of the problems the agency is expected to deal with. Analysts have the tools to merge both statistical data and intelligence to create a comprehensive picture of what is occurring at that time. Additionally, a trained and experienced analyst will be in a position to make assessments as to what is likely to occur in the future with regard to the matters under discussion. (The idea that an analyst provides only statistical analysis based on agency records is flawed and is discussed at length in Chapter 8.) While setting agency priorities is the responsibility of senior managers, expert interpretation from the relevant intelligence professionals will go a long way to informing their decisions.

Senior managers need to have a clear picture of what is occurring in their area of responsibility. This information can be provided to them in a number of ways, including written report or in diagrammatical form. Diagrams can help create better understanding, particularly when making comparisons. The many ways information can be presented aids understanding, but

---

* Imagine the difference in terms of priority how low the local police are likely to view the theft of your pet dog and how high a priority you are likely to see it as. And how annoyed you will get when they do nothing!

remember that regardless of how the information is presented, an analyst is often needed to interpret what is there.

The data that is available from the agency's record management system is often seen as the driving force in identifying agency priorities. Using this type of data may seem like a logical way for a Chief to make resourcing decisions—that is, until one considers that the information contained is mainly statistical data and one returns to the old adage "lies, damned lies, and statistics." If decisions are made based only on statistical data, without greater exploration of that data and the background context of the data, there will be the potential for the decisions to be made from a distorted perspective, leading to flawed decision-making. The purpose of including intelligence at a strategic level is to greatly enhance this picture. As McDowell (2009:221) says,

> Gathering and modelling statistical data to establish trends and patterns can be extraordinarily useful, but the analyst should never assume that such data would always be complete, reliable or even representative of the whole phenomenon under scrutiny.

To further illustrate the benefits of using an analyst to assist in identifying priorities, let us assume that the most prevalent crimes for an agency are house burglaries and shootings. A logical response to addressing these problems would appear to be one that identifies the hot spots for these crimes and then increasing patrolling in those areas at relevant times. However, this fails to give any idea of what the causes of those crimes are or the perpetrators. When the analyst integrates this data with intelligence, it may reveal that the crimes are drug related, and only by making drugs a priority will the other crime problems be addressed.

Where the agency's intelligence capacity is limited, crime data may be all that management has. With that said, crime data, comprehensively and properly presented, provides a picture of what is occurring in an area and should not be ignored. Crime data can provide the following:

- Crime types
- Locations of crimes
- Offenders made amenable
- Victim details
- Modus operandi (to a limited extent)

Analysis of this data can identify the following:

- *Crime trends:* If there is a yearly increase/decrease in crime type based on the statistics, if the commodities involved in crime are changing, and so on.
- *Crime hot spots:* Data will often point to crime occurring in a particular geographical area or a particular type of area.

- *Prolific offenders:* Provided that they are among the offenders caught, care must be taken here as what appears to be a prolific offender just because he is caught a lot may just mean that the individual concerned is unlucky or an idiot or both, while the actual prolific offender remains at large.
- *Potential future victims:* If crime data identifies a stereotypical victim of a certain crime, then steps can be taken to warn such potential victims before a crime occurs. For example, if a number of elderly people have been the victims of fraud by "cowboy" builders, then steps can be taken to warn other potential victims.

Crime data can help educate management as to the questions they should be asking of their intelligence staff and may go a significant way towards identifying intelligence gaps. Quite simply, if 20 high-value cars are being stolen a month, and the intelligence manager has no idea about who is doing it or where they are going, then there is an intelligence gap. Using this example highlights another problem that occurs in law enforcement because of poor priority setting. In the example given, it discusses the theft of 20 high-value cars, the loss of which is likely to be (for discussion purposes) in the region of half a million U.S. dollars. This is a huge sum of money, but law enforcement often chooses to deploy resources against other more visible problems, such as street-level drug problems. The danger here for any agency is that the decision as to which one of these two should be the priority is not an evidence-based decision but made on agency norms and what the members enjoy doing. In drug work, it is relatively easy to get results (we look like we are busy) and it is a lot of fun! And the public really want to see drug busts. Stolen vehicles—yawn! Where do I start? And why would I bother? The insurance company will pay out anyway, so no one loses. While these comments may appear flippant and the example given oversimplistic, the fact remains that there are many hurdles, realized or not, where the agency can falter in deciding the correct priorities. The more accurate data and intelligence that the Chief has will reduce the potential for such errors occurring and increase the chances of identifying the correct priorities.

There are many tools that can be used in deciding priorities. For example, a simple matrix such as that illustrated in Figure 6.4 allows management to categorize and compare the various problems and decide which ones to prioritize. The utility to this matrix lies in its simplicity. Furthermore, the creation of crime-mapping products and other similar visualization products by the analyst will help correctly identify priorities.

The agency's strategic priorities should be as follows:

- Be specific and clearly articulated in writing.
- Be evidentially based.

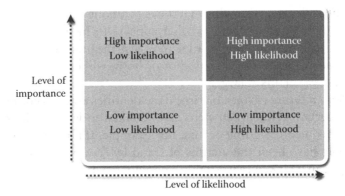

Figure 6.4 A simple prioritization grid.

- Address local issues but be integrated with both regional and national priorities.
- Be set for a yearly basis, with a built-in review after six months. These are realistic time frames for most agencies and from a practical perspective, allow trends to be clearly identified and the success or failure of tactics deployed to be realistically assessed.
- Be limited in terms of number as to what can realistically be achieved by the agency. It is not a wish list or one made to appease all comers.

In law enforcement, a major problem in deciding the priorities of the agency exists because the agency is likely to have responsibilities to contribute toward local, regional, and national problems. Before local agency priorities are established, clarity should be sought as to what regional and national priorities have already been established. In many cases, there is likely to be a degree of competition for resources between the local priorities of the agency and these externally based priorities.

National and regional priorities need to be integrated into each agency's priorities, but this is not always easy to achieve. One specific problem that local law enforcement leaders face is political pressure to address only local needs. Ratcliffe (in press) comments,

> Mayors, police Chiefs, mid-level commanders, and individual officers often appear to have free rein to make significant decisions regarding crime policy without recourse to objective analysis of the issue, or even a partial understanding or knowledge of the problem. When done in response to newspaper articles or stories on the nightly news (as appears to sometimes be the case) it is often an example of media-led policing.

In the United States, this problem is particularly pronounced due to the plethora of small police departments and the huge pressure that local government is able to exert on police Chiefs and sheriffs. While it may be understandable that local officials focus on local problems (they are after all accountable to the electorate), concentrating exclusively on local issues has the potential to detract from attention that should be given to problems that affect the region or nation as a whole. When identifying agency priorities, agency leaders must take account of problems at the regional and national levels and gather intelligence to address these problems.

Integrating regional or national priorities is not as difficult as it may first appear. Quite simply, when the senior management team is meeting to identify the strategic agency priorities for the incoming year, the list of potential priorities should contain those priorities that have been submitted to that agency from the relevant regional or national body. The intelligence manager presents to the senior management team a briefing in relation to how both regional and national problems manifest themselves within the local community. If these problems are evident within the local community, there is less of a chance that the senior management team will object to deploying resources against these problems. If, however, there is no evidence of activity related to the national or regional problems, the temptation arises to push these problems to the side and deploy only token or no resources to addressing these problems. However, this leaves the wider community vulnerable to what will be serious threats. For example, few small communities would see the potential for terrorists to be active within their midst, yet this is exactly what occurred in the run up to 9/11. Failure to address regional or national priorities means that the one section of the population is in effect being favored, to the detriment of other sections of the population.

Where a number of smaller LEAs have responsibility for geographically connected areas, it may well be of benefit to identify priorities on a regional basis. It should be remembered that the use of intelligence only forms a part of the agency's overall strategy to address these priorities. Other components including the use of problem-oriented policing and community policing will support and be supported by the intelligence component.

6.7 Tactical Priorities

Tactical priorities are the offspring of the agency's strategic priorities and are identified in a similar manner. Essentially, it is about drilling down into the strategic priorities and identifying what needs to be done tactically to address the matter. For example, the strategic priority may have been set as reducing the presence of methamphetamine availability within the community, with the corresponding tactical priority being to tackle the McKenna Crime Gang, whose members are the main suppliers of methamphetamine. Tactical priorities are identified by the agency's branch, with the lead for investigating the business area identified as a priority by senior management;

a drugs strategic priority is likely to go to the agency's narcotics branch. They will take the lead and set tactical priorities. The nature of criminality means that the same criminals may be engaged in many different aspects of crime, which may necessitate a joint approach between different sub-branches within an agency.

6.8   Intelligence Requirements

Intelligence requirements are a statement clearly listing the matters on which the agency has decided that they want to obtain either more intelligence or specific intelligence. Intelligence requirements are set, and information is then collected against those requirements. The information-collection process needs to be focused, so that resulting intelligence products meet the specific requests of the customer or are as close to that as is practically possible. In essence, the gap between what is known and what is desired to be known forms the intelligence requirement, hence the often-used phrase "the intelligence gap." Intelligence requirements are not the same as agency priorities; they are derived from the priorities and there will therefore be both strategic and tactical requirements.

Many intelligence collectors view strategic intelligence requirements as belonging to senior management or only being of interest at a headquarters level. This is understandable for the following reasons:

- Generally speaking, lower ranks have little real understanding of how an LEA is managed and the resource constraints placed on senior management. Furthermore, they have little empathy for the senior management role. To paraphrase, a "them and us" attitude prevails with little incentive to bridge the gap.
- Strategic intelligence requirements are often conveyed in a way that has little to do with the reality that officers are facing at a tactical level.
- Officers working at the tactical level receive little or no training in intelligence management and therefore do not know what information assists in preparing a strategic assessment, nor do they have a real understanding of the techniques used in preparing such an assessment.
- The performance of tactical officers is often judged on simplistic indicators such as number of arrests made and the amount and value of contraband recovered. There is little incentive to provide intelligence required to address strategic problems.
- Many tactical officers fail to comprehend the benefits in taking a broader view of a problem. They have little or no connection with legislatures, or other parts of the criminal justice system, and therefore

they confine their view of the problem to what directly affects their day-to-day work. However, this in turn limits potential solutions and is contrary to approaches such as problem-oriented policing. Intelligence gathering must go beyond the arrest/convict mentality if it is to provide others who have a shared responsibility for addressing the problem to play their part.

Many potential collectors pay only lip service to tactical intelligence requirements. This is most likely to occur when the officer's role is not exclusively one of intelligence gathering. In such circumstances, the officer is likely to seek out only the intelligence that is necessary to further their investigation or to help them "make their case."

6.9   Setting Intelligence Requirements

Experienced intelligence collectors are all too familiar with being placed in a predicament where the intelligence customer is uncertain what they want specifically. It is not unusual for collectors to be asked to "Find out what you can about Miguel Acosta" or "Concentrate on the meth dealers." No such tasking is acceptable. Intelligence collectors should work only against previously agreed intelligence requirements. As McDowell (2009:220) comments in regard to intelligence collection, "Collection of information needs to be driven largely by the need for specifics, not by the opportunistic collection of whatever happens to be available." Intelligence requirements should be discussed with the intelligence customer and put in writing before the commencement of any intelligence-gathering operation. The reasons for requirements being specific are many and include the following:

- The collector needs to know what resources to deploy to get the intelligence.
- The collector needs to be able to estimate how long it will take to get the intelligence and therefore be able to estimate the expenditure involved.
- All parties need to be aware of the parameters with regard to what techniques may or may not be used.
- All parties need to agree what the ultimate goal is—is it for prosecution, disruption, or merely to increase knowledge? Each of these can open options or close options for the intelligence collector.

Intelligence requirements should:

- Be in writing. If a requirement is not given in writing, it creates the potential for there to be significant misunderstanding between the customer and the collector that leads to wasted resources and/or the failure to investigate or prevent crime.

- Be specific. In most cases, if requirements do not state the scope of collection, then time will be wasted in collecting information that is of little or no use to the customer.
- Be prioritized. The customers must decide what they want the most or what they want first.
- Establish a legal basis to justify any interference with a person's rights. Intelligence requirements will often focus on individuals, with such individuals being referred to as "targets" and the process of gathering intelligence on these targets as targeting. Such intelligence requirements most often occur at the tactical level. Setting an intelligence requirement that targets an individual will, in most jurisdictions, be unlawful, unless there is reasonable suspicion of that person's involvement in criminality, now or in the future, or that the person is a threat to public safety. Care must always be taken in setting intelligence requirements in relation to a person that the reasons for targeting the person are evident.
- Have a realistic timescale. The information collector needs to know how long he has to collect and process the information, as this may well dictate the methods used to collect it. In addition, the timescale must be realistic: too short a time means the desired results will not be achieved or unnecessary risks will be taken to collect the information; too long a time means the waste of resources and potential loss of focus.
- If possible, be measurable. As with any business performance, measurement provides accountability and can drive productivity. If there is no way of measuring what has been achieved, it can be more difficult to justify the resources used to achieve the end results. Many covert methods can incur significant expense, and any LEA is likely to have some level of scrutiny regarding the expenditure of the citizens' taxes. The opportunity to evidence results should not be overlooked. Performance indicators should be set against the intelligence requirements.
- Take cognizance of the feasibility of collecting the desired information. There needs to be an exchange between those issuing the requirements and those charged with collecting against the requirements to ensure the requirements can be realistically achieved.

In the course of an investigation, the intelligence requirements are likely to evolve as the investigation progresses with some existing requirements being satisfied, intelligence gained being exploited, and intelligence indicating other more productive options are available. With each change in the intelligence requirements, the collection plan must be revisited to ascertain if it is suitable to meet the new requirements. Often the initial requirements will revolve around understanding the nature of the criminality or the gang involved and identifying vulnerabilities. The next set of requirements is likely to move toward gaining information that can exploit those vulnerabilities to damage or shut the enterprise down. In short, plan 1, understand their weaknesses, and plan 2, exploit those weaknesses. It is common for an agency to work through the cycle a number of times before the agency priorities have been met. It is far from unusual for the agency to continue with the same strategic priorities for many years with the intelligence cycle seeming akin to a merry-go-round. On a tactical level, definitive results are more likely to be achieved, with one criminal enterprise being eliminated but the cycle beginning anew as someone else takes up the mantle, where the previous gang left off. This necessitates new tactical requirements being set.

6.10 Practical Application

Figure 6.5 illustrates how an agency, having identified its priorities, then begins the process of working to translate these priorities into definable intelligence requirements.

In the example, we will consider the agency has identified reducing narcotics supply as one of the agency priorities. Having completed a strategic analysis of the drug problem, the agency has identified the "Redcoats," an organized crime gang, as being at the forefront of the drug supply.

Before defining specific intelligence requirements for the collection operation, we must first have a clear understanding of the structure and ethos of the target organization, in this case the Redcoats gang. In other aspects of society, people look at how an organization functions with the intention of identifying ways in which that organization can be more efficient. As law enforcement officers, the intention is not to improve the criminal organization but to disrupt its activities. The agency must take away what makes the crime gang efficient. The ultimate goals may be to prevent a crime from occurring and bring all the conspirators to justice, pragmatically; much less may have to be accepted. Goals may involve the disruption of individual operations or the thwarting of long-term strategic objectives. Many of the options will be dependent on the quality of the information being received, the timelines of that information, and the agency's operational capabilities.

Before establishing the goals, the agency must have a clear view of what is happening within that gang. Analysis of the target organization must be comprehensive. The first step is getting the analyst to see what intelligence already exists in relation to the gang. The investigation team needs a clear understanding of the organization, its structure, the members, and their roles. This analysis

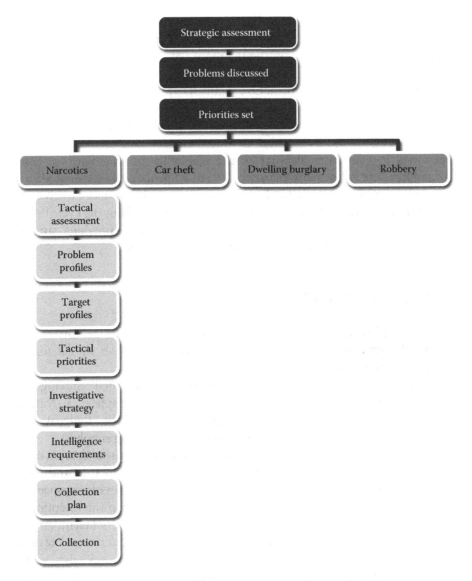

Figure 6.5 From priorities to collection—a practical example.

should identify where intelligence coverage of the target exists and where there
are gaps. The analysis should look at all levels and parts of the organization.
It is where the intelligence gaps are identified of which the intelligence collectors will attempt to obtain coverage. Often, the most glaring gaps in intelligence will be in the support aspects of the gang's activities, such as money
laundering and communications. Another often-overlooked vulnerability, in
any gang, is the personalities of the gang members. Rarely are they recorded in
any depth, aspects such as group dynamics and internecine rivalries, yet these

can readily be exploited to impact the gang's functioning. Having established what is known about the Redcoats, the first set of intelligence requirements can be created. These will normally focus on the gaps that have been identified relating to the strategic structure and functioning of the gang.

Each set of intelligence requirements must be clearly defined in order that the most appropriate operational methodology be used to collect the information. As more intelligence is created, the investigator and intelligence staff must work closely to redefine intelligence requirements and the methods to be used in collection. There is little point in recruiting a source who can supply information on the identities of Redcoat drug dealers, if the specific need is for intelligence in relation to the laundering of the proceeds of the drug dealing. The requirements should also clearly identify the time-scale in which the intelligence product is required, as a limited time frame will undoubtedly restrict the options available. There is always a chance that events will overtake the plan. Those planning the collection need to take stock of what assets already exist around the target organization. These may vary from limited reporting of an overt nature to phone tapping, surveillance, and other human-source coverage. An assessment of the existing assets is critical at this time, so that time and resources are not wasted.

Having identified how the Redcoat gang functions at a strategic level, the investigator moves to providing intelligence requirements of a tactical nature. These requirements are likely to be things like dates and times of drug movements or the locations of storage facilities. All parts of the investigation have to be interwoven with other aspects of the investigation and/or intelligence gathering. A centralized intelligence management system means that in complicated investigations, someone at a senior rank has the ability to oversee all aspects of investigation and collection, and all the intelligence is found in one place, avoiding intelligence requirements being reissued when some section already has the answers. Comparisons between the intelligence requirements and how those requirements have been met can be used as effective performance indicators.

6.11 Common Issues in Addressing Intelligence Requirements

There are a number of problems that regularly occur in the transfer of intelligence requirements to those tasked to provide the intelligence and in the subsequent return of that intelligence to those requesting it. These include the following:

- The intelligence provided does not match the requirement in terms of *specificity*. What may have occurred here is that the initial requirement in itself lacked clarity or detail about what was desired. If poor communication was the cause, then the requesting party is responsible and should realize that the opportunity to obtain the specifics may have been squandered. Alternatively, the information provider (be it officer or citizen) may have been unable to provide the specific information as requested. If an officer with responsibility for addressing an intelligence requirement is unable to obtain the specific intelligence requested, she should tell those requesting it that she is unable to obtain it. This allows the requesters to then seek alternative providers.

- The intelligence requested does not reach the requester in a *timely fashion*, perhaps because the requester has neglected to include the relevant time period to obtain the intelligence, the provider has been unable to obtain the intelligence within the relevant time scale, the provider has been lackadaisical in obtaining the information in the relevant time, or the information has failed to progress through the intelligence system in a timely manner. The last two of these are strong indicators of flaws in the intelligence management system that need to be corrected.

- The intelligence provided appears to be *tainted or skewed* or in some other way inconsistent with what could be reasonably expected in answer to the request. This may be the result of the provider having some agenda or having an incorrect understanding of what they have been asked for. It must be remembered that there is the potential for distortion as the number of people involved in processing the information between where it originates and where it is finally received as an intelligence product increases. Most readers will be familiar with the game of "whisper down the lane" and the distortion in message from beginning to end. Alternatively, sometimes what is expected is not what is received. In such a case, it is foolish to dismiss the new and different intelligence out of hand.

6.12   Unplanned Collection

There are two aspects to collection, both of which the agency needs to manage. The first of these is "unplanned" collection. Unplanned collection refers to the effective processing of information that has come to the agency as a matter of course. As part of their normal responsibilities, law enforcement collect huge amounts of information, originating in many different ways, including crime reports, investigations, calls from the public, observations of members, and arrests. Each piece of information that the agency receives, through this unplanned collection, has the potential to contain something that may be of intelligence value. The agency must have in place structures where every member of the agency is cognizant of the fact that the agency needs intelligence, and how that member can contribute to addressing that need while carrying out their role. Furthermore, there must be a process to get that information to a person who can decide whether it has merit for intelligence purposes. Processing such information, while not guaranteeing the collection of the right intelligence, often provides valuable pieces of intelligence. Unplanned collection is all that a significant number of agencies do at present.

Information collected that is not in sync with the agency's priorities should be processed in the usual manner, but thought must be given to what is done with the intelligence product after it has been reposited. If the intelligence is deemed to be "actionable intelligence," then the balance will tip strongly in favor of taking action. If the intelligence is deemed otherwise, then the balance will shift toward no further action.

6.13 Planned Collection

The second type of collection is "planned" collection. Planned collection is a proactive approach and involves the agency deciding how and where they are going to obtain the information that can be processed to satisfy the intelligence requirements. A collection plan is one "that directs the collection of information to satisfy an intelligence requirement." Having a collection plan means that the right information is collected, in a timely and cost-effective manner. If there is no collection plan, the intelligence requirements are likely to become little more than aspirational. A collection plan includes the following:

- An agreed list of collection options
- An estimated time frame for the collection process
- Names of those responsible for ensuring that collection is achieved
- Details of the agency resources to be used
- A statement of collection parameters—what can and cannot be done
- An estimate of the cost of obtaining the information
- Details of any potential problems or conflicts of interest
- Where the collection involves recourse to another agency, a copy of the agreement with that agency

Collection plans must be realistic in relation to what can be achieved. Taking into account the resources the agency has to deploy, the pertinent timescales, and the nature of the problem faced, the desired outcome may be some distance from what a realistic outcome would be. It is foolhardy to create unrealistic expectations about what can be achieved. Those involved in supervising collectors need to ensure that information-gathering operations remain focused on the requirements. It is extremely easy for an operation to lose traction or be diverted onto a course away from what it was originally designed to achieve. Line managers should view information submissions and compare what is being submitted with the identified intelligence requirements.

The benefits of a collection plan include the following:

- It provides clarity with regard to the type of material to be collected and the amount of material to be collected.
- It reduces the amount of time spent collecting material that is of limited or no worth.
- It identifies to collectors why the material is being collected and the methods they are permitted to use in the collection.
- It enables those collecting it to know what purpose it is being collected for. The use for which the intelligence is ultimately intended may prescribe certain collection avenues. For example, collectors may not use a human source where subsequent legal requirements are likely to compromise that source's identity.
- It ensures that the information is collected in a systematic manner, reducing the chances of tasks being duplicated and resources wasted.
- It allows everyone to know what resources are available and to judge if they can undertake and sustain the task. Many agencies commence a job with little real understanding of the cost of the resources involved and the ability of the agency to sustain a long-term deployment. What happens is the agency ends up putting everyone and everything in jeopardy, or calling for action far too early, taking what they can get, regardless of the potential harm caused. This kind of poor operational management leads to bad feelings.
- Customer expectations are better managed. Intelligence customers are often unrealistic in their expectations, making the assumption that those involved in intelligence can find out exactly what the target intends to do and when. The flaw in this reasoning is that it assumes the target actually knows what he is going to do. Expectations must always be managed.

6.14 Collection

There are two aspects of collection. First, there is collecting the information into the agency, and second, there is the problem of collecting it all in one place. Considering the many different places and ways that information will have come into the agency, the biggest problem facing the agency is often not the getting it, but how to get it into a central place where the raw material can be processed into intelligence. If we return to the connecting-the-dots metaphor, there are many times when an agency has collected lots of dots, but they are never connected because the agency fails to gather all the information in one identified place. The agency needs a mechanism to do so, where it can be processed and the dots connected. The mechanism used to do that is an "information submission."

6.15   Information Submission

It is probably necessary at this stage to remind the reader of the difference between information and intelligence. We collect information, which then goes through an identified process, and on completion of that process, it becomes intelligence. This section deals with how the information gets to the start of the process. Using the metaphor of a bakery, information is the flour that arrives in the back door and intelligence the bread that goes out of the front door. And in the middle is the baking process. An "information submission" is the mechanism we use to get the flour to the back door of our bakery.

Information comes to law enforcement in different ways and from different origins; therefore, the mechanisms for submitting information will vary depending on the origin of the information and the nature of that information. Information that has not been submitted correctly is all but impossible to evaluate with any degree of accuracy at a later stage. We will begin by discussing the more simple forms of information submission and then move to the more complex, which are usually associated with specialized operations. The first thing we will do is define the meaning of an information submission. An information submission is an obligatory process by which information enters the intelligence management system and that includes four sections:

1. Details of the submitting member
2. The origin of the information
3. The unabridged text of that information
4. How that submission was managed

As far as practically possible, information submissions should be in a standard format, although it is accepted that the nature of some information may make the standardization of all submissions difficult.

Most "information submissions" should be entirely electronic, as this allows the rapid transfer of information into the intelligence management system and provides full accountability. The agency should provide a standardized information submission format that allows untrained staff to submit any information they obtain to the Intelligence Unit, with little or no need for advice. Another key benefit of electronic submission is it forces submitting officers to complete "mandatory" fields in the information submission, thus reducing errors and omissions and saving time for Intelligence Unit members.

Information that comes to the agency as part of the agency's normal functioning can all be submitted using a simple submission mechanism. Although the method discussed here is electronic, should an agency choose to be paper-based, the mechanism remains similar, the only differences being speed with which information is processed, the potential risks this creates, and the waste of resources in doing so. The submission should be self-explanatory but if using an electronic format, then "Help" links should be included as standard. Expanding from its definition, the information submission is likely to contain the following:

1. *Details of the submitting member.* An information submission can be completed only by a member of that agency. If an electronic mechanism is used, then as soon as that member opens the software program, it will automatically register the submitting member's details. If the software is of an appropriate standard, the submission will be to evidential standards. Details of the submitting member are required should further clarification of the information be needed. A further benefit of having appropriate software is that the submission can be automatically returned should rework be necessary. The submitting member's details are also necessary should the information be used at a later stage, in an evidential capacity.

2. *The origin of the information.* This refers to the where and under what circumstances the *member* obtained the information and includes the "information route."* (This is different from the "provenance† that describes where and how the information came to the information provider" the provenance being included in Section 3 of the information submission.) It may be as a result of the stop and check of a suspect, a police investigation, or from a member of the public (MoP), to name but a few potential origins. Given the fact that

---

* The "information route" refers to where the information was obtained from by the agency and under what circumstances.
† The "provenance" of a piece of information refers to origin of the information and how the information provider obtained it. This is distinguished from the "information route," which refers to from how the agency has obtained the information. The word provenance is derived from the French word *provenir,* "to come from," and refers to the origin of material. Here, the question provenance answers is "Where did this information come from?" and not "Who brought it here?"

there are a number of different circumstances in which a member can obtain information that may be of use for intelligence purposes, an electronic submission mechanism should have a number of drop-down options to address all of the likely contexts in which information is obtained. Many of these will be similar, so the number of possible options is limited. This section of the submission should allow the officer to make their observations on the circumstances in which they obtained the information. This may include comments on why the person is passing the information or the likely veracity of that information. This part of the form should also allow the submitting member to make comments about any potential risks associated with the origin of this information. The expectation is that such risks will be written in lay terminology.

3. *The unabridged text of the information.* The full unexpurgated text of the information is included here. Depending on the origin of the information, several subheadings may be included to prompt a more comprehensive submission. A good information submission will include the answers to every question that should have been asked by the member receiving the information, such as accurate subject details, accurate addresses, and good descriptions of people and/or vehicles. A separate entry should be made for each piece of information provided. With a computerized system having an icon that creates a new panel for each entry, the number of entries becomes unlimited. In each of these entry panels, there will be a standard formatting that includes the provenance of the information, the risks associated in disseminating that piece of information, and a space for comment by either the submitting officer, the originator of the information, or both, although obviously it must be made clear which is which. When information is received from a citizen, a separate prompt should ask, "How did the person become aware of the information they are providing?" A suitable prompt at this stage means that submitting members are likely to remember to ask this question. Moreover, questioning of this type helps to identify any risks involved and to establish what dissemination is later appropriate. Any attachments should be attached to this section or details of how they will be forwarded, if not in appropriate electronic format.

4. *How the submission was managed.* Deciding what to do with information falls primarily to the Intelligence Unit, but such decisions will often require consultation with the officer submitting the information to identify any specific risks attached to the information, particularly in regard to how the intelligence produced from the information can be disseminated. All such discussions should take place on a professional basis with the intelligence manager being the

decision-maker. When a dispute arises that cannot be resolved, and there exists the potential for real harm, then the matter should be referred to the senior responsible officer for intelligence for a decision. It should be clear from this section of the submission exactly what was done with the information and why. Furthermore, there should be clear linkage to any intelligence reports that have been created. If it has been assessed that the information is of no value, it should be noted and an explanation included. As no further action is likely to occur with many stop/checks, a simple comment such as "no intelligence value" should suffice. The information submission will not include how any intelligence report created from the submission has been "assigned"—assigning being what happens to the intelligence report after it is created and reposited (see Section 6.33).

Information originating from the following areas can be submitted using this simple standardized mechanism:

- Police stop checks.
- Officer observations of activity or a suspect.
- Information from MoPs obtained in investigations. This includes information received as a legal obligation, such as that imposed on the financial industry in relation to suspicious transactions and on the pharmaceutical industry in relation to precursor chemicals for illicit drug manufacture.
- "Crime stoppers" and information received from similar programs.
- Information from other agencies. The original report from the other agency should be attached to the information submission where a paper-based system is used or a copy scanned as an attachment in an electronic system.
- Information obtained from the agency records management system such as an incident of note, results of a search or an arrest.
- Open source reporting.
- Anonymous information. This category should only be used where the submitting member does not know who the person providing the information is and not as a device to "protect" the person giving, as in reality this creates as many risks as it allays.
- As a covering missive for the submission of photographs, video, or some other electronic information.
- Information obtained as a result of an investigation such as the forensic examination of a computer or firearm.

In all these cases, the pathway for an information submission will be *directly* to the Intelligence Unit, except for when it actually originated from staff in the Intelligence Unit and is the result of research they have carried out in-house. In such circumstances the information submission begins its journey from within the Intelligence Unit. An information submission should always be created. Intelligence should not be entered into the intelligence repository, as such documents should not contain explicit details of the origin of the material. Where a person is stop checked by a police officer and then provides information to the police officer, the information-submission mechanism must allow these two separate strands of information to be appropriately recorded. The first strand is the stop check as a potential piece of intelligence in itself, and the second strand is the information obtained from a MoP and the potential intelligence obtained from that. For practical reasons, it may be too much to ask the submitting officer to complete two separate submissions, but the submission must be capable of division once received in the Intelligence Unit.

Using technology to its maximum, information submission for much of this type of material can be done using a handheld device such as a smartphone or tablet, provided that there is suitable built-in security on such a device and the content is immediately uploaded to a central secure server. Advantages of using handheld technology for information submissions include the following:

- Speed of transmission.
- Officer can remain on the ground.
- Security. Built-in security means that such devices are much more secure than paper records.
- Audit. Such mechanisms create an automatic auditable record.
- Geocoding. Devices such as these that constantly send the location details of the device at time of submission may be of relevance or prove relevant at a later time such as judicial proceedings.
- Photographic, audio, and video attachments. Given that smartphones and many tablets can take photos and make audiovisual recordings attaching these to a submission may be of assistance. For example, photos taken in a public order situation could be submitted and then linked, using facial recognition technology, to photos of persons whose details are held in the intelligence repository.

The four sections of an information-submission mechanism are illustrated in Figures 6.6 through 6.9. The layout is shown to provide the reader with general principles involved. Attempting to illustrate what can be achieved on a computer is all but impossible, the main achievement being to illustrate the limitations of paper storage methods compared with using computers. Software developers can add significantly more functionality than is described here and make it look a lot prettier.

Figure 6.6 shows the opening screen of an electronic information submission. There are a few points to consider in completing section 1 of the submission.

- Properly constructed software will self-populate the member's details. The member only has to put in the date and time the information was received and select the nature of that information.
- Software will also create a unique reference number (URN) known as the information submission reference number. This number is embedded in each section of the form and facilitates each section being capable of "standing alone," should the need arise. This number is also included in every "intelligence report" that is derived from the information submission.
- The date and the time that the information is actually submitted would also self-populate when the member completes and "sends" the document to the Intelligence Unit. Completion of such data is important from audit and integrity perspectives.
- The submitting member then clicks the icon that relates to the origin of the information.

Worthy of noting for those involved in intelligence gathering in the United States is that this method of information submission is ideal for all types of information submitted under the Suspicious Activity Reporting scheme.

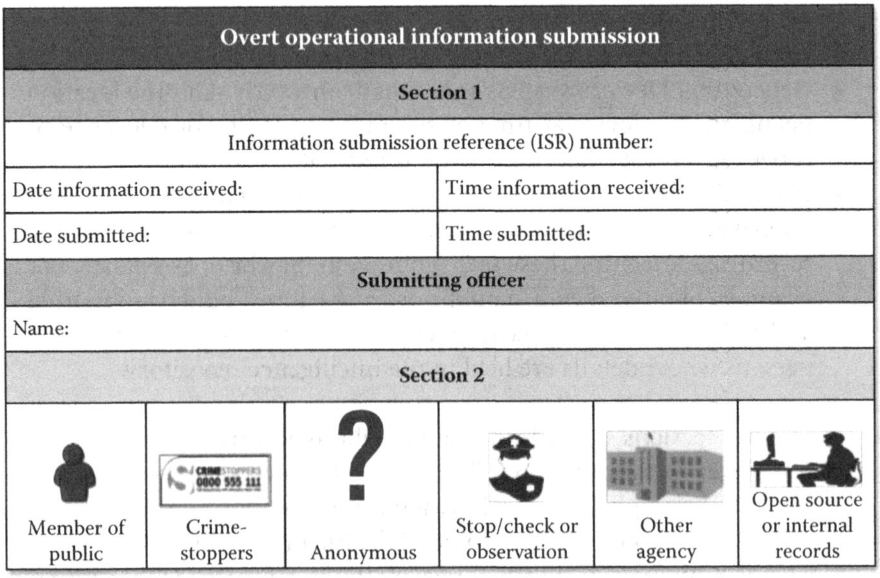

Overt operational information submission	
Section 1	
Information submission reference (ISR) number:	
Date information received:	Time information received:
Date submitted:	Time submitted:
Submitting officer	
Name:	
Section 2	

Member of public	Crime-stoppers	Anonymous	Stop/check or observation	Other agency	Open source or internal records

Figure 6.6 Example of opening screen of overt operational information submission.

- It encompasses all possible origins of material.
- It provides an audit of how and where the information was collected to evidential standards.
- It delivers the information promptly to an intelligence professional, where it can be assessed and disseminated or if of no intelligence value purged.
- It is submitted in a manner that ensures compliance with "28 CFR 23" (government guidance).

Figure 6.7 illustrates section 2 of an information submission. A few points about completing section 2 of an information submission follow:

- The screen shown assumes that the submitting member has clicked the Member of the Public icon contained in the opening screen illustrated in Figure 6.6.
- The example given in Figure 6.7 is for an information submission from a "Member of the Public." The format will vary according to which icon the submitting member has pressed in section 1 of the form, or where it is from specialized activity.
- The information route provides the history of how the information came to the agency. The four route boxes are written in free text and are expandable.
- None of the details given in this section are entered into the intelligence repository as entities, even if the person providing the information or their address already exists as an entity. To discharge the agencies' duty of care to this person, the information submission is the only place where the person's details will be stored.
- Every country has standardized address formats. These should be used. If the computer system being used has been constructed with geocoding in mind, it will self-populate this field on entry of the address.
- The example shows both home addresses and business address. This is important when identifying if this person is giving information to different members on a regular basis.
- The "±" button indicates you can add a similar box. The "i" is a hyperlink to a help screen that tells the member what to write.
- The "why" box is included to provide suggestions as to what the person's motives for providing the information may be. The word motive is not included, as few have anything other than a simplistic understanding of the concept. A drop-down menu of "motives" should *not* be used. Free text is much more likely to be accurate. Where there is any expectation of reward of any type, this should be included in the "why" box.

Overt operational information submission		
Member of the public		
Section 2		
Information submission reference (ISR) number:		
Person details		i
Forename:	Middle name:	Family name:
Alias:	Maiden name:	Nickname:
DOB/Age range:	Occupation:	How verified:
Contact details		
Home number:	Mobile number:	Business number:
Email:	Other (state):	Fax/Pager:
Home address		± i
Apartment number:	House number:	Building name:
Street:	Locality:	Post town:
County:	Country:	Post code:
Geo-code:	Additional information:	
Business address		± i
Business name:	Business type:	Owner:
Apartment number:	House number:	Building name:
Street:	Locality:	Post town:
County:	Country:	Post code:
Geo-code:	Additional information:	
Information route (circumstances information obtained)		
How was the information obtained:		i
Where did the submitting officer obtain the information:		i
Why is the person passing the information:		i
Are there any risks associated with this person:		i
		Continue

Figure 6.7 Example of section 2 screen information submission.

Figure 6.8 illustrates section 3 of the information submission. A few points about completing section 3 of an information submission follow:

- The entire "information to be considered for intelligence purposes box" is duplicated for each separate piece of information with the relevant entities being included with each information entry.

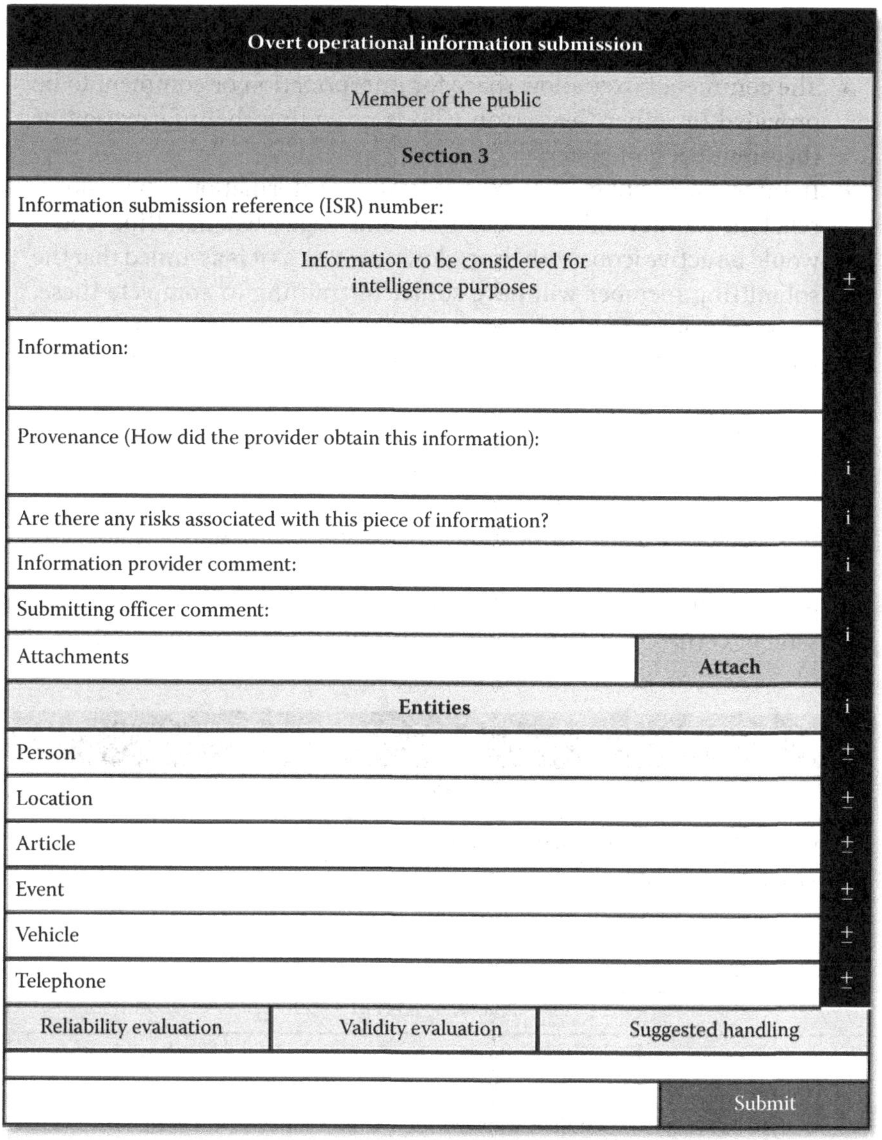

Overt operational information submission	
Member of the public	
Section 3	
Information submission reference (ISR) number:	
Information to be considered for intelligence purposes	+
Information:	
Provenance (How did the provider obtain this information):	
	i
Are there any risks associated with this piece of information?	i
Information provider comment:	i
Submitting officer comment:	
	i
Attachments	**Attach**
Entities	i
Person	+
Location	+
Article	+
Event	+
Vehicle	+
Telephone	+
Reliability evaluation Validity evaluation Suggested handling	
	Submit

Figure 6.8 Example of section 3 screen of overt operational information-submission mechanism.

There can be one or many, all submitted in the one information submission.

- The submitting member should attempt to confirm the full details of the entity including the entity's URN. The entities that they will be able to see will be dictated by the member's access-level status. (Entities are discussed further in Chapter 7.)

- Additional entities in each paragraph are created by means of the ± icon.
- The comment boxes allow space for interpretation or comment to be provided by either the person who is providing the information or the submitting member.
- In information submissions for specialized information submissions, reliability and validity evaluations and suggested handling codes would be active icons with drop-down menus, as it is assumed that the submitting member will have sufficient training to complete these. These buttons will also be active when a member of the Intelligence Unit is the submitting member. Where the information submission originates from another agency and they have put in an evaluation, this should be included in section 3, as it cannot be assumed that the agency from which it has been received is using exactly the same matrix. The icons are shown here for illustration purposes and would be disabled in the working system for overt submissions.

Figure 6.9 illustrates the final screen in an information submission. A few points about completing section 4 of an information submission follow:

Overt operational information submission			
Section 4			
Information submission reference (ISR) number:			
Date information received:		Time information received:	
Date processed:		Time processed:	
Processing officer			
Name:	Rank/Grade:		Number:
Is a risk assessment necessary for this submission?			
Process options			
No further action For disposal	Intelligence product reposited For reference only	Intelligence product reposited For development	Intelligence product reposited Advisory issued

Figure 6.9 Example of section 4 screen information-submission mechanism.

- The fourth section deals with the Intelligence Unit and records how the submission has been dealt with.
- With any information submission, there is the potential for risks to be identified. The "exclamation" icon will open a copy of the agency's standard risk assessment/risk management form for a processing officer to complete. This will then be embedded in the information submission.
- The process icons provide four options for the intelligence manager. The content of the information submission will dictate what future action will be needed. Each of the four options offered will have additional subsections to complete.
- Subsections will include reference numbers of any intelligence products created and details of any person.

Certain aspects of law enforcement, especially covert activities, require that there are additional management structures in place as information is received by the agency. Where such structures exist, it is likely that the information-submission mechanisms will require different mechanisms from the standard formatting described in Section 6.15. Such mechanisms will be required to address the volume of information obtained and the potential complexities associated with such information. These circumstances will most likely occur in covert law enforcement and include information gathered as a result of the following:

- Surveillance. Covert observation or tracking. Problems here include the submission of mapping records and interpretation of events.
- Interception of telecommunications, including telephones, instant messaging, and computer-based communication. Problems here include linking of cell/mobile phone location at time of conversation to location and sensitivities around methodology involved. Also likely to crop up are the various legal constraints found in many jurisdictions. This will also include the examination and seizure of Short Message Service and Multimedia Messaging Service that are held on mobile phones, as there are statutory obligations in many jurisdictions to examine these. Where there isn't legislation, common sense would suggest that law enforcement should not be able to examine what are often very personal messages, without some form of authorization process. As a matter of good practice, the agency should establish procedures for examining handheld devices.
- Telephone records, that is, subscriber checks, records of numbers called, and duration of calls.
- Listening devices in premises and vehicles. Problems here can be sheer volume of material obtained.
- Human sources.

- Undercover operations.
- Witness protection. The most likely problem here is keeping the person's new identity totally separate from their old identity and the potential crossover in submitting information on their past activities.

With all these types of operations and other similar ones, there is likely to be a document on which the members involved initially record the information. Due to the nature of the material and the context in which it is recorded, direct input to an information form is not possible or inappropriate. The following are given as examples of processes to aid understanding but should not be looked on as the only solution. In building an intelligence management system, each agency must build individual processes that meet their circumstances and then test the whole system to see that it works, modifying it as it becomes necessary. In the following suggestions, the term "requesting officer" is the officer who has requested that the specialized operation be carried out. This officer may be an investigating officer, or from within an Intelligence Unit, or have some other role, but not the officer who carries out the specialized function.

- In surveillance, there should be a "surveillance log" completed by a log keeper that records all the movements of the target and any attendant operational aspects. This document is potentially supplemented by handwritten notes made by each surveillance operator. From this log, a surveillance officer should complete a "surveillance debriefing report" that gives an unabridged account of the surveillance period including tactical aspects and information. This surveillance debriefing report stays within the surveillance records, but from it an information submission for the operation is prepared. An information submission for surveillance will do the following:
  - Be submitted by an identified officer, normally the requesting officer. There is often a conflict here as to who is the best person to prepare the submission. The argument being made is that those observing the action may not be able to identify relevance in certain events. Generally speaking, the submission should be made by the requesting officer. This submission should be based on the "surveillance debriefing report" prepared after the surveillance by a surveillance officer. This achieves what is desired without overexposing methodology. Much of what is contained in a "surveillance log" alludes to how the surveillance is done and requires much greater protection than the fact that it is being done.
  - Contain details of date and time and nature of operation and its code name.

- Be a comprehensive record containing all the relevant information from the surveillance debriefing report. In other words, "what happened" during the surveillance and how it can be interpreted. A separate entry (paragraph) should be made for each piece of information that has been extracted from that surveillance run. With a computerized system having an icon that creates a new panel for each different information entry, the number of potential entries becomes unlimited. In each of these entry panels, there will be a standard formatting that includes spaces for the evaluation of *that* piece of information, the risks associated with *that* piece of information, and any added comments by the surveillance officer or the submitting officer intended to clarify or interpret an event. A further space will provide suggestions as to appropriate dissemination.
  - Detail what was done with the information supplied and by whom. This will include details of what was reposited in the intelligence repository.
- In the interception of telephone calls, the raw product will often be a verbatim transcript, sometimes augmented by geographical positioning data from a mobile phone and/or with subscriber details of the other party. Given that it is often the experience of the transcribing member that will identify the parties involved, if voice recognition technology is unavailable, the transcription is likely to include an indication as to the degree of certainty surrounding such. Preparing an information submission for such can require prior knowledge of the targets, their style of communication, and code words they use. An additional complication is that such calls may have been made in a foreign language and are transcribed and translated by a linguist. In such circumstances, the agency needs to retain both the original transcript and the translation of it. The information submission for interception will consist of the following:
  - Be submitted by an identified officer, normally the requesting officer. Again there is often a conflict here as to who is the best person to prepare the submission. The argument being made is that those transcribing may not be able to identify relevance in certain comments, and there is much evidence to support this standpoint. Other arguments are often raised around who is legally entitled to see or hear what. Generally speaking, the submission should be made by the requesting member and their interpretation added in the information submission. When a foreign language is involved, and given the potential for meaning to get "lost in translation," there should always be discussion between the transcriber and

the requesting officer. There can be many subtle nuances involved, and these may be overlooked by either party.

- Contain details of date and time and nature of interception and duration of call.
- Be a comprehensive record containing all the relevant information from the communication leaving out irrelevant information such as methodology. In other words, "What was discussed during the call?" A separate entry (paragraph) should be made for each piece of information that has been extracted from that surveillance run. In each of these entry panels, there will be a standard formatting that includes spaces for the evaluation of *that* piece of information, the risks associated with *that* piece of information, and any added comments by the surveillance officer or the submitting officer intended to clarify or interpret an event. A further space will provide suggestions as to appropriate dissemination.
- Detail what was done with the information supplied and by whom. This will include details of what was reposited in the intelligence repository.

- Telephone records and subscriber checks will usually be returned either as a paper record or in electronic format from the relevant provider. Ideally they should come electronically from the provider through a portal and into the relevant computerized process that the agency uses to apply and authorize requests for such data from the provider. Like much of the information gathered by law enforcement, it may have both an investigative and intelligence potential. The information submission for telephone records will have the following characteristics:
  - Be submitted by an identified officer. This should be the officer requesting the records as they will have the context in which the records have been requested. However, such records will often benefit from analytical interpretation and this should be carried out before the information submission.
  - Contain details of the provider, the nature of the investigation, and the relevance of the records.
  - Be a comprehensive record containing all of the relevant information that can be ascertained from the records. It may be a very short paragraph giving the number and who it is registered to and/or who is believed to be using it or may be an analytical report including a network analysis. Note, where an analyst has worked on the raw records, these should *not* be reposited directly by the analyst but should form an attachment to the information submission, and if necessary will be reposited by the Intelligence Unit. This avoids cluttering the intelligence repository. A separate

entry (paragraph) should be made for each piece of information that has been extracted from the records. In each of these entry panels, there will be a standard formatting that includes spaces for the evaluation of *that* piece of information, the risks associated with *that* piece of information, and any added comments by the analyst or the submitting officer intended to clarify or interpret an event. A further space will provide suggestions as to appropriate dissemination.

- Detail what was done with the information supplied and by whom. This will include details of what was reposited in the intelligence repository.

- Listening devices can provide significant amounts of information. When they are placed in vehicles, the associated geopositioning data can have significant relevance. The information submission for listening devices will have the following characteristics:

  - Be submitted by an identified officer, normally the requesting officer. Again, as with interception, there is often a conflict here as to who is the best person to prepare the submission, the argument being made that those transcribing may not be able to identify relevance in certain comments. There is much evidence to support this standpoint. Other arguments are often raised around who is legally entitled to see or hear what. Generally speaking, the submission should be completed by the requesting member and their interpretation added in the information submission. When a foreign language is involved, and given the potential for meaning to get "lost in translation," there should always be discussion between the transcriber and the requesting officer.

  - Contain details of date and time and nature of interception, duration of the call, and the operational name.

  - Be a comprehensive record containing all the relevant information from the conversation, where possible, avoiding details of the location of the device. This should read like a story and not the script of a play (i.e., "he said, then she said, then he said, etc."). A completely new information submission should be submitted for each conversation with all the information from that conversation contained in that information submission. However, a separate entry, in section 3, should be made in an information submission for each different topic of conversation that is collected. In each of these section 3 panels, there will be a standard formatting that includes spaces for the evaluation of *that* piece of information, the risks associated with *that* piece of information, and any added comments by the transcriber or the submitting officer intended to clarify or interpret the information. A further space will provide suggestions as to appropriate dissemination.

- Detail what was done with the information supplied and by whom. This will include details of what was reposited in the intelligence repository.

- Human sources can provide huge amounts of information but are in continual danger of having their role exposed. One of the most frequent reasons for this is the overexploitation of the source stemming in no small part from poor intelligence management. Dealing with information submissions for human sources can be further complicated by the sheer volume of material a good source produces and the frequency with which it is produced. The information submission for human sources will undergo the following procedures:
  - Be submitted by the source handler through the source controller (manager for source operation).
  - Contain the date and time the information was received and the agency's URN for the source.
  - Be a comprehensive record of all the information that the source has provided and how that information was obtained by them. A new information submission should be used for each source meeting or contact, with all the information from that meeting in that information submission. However, a separate entry should be made in section 3 of the submission for each different topic or incident described by the source. There can be many section 3 entries from one meeting and this is why with a computerized system having an icon that creates a new panel for each different information entry, the number of potential entries becomes unlimited. In each of these section 3 panels, there will be a standard formatting that includes spaces for the evaluation of *that* piece of information, the risks associated with *that* piece of information, and any added comments by the handler intended to clarify or interpret an input. A further space will provide suggestions as to appropriate dissemination.
  - Detail of what was done with the information supplied and by whom. This will include details of what was reposited in the intelligence repository. This part has particular relevance, as there will need to be a feedback loop to the source management team to ensure appropriate rewarding for the source.
- Although undercover deployments are primarily aimed at gathering evidence, they also can provide huge amounts of valuable intelligence. Each time an undercover officer meets with or contacts their cover officer, a comprehensive "undercover debriefing report" should be prepared containing both operational details and the information

obtained. From this report, the information submission for undercover is prepared and will

- Be submitted by an identified officer, normally the cover officer,
  for the undercover officer. This should be done whenever possible
  in consultation with the undercover officer.
- Contain the date and time the information was received and the
  name of the operation.
- The information submission will contain all the information
  received during the debriefing of the undercover officer even if
  it will also be used for evidential purposes. Care must be taken
  that there is no contradiction between what is placed in any information submission and what has been written in a statement
  of evidence, as both are likely to be disclosed at trial. With one
  debriefing, there will be one information submission. A separate
  section 3 entry should be made for each piece of information that
  has been extracted from the debriefing of the undercover officer.
  In each of the section 3 entry panels, there will be a standard formatting that includes spaces for the evaluation of *that* piece of
  information, the risks associated with *that* piece of information,
  and any added comments by the surveillance officer or the submitting officer intended to clarify or interpret an event. A further
  space will provide suggestions as to appropriate dissemination.
- Detail of what was done with the information supplied and by
  whom. This will include details of what was reposited in the intelligence repository.

For any other aspect of specialized law enforcement, such as witness
protection or covert Internet investigation, the information-submission
mechanisms should be integrated with the existing management structures
for that business area. This makes the assumption that the existing management structures already demonstrate that any information being obtained
from such processes is being gathered lawfully and addresses any civil liberty
and privacy issues. No information should be submitted using methods that
deviate significantly from the format outlined here.

Where the information submission is completed by a trained officer,
such as a source handler or intercept case officer, the information submission may contain the exact wording to be used in the intelligence report.
In such circumstances, the submitting officer may be in the best position to
sanitize the information with the added benefit of saving time for the staff in
the Intelligence Unit. However, there exists a risk that such officers may be
overprotective of their asset and fail to include sufficient detail. The situation
needs to be monitored on a continuous basis by the intelligence manager, with
a right of redress where it is believed that there are unnecessary omissions.

Regardless of which member performs the sanitization, the intelligence report will always be prepared and reposited by staff in the Intelligence Unit.

6.16   Purging Information Submissions

The subject of "purging" or weeding documents in an intelligence management system is dealt with in depth in Chapter 7. However, at this juncture, it is worth drawing attention to the fact that some of the key benefits of having a structured information-submission process is that it reduces the amount of inaccurate or spurious intelligence that is reposited, and it allows the agency to maintain management records pertaining to their involvement in information gathering, even though the final product (in this case, an intelligence report) has been purged from the repository. Purging unsubstantiated or false intelligence from intelligence repositories is a legal requirement in many jurisdictions and good practice.

6.17   Integration and Evaluation

The terms "integration" and "evaluation" are found in many versions of the intelligence cycle and even if they are not used categorically, the work that is associated with them is implicit in the misuse of such terms as "analysis."

Attempting to separate the steps of integration and evaluation can be tricky and is, at best, difficult to understand, as the two are intrinsically linked. As part of the information-to-intelligence process, information has to be evaluated. An original evaluation may have been carried out by the officer submitting the information. That officer may or may not have had access to all other intelligence that is currently held. To evaluate the new information correctly, it has to be regarded alongside the intelligence that is already in the intelligence management repository. This occurs while the new information is not actually in the repository. Additionally, once evaluated and placed

Figure 6.10 Collation/evaluation paradigm.

in the repository, there may be a need to further re-evaluate its worth. This interconnectivity creates a simple paradigm illustrated in Figure 6.10.

Fortunately as this part of the process requires the input of a person trained in intelligence management, it is not actually as complicated as it may first appear. It is the responsibility of the Intelligence Unit to ensure that intelligence is entered correctly into the intelligence repository, and this involves both evaluating and integrating the information before repositing. The switching nature of evaluation and integration means that useless, irrelevant, and incorrect information is removed before time is invested in making links, and so on.

By way of an example, we will consider a simple scenario: A uniform patrol officer stops a person late at night in the vicinity of an industrial complex where there have been a number of break-ins. She submits this information through the identified process, and it arrives in the Intelligence Unit. In the Intelligence Unit, an intelligence officer looks at the information and evaluates it as factual as the person is positively identified. They then search the intelligence repository to see if the person has been previously recorded. On finding that the person is a known thief, they submit an intelligence report into the intelligence repository. In repositing this report, the intelligence officer links the person on the intelligence report to the entity already held on the system (they are synonymous) and links the premises where the person was stopped to the premise details already in the repository. If the premise is not present, a new entity is created. This is an example of "integration."

6.18   Integration

Collation is a term often used in the intelligence cycle. In general usage of the word, it means to examine and compare new material with old material, note points of agreement, and assemble the material in a logical sequence. In effect, it is about the *integration* of new material with old material, while attempting to verify it through careful examination throughout the processing of the new material. As the word integration has more clarity, it is chosen in the model to replace the somewhat outdated term "collation."

In intelligence management, integration is the linkage of new "information" to existing "intelligence," so that there can be accurate evaluation of it and subsequently easy and rapid retrieval of it. Integration includes sorting the information so that relationships between the new information and existing intelligence can be determined. Integration also includes reconciling the entities that will be contained in new intelligence products with existing entities held in the repository. When new intelligence is created and placed in an intelligence repository, care must be taken to avoid the duplication of entities. This comes about because of a number of factors that the integration process is intended to mitigate. They include the following:

- *Poor information reporting.* The submitting officer takes insufficient care to obtain the full correct details at time of submission. This includes information that had the officer asked the right questions they would have obtained, such as obtaining a person's date of birth and incorrect spelling of a person's name, especially where it is of foreign origin or there are a number of similar-sounding names.
- *Insufficient information available.* The submitting officer was unable to obtain the correct details from the information provider.
- *Uncertainty about information.* There is ambiguity or confusion about whether the new information definitely relates to an existing entity. In such circumstances, it will be misleading to directly link the two unless the caveat is placed on the intelligence to say that there is doubt that it is definitely that entity.

The various types of entities likely to be found in the intelligence repository are discussed in detail in Chapter 7.

Integration can be a time-consuming business, and it is incumbent upon the agency to make sure that officers submitting information provide the most complete and accurate details available to them at time of submission. Where incomplete or inaccurate submissions have been made, they should be returned by the Intelligence Unit to the submitting officer. If the problem continues, the line manager for that officer should be informed as the officer is obviously in neglect of his duty.

6.19   Evaluation

It would be very easy if intelligence officers could decide if a piece of intelligence is either true or false. Unfortunately, accepting information at face value is rarely a viable option. Information originates from many places, and one has to raise a question mark as to whether or not information arriving from a particular place can be trusted and to what extent it should be trusted. Furthermore, although we may be able to attach a value for the level of credibility we place in where the information originates, we must also make a decision on each piece of information that originates from the same place. The process involved in making such judgments is known as "evaluation" or sometimes referred to as "grading." Evaluation can be defined as "an assessment of the reliability of the provider of the information and the validity of the information provided." Evaluation requires separate assessments of both of these factors; that is, first, we assess the reliability of the provider of the information, and then we make an assessment as to the validity of each piece of information received from that provider. Evaluation is a critical part of the information-to-intelligence process. Its purpose is to give the end users of the intelligence product as accurate as possible guidance on the worth of the information in front of them.

Evaluation can be thought of as an objectively based judgment or can equally be viewed as a professional opinion. What must be considered here is the assessing officer's ability to make such a judgment and on their ability to express how and why they arrived at this judgment. Too many of those involved in intelligence management have an insufficient understanding of the aspects that are central to the evaluation process. This is often because of a lack of proper training.

To have a clearer understanding of the evaluation process, it is necessary to examine both parts of it. We begin with reliability. *Reliability* refers to our ability to trust the consistency of the provider's information. This assessment can only be made over a period of time and a number of encounters. It should be noted that an assessment is not being made of the "provider as a whole," merely the consistency of their information. The judgment being made is whether the information normally obtained from this provider is reliable or not.

The distinction between the provider as a whole and the consistency of the provider's information is an important distinction to make, as many of the individuals that law enforcement obtain information from would, if an objective assessment was made based on the whole, be far from reliable. Take, for instance, a heroin addict; as a whole, they are not "reliable" as a person, but as a provider of information they may consistently provide accurate and detailed information. Such a person would have a high grading when it came to reliability. In making a judgment in relation to the reliability factor, what is being evaluated is based solely on their history in providing information. It is not an evaluation of that person. For example, there should be no difference in the grading attached to the head teacher of a school and a drug dealer, if neither has previously given information.

Factors to take into account when considering the reliability of information providers include the following:

- What is their history in relation to providing information?
- Is there consistency/inconsistency with information provided on previous occasions and what is now being reported? One week they say one thing and without explanation their account changes the following week.
- What may affect the partiality of the provider? Many providers will taint information to address their agenda, for their benefit, or to cause harm to another.

- What may be motivating the person to provide the information? (This makes the assumption that the evaluating member has a proper understanding of human motivation.) Is there a reason why they may provide false information?
- How accurate has the person been in relation to the information they have provided? Has the information provided been the "best quality and quantity of information ...?" (Milne and Bull 2006:8). If a provider has supplied a huge amount of accurate information, then that will speak toward their reliability.

We now move on to the validity of the information. *Validity* refers to the believability of the information that has been provided. Each piece of information should be assessed to identify the accuracy of *that* particular piece of information. Note each separate piece of information is assessed for validity, regardless of it being presented to the agency at the same time from the same provider as many other pieces of information. This is because the provider will often have obtained the information in different ways and under differing circumstances, each of these factors being likely to affect the validity of the information. An information validity assessment must be done no matter who supplies the information and regardless of the stated reliability of that provider. It should be an objective assessment and those making it must take care that their views of the provider do not cloud their assessment of the information.

Factors to consider when assessing the validity of the information provided include the following:

- How does this piece of information fit with what is already known?
- Is there information to contradict this information? How valid is it?
- Under what circumstances did the provider obtain the information (the provenance)? How might those circumstances have influenced perception of the event being recalled?
- Is the information consistent with itself?
- Does it appear impossible or highly improbable?
- Is the event being misrecollected? Human memory is far from perfect. Often events will not be recalled correctly despite the best intentions of the individual.
- What parts of the information can be independently verified? Although the core of the information may be impossible to verify, the parts surrounding it may be verifiable by other means. If parts of it are true, there is a better chance that it as a whole is true than if no part can be verified. For example, if a human source reports that he saw a drug deal take place on Windsor Road at 18:30 hours on November 24 and included in his report is that police were in the

area at the time investigating a vehicle collision. The part about the vehicle collision is verifiable and so points to the rest being valid.

- Are details missing that should be there if the information is valid? Care must be taken that these omissions are not due to the incompetence of the reporting officer.

In evaluating any piece of information, the possibility should always be considered that no matter how ridiculous or incredible what is being reported may seem—no matter how out of step it may seem to be with all other known information—that piece of information may be true. Some things are true whether you believe them or not! And care must be taken if the information contains something that we do not want to hear or that we do not want others to hear, so that the evaluation does not reflect our prejudices or agenda (Figure 6.11).

Many involved in evaluating intelligence fall into the trap of repeatedly putting the same grades on different pieces of information, purely because they originate from the same place/person. This comes about both from laziness and because they believe that if they grade the validity of a piece of information as being low, this damages the overall reliability of the person providing the information. Such errors in judgment should be addressed by supervisors and/or those involved in processing the information.

Evaluation should be carried out as close to the origin of the material as possible and should be conducted simultaneously with or immediately after its acquisition. This is because this is where and when the information is in its purest form. For example, it is entirely appropriate that the officer managing a human source grades the information provided by that source, as they will have a much better grasp on aspects such as the nature of that person's relationship with the agency, their previous encounters with the agency, and what may or may not be driving their behavior. Notwithstanding this, the grading that they may place on the validity of the information they submitted may be reevaluated by an intelligence officer who has access to the bigger picture or other relevant information. Care must always be taken with reevaluation and is often better achieved through consultation. One of the key benefits of the evaluation system is that when an intelligence product is disseminated, it makes it easier for those receiving it to then make an educated decision as to how act upon it, without having a need to know where that intelligence has originated. The ability to withhold the origin of the information from

Figure 6.11 Evaluation.

a person or persons, the circumstances under which it was obtained, or the method used to obtain it obviously makes it easier to disseminate intelligence, as the risk of compromise to the origin is significantly lessened.

Many agencies now use an alphanumeric matrix to describe the information once it has been evaluated. The letters in the matrix refer to the reliability of the information provider and the numbers to the validity of that piece of information. Perhaps one of the best known of these matrices is the "Admiralty System" that is employed by the North Atlantic Treaty Organization, but most matrices share a common structure—the two main variables being the number of gradings for reliability and validity and the amount of explanation that accompanies each grading. Generally speaking, the matrices will be in the form of 4×4, 5×5, or 6×6. The advantage of a 6×6 matrix is that it allows for a clearer expression of both elements. The argument could be made that it is too cumbersome, but given the huge number of variables that potentially affect the information, presenting more options for evaluation would seem to be a logical solution. However, what is most important is that each member involved in the management of intelligence knows what matrix is being used and the meaning attributed to each grade. When an intelligence product containing evaluated intelligence reports is passed outside the agency, then an explanation of the matrix values used should accompany that product.

Table 6.1 gives the designated grade, the meaning of that grade, and a brief explanation of what the term used means. These three columns are necessary when evaluating information. A fourth column entitled Spontaneous Interpretation is added to aid in understanding how those gradings are likely to be as to interpreted by a recipient. It is likely that most recipients will take an extremely brief look at the evaluation and in those seconds make an assessment as to what that evaluation conveys. The spontaneous interpretation is intended to convey the meaning they are likely to attach and stress the importance of accurate grading. Recipients reading anything evaluated as A1, A2, B1, or B2 are very likely to accept the content as being true and then act accordingly. While this may not be wholly acceptable and in some cases unacceptable, it is worth bearing in mind.

6.20   Reliability of the Origin

Table 6.1 illustrates suggested values for the reliability of the origin of the information. These values can be of critical importance, and although displayed in tabular form here for convenience, they should be fully explained in the agency's intelligence procedures, so that any ambiguity is removed. Because the values are in essence just an "opinion," albeit that of a professional, there is no room for wide interpretation in their meaning, and any member assigning these

Table 6.1 Reliability Values

Designated Grade	Reliability	Explanation	Spontaneous Interpretation
A	Completely reliable	There is no doubt regarding authenticity or competence of this provider. The provider has a prolonged history of being complete reliability	Gets it right all the time
B	Usually reliable	Provider has a history of reliability having been incorrect on only one or perhaps two occasions during a prolonged period	Right more often than not
C	Fairly reliable	Provider has a history of being correct much more often than they are incorrect and the history will indicate that some of their reporting has been inaccurate	Take a bit of time to be sure
D	Usually not reliable	The provider has supplied information in the past that has been incorrect or unacceptably inaccurate	Read it but do not put a lot of faith in what is said
E	Untrustworthy	There are serious concerns about the information provider. The provider may have a history of providing false or misleading information or is strongly suspected of doing so. The provider of this information may have been designated as "hostile" and/or "intelligence nuisance"	Danger. Be careful with this individual. They have the potential to cause harm
F	Cannot be judged	The provider cannot be judged. This grading will be used when there is no or little history of providing information.	Do not know—take the information as it is

values needs to be fully trained in them. Any member using the intelligence of which these values form part also needs to understand what the values mean before they use the intelligence. The agency should include in its procedures words to the effect that intrinsic to the use of the intelligence is the member's full understanding of what the evaluations mean. Failing to do this creates situations where something goes wrong and the member uses the excuses "I thought it meant…" or "I didn't know; if I had, I wouldn't have blah, blah, blah… ."

6.21   Validity of the Content

Table 6.2 illustrates suggested values for the validity of the content of an intelligence report. If the information is a report of an incident that took place—for example, the recovery of contraband or a shooting attack that police have attended—this should not be evaluated using this matrix (Table 6.2). It should be recorded as "fact" and the grading aspects left blank.

Table 6.2   Validity of Content

Designated Grade	Reliability	Explanation	Spontaneous Interpretation
1	Confirmed	The content has been confirmed by other independent reports. It is logical in itself and is corroborated by other existing intelligence on the subject	This is *true*
2	Probably true	Although the content has not been confirmed independently, it is logical in itself and agrees with other existing intelligence on the subject	More than likely *true*
3	Possibly true	Although the content has not been confirmed, it is reasonably logical in itself and it is, in at least part, supported by other intelligence on the subject	Not sure. Calls for judgment in action
4	Of doubtful truth	The content is unconfirmed and while not illogical it is assessed as being incorrect. The information is not believed at time of evaluation, but it remains possible that it is true	Not true
5	Believed to be false	There is reliable intelligence available that contradicts the content. It appears illogical in itself. The manner or circumstances in which it was reported gives strong indications that it is false	False. Handle with care
6	Cannot be judged	There is insufficient knowledge to make a judgment on the validity of the information	No idea

There are a number of difficulties that are commonly found in evaluating information because of the origin of that material. Perhaps the simplest example is with regard to stop checks of a person of interest to law enforcement. If a police officer physically stops and checks the individual or knows him and has a clear view of him and is certain of that person's identity, then this should be evaluated as a fact. However, if the officer merely observes the individual, then the information has to be graded, as there can be an element of doubt as to whether or not it was the person. Such a piece of information is likely to be graded "A" as the officer is reliable and then assigned an appropriate value for validity, dependent on how certain the officer is following the observation and how that observation fits with other information. Similar dilemmas regularly occur with the reporting of surveillance operations when the surveillance operator may only have had a limited view of a person. The way in which the subsequent intelligence report is written will go a long way to adding clarity to the validity evaluation. One of the most complex forms of information to evaluate is that coming from the technical intercept of a telephone or a listening device in a property. The initial problem is often in deciding what should be considered the origin of the material—against which to assign a reliability value. Is it the listening medium itself, the person speaking that is heard through the medium, or the officer reporting the content of the medium? Taking a step back and making a logical choice, one can rule out the reporting officer, as all they should be doing is relating what has been said. The question is then: Is it the reporting medium or the people whose conversation is being monitored using the intercept? Many monitoring operations are likely to be in place for prolonged periods and are often given an operational name. For ease of explanation, let us call our intercept operation "Operation Sunshine." The reason that such operations are put in place is that they are intended to provide high-grade information and/or evidence. Those conversing through these media are likely to vary. The reliability grading should be applied to the intercept medium and the individuals conversing on it if and when identified and will be part of what goes toward evaluating the validity of each piece of information. Over a period of time, we will be able to establish the level of consistency for the information that comes through Operation Sunshine. Factors likely to affect this are how safe those being monitored feel—the safer they feel the more they will talk—the more reliable Operation Sunshine will prove over time, and the higher grading it will attain. The validity grading will be dependent on other things such as who is talking, what they are saying, and the *way* they are saying it.

The importance of accurate evaluation cannot be overstated. Decisions affecting life and death will be made upon intelligence products. If these products are not accurately graded, wrong decisions are made, possibly resulting in harm that could have been avoided. In addition, many actions carried out by law enforcement are done based on intelligence. These include arrests, searches, and seizures. Poorly evaluated information can lead to wrongful arrests and evidence being ruled inadmissible in court. Such incidents not only have consequences for those directly involved but can also have serious ramifications for the LEA and the wider criminal justice system.

6.22 Deception

Those involved in intelligence evaluation must always recognize the potential that they are being deceived. Deception can come in many forms:

- Deliberate misinformation placed on the Internet
- Deliberate misinformation passed through a human source that is in reality continuing to work for the criminals
- Deliberate misinformation knowingly passed over a telephone the criminals believe to be intercepted
- Deliberate misinformation spoken by criminals in a location that they believe that law enforcement has bugged
- Deliberate misinformation by an officer involved in a corrupt relationship
- Deliberate entering of information into the system by an officer to mask their incompetence or lack of work
- Misleading information entered into the system by an incompetent officer

The more credible the information passed appears to be, the more likely it is that those receiving it will believe it. The more sophisticated and experienced the criminal organization, and the less experienced the officers involved, the more likely the deception is to succeed. The greatest difficulty for law enforcement occurs when lies are intermingled with material that is known to be true. Those involved in intelligence management should continually ask themselves if each and every piece of information is accurate. One unfortunate aspect is that if staff have invested heavily in intelligence that they believed to be true, and subsequently suspect its veracity, it becomes increasingly difficult to fess up and admit their doubts the longer the commitment continues and the greater that commitment has been.

6.23 Information Overload

Evaluation is not restricted to the grading of information but also includes decisions as to whether or not information ever gets to being recorded as intelligence. Significant volumes of information will pass through a law enforcement agency on a daily basis, not all of which has value from an intelligence perspective. Part of the evaluation process carried out in an Intelligence Unit is to decide what should be included and what should be discarded. The fact is that most LEAs already cannot deal with the volume of intelligence they have, and all that adding further to it does is to make it impossible to see the fire because of the smoke. Objective judgments must be made as to what should be included in the intelligence repository and what is to be discarded to reduce the chances of information overload and to ensure that privacy rights are protected. Before repositing intelligence, the role of the Intelligence Unit is to ensure that irrelevant, incorrect, and otherwise useless information is weeded out or purged. If an intelligence repository has too much intelligence in it, future weeding of it becomes logistically impossible. Ultimately, criteria for inclusion in the repository will be decided by the agency's senior intelligence manager and laid down in procedures. However, such decisions are likely to be made on a daily basis by intelligence officers working in the Intelligence Unit, as this is where a significant volume of information will be available for evaluation. Given the importance of not missing a piece of information that is relevant, it is obvious why intelligence officers need to be well trained and competent in their role. Making the call as to what is relevant and what is not will often rely heavily on the member's professional judgment and experience, but guidelines as to what is to be considered should be in place within the agency's intelligence management procedures.

Part of the evaluation process involves prioritizing information as it comes into the Intelligence Unit. This will involve sifting through all information in a manner similar to that of triage at a hospital emergency ward. Once the information that has been received has been through this "triage"-type process, decisions can be made as to what is required to be put into the intelligence repository and what is unsuitable for inclusion in the repository. The idea of triage is to identify what requires the most urgent attention and deal with it first. Intelligence management cannot function properly unless new information is sifted to identify material that needs immediate action, such as a threat to someone's life or the imminent opportunity for an arrest and seizure.

6.24   Role of "Intelligence Unit" in the Cycle

When one observes the intelligence cycle as illustrated in Figure 6.3, it should be apparent that all information must be integrated and evaluated and therefore passes through the Intelligence Unit before being reposited in the intelligence repository. There should be *no* direct input into the intelligence repository by any other member. This is done for a number of reasons:

- The Intelligence Unit can ensure that poorly prepared or incorrectly evaluated intelligence reports do not find their way into the repository, thus maintaining standards.
- All intelligence is entered at the correct level in the repository, thus ensuring greater security.
- There is a central point for those requiring access to all relevant intelligence where they can obtain that intelligence.
- Intelligence to be disseminated is sent to the right people, in the right form, and in an expeditious manner.
- Those exploiting disseminated intelligence have one point to report back the results of taking action because of that intelligence.
- Staff in the unit are able to see all intelligence relevant to their role on an ongoing basis without the need for continually searching the repository. This creates invaluable expertise.

It is recognized that many members—such as those involved in managing human sources, undercover operations, and surveillance operations— will have had training in intelligence management and that these members may be well capable of completing intelligence reports. Nevertheless, while it may be totally appropriate for that officer to create intelligence reports, no intelligence report should enter the repository without passing through the Intelligence Unit.

The Intelligence Unit is responsible for a significant amount of work in the intelligence cycle. Figure 6.12 illustrates its central role in the intelligence management system. Some may view the role of the Intelligence Unit as merely a clerical role, dominated by sorting through and filing records; it is, in reality, the linchpin in the information-to-intelligence process. It is the role of the Intelligence Unit to take information and process it into intelligence. Inevitably this will involve discarding some material that is provided to the unit because it is of no intelligence worth. The processing involves converting the vast amount of information collected by the agency to a form that is usable by intelligence customers. The process requires professional decision-making that can only be carried out by trained and experienced staff fully supported with adequate resources, including a computerized intelligence management system. The structure of Intelligence Units is explained further in Chapter 7.

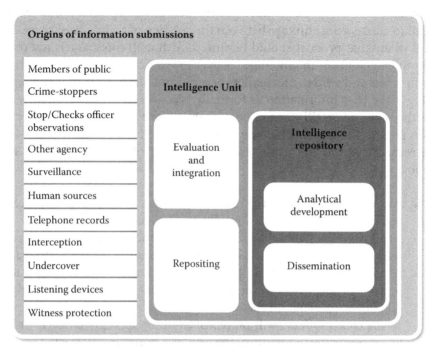

Figure 6.12 The intelligence management system.

6.25   Interpretation

Part of the integration process can involve interpretation of the information that is provided. Distinct from interpretation from one language to another, interpretation in this context means changing the information from its raw state into a format that can be understood by customers. Often information will be collected in a way that if left in its raw state, it would be of little use to many potential customers. It is the role of the collectors, the Intelligence Unit, and sometimes the requesting member to interpret what is related and give it meaning. This is done through a variety of methods including consultation, translation of slang, the decoding of words used by the criminals, and using prior knowledge of the parties involved. Care must always be taken by those involved in the interpretation that they are only elucidating what is already there and neither adding to or detracting from the content of the initial information.

6.26   Repositing

Repositing is the process of entering an intelligence product into the intelligence repository. It is derived from the word "reposit," which means "to put away, deposit or store up" (Free Online Dictionary) and refers directly to lodging the intelligence product in the intelligence repository. The word is used to create a clear linkage between the creation of an intelligence product and where that product should be stored. Although this stage is not found in other versions of the intelligence cycle, it is included here to add clarity as to when and where information becomes intelligence. It is at the repositing stage that information is formally recognized as being intelligence. In the revisited intelligence cycle, illustrated in Figure 6.3, once information crosses the dashed line and is logged into the repository, it can then be regarded as intelligence. There are a number of factors associated with repositing:

- All intelligence products must be reposited, including intelligence products created through analytical examination.
- Intelligence will always be reposited in a structured (indexed, cross-referenced) way that permits rapid and accurate access and retrieval.
- All intelligence reports will be sanitized before being reposited to protect the identity of the origin of the intelligence and/or the methodology used to obtain that information.
- Intelligence products will be reposited at an appropriate level, with awareness of the sensitivity of the intelligence and any associated risks.

6.27   Repositing Protocols

Protocols are codes that dictate the correct way to do something. Intelligence should only be entered into the repository against agreed protocols as defined by the senior intelligence manager. If intelligence is not properly filed, it becomes increasingly difficult to find what is required and to use the intelligence with as much certainty with regard to its authenticity. Typical of a poorly managed repository are numerous separate entries referring to the same person or place, a variety of spellings for names, and different vehicle numbers for the same vehicle. To give an idea of some of the issues that will need to be addressed in submission protocols, the following suggestions are included. They should by no means be considered a definitive list:

- All landline telephone numbers should be linked to a geographic location, and cell/mobile phones should be linked to the International Mobile Equipment Identity (IMEI) number of the handset to which the number is associated. (Note: The IMEI number and associated SIM card may change at some point. This should be recorded.)
- All geographic locations should be identified by a full postal address and its position recorded in the intelligence repository through geocoding.

- All entities should be reposited in a way that they can be searched against synonyms. For example, when the name "Charles" is entered, the search should return Charles, Charlie, Charley, Chuck, and so on. Similarly, if "Cocaine" is entered, returns will include Cocaine, Coke, Ice, Crack, Charley, and so on. However, with the examples given, if the entity is not categorized correctly as a name or a commodity, it can create errors.
- All past and present names, aliases, and nicknames for a person should be linked. Many criminals will use false names and/or nicknames—these names need to be linked so a search brings back all intelligence relating to that person, regardless of name used. In addition, the very nature of intelligence means that reporting is often fragmented, and an investigator may not have the luxury of having a full or wholly accurate name. Effort must be made to keep the number of such partially identified persons to a minimum. Where it is believed partial identification refers to an identified person, the link should be established between the reporting and that individual, but with a warning with regard to the incompleteness of the information.
- All past and present names and nicknames for geographic locations should be linked. For example, bars often have formal names, but they also have nicknames that are used in common parlance, and they often change their names as they change image or ownership. It is important that a search for one name brings up the intelligence associated with all the names.
- The quality of inputted material should be monitored as a matter of routine to maintain input standards. Common faults that should be identified include typographical errors, poor punctuation, unexplained abbreviations, and incomplete or omitted fields.

6.28 Sanitization

Sanitization is defined as "The practice of removing or altering the content of a document with the aim of protecting sensitive sources and/or methodology to arrive at a form appropriate for dissemination" (Association of Chief Police Officers 2005). If intelligence is to be of any use, it must be shared, even if there are risks involved with sharing it. Sanitization is a control measure to reduce the risks in sharing intelligence. Sanitization is not an easy task to achieve. It involves significant thought, and for want of a better word, guile to remove all traces of where and how intelligence has originated, without losing content, accuracy, and the essence of what was originally reported. As

Harfield and Harfield (2008:202) comment, "The watchword is sanitization rather than sterilization." Additionally, care must be taken to avoid creating ambiguity for those using the intelligence, as ambiguity has the potential to cause serious harm in an investigation. Sanitization is performed at the repositing stage because, as will be seen in Section 6.36, intelligence is automatically disseminated on repositing. Sanitization can be achieved using a number of techniques including the following:

- *Editing.* The removal of certain words or sentences is the most common technique used in sanitization. For example, "Source states ..." The intelligence is obviously from a human source. Edit the two words and leave only what the source has stated. "Source states his brother..." In this case it is not too difficult to work out that it's a human source and who it is. Edit all and leave only the text.
- *Language modification.* Often the language used in an information submission will make it apparent where the information has originated. By changing the words used, the origin becomes vague. "Jack Thompson called his brother to say..." This is probably from an intercept. Change to "Jack Thompson told his brother..."
- *Separation.* The separation of the information into two or more intelligence reports even though it addresses the same subject matters. Note where an information submission contains reporting on a number of subjects. These should, as a matter of course, be separated into individual intelligence reports. This reduces the risk of exposing the origin of the content as collectively the origin may be very apparent.

It is the responsibility of the intelligence manager to ensure that all intelligence has been properly sanitized before it is reposited.

6.29   Repositing at the Correct Access Level

Part of the repositing process involves ensuring that intelligence can be accessed at a later stage, by those who need access to it, and not be accessed by those unauthorized to see it. Care must be taken that an intelligence product is reposited at an appropriate access level within the intelligence repository. The lower the access level at which a product is reposited, the more people will have automatic access to it, and the higher the access level, the fewer people will have automatic access to it. A simplistic view of access-level repositing is illustrated in Figure 6.13. Although deciding on the access level for each intelligence product can be time consuming, it is essential to preserve security while at the same time facilitating access.

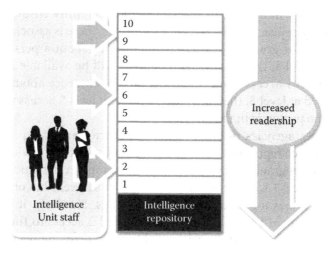

Figure 6.13 Access-level repositing.

6.30   Levels of Access

The agency's computer must be able to provide numerous levels of access and make access available to different group types. There are some general points to consider as follows:

- There will normally be a correlation between the access levels in the agency's repository and the national government's protective marking scheme with access levels ascending as the weight of the protective marking increases. Given the likely nature of some of the intelligence that will be stored, serious consideration must be given to IT security. However, the most sensitive aspects of intelligence management are not often the intelligence products but the methodology used and the origins of the information for which the intelligence was derived.
- Normally, the existence of an entity will be visible to all having access with the capacity to hide the content of associated intelligence products at higher levels. A member with access to level 1 may see that Joe Smyth is in the intelligence repository but because all intelligence about Joe Smyth is at a higher level, that member would not be able to read it.
- Care must be taken with the opening screen of any entity to ensure that intelligence reposited at a higher level does not appear at a lower access level. For example, the new address of a terrorist may be very sensitive and be reposited at level 6 but the opening screen is populated with that address.

- The facility must exist to completely hide an entity ensuring that it will only appear at the lowest level to which there is associated intelligence. For example, if there is intelligence about a person reposited at level 1, then that person's details will be available to anyone with level 1 access. However, if the only intelligence about a person is stored at level 5, then only members with level 5 access will know that the person is in the system.
- In larger agencies or where smaller agencies are using a regional intelligence repository, it will be necessary to further divide the levels on a geographical or unit basis. For example, a narcotics member having level 3 access may see all the entities at level 3 but only be able to see level 3 intelligence relating to drugs. Similarly, if an officer from Tintown Police Department has level 2 access to the regional intelligence repository, he will only be able to read intelligence reposited for Tintown readership. Each agency must take the time to work out how the levels and groups are to be configured, but the software must have been built with this in mind.

What can be seen from many of these comments is the importance of getting the software right. Few software manufacturers have the knowledge to build programs that will include many of these nuances. Unfortunately, what happens is that software companies often only employ one or two former officers who then design a program that mirrors how they did it in their former agency, with the limited adaptability and aptitude that this creates. Furthermore, nothing here is set in stone. One of the difficulties in building an intelligence management system is identifying all the potential options for a structure and then working through all consequences of each.

6.31   A 10-Level Repository

To have a clearer picture of what the access levels in a repository are likely to look like, the following are suggestions of the likely readership at each level of a 10-level intelligence repository illustrated in Figure 6.14.

Level 1: All sworn officers and support staff requiring access
Level 2: Line managers of all sworn staff and support staff having access
Level 3: Middle management of all sworn staff and support staff having access including area commanders
Level 4: Detectives and those involved in the investigation of serious crimes
Level 5: Detective supervisors

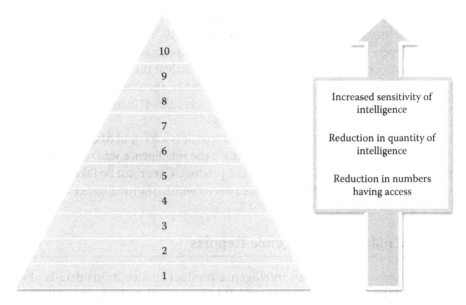

Figure 6.14 10-level intelligence repository.

Level 6: Intelligence Unit staff
Level 7: Intelligence manager
Level 8: Internal investigation
Level 9: Those involved in national security/counterterrorism who have
        a high security clearance
Level 10: An extremely limited number of staff, as this is where the most
        sensitive intelligence is stored

There are a number of points worthy of note in relation to identifying access levels. First, access levels refer only to access to the intelligence repository; it does not give staff access to software programs that manage covert operations, nor will the repository disclose the origin of any intelligence (provided the entire intelligence management system has been correctly built!). Second, access levels are based on "the right to know, need to know" principles. Unless both these criteria are met, access should not be granted as a matter of routine. When a member needs to see specific material at a higher level than their access level status allows, access to that material can be granted on a one-time basis; the member's access status should not be increased as they have neither a need nor a right to see other material at that level. Even being Chief should not automatically confer access to all levels. The Chief has a right to know, but does not need to know. Third, intelligence relating to internal investigations should always be stored at a high access level and the internal investigation material ring fenced at that level, so only those involved in internal investigation can see it even if they have higher access status. Fourth, as a member's access-level status rises, so should the level of vetting to which they are subjected. Fifth, intelligence stored at the highest levels is likely to be of the most sensitive nature, with a significant amount of it coming from external agencies. Only if the receiving agency can ensure the safety of such intelligence will other agencies continue to share intelligence with them. Lastly, too few levels allows insufficient flexibility, and too many levels become meaningless.

Remember, when intelligence is reposited, it is a form of dissemination. All those who have access to the level at which the intelligence was reposited automatically have access to that intelligence product. Care must be taken to reposit intelligence products at the correct access level within the intelligence repository.

6.32   Creating Intelligence Reports

An intelligence report is an intelligence product that contains details of an entity or intelligence about an entity. It is prepared by a trained intelligence officer in order that the content can be reposited in a format that protects the identity of the origin yet facilitates the dissemination of the intelligence contained therein. Intelligence reports are the mainstay of any intelligence repository. They are stand-alone documents; that is, they do not need any other documents to explain them. Intelligence reports will always be in a single standardized format, regardless of the origin of the intelligence contained therein. Intelligence reports will be completed by a *repositing member* (a member of the Intelligence Unit) and be derived from the information submission that was hitherto completed by a *submitting member*. An intelligence report will exhibit the following:

- Contain a topic heading and a subheading selected from a prepared list. Such headings allow for easier searching. For example, the topic heading may be "burglary" and the subheading "commercial premises."
- Contain a topic title and a list of keywords. The topic title should be concise but a clear indication of the content of the report. For example, "McPherson Gang—Robbery Plan." The number of keywords should be limited.
- Contain only the name of the repositing member. The inclusion of the submitting member's name means that many others within the agency will be aware of the means by which it was obtained. Knowing where intelligence has come from and who has submitted it has the potential to prejudice the customer's subsequent actions in relation to that intelligence; prejudice being the key word here! Furthermore, should the intelligence report be disclosed, it provides

an unnecessary opportunity for a defense lawyer to follow, in the hope of derailing the case to which the intelligence relates.

- Contain an evaluation of the intelligence within that references both the reliability pertaining to the origin of the content and an assessment of the veracity of that piece of intelligence.
- Have a URN from which its origin can be traced. Such tracing will only be permitted by an authorized member. The origin of the content and/or the method used to obtain it must not be apparent to any casual reader.
- Be marked in accordance with the relevant government's protective marking scheme *and* the level within the repository at which it has been deposited. It is for the repositing member to decide the appropriate protective marking.
- Contain only one piece of intelligence relating to one topic, even though there may have been other content contained in the information submission from which it originates. This is to minimize the harm should the intelligence report be disclosed. Intelligence reports are the intelligence product most often used in the preparation of warrants or as a basis for arrests. As such they are more likely to be vulnerable when it comes to the disclosure regime.
- Be sanitized to protect the origin of the material. However, care must be taken to ensure that the remaining content does not become so insipid as to be worthless.
- Only be reposited when all the entities contained within have been checked against those already existing in the repository and identified as far as it is reasonably practical to do so. Each entity contained therein will be identified by its relevant URN.
- Permit comment by the repositing member and/or the submitting member. Such comments should not betray the origin of the intelligence: for example, "Source tasked to further investigate." In this case, what should be said is, "Submitting member tasked to further investigate." Such comments provide input for the expertise of the officers involved in managing the intelligence and can provide valuable insight.
- When it is necessary for the intelligence customer to have numerous pieces of intelligence from one information submission all in one place in order to contextualize the content, a "protected intelligence report" should be created. Protected intelligence reports will always be stored at the highest levels of the intelligence repository. Numerous other intelligence reports can be created from a protected intelligence report. The URNs of each intelligence report will be contained on the protected intelligence report, but no reference whatsoever will be made to the protected intelligence report on any of the other intelligence reports. The protected intelligence report will be

clearly endorsed that it is protected, the most effective means being watermarking.

- Contain details of how the intelligence report has been assigned.

6.33   Assigning Intelligence Reports

As information passes through the intelligence system, it moves progressively toward the position where the intelligence manager has to decide what needs to be done with the finalized intelligence product. In respect of each intelligence report, the intelligence manager can assign it one of three options:

1. Reposit the intelligence report in the intelligence repository "for future reference." In essence, the manager makes the decision that the intelligence contained therein needs no further action carried out upon it, but that the intelligence is worth retaining and can be lawfully retained. An example of this would be an intelligence report that states that Tony Bishop (a habitual criminal) has purchased a new vehicle, the report also including the description of the new vehicle. Nothing needs to be done at present, but the intelligence may prove useful in a future investigation of Bishop. The intelligence report is reposited "no further action required."

2. Reposit the intelligence report in the intelligence repository and allocate it to a relevant party "for further development." This development may include further research or operational development. An example of this would be intelligence that states that Tony Bishop, a habitual criminal and identified target, is dealing large quantities of cocaine from a warehouse in the area of the local docks. Law enforcement may wish to place Bishop under surveillance to identify the warehouse and/or a researcher may be tasked to search public records to identify the warehouse, either of which could be the next logical steps toward indicting Bishop for the possession of illegal drugs. The intelligence report is reposited and a link sent to the unit or person responsible for dealing with it. The intelligence report is marked "for further development."

3. Reposit the intelligence report in the intelligence repository and "issue an intelligence advisory" (see Chapter 7) to the relevant customer. There are three potential situations relating to intelligence advisories and the intelligence manager must indicate which one of the three is most appropriate. Given the circumstances:
   a. There is a threat to life or property. Each agency will have its own procedures to deal with such.

b. The advisory is issued in the expectation of executive action. This will be done when the intelligence report contains actionable intelligence. An example of this would be Tony Bishop, a habitual criminal and identified target, has a kilo of cocaine at an identified warehouse. The expectation is that the intelligence customer, having asked for such intelligence, will then take action on receipt of that intelligence. The result of the subsequent action or the lack of action and the reason why no action was taken must be reported to the Intelligence Unit within an identified period. The intelligence report is marked "for action."

c. The advisory is issued with potential for executive action. This will be done when the intelligence report contains actionable intelligence but intelligence that the customer may not wish to act upon. This is likely to occur when the intelligence relates to something that is not a strategic or tactical priority. An example of this would be Tony Bishop, a habitual criminal but not an identified target, has a limited quantity of cocaine that he is selling from his home. The expectation is that the intelligence customer, although not having asked for such intelligence, is in the best position to decide what to do with regard to exploiting that intelligence and to account in writing for that decision. The intelligence report will be marked "for decision as to action."

Because of the sheer volume of intelligence reports that will pass through the Intelligence Unit, it would be unrealistic to expect the intelligence manager to make a decision as to what needs to be done with each intelligence report. When staff have any doubt as to what should be done, the intelligence report should always be shown to the intelligence manager. When an intelligence advisory relates to a threat to life or property, this should always be authorized by the intelligence manager or his deputy.

6.34 Specified Handling Limitations

A section on the intelligence report should be reserved for specified handling limitations. Specified handling limitations inform the reader what they are not allowed to do with the content of the intelligence report (or other product). Specified handling instructions are necessary for the exchange of intelligence between agencies. The various national protective marking schemes (discussed in Chapter 7) do not offer sufficient flexibility to address the complexities of sharing intelligence, and unless there is a direct correlation between agencies in regard to the access levels in their respective repositories, additional guidance has to be provided as to how the recipient should deal with the intelligence they are receiving. The presumption should always be that, in passing intelligence to another agency, the control of that information is being ceded. This is because there is little, if any, punitive action that an agency can take against the recipient if they mishandle the intelligence. Specified handling limitations make it clear as to how the originating agency expects the recipient to behave in regard to handling the intelligence. These handling limitations should be written in clear concise language and in bullet-point form. For example,

- "For information narcotics unit. No further dissemination permitted." The intelligence is for the information of a particular unit within the receiving agency and should not be shared any further within that agency. Furthermore, no action should be carried out in respect of the content.
- "For agency use only." The information can be used internally by the receiving agency as it sees fit, but it cannot share the intelligence with anyone else.

Specified handling limitations mean that the receiving agency is not left in limbo as to what they can do with a piece of intelligence. Discussing this problem, Fowler (2011) raises the problem of an agency having been given intelligence but not being given the "authority to release" the content to those it deems as needing it.

U.K. law enforcement has a series of five "handling codes" that were created in an attempt to address the disconnect between access levels within an agency and what can be done with intelligence when it is disseminated to another agency (ACPO 2010). They are as stated in quotation with commentary following:

1. "Permits dissemination within the U.K. police service and to other law enforcement agencies as specified." This means the intelligence could go to anyone within any U.K. police service. This is an extremely wide readership.
2. "Permits dissemination to U.K. non-prosecuting parties." This permits sharing the intelligence with other non-law-enforcement bodies such as banks.
3. "Permits dissemination to foreign (non-EU)* law enforcement agencies." While addressing dissemination to non-European-Union states, it does not say anything about sharing with member states.

* EU = European Union.

4. "Permits dissemination within originating force/agency only; specifies reasons and recipient(s). Review period must be set." Agency access levels address this issue.
5. "Permits dissemination but receiving agency to observe conditions as specified." This handling code is the same concept as the specified handling limitations already discussed.

Unfortunately, because of the way they are constructed and the way in which they jump about with regard to who can see the content, these handling codes are poorly understood and they have, arguably, become meaningless. They are discussed here only to illustrate the difficulties in finding an effective way to share information. The position we adopt is as follows:

- Internal dissemination is dictated by the reports' "access level."
- External dissemination is dictated by "specified handling limitations."
- These are clearly stated in the relevant space on an intelligence report.

Specified handling instructions will normally be used only when the intelligence report is being shared with an external agency. However, internally, there may be occasions when in addition to it being reposited at an agreed level, it is necessary to emphasize the sensitivity pertaining to some aspect of that intelligence report for the benefit of internal readership. This should be the exception rather than a rule.

6.35 Analytical Development

Stemming from its roots in the world of the intelligence community, there is without doubt confusion over the role of the analyst within law enforcement. The problem has been exacerbated by the attitudes and lack of knowledge of some within law enforcement. The role of the analyst is discussed at length in Chapter 8. However, for the sake of continuity, a brief outline of where analytical work sits within the intelligence cycle is needed. The most important aspect is the removal of the word analysis from within the circuit that normally describes the intelligence cycle. This inferred that intelligence could not be produced without analysis. Most versions of the intelligence cycle have analysis as one of the main steps. If one was to dig deeper into many of these versions to see what was meant by the term, it becomes apparent that it is not analysis by a trained analyst but "processing." This stage in the revisited cycle recognizes and emphasizes the fact that a trained analyst does not need to be involved for information to become intelligence. However, a trained analyst can make such a significant contribution to intelligence management that to omit their input would be absurd. The role that is envisaged for the analyst within the revisited cycle is twofold. The first function is the formation of new intelligence products created by combining the crime data from the agency's record management system with the intelligence taken from the repository and with material from other research avenues. These new intelligence products are then reposited in the repository to be used when required by the various intelligence customers. Such products will vary from gap analysis to problem profiles, and from network analysis to market profiles. The second function is that of analyzing the intelligence that already exists. Although the result of any analysis will be the creation of another intelligence product, what is referred to here is the ability and training that analysts need to have to link disparate pieces of intelligence and then find meaning from these combined threads. It is about the ability to interpret what is occurring and predict what is likely to occur in the future. All intelligence products created by an analyst should be reposited using a standardized four-section information submission outlined in Section 6.15.

These two strands of analytical development have the potential to add significant benefit as the intelligence progresses toward dissemination, and in many cases the customer will favor the intelligence products developed by the analyst.

6.36   Dissemination: A Risk-Based Approach

Intelligence is of no worth unless it can be used. Dissemination is about making intelligence available to those who can use it. An agency should adopt a risk-based approach to the dissemination of intelligence. This means that before any intelligence is disseminated, the risks of dissemination need to be considered. Creating a cohesive system from receipt of information to dissemination of any final intelligence product, while in itself is an effective control measure, is insufficient to identify and control all the potential risks. The officer who obtains and submits the information (the submitting officer) must identify any potential risks in its exploitation, albeit with untrained staff such a risk assessment is likely to be very basic. In more complex scenarios, such as managing human sources, the officers involved should be sufficiently trained to identify risks to the source if the intelligence is used and will be expected to assess the risk in dissemination. The expectation is always that they will make a preliminary judgment in relation to the risks of dissemination for each separate piece of information contained in an information submission.

There is often a perception held by those who have gathered the intelligence that it is so super-secret that it can be shared with no one. This is rarely the case. In reality, with a bit of thought, the vast majority of intelligence can be shared with those who need it to carry out their role. Therefore, the balance should always weigh toward sharing, with a limited amount being withheld and even that for a limited period only. Dissemination requires getting intelligence to those who have the need and the right to use it, in whatever form that is of most use to them.

Members are often reluctant to share intelligence, because they view it as a valuable possession—possession being theirs and the value being to that member, as opposed to it belonging to the agency and of value to the agency. The old adage "He who has knowledge has power" not only is alive in the law enforcement psyche, but "doing very nicely, thank you"! Members are all too aware that in many agencies the person who holds the intelligence or has access to the origin of valuable information has significant power. When they do give it away, their expectation will be that they will get something in return. If an agency's intelligence system is working properly, the benefits for each and every member using that system should be apparent. Even then some officers will fail to adhere to the procedures necessary to make the system work for all. Procedures need to be in place to address these issues and to deal with these officers in a robust way.

Given that the term "dissemination" is found widely in intelligence management, it is often assumed its meaning must be clear to all. However, it can be argued that this is not the case. The general consensus is that dissemination occurs when intelligence is "given" out to those who need to have it, but a significant number are "blind" to the ways in which intelligence can be "let out" of the system. Members often think that when they put something into the intelligence repository, it is safe there, unless there is a conscious move made to give it out. The reality is that if another person has appropriate access, they can come in and get that intelligence whenever they want. No giving out is required. Likewise, others are so concerned about intelligence being "let out" that they refuse to put intelligence into the repository. To address both these concerns, clarity must be established as to how intelligence will move out of the repository to a wider audience. We begin by defining dissemination.

Dissemination is "the release of intelligence products, under identified protocols to those that have both a right and a need to have them." Intelligence is disseminated in one of two ways:

- Authorized access (This can only take place when a properly configured computerized intelligence repository is used.)
- Mandated exchange

If intelligence leaves the repository other than by one of these two methods, there is a problem with the system.

When intelligence is disseminated by means of "authorized access," the sharing of intelligence is automatic. Intelligence is placed in the repository and it can be accessed, when it is desired, by a member up to the level to which that member is authorized to have access. The higher the level of authorized access (their access-level status), the greater amount of intelligence the member will be able to see. In addition, depending on the software configuration, as a member's level of authorization is increased, the ways in which they can access the intelligence is likely to increase. For example, a member that is authorized to access level 1 of the intelligence repository may be able to see only that a person is on record, whereas a person with level 5 clearance may be able to access many intelligence products associated with the person and then link directly to details of other persons named in those products. Authorized access is the way in which most intelligence is disseminated. The benefits of this method of dissemination are many:

- The intelligence is continually available. Law enforcement is a 24/7 role and not being able to access intelligence in a timely manner reduces the agency's capabilities. More importantly, it increases officer safety. Police officers encounter potentially dangerous situations on a daily basis. Having ready access to intelligence means that an officer can be made aware of any relevant intelligence that indicates a potential threat before engaging in the situation.
- It reduces time being wasted in sending and reading intelligence that may not be of interest at that time. Everyone is familiar with the amount of unnecessary e-mails they receive and the amount of time spent reading them.
- It negates sending paper copies of the intelligence, thus avoiding both security and storage problems.
- It facilitates further inquiry without the need for request.

Problems with this type of dissemination include the following:

- Maintaining correct access levels for staff can require significant thought and effort in large agencies.
- Staff will often push for greater access than they require and unless expectations are managed, a situation can evolve where staff become resentful at not getting the access they feel they should have. At the same time, management has to restrict access from a security perspective.
- If the levels are not correctly set, collectors will withhold information, because they fear compromise of their assets. This problem was highlighted by International Association of Chiefs of Police on Criminal Intelligence Sharing (2002), and while referring to interagency sharing, the comment refers equally to internal sharing. "Individuals with information must be able to trust the system (that it cannot be breached) and the system's users (that they will not inappropriately share data) before they will use it as a sharing tool for the

data they hold." Ratcliffe and U.S. Department of Justice Office of Community Oriented Policing Services (2007) also highlight concerns that many officers have in relation to lodging intelligence in a repository: "Intelligence officers often retain their intelligence within their teams or squads, under the often mistaken belief that this is necessary for operational security and because of government rules." Unsupervised access creates a risk of inappropriate use by members. Software must have a full audit facility to discourage fishing expeditions by staff.

Authorized access will be available to the following:

- Members of the agency.
- Nominated members of other agencies working regularly in partnership with the agency that owns the intelligence. This is often necessary in joint task forces and similar arrangements. Any member of an agency having rights of access to another agency's intelligence repository should be instructed in the agency's procedures relating to that repository and the conditions under which they may access the repository and use the material within should be acknowledged in writing. This is very important from a citizen's privacy perspective and also to ensure compliance with many of the laws surrounding data protection, which are present in the various jurisdictions.

6.37 Mandated Exchange

Mandated exchange refers to circumstances under which legislation or the agency's policies dictate that certain types of intelligence must be disseminated to previously identified parties. Mandated dissemination makes the assumption that these parties will not have access to the intelligence as a right and therefore they need to be specifically provided with it. The format for mandated exchange is likely to vary according to the nature of the various agencies involved and the context in which they are sharing intelligence. The following points are worth bearing in mind:

- Many countries have legislation that places a legal obligation on agencies to share intelligence in respect to certain matters. Most legislation of this type deals with the potential threat to someone's life or harm to children. The agency needs to have structures in place to meet the demands of the legislation.

- There will be many circumstances where specific units within an agency need to be informed of a piece of intelligence which they do not have a right to access normally. Structures need to be in place to make sure this is done. It will normally be done by the Intelligence Unit sending a notification to the person with a link to access the specific document. The software must be constructed in such a way as to allow this. As a matter of good practice, even if a person already has access rights to see a piece of intelligence, if it has particular relevance to them, the Intelligence Unit should notify them of its existence.
- Sharing information with any other agency should be done only when there are agreements in place and structures to share the intelligence securely.

The main problem with mandated exchange is often getting the intelligence from one agency to another effectively and securely, particularly if it is of a sensitive nature.

6.38   External Dissemination

Disseminating intelligence outside the originating agency brings with it issues, additional to the internal issues, that must be considered before dissemination.

- Once intelligence is given out, it cannot be brought back.
- When intelligence is given to an external agency, de facto, the ownership of that intelligence is also given; the external agency has the power to do with that intelligence what they want. Well-constructed memorandums of understanding around intelligence exchange and adherence to them hopefully obviate many concerns, but the reality is that in tandem with passing the intelligence is passing the power to do with it as the recipient wills. On whatever form the agency uses to pass intelligence, there should be a section called "specified handling limitations" where the originating agency specifies any limitations on further dissemination. Any external agency that receives intelligence and uses it contrary to the express wishes of the provider is likely to receive little in the future and rightly so as this constitutes a breach of trust. The unfortunate thing is that every agency has idiots, and so often it is the agency idiot who ends up in possession of intelligence and uses it wrongly for their own ends.
- Sharing with any external agency should only be done through one specified point within the originating agency, to another

specified point of contact within the external agency. This provides an audit trail and holds both agencies accountable for their actions. Furthermore, it reduces the chances of intelligence that shouldn't have been passed being passed or where intelligence was meant to be passed but was passed to the *wrong* person. The idea that an officer calls his buddy in the other agency and they exchange intelligence is flawed and in some jurisdictions a criminal offense.

- Sharing intelligence with other government bodies should always be done through a memorandum of understandings. Most countries have legislation surrounding sharing data, and care needs to be taken about what is shared, with whom, and, most importantly, why.
- Sharing intelligence with the private sector should always be done at the highest level possible within the company or with a designated individual. As with any organization, there are likely to be internal conflicts and politics, and knowledge can be a powerful commodity. Passing intelligence relating to threats from crime and/or terrorism will be a regular event with many businesses in the private sector: for example, airlines and airports in relation to terrorism and shopping malls in relation to theft.
- If intelligence has to be passed to the private sector and the recipient company has many branches in different locations, the information should be shared with the head office and distributed by them. In a similar vein, if there are many LEAs that potentially could pass the intelligence, one LEA should be designated as being responsible for sharing that intelligence. This avoids different agencies telling representatives of the same company different versions of the same intelligence, showing law enforcement in a very unprofessional light.
- Sharing intelligence with individual citizens is most likely to occur in discharging an agency's legal obligations to protect that individual or their property, for example, when intelligence indicates there is a threat to the person's life. The assumption should always be made that people will share whatever they are told with "every man and his dog." While law enforcement can hope that the recipient will not tell anyone unnecessarily or ask the recipient not to tell anyone other than is necessary, the reality is that the majority will tell too many. Some people will go straight to the media as soon as the officer passing the intelligence is out of the door. Such intelligence should always be passed in written format that has been well considered beforehand and it should be delivered only by a supervisory rank.

6.39   Dissemination: Intelligence Recipients

Understanding who is likely to be receiving intelligence is important when establishing protocols and mechanisms for dissemination.
Intelligence can be disseminated to a broad spectrum of people including
the following:

- Senior management team. They will normally require strategic intelligence products. Senior management will often prefer written copies
  of documents, especially if the content is under discussion at a meeting they are attending. This practice should be kept to an absolute
  minimum, as it presents a security risk in relation to the documents
  being lost. To combat the risk of loss of documents, numbered copies
  should be given out against signature.
- An investigator in charge of a particular investigation. Sending a link
  or a notification of new intelligence in the repository will generally
  be sufficient, with no need to send either a hard copy or electronic
  copy. Care must be taken with the content of any notification as it is
  likely to be subject to any disclosure regime.
- An analyst who is in the process of creating additional intelligence
  products. As with the investigator, sending a link or a notification of
  new intelligence in the repository will generally be sufficient with no
  need to send either a hard copy or electronic copy.
- The person within the agency who has a legal obligation to take
  action on receipt of the intelligence. For example, intelligence that
  includes the threat to the life of a person living within the area for
  which they have responsibility (see Section 7.30, Chapter 7).
- The person within the agency who has the lead for the particular
  business area to which the intelligence refers and the expectation is
  that action will be taken upon receipt.
- All members of the agency are likely to receive various briefing
  products. Many agencies use electronic briefing, as this is the most
  effective and most secure method for distributing intelligence to
  large numbers of staff. This can be done easily through authorized
  access with the added benefit that accessing groups are already
  selected.
- Any external agency that has the lead in a particular field such as
  national security or computer crime.
- Other LEAs working on joint projects, such as in High Intensity
  Drug Trafficking Area task forces.
- Other LEAs to which the intelligence relates.
- Central and local governments.

- Private sector partners.
- Citizens.

Nothing in dissemination procedures should limit the dissemination of intelligence to any individual, when such dissemination is necessary to avoid imminent danger to life or property.

6.40   Exploitation

The exploitation point in the cycle is the point at which the intelligence gathered is put to use. While many in law enforcement view exploitation in terms of executive action, there are many other ways it can be used. In building an intelligence management system, the agency must put in place methods of recording when and how intelligence was used. If no such mechanism exists, then the agency cannot see if their strategies are being successful or to what extent. Moreover, it has the potential to cause division in the agency with those uninvolved in intelligence failing to recognize the benefits and those involved in intelligence feeling their efforts go unrecognized.

The following lists a number of ways that intelligence products can be used:

- Executive action. For example, arrests, searches, and seizures.
- Strategic planning.
- Problem-oriented policing. Intelligence can be shared with partner agencies to develop a more comprehensive strategy to address the problem.
- Crime prevention strategies.
- Officer safety.
- Threat advisories to citizens, government, and the private sector.

The agency should keep a record of each time intelligence has been exploited and in what way it was used.

6.41   Review

Review is the stage in the cycle where the effectiveness of the intelligence produced is reviewed. Part of this review will come from the intelligence customers, and the other part will come from within the intelligence management system. In reviewing intelligence, it is not always easy to separate its intrinsic worth from the overall worth of the investigation or strategy to which it relates. The most critical question to those involved in intelligence management should be, "How well did we meet the intelligence requirements?" From this, those involved can learn what works, what did not, and why.

One way to review intelligence is to include a feedback loop with each product that is disseminated. This places an onus on the customer to explain what they have done with that product, and this feedback can then be sent back, ultimately to the origin of the information from which the product stemmed. An additional benefit of the review process is that any failings in the functioning of the intelligence management system can become apparent.

6.42   Continuation

The final step in the intelligence cycle is a return to the setting of the priorities or to a redefining of the intelligence requirements. It should be noted that although there are a number of stages identified within the intelligence cycle model, the delineation between each stage is not definitive. While processing the information, the Intelligence Unit is likely to identify intelligence gaps and the intelligence requirements may have to be revisited to address these. In a similar vein, the analyst may identify previously unidentified connections and the collection plan may have to be revisited to address these. In addition, intelligence obtained or events on the ground may necessitate a change in the agency's priorities. Exploitation of one intelligence product may lead to the necessity to gather other intelligence or may create the opportunity for further collection. Generally speaking, there is nothing to prevent any stage from being revisited before advancement to the next, and such is the nature of operational law enforcement that these fluctuations may occur with great rapidity.

6.43   Conclusion

This chapter has explored the concept of intelligence management using the intelligence cycle as a model to help understand what occurs. It has outlined a theoretical framework on which to build an effective intelligence management system for LEAs. The intelligence cycle is a model and as such is intended only as a map. And just as having a map does not give you the ability to drive from A to B, it does help! Now that we have that map, we can start to drill down into the practicalities of creating such a system and to identify some of the problems likely to be encountered.

References

Association of Chief Police Officers (ACPO) (2005) *Guidance on the National Intelligence Mode*. U.K: Centre for Policing Excellence (Centrex).

Association of Chief Police Officers (ACPO) (2010) *Guidance on the Management of Police Information*. 2nd ed. U.K: National Police Improvement Agency.

Commission on Accreditation of Law Enforcement Agencies (CALEA) (2002) *Standards for Law Enforcement Accreditation, Standard 51.1 Criminal Intelligence*. Washington DC: Commission on Accreditation of Law Enforcement Agencies.

Federal Bureau of Investigation (FBI) (2012) Intelligence cycle. Available at: http//www .fbi.gov/about-us/intelligence/intelligcence-cycle (accessed April 2012).

Fowler, R.D. (2011) Dissemination in criminal intelligence. In: Wright, R., Morehouse, B., Peterson, M.B. and Palmieri, L. Eds. *Criminal Intelligence for the 21st Century: A Guide for Intelligence Professionals*. Sacramento, CA; Richmond, VA: Law Enforcement Intelligence Units (LEIU); International Association of Law Enforcement Intelligence Analysts (IALEIA).

Harfield, C. and Harfield, K. (2008) *Intelligence: Investigation Community and Partnership*. Oxford: Oxford University Press.

International Association of Chiefs of Police (IACP) (2002) *Criminal Intelligence Sharing: A National Plan for Intelligence-Led Policing at the Local, State and Federal Level*. Available at: http://www.ncirc.gov/documents/public/supplementaries/intel_sharing_report.pdf (accessed December 2012).

McDowell, D. (2009) *Strategic Intelligence: A Handbook for Practitioners, Managers, and Users*. Lanham, MD: Scarecrow Press, Inc.

Milne, B. and Bull, R. (2006) Interviewing victims of crime, including children and people with intellectual disabilities. In: Kebell, M.R. and Davies, G.M. Eds. *Practical Psychology for Forensic Investigations*. Chichester: John Wiley and Sons.

Ratcliffe, J.H. (In press) *Intelligence Led Policing: Anticipating Risk and Influencing Action*. To be published by the International Association of Law Enforcement Intelligence Analysts. Available at: http://jratcliffe.net/papers/Ratcliffe%20(draft)%20ILP-Anticipating%20risk%20and%20influencing%20action.pdf (accessed September 2012).

Ratcliffe, J.H. and U.S. Department of Justice Office of Community Oriented Policing Services (2007) *Integrated Intelligence and Crime Analysis: Enhanced Information Management for Law Enforcement Leaders*. Washington, DC: Police Foundation.

Standing Committee on Crime and Criminal Intelligence (SCOCCI) (1997) *Guiding Principles for Law Enforcement Intelligence*. Australia: SCOCCI.

Turner, M.A. (2006) *Why Secret Intelligence Fails*. Washington, DC: Potomac Books.

Building an Intelligence Management System

7

... we're pretty much making it up as we go along, and half the time we're not even certain what the law is, so it can get interesting.

Commander Samuel Vimes, Ankh Morpork City Watch[*]

7.1 Introduction

Regardless of how much guidance is put out to agencies, and the numerous benefits that have been expounded with regard to taking a more proactive approach to gathering and exploiting intelligence, the inability of many agencies and their members to change to meet evolving circumstances means that they continue to cling to the outdated methods of the past. As the old adage says, you only get out of it what you put into it. Every agency needs mechanisms to lawfully collect information for intelligence purposes, to process that information as it is received, to integrate and evaluate it, and then to lodge the intelligence that is produced in an intelligence repository. The information received will originate in many different places, and processes must be established to deal with these varied circumstances. Intelligence must be created and reposited against agreed criteria and in a standardized way. This chapter builds on the framework outlined in Chapter 6 on the intelligence cycle. There are four parts. The first part deals with the practicalities and benefits of building an effective intelligence management system. This involves drilling down into what is required and how to build a system. The second part puts the "meat on the bones" of the newly created system, identifying further steps that need to be taken and considerations to be made. The third part discusses the computerization of the system, and the final part looks at security implications. While it is impossible to outline every possible step that needs to be taken to create an effective system, the chapter provides clear indication of the volume of work that needs to be undertaken and the depths that need to be gone to.

---

[*] From the book *Feet of Clay* by Terry Pratchett (1996), published by Harper Collins Publishers.

7.2   Starting the Journey

Having discussed much of the theory surrounding intelligence management, we now progress to the practical aspects of creating an effective intelligence management system. Undoubtedly, undertaking such a proposition is not without difficulties, but the benefits for the agency will rapidly become apparent. What should be recognized at the outset of reengineering intelligence management within an agency is that it should not be viewed as a criticism of what has gone before, but merely as a better way of doing things. There was nothing wrong with the horse and cart but with the opportunities that were presented by the motor vehicle, progress was inevitable.* A statement of this position can help ease the path to the new, avoiding what can be significant backlash from those comfortable in the old ways. Much of what will be suggested in the forthcoming chapters is not new; it is merely a more effective way of achieving what law enforcement officers want to achieve. The end goal has not changed, merely the pathway there. We are not trying to go somewhere different; instead, we are just trying to find a better way of getting there. As the author Henry Miller writes, "One's destination is never a place but a new way of seeing things."

7.3   Identifying the Problems

On examination of the methods that a law enforcement agency (LEA) uses in managing intelligence, it is common to find many instances of what can only be described as bad practice. These include the following:

- Many agencies are still using "stand-alone" computers for certain parts of their business, including to manage covert processes, or to hold certain types of information. This is done for a number of reasons. There often exists the genuine belief that a stand-alone computer, unconnected to any network and accessible by only a few, is more secure than a networked system and in intelligence work, security is a key factor: for example, undercover policing. While the security concerns are understandable, the thought process in selecting a stand-alone solution is flawed from two perspectives: namely, only a limited few can see the contents of a stand-alone computer, and there are usually severe limitations on the functionality of the software used. These limitations include the fact that when information is entered into a stand-alone system, it is never shared or that which is to be shared has to be

---

* Given the number of people killed by motor vehicles each year and the destruction caused by vehicle pollution, the notion of progress is open to some debate.

expensively rekeyed into another system. Furthermore, where software is specifically built for a particular agency, the member instigating the software has it built to suit their particular preferences. Unfortunately, while this may sound like a great idea, what often happens is the person who had it built to their preferences moves on, leaving a product that only they liked and/or understood, and those that are left have a tool that has limited usefulness. Any person competent with computers can create an Excel spreadsheet with a few hyperlinks, but this does not mean they have built a software program. Good software is expensive to design and takes considerable time. However, of greatest concern is the fact that it is a myth that a stand-alone computer is secure. At the end of the day, if someone really wants the contents of a stand-alone computer, it is easier to lift the whole computer and walk out the door with it, as opposed to when the material is loaded onto a secure server.

- Some agencies are still using paper to manage many of their information-gathering processes, including the financial management for operations.* Failure to use the available technology wastes resources and leads to numerous and varied risks not being managed properly.

- Some agencies still allow members to create their own "folders" accessible only by that member, while others may allow members to keep personal paper records of events relating to information collection or storage. This has the potential to create significant problems for the agency. Often, no one other than the member creating those files knows those records exist, and no one else knows what they contain. The potential for information to be lost is huge, disclosure is impossible, and there often arises questions as to why the member creating those files is keeping them hidden. There is always the temptation for a member to keep records or details of an event "just in case they might need it." Such records are often kept as a result of internal disputes or wrongdoing that is being covered up. Some members have even been known to keep material relating to work on their personal computers (PCs) or in their homes. The agency should put in place procedures that clearly state where all records are to be kept and where they will not be kept and rigorously enforce these rules. The agency also needs to understand why it is happening as often as it is; surely the agency will see that it will be a result of its failing to create structures that are effective and user-friendly.

- Needless copying of intelligence-related documents. Many people like to have a paper copy of something they are reading—this is understandable. However, in intelligence management, this carries

---

* Hello—it is the twenty-first century! The guy putting tires on your car uses a computer to make his work easier. What century are you living in?

risks with it. The fact that copies of records are printed increases the risk that they may be lost or all too easily handed to those not entitled to have them. If the agency has an effective intelligence management system, only a limited number of staff should have print privileges, and there should be strict guidance as to when documents may be printed off and how they will then be handled and subsequently destroyed. A further stimulus for curtailing printing is a cost analysis that will identify just how much money is being wasted by the agency with needless printing.

- Information-gathering processes have often been allowed to evolve within an agency with no defined structure to each process. Alternatively processes have been developed that are entirely independent of each other. When nothing joins up, time is wasted, and lives are put in danger.
- A failure to recognize the risks the agency is running. Few agencies have an idea of the real cost of compromising assets and therefore continue to run a level of risk tolerance that they only realize as unacceptable when it is being pointed out to them in a lawsuit.* This type of neglect not only harms an agency but also harms every other LEA. It discourages people from providing information, shows law enforcement as being incompetent, and can end up costing taxpayers considerable sums of money in subsequent lawsuits. Furthermore, it compromises methodology that many other agencies rely on. One poor piece of work by a solitary agency can bring the proverbial house of cards down for many other agencies.

7.4   Looking Again

As we have already alluded to, one of the biggest problems is admitting that things might be wrong in the first place. This will be hard to accept at all levels of the agency, and even mentioning the fact that things might need changing will often be met by significant hostility. However, unless an agency has built a structured intelligence management system that has been the subject of continual review since its inception, then it is likely that the agency will benefit from a review of how they are managing intelligence. The nature of the law enforcement business means that the only time an agency is likely to

---

* An all too tragic example of a poor (or nonexistent?) system at work occurred in 2007 and involved the Tallahassee Police Department and a young informant Rachael Hoffman (1984–2008). The mismanagement of this young woman resulted in her death, a $2.6 million lawsuit, and change in legislation for every police agency in the state of Florida.

review its processes is when it has been caught metaphorically with "its pants down" and the public is asking "What the hell is going on?"

Reviewing how things are being done is common business practice and is often referred to as business reengineering. Business reengineering is used to redesign how an organization works to improve efficiency and effectiveness, often with the additional benefit of cost reduction. It is necessary in any business to keep up with changing circumstances, and progression is critical to running a successful business. Hammer and Champy (1993), two of the leading proponents of reengineering, write as follows:

> Reengineering is the fundamental rethinking and redesign of business processes to achieve dramatic improvements in critical, contemporary measures of performance, such as cost, quality, service and speed.

Successful reengineering can involve radical changes in how a business operates. Reengineering starts with identifying the desired outcome and working step-by-step to establish the processes that can bring about that outcome. It needs to be vision led by upper management and involves not only changing processes but also attitudes and behaviors of staff. When attempting such change, one will often be met with complacency and resistance and an often genuine fear of what the implementation of such new methods will mean for those involved.

The International Standards Organization (ISO) (2005) has identified how to evaluate any management system. It necessitates asking four questions in relation to every process that forms part of the management system. The questions are identified below in quotations, with supplementary questions applicable to intelligence management:

1. "Is the process identified and appropriately defined?" Can everyone within the agency see clearly what must be done under a given set of circumstances?
2. "Are responsibilities assigned?" Who has specific responsibility for each action within the process? Is it clear to all involved? Can individuals be held accountable if there is a failure?
3. "Are the procedures implemented and maintained?" Are there comprehensive and joined-up procedures for each of the processes involved and are these regularly updated?
4. "Is the process effective in achieving the required results?" Does each process work effectively and consistently? Do things happen by design or chance? Are all the processes interlinked, creating a fully functioning system?

One of the easiest ways to establish if an agency's intelligence management system is up to scratch is to select *any* process where information of a potential intelligence value enters the agency. The second step is to examine that process against the questions asked above and establish if that process would be deemed as effective if checked by external auditors. The third step is to do the same with each potential avenue for intelligence and then examine how the intelligence products created from this information would be disseminated both internally and externally to law enforcement partners. Examining the process from the perspective of an external auditor assists in avoiding a defensive and self-justifying attitude and facilitates more critical scrutiny.

Undertaking such a review is not easy for many reasons. The problem with turning over a rock is that you cannot know what is going to crawl out, but all too often it is the knowledge of what is likely to "crawl out" that has made damned sure that no one has turned over the rock up to now. If there was an in-depth examination of any agency's intelligence management systems, at least some of the following will be uncovered:

- Significant waste of resources including duplication of work, double keying of records, and the limited exploitation of intelligence that has been obtained.
- Many gaps and inconsistencies in the flow of information to intelligence and the subsequent dissemination of that intelligence. Vital intelligence does not get where it needs to go.
- "Black holes." Referring to the concept in astronomy of a black hole, where gravity prevents anything from escaping including light, many agencies would be surprised to find how much information of intelligence value is "hidden" in various desks, cupboards, stores, and stand-alone computers. It is not uncommon for individual officers or sections to "file" material where it will never again see the light of day. Often this is done with no thought whatsoever, it being just the social norm. This is clear evidence that the individual process for that business area or the system, as a whole, is broken. An effective process or system makes these occurrences rarer and easier to detect before they get out of control.
- "Too difficult to deal with" trays. Law enforcement officers are extremely inventive at finding ways to "file" away information that they do not know how to deal with or cannot be bothered dealing with. "I will just file that in the 'too difficult to deal with' tray, where my successor will probably find it, but that will be long after I am gone."
- Corruption of various shades.
- Poor security of records creating threats to the lives of citizens and members and embarrassment and lawsuits for the agency.
- Processes not reaching necessary legal or evidential standards thus jeopardizing investigations.

- Staff who resent inquiry into their work practices.
- Frustrated staff. Good people resent having to work in bad systems.

What will also be found are as follows:

- Staff wanting to make changes that will improve how intelligence is managed.
- Opportunities to improve how the agency works to the benefit of citizens.
- Opportunities for self-development. This can be a strong motivator for individuals who are prepared to reengineer the agency's processes and system.

7.5   Why the Agency Needs a System

There will always be members who question the benefit in making changes in how an agency should manage intelligence, failing to see the need to undertake such a project. Common attitudes found include the following:

- *Lack of understanding at a senior management level.* If the people at the top do not understand they have a problem, they are very unlikely to make available the resources to make change happen.
- *Selfishness and empire-building.* All too often it suits certain people not to make change. The way things are at present allows them to be emperor in their empire. Change will remove their power and may expose failures in how they have been operating.
- *Lack of thought.* No one has actually ever thought that what they are doing might not be efficient.
- *Make-do approach.* This attitude is prevalent in law enforcement and very understandable, given that people are by nature lazy and inclined where possible to take the easiest route. This is about accepting less than can be achieved. It is about being resigned to a state far from the one that is desired. It is about knowing winter is coming but not really caring enough to make preparations in the fall. It is lacking in both imagination and motivation. Often it can be used as a cover to mask other attitudes: "If we need to pass information we will make do with the telephone." (Read into this the underlying theme of having control.) "We will make do with a standalone computer." (Read "selfishness" for no one else will see what they have.) "We will make do with handwritten records." (Read "I don't want others to know what I am doing!")

Criticisms of "broken" intelligence management systems are all too common. Highlighting shortcomings in connectivity and analysis in U.S. law enforcement, Ratcliffe and the U.S. Department of Justice Office of Community Oriented Policing Services (2007), remark,

> Even with the introduction of fusion centers in the U.S., few managers have analysts that are tied into local networks that enable police leadership to access intelligence on the crime picture in neighboring jurisdictions. Internally, agencies that have only crime analysts often lack a detailed understanding of recidivist individuals and gangs and their motivations, while agencies that have only intelligence analysis get detailed information on individuals and networks but little indication of the crime context in which these people operate.

Advocating the use of agency-wide intelligence management, renowned English Barrister Michael Mansfield in his summation at the inquiry into the police handling of the murder of Stephen Lawrence (MacPherson 1999:11055) stated,

> In summary, there plainly has to be a compendious and effective local intelligence gathering operation in existence.... The information itself should be categorized in such a way that it can be called up by reference to name, or description, or address, or offences, or modus operandi or vehicle or associates. Computerization must clearly have made this possible for the future.

Of particular interest should be Mansfield's comment with regard to computerization. Arguably, Mansfield was articulating the public view as to expectations of behavior in law enforcement. Given that his comments were made in 1998, the question could be asked as to how any agency can expect to escape criticism if they are still using paper-based systems.

In discussing what many involved in intelligence may initially dismiss as errors made by individuals, Cooper (2005) highlights that such occurrences are likely to be indicators of a much deeper problem, one that is all too relevant in intelligence management and one that requires in-depth examination:

> ...a series of "idiosyncratic" errors by individuals and small groups within an organization are, however, more likely to be symptoms than root causes, A pattern of repeated errors is often a signal of seriously dysfunctional methods—fundamental and systematic failures of procedures and processes throughout an organization. From this perspective, the proximate causes of the failures identified in both the report of the 9/11 Commission and the SSCI report on Iraqi WMD hardly appear to be convincing root causes of these recent intelligence failures. A more accurate diagnosis of the sources of our intelligence shortcomings requires a deeper and more thoughtful analysis of why organizations make mistakes.

Continuing his critique, Cooper comments on how habits within an agency have a way of developing into what he refers to as "rigid routines," ways of doing business that give the superficial appearance of being satisfactory. Comparing the failure of dinosaurs to adapt to a changing environment, he highlights the potential risks that are created by continuing with such practices:

> Not unexpectedly, these routines "work" for the specific conditions they were developed to address. They rarely perform well for off-design conditions, however, and, often, the better they work for the design conditions, the more narrow the set of conditions for which they are appropriate. Paradoxically, the better they work, and, therefore, the more efficient the organization at its routine tasks, the greater the danger that the organization will fail to be sensitive to its environment and changes occurring there. As with the dinosaurs, scores of major American corporations have fallen victim to this pattern of "over adaptation" and "change blindness." The Intelligence Community runs the same risk.

Some of the benefits of a purpose-built intelligence management system are as follows:

- It allows members to find what they need to know and when they need to know it. Intelligence is stored in one central repository, where access can be regulated. This is a major problem for law enforcement, and it is one of the primary failings that Michael Mansfield brought to attention in the previously mentioned Lawrence inquiry.
- It reduces conflict within investigations and covert operations.
- It provides management with timely and accurate intelligence on which to make defendable decisions.
- It reduces duplication of work and wasting of resources.
- It provides standardized and fully accountable means of gathering and managing intelligence ensuring that such activities are done in a lawful manner.
- It ensures that the agency is working as a team against an agreed set of goals as opposed to individuals and individual units working to their own agendas.
- It maximizes quantity and quality of intelligence produced and allows it to be used for the benefit of the whole agency and other partner agencies.

7.6 Defining System and Process

Throughout this book, we refer to the intelligence management "system" and also to various "processes." The words "system" and "process" are often used interchangeably, but the intention here is to draw a clear distinction between them. Perhaps the easiest way to understand the difference is to remember that "processes are components of a system, and it takes the whole system to produce the desired result." The system is a mechanism that links and binds the various processes together. Identifying, understanding, and managing interrelated processes and the system as a whole contribute to the organization's effectiveness and efficiency in achieving its objectives.

A simple illustration of a system is in the manufacturing of a car. There are many diferent processes to create and fit the different parts of that car. The car assembly system incorporates all aspects of these from acquiring the raw materials to when the end product rolls off the assembly line. However, manufacturing a car is not just about the construction; it is about the design before production, the sales, and the support that follows. There will be a manager and workers for each separate construction process and a manager and workers to ensure that the whole system works sequentially and effectively. So it is with an intellgience management system. The intellgience management system produces intelligence, but it needs to follow a design set by the agency. Once intelligence has been produced, it needs to be provided to customers, feedback gained from them, and further support provided. Intelligence management is not just about producing intelligence; it is about producing the right intelligence for the customer and providing continuing support for the customer. This is what an agency's intelligence management system must be built to achieve.

Understanding the breadth of functioning that is required, we can now define an intelligence management system as "a complete set of interlinked processes aimed at ensuring that the provision of intelligence to assist in discharging a LEA's priorities." Using this definition, we can start to explore some of the other steps an agency needs to take in building such a system.

Continuing with the manufacturing analogy, the intelligence management system assembles intelligence products, but this is possible only because of a number of processes contained within it such as the analytical process, the process for collecting information from undercover officers, and the process of evaluating information. Different people will be involved in working in each process, with a different manager ensuring that a process works effectively to produce the desired results in a safe and effective manner. These end results are then fed into the intelligence management system.

People working in the different processes should have a good understanding of the overall system, with managers of processes needing to know how and where their process interacts with the whole system. Failure in any process can cause damage to the whole system. For example, the poor management of a human source may produce incorrect information that is then processed into a flawed intelligence report on which an evidence-gathering search is based. The defense lawyer later undermines how the information was gathered for the search warrant and the whole prosecution case is lost, with attendant criticsm of the LEA. In this case, because the collection process was not managed properly, regardless of what was done at a later stage, everything was bound to fail. If the process for fitting brakes in a car fails, the whole car will be lost! This can be summed up as "process failure—system failure."

Those managing processes must ensure that all aspects of each process are working effectively and that they are producing the requested outputs to a suitable standard. The person responsible for managing the intelligence management sytem must ensure that the interactions between all processes work effectively. This is one reason why there must be a senior officer within the agency who has overall responsibility for all intelligence management. This officer is known as the "senior responsible officer." The senior responsible officer must be in a position to direct changes in processes across the entire agency if such change becomes necessary. In car manufacturing, you cannot have the manager in charge of making the car brakes telling the Chief executive officer of the car company that the way they make car brakes is "not changing." Unfortunately, it is not uncommon for some working in specialist processes in intelligence management to try and dictate to others, including the Chief, how their aspect of work will be carried out. "I am the undercover expert; you can't tell me to change how I am doing things."

The intelligence management system that is suggested here is a system composed of regularly interacting processes or groups of processes, each of which has the potential to impact the other. Constructing such a system may appear a daunting task, but it is one that can be achieved if sufficient thought and effort is put into it. Unfortunately, the very nature of law enforcement and the history of intelligence management in law enforcement mean that sometimes it is first necessary to undo what was created in the past before a new and bettter process or system can be implemented. If the desired outcome is an effective intelligence management system, then each process that contributes to that system must be examined to establish if it is fit for purpose and/or how it can be improved. It is rare indeed to find any process that does not require ongoing maintenance and that cannot benefit from some measure to make it more robust or effective.

7.7 Management Leadership

When attempting to put in place any intelligence management system, one of the first problems likely to be encountered is convincing the senior management team of the need to create a new intelligence system or to change the existing intelligence system. Unless there have already been negative consequences for the agency as a result of poor intelligence, management are unlikely to perceive they have a problem and therefore reluctant to make the investment in change. Even when one convinces management of the need for change, getting adequate resources to facilitate the change becomes the next problem. Ultimately, an effective intelligence management system will save the agency money, but it is not always easy to convince the purse holder of this.

If management does not buy into the idea of building an agency-wide system, each group of officers or sub-branch will create their own processes, using whatever resources they have at hand, addressing whatever their specific requirements are. This will be done with little consideration for the needs of others within the agency, or the agency as a whole, let alone addressing the needs of partner agencies or national requirements. Allowing units to build a process in isolation has a number of consequences:

- Nothing joins up, and the agency then has to spend more if it later want things joined up. While there may be nothing inherently wrong with any process created by the experts in a business area, the fact that it is not joined to the rest of the agency is fundamentally flawed.
- Each process is built to different standards in terms of both performance and agency regulation.
- Each process will be built with limited imagination. Most projects benefit from the creativity that others, external to the process, can provide. When we are caught up in the middle of something, our views of it lose objectivity, and we become blind to opportunities for improvement.
- Waste in resources spent on developmental costs.

7.8   Starting to Build

Starting to build an intelligence management system is very similar to starting any piece of work, and measures include the following:

- A statement from the senior responsible officer outlining the intention to review the intelligence management system and any parameters in regard to that review.
- The appointment of a "program" management board to oversee and direct the program of work. This will normally be composed of three to four members of the agency, the majority of whom will have direct involvement in the business area. This group will identify the various "projects" that need to be undertaken to complete the program.
- The appointment of project managers for each identified project. The project manager will be responsible for making sure each project is completed in a timely and efficient manner.

- The early involvement of the agency's IT department. IT forms a critical part of any intelligence management system, and specialist knowledge of what is available and what can be done should be sought from the outset.
- The involvement of staff from different backgrounds to maximize knowledge available and avoid problems caused by such mind-sets as groupthink.
- Members of the agency must be engaged from the beginning because if they have no input in building the system, they will feel alienated from it. Furthermore, they are likely to resist any changes. Antagonism is often a result of an inability to reconcile the methods used in the past with what is required now and in the future. Internalizing that what was done in the past was wrong leads to the feeling of being criticized, and this leads to resentment of those involved in creating the new system. This is often compounded by a reluctance to share knowledge with others perceiving they will be giving up their power. To overcome these misplaced perceptions, the intelligence management system must provide clear benefits for all.

There are many techniques that can be used to aid in the development of an intelligence management system:

- *Questionnaires.* A good way of starting is to ask different parts of the agency what their problems are and what they would want in an ideal world. Such questionnaires should start with fairly open questions and then be tailored to elicit more specific information.
- *Workshops.* Workshops are a way to formalize brainstorming. At the end of each workshop, there should be a clear record of what was achieved during the session. Workshops should not be used as mere talking shops or allowed to deteriorate into destructive discourse. Workshops are time- and resource-intensive and often fail to achieve the desired results because of the lack of a "neutral" facilitator. While it is necessary and effective for key players from many departments within the agency to be involved in workshops to develop a system, one major hurdle that is encountered is that it can be very difficult for them to contribute their knowledge to such discussions without that knowledge being accompanied by their personal agenda, their values, and unfortunately their egos. Such is the reality of life, that if you put a group of opinionated, knowledgeable individuals into a room to discuss something of importance to them, the possibility of destructive conflict is high. One way to minimize this is through the use of a facilitator to chair these workshops, but finding someone within the agency to facilitate such a meeting can be difficult, because that person can be

"tainted" by their history or their perceived agenda. One solution is to use a facilitator from outside the agency. An independent facilitator has no stake in the outcomes and this helps create a more neutral environment, where each attendee is facilitated in articulating their concerns without personalities being allowed to dominate. The neutrality of the facilitator helps modify behavior that may tend to be inappropriate when tension rises. A competent facilitator will do the following:

- Have clarity with regard to what is to be achieved in the workshop and a plan for achieving it within the agreed timescale.
- Create a neutral environment and put all the attendees at ease.
- Provide clear explanation of the format of the session.
- Give each attendee an appropriate amount of time to articulate their issues and make sure that each attendee remains involved.
- Clearly identify points where there is agreement and where there is disagreement, and keep a record of all relevant matters. (Note: A trained minute taker is often of significant benefit to assist the facilitator.)
- Remain calm when conflict arises, identifying and reducing conflict.
- Deal with inappropriate or personal comments.
- Keep the group focused and motivated with regard to the task at hand.
- Bring to the surface difficult issues and help others to do so.
- Actively listen to all participants and take cognizance of the various personality types attending.
- Use appropriate questioning skills to elicit and confirm information.

- *Working groups.* There is a need to get the right staff on board; staff that have both the knowledge to make change happen and the willingness to drive that change. Setting up working groups for each project can move things rapidly forward, if the right people are involved.
- *Using a consultant.* There are many reasons an agency may choose to hire a consultant to develop an intelligence system. These include the following:
  - Depth and breadth of knowledge
  - Cost-effectiveness
  - The ability to reduce internal conflict with regard to change by depersonalizing it

If agency does hire a consultant, a few things should be borne in mind:

- Checks need to be done to gauge both the depth and breadth of their knowledge. Unfortunately, there are many self-styled consultants who have a very limited depth of expertise or who lack sufficient breadth of expertise to consider all the aspects of setting up an intelligence management system. A good balance of practical experience of the craft should be present, not limited to one agency type or geographical area, and this practical experience should be accompanied by relevant training and education. All this should be evidenced before engagement. Furthermore, the consultant needs to be aware of more general issues surrounding such matters as project management and procurement, as these attributes will greatly assist in the overall smooth running of the project.

- The agency needs to put in place measures to capture the consultant's knowledge while they are present. Failure to do so means that the agency is reducing the benefit they could get from their investment.
- Consultants are often retired law enforcement officers and know enough to bluff knowledge but can add little other than their opinions.
- Be wary of costs. Be conscious of perpetuating a gravy train, where the consultant identifies more and more needs while at the same time offering themselves as a solution.
- Be wary of costs. Consultants hired through employment companies often cost twice what the consultant themselves charges with the employment company taking a large piece of the pie with no added benefits for the service.
- Be wary of costs. Some consultants are all too ready to milk the golden cow dry by submitting extortionate "expense" claims!

7.9 Creating a System

Even if the desire exists, there often remains uncertainty as to how to start to construct the processes necessary for an effective intelligence management system. Creating any management system is governed by a number of general principles identified by the ISO. These principles are valid regardless of the nature of the business environment; as the International Standards Organization (2008) states, "Requirements for quality management systems are generic and applicable to organizations in any industry or economic sector regardless of the offered product category." Highlighting that the adoption of a system should be "a strategic decision of an organization," the document articulates the requirements for building a management system (quotations as indicated):

- Determine the processes needed for the management system and their application throughout the agency. For the system to function effectively, the agency "has to identify and manage numerous linked activities."

- Establish the "processes necessary to deliver results in accordance with customer requirements and the organization's policies."
- "Determine the sequence and interaction of these processes." Recognizing that output from one process directly forms the input to a sequential process, management must ensure not just the effectiveness of each process but the linkage between the various processes.
- "Ensure the availability of resources necessary to support the operation and monitoring of these processes."
- "Implement actions necessary to achieve planned results and continual improvement of these processes."

Often there can be a problem of translating concepts into realities. The concept of building an entire intelligence management system may appear simple to many, but when one starts to drill down into the details, the complexities become more apparent. The agency has to work out the order in which different processes are carried out and how they relate to one another. Often we will think that what is required in a process is obvious and then discover as we construct it that running in tandem with it is another process that directly conflicts with it.

The agency needs to detail the specific results they expect each process to produce, how these processes will function; for example, What will an undercover operation produce in terms of intelligence? How will that information be processed? In what format will it come through to those who need it? Are there legal considerations? What if …? Answering each of these questions leads to more questions and this must be done for each process. The system must be capable of effortlessly exchanging intelligence horizontally across the agency and upward and downward through the agency. Given the number of processes that need to be interlinked, constructing such a system is not easy. As with the construction of anything, there are tools that will help. Two such tools are as follows:

- Process builders
- System testers

7.10 Process Builders

Simply put, process builders are written examples of scenarios likely to be encountered in real life for which one is attempting to build a standardized process. They answer the question "How …?" For example: If we are constructing the information-submission process for patrol officers, a scenario they are likely to encounter is the "stop/check" of a person acting suspiciously. The question to be answered is, "How does an officer submit such details so that the information can be captured, examined, and a decision made as to what should happen to that piece of information?" Process builders are based on real-life occurrences. The agency starts with the most simple of possible scenarios and builds through increasingly complex scenarios with each new process builder creating a stem from which a number of branches can grow. The stem is merely a basic scenario, and the branches are various possible twists or adaptations to that stem, each of which is likely to occur and having the potential to need further adaptations to the process or the overall system. In using process builders, the agency is starting from scratch. If attempts are made to integrate with the existing setup, it will not work. Some terminology may be borrowed and some processes may remain very similar but all must be reexamined. As each builder is completed, the rules and terminology for the process evolve. The idea is to keep both of these as simple as possible. The same words or terminology *cannot* be used for two different functions. To design a basic information-submission process, the agency will probably need 30 or 40 different process builders each increasing in complexity. A working group of suitably experienced members are required to design each process and must include a trained policy/procedure writer, as this person should have the experience in creating structures and avoiding ambiguities. Building any process can be frustrating, because the authoring of process-builders can be very time-consuming. A good place to start is with uniform patrol submissions, as these are often relatively simple. A lexicon of standard terminology can also be established as far as possible before commencing, although this in itself can take some discussion. This lexicon includes definitions such as that for "information" and "intelligence" and for such things as the "Intelligence Unit" and where intelligence will be stored (i.e., "intelligence repository"). Although such definitions and terminology have all been included in this book, the agency may wish to design its own. This is all part of building a process. Figure 7.1 illustrates a process builder. The typing shows what is to be included and the writing gives an example. Each process builder works sequentially. If one process builder further along in the sequence causes changes in what has already been established, it necessitates a return to the earlier process builders and a reworking of everything from that point on.

The processes outlined in Chapter 6 for information submissions have been constructed using process builders. While the information submissions suggested there are of a general nature, they will work for the vast majority of agencies. Separate processes must be established for all aspects of the intelligence management system. Such processes include the following:

- Information submission
- Evaluation, collation, and repositing
- Analysis
- Undercover operation
- Human source management

Process Builder	
Process: Intelligence Submission Stem Number: 1	
Stem Details	State details of scenario and what has to be achieved Constable Hanks observes John Alpha from Anytown acting suspiciously at the rear of an electric store in High Street Anytown at 4am. Alpha is unknown. Create basic submission.
Process	Insert the process designed here:
Branch 1:	How can the theme of this builder change Alpha is a known criminal Update a record
Process:	Insert the second process designed here if first does not accommodate the change in circumstances:
Branch 2:	What other change in circumstances may there be? There have been a number of burglaries in High Street Anytown Disseminate to other department
Process:	Insert the third process designed here if previous does not accommodate the change in circumstances:
System Rules Established	State the system rules you have now identified
Terminology	Write in new terminology established:
System Conflicts Identified [refer by Stem Number]	Are there conflicts with any previous stems? (If we go back to them and redo all from there.)
Notes:	Any additional comment:

Figure 7.1 An illustration of a process builder.

- Surveillance operations
- Interception of communications
- Dissemination (internally and externally)
- Handling of threats (to citizens, businesses, officers, etc.)
- Handling "classified" material

- Disclosure relating to intelligence
- Auditing
- Internal investigation access and use

All these processes must use standardized terminology and must be connected. It should be noted that even the words used in the preceding list must be clarified by the agency in the process building stage. If everything is disconnected, the agency does not have an intelligence management system. When constructing such processes, it must be borne in mind that the intention should be that the end result will be computerized. An idea of what is in the marketplace is worth establishing before commencing to design each process. However, as we will explore later in Section 7.33, it is up to the agency to dictate the process, not an IT company.

Once the working group has established processes for all aspects of the intelligence management system, then that system has to be tested.

7.11 System Testers

System testers are exactly what the name implies. They are scenarios designed to test if the system functions as it was designed to do. System testers are required for each process. For example, just because the undercover process works all the way through, it cannot be assumed that the surveillance process will work properly. The easiest way to test the system is to take a large number of real-life scenarios and push them through the system, from start to finish. For example, if a month previously a human source brought in information on a vehicle being used by a criminal, the system can be tested by taking this piece of information and checking how it would be managed from start to finish as it progresses through the system. The final checks will include checking did it get where it was meant to go in the desired format and in a reasonable time period. The system should be tested numerous times with ever increasingly awkward scenarios, particularly if the agency is intending to use computerization. It is much better to iron out problems and have the business processes established before investing in the IT.

7.12 Fundamentals

Regardless of size of the agency, the fundamental principles of intelligence management remain the same namely:

- The agency must have comprehensive procedures for all aspects of intelligence management.
- All intelligence must be contained in a central repository.

- All intelligence should be submitted to that repository in a standard format.
- The most common (and simplest) product stored in the repository will be an intelligence report. An intelligence report comprises one or more pieces of processed information.
- All documents within the intelligence management system should have a unique reference number (URN).
- All entities within that system must be categorized and have URNs.
- Documents should always be linked to entities.
- The intelligence repository will have a significant number of access levels with the more sensitive products being stored at the higher levels.
- A strict regime must surround access control to the computerized system, and there must be a comprehensive auditing facility built in.

7.13   Infrastructure

When constructing the system, the agency must identify the infrastructure that will be required. This includes the following:

- Buildings, office space, and all the associated practical requirements.
- Equipment including hardware and software and also specialized equipment such as recording devices and covert cameras.
- Supporting services such as transport and communications.
- Human resources. In building an effective system, there will be implications for human resources including working conditions and practices and the potential redeployment of some staff.
- Funding streams. Nothing is free and how the various projects will be funded will need expert input.

Having discussed the more general aspects of building the system, we now begin to drill down into specifics.

7.14   Intelligence Unit

At the heart of any agency's intelligence management system will be the Intelligence Unit. This unit will be responsible for gathering together *all* information, processing it into intelligence, and ensuring the appropriate dissemination of that intelligence to the relevant intelligence customers. The Intelligence Unit will be the first point of contact for any member wishing to submit information for intelligence purposes or having a query about anything intelligence related.

Figure 7.2 outlines the typical composition for an agency of 300 officers or more. The number of posts and nature of the posts will vary according to agency size, but the example given is realistic for the expected work load.

While the composition and staffing levels of each Intelligence Unit will vary from agency to agency and even within an agency, suggested functions of each members are outlined as follows:

- *Intelligence manager.* This member will normally be at least two ranks/grades up the agency's structure and have considerable decision-making responsibilities.
- *Deputy manager.* This member will normally be of first-line supervisory rank and will perform the functions of the manager when that person is not present.
- *Analyst.* The role of the analyst is discussed fully in Chapter 8.
- *Intelligence officer.* The primary function of this person is to carry out the processing of information into intelligence. It is a person who will do the vast majority of the work needed for information to become intelligence. Computers may make the work easier, but it is the human mind that converts information into intelligence, and the importance of the role of the intelligence officer cannot be overemphasized. She will also deliver briefings to staff and have in-depth knowledge relating to crime in her area of responsibility. Because of the nature of the role, she will normally be a sworn officer. Intelligence officers must be trained in their role and certified as such.

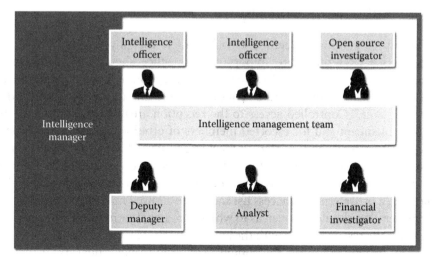

Figure 7.2 An example of Intelligence Unit staffing.

- *Support staff.* The requirement for staff to support intelligence officers will be limited to as much of the work that would previously have been done by support staff. Routine filing will be carried out by computers. However, consideration should always be given to potential financial savings that can be made by removing some duties from sworn members.
- *Financial investigator.* Financial investigation can contribute significantly to the intelligence picture, and a trained investigator can be a valuable asset in any Intelligence Unit.
- *Open source investigator.* Open source information collection is a specialized role and is discussed further in Chapter 9. The Intelligence Unit is a natural place for such an investigator to sit.

Selecting staff for the Intelligence Unit must be done with care. Staff should possess the following qualities:

- Have a sufficiently high-level relation to their intelligence quotient.
- Have the ability to write clearly and concisely.
- Be able to think objectively.
- Be professional in all aspects of their work as they are likely to be the interface between all involved in specialized intelligence roles and the other agency staff.
- Be approachable and have good communications skills.
- Must have integrity and be able to work as part of a team. Those who are continually disruptive or will not work to expected standards should be removed.

7.15   Intelligence Unit Offices

While it may initially seem a trivial matter, the physical aspects of an Intelligence Unit office are important. The office should be divided into a reception area and a restricted area. The reception area will be situated at the entrance to the office and be subdivided into an "interview room" and a "waiting area." Controlled access to the reception area will be allowed for all agency members and for escorted members of other agencies. The interview room allows intelligence officers to meet in privacy with visitors. Those sitting in the waiting area should not be allowed to hear conversations taking part in the restricted area. No one other than staff from the Intelligence Unit and those on a predetermined access list should be allowed into the restricted area. Consideration should be given as to whether or not cleaning staff will have any access to the restricted area with the balance leaning toward no access. If cleaning staff are allowed access, this should be done only under supervision, outside normal working hours, and where a clear desk policy is strictly enforced.

The Intelligence Unit may also be the best place within an agency to manage knowledge assets relating to intelligence. Another viable option is within an intelligence training unit, should the agency have one. Knowledge assets include the following:

- Current legislation and case law
- National and agency policies and procedures
- Manuals of guidance and good practice
- Intelligence-related literature

7.16   Intelligence Departments

Where due to size or role an agency requires more than one Intelligence Unit, the structure of a single unit is merely replicated throughout the agency either on a geographical, departmental, or subject-specific basis. If modifications for functionality are required, these can be readily adapted but all should have a nominated intelligence manager and work to the same procedures. To ensure standardization of the intelligence function across the agency, multiple units should be managed as an intelligence department. Figure 7.3 illustrates the composition of an intelligence department.

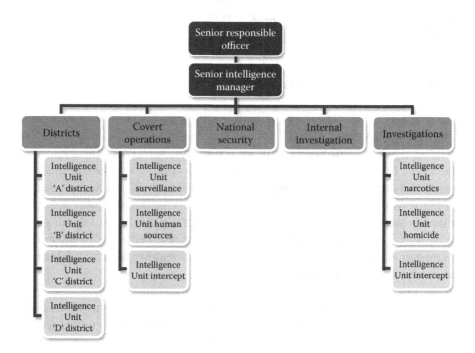

Figure 7.3 An intelligence department.

7.17 Senior Intelligence Manager

Where an agency has a number of Intelligence Units, it will by default have a number of intelligence managers, intelligence officers, and analysts. There needs to be one person appointed to oversee and direct the intelligence management system. For the purposes of this book, we refer to this individual as the "senior intelligence manager." In other agencies, such a person is commonly referred to by titles such as "head of intelligence" or "director of intelligence." What must be clear in agency procedures is that this person has responsibility for managing intelligence on behalf of that agency and their full-time role relates to the intelligence function. It is recognized that some operational aspects of the intelligence collection will fall outside their remit: for example, managing the activities of uniform police officers or undercover operators. However, once these persons have submitted the information, the actual processing of that information into intelligence and the subsequent management of that intelligence all fall under the remit of the senior intelligence manager.

The senior intelligence manager in an agency will be designated as the point of contact for all intelligence matters within the agency. This is the person to whom external agencies may direct inquiries and advisories. Furthermore, it is this person who has the authority to release intelligence to other agencies. This person must have sufficient training to understand the language, processes, and regulations incumbent on the law enforcement intelligence community.

7.18 Staff Development

Getting and developing the right staff is an integral part of any intelligence management system. All staff for intelligence-related functions should be selected against identified criteria for the specific role. Once the staff members have been selected, they should undergo a comprehensive training program. All too often the training of staff involved in intelligence management is left to what is commonly referred to as learning "on the job." There are many problems with this attitude, and yet we rarely think about it: imagine if your doctor was expected to solely learn on the job! Learning on the job is a management cop-out. It is a concept filled with mistaken beliefs and destined to fail for a number of reasons:

- On-the-job training is often viewed as being similar to that of a tradesman serving an apprenticeship. First, in those circumstances, the tradesman to whom the person is apprenticed is already qualified to recognized standards. Second, the apprentice will normally only be as good as the tradesman under whom they learn, and third, apprentices generally follow a structured path with both on-the-job practice and theoretical schooling.

- On-the-job training makes the assumption that there is an officer from whom a person new to the role can learn.
- On-the-job training means that the new person is often taught the bad along with the good.
- On-the-job training produces huge inconsistencies across an agency with the creation of little empires based on what is done in a particular office or section being viewed as the only way to do something.
- On-the-job training offers little value for the money because the member only learns if and when someone chooses to teach them and whatever that other person chooses to teach. On-the-job training is slow to develop a competent member.

Lack of training in intelligence management is an international problem as O'Shea and Nicholls (2003) remark: "Training—or more specifically the lack of training—is a perennial issue for law enforcement agencies (LEAs) law enforcement agencies in many countries." Too many agencies do not provide adequate training appropriate to the role. Training should be structured and delivered at the earliest possible opportunity. Structured training should include the following:

- Relevant legislation and the correct interpretation of that legislation
- Agency policies and procedures relevant to a role
- An understanding of human rights and civil liberty issues as they relate to intelligence management
- Ethics
- Common definitions used in intelligence management, and the structure of the intelligence management system

Delivering training as staff commence their roles is important but it is not the end of the process. Staff will need both ongoing refresher and developmental training if the agency is to obtain the maximum benefit. Furthermore, managers should always be on the lookout to identify intelligent, industrious, and intellectually curious members of staff that are likely to benefit from enhanced development and then use the skills they have acquired for the benefit of the whole agency. A limited number of people will show real flair for intelligence work and such individuals need opportunities to develop. Such opportunities will include enhanced training and working with other agencies working in a number of different aspects of intelligence. Far too often, insufficient investment is made in staff members who show real potential, and they are left to wither on the vine.

Getting the human aspect of the intelligence management system right cannot be emphasized enough. Intelligence management is a difficult role and staff issues need to be continually monitored. A good understanding of the human aspects will help negate many potential problems. Some aspects worth bearing in mind include the following:

- Rank does not indicate expertise in the field of intelligence.
- If officers who have gone out of their way to develop themselves and make contributions to the system are not rewarded, the agency will ultimately lose their commitment.
- If intelligence is not written down and the member who has it in their head leaves the agency, the intelligence walks out the door with them.
- As with most aspects of life, desired behaviors that are recognized and rewarded will prosper and continue, while those undesired behaviors that are ignored and punished will gradually be eroded and end.

While the head of an agency will have the entire agency to manage, there are a few matters specifically relating to the intelligence management system that they need to take care of:

- They must understand the basic concepts of intelligence management and the benefits it will bring to an agency.
- They must allocate a senior responsible officer for intelligence-related matters.
- They must actively promote the intelligence function within their agency, fully integrating it into strategic and tactical decision-making.
- They must be proactive in establishing links to other agencies in regard to intelligence sharing.

Moving on from the responsibilities of the agency's head, there are a number of responsibilities that will fall to senior management:

- They must demonstrate support for the use of intelligence within the agency and be clear about what they want it to achieve.
- They need a clear understanding of the legal and privacy constraints that relate to intelligence management.
- They need to ensure that their staff members, regardless of their specific roles, have sufficient training to support the intelligence management system and to maximize the benefits of it.
- They must ensure adherence to the policies and procedures relating to intelligence management.

- They must ensure sufficient resourcing for the intelligence function within their areas of command.

Unfortunately some senior managers do not recognize their lack of knowledge of how intelligence is supposed to work or the benefits it can produce and so continue to make poor decisions based on that knowledge dearth. Others have difficulty in seeing the need to improve the intelligence function or fail to instigate the change that is required. For them, the necessity for change is brought about only by some impending crisis and in many cases a crisis that should and could have been avoided. While this adversity to change affects many people, the problem with it being held by a senior manager is that it stifles the entire agency.

7.19   Forms

Another difficult aspect of building an intelligence management system is creating the various forms that are necessary.* The standardization of forms is important for a number of reasons:

- Named forms facilitate writing effective procedures. It is much easier to tell someone what they have to do if you can refer to each form by an identifiable name. In naming forms, it is beneficial to reflect what the purpose of that form is, as opposed to referring to it by a number. Care must be taken with nomenclature to reduce the chances of confusion if the name of the form is reduced to initials to ensure that two forms do not have the same initials.
- Standardized forms speed the processing of intelligence.
- Forms reduce the chances of errors and omissions and guide the user through the relevant process.
- Using standardized forms reduces the time it takes to complete each form. Officers do not have to learn how to complete different forms, and if they have only a limited number to use, they become increasingly familiar with them again reducing time.
- Standardized forms are easier to read, thus increasing efficiency.
- Standardized forms create a more professional impression when used in judicial proceedings or when sharing intelligence with other agencies.

* While the term "form" is used here, it is intended to include electronic forms/formatting.

Different forms containing similar information types should not be used simply because the origin of the information varies. Forms should be developed so that they can for the most part be used regardless of where the information originates. The following are examples of forms that will be found in any intelligence management system:

- Intelligence report
- Tasking request to gather information
- Request for access to the identity of origin intelligence
- Finance reports of varying types
- Performance return
- Audit report

7.20   Intelligence Repository

An intelligence repository provides centralized storage for all the agency's intelligence products in a single database sometimes referred to as an intelligence database. For the vast majority of agencies, it will be a computerized system. Some smaller agencies may feel for economic reasons that they should use a paper-based system or software with limited functionality; both solutions are for all intents and purposes, unacceptable for the majority of LEAs working in affluent nations in the twenty-first century.

Before addressing the need for a computerized system, we examine why all intelligence should be stored in one central repository:

- It is the most cost-effective way to store the information. There is no need for an agency to spend money on constructing or purchasing a number of different solutions, when one properly constructed solution will suffice.
- Retrieval of intelligence is much easier if there is only one place to look for it, thus saving valuable resources on a daily basis. Where time becomes a critical factor during enforcement operations, it is much easier to check one place than many places for relevant intelligence.
- There is less chance of important intelligence being missed if it is stored in one place as opposed to in a number of places.
- A single repository is easier to control and audit than a number of disparate systems, thus reducing the potential for corrupt use of the intelligence going undetected.
- A single repository encourages standardized submission of intelligence products and thereby increases the quality of the final products.
- A single repository, supported by identified intelligence submission mechanisms, reduces time spent in training staff in how to access the repository and retrieve the intelligence they need to retrieve.

The following are suggested as good practices in relation to the intelligence repository:

- Members should have a unique login identity and an associated password. A preset login identity will dictate their access rights.
- Members are not allowed to pass information they have accessed to anyone else, save where their role allows for it: for example, an officer briefing a team before an operation.
- Members cannot provide intelligence to any person, where the recipients' access-level status does not already allow them to access it themselves. For example, an inspector cannot go into the repository at their access level and then brief out intelligence to a constable who is not entitled to read it for themselves. This is a significant problem in intelligence and has the potential to cause real harm. Where this occurs, disciplinary action should be taken.

If an intelligence repository is to work effectively, the contents of it must be codified in a way that they can be readily accessible to those who need access to the content. Such codification benefits from simplicity. Files need to be created in a way in which the nature of their existing content is readily apparent and in a way that it is also apparent where new items should be placed. Such simplicity is not always easy to achieve. If procedures and technology do not prevent it, there can be a tendency for members to create files other than those created through corporate designation. File "types" should be authorized only by the senior intelligence manager. Furthermore, duplicate files relating to intelligence should not be permitted.

Using the URN embedded in each intelligence product contained in the repository, it must be possible to identify the origin of that product, the members involved in its creation, and the pathway from origin to repositing. This is necessary to ensure the integrity of the content and to enable adequate investigation as to its origin, should the need arise.

No piece of information should be acted upon without that information being submitted through the intelligence management system, except where the information is time critical and any delay in acting upon it is likely to lead to the loss of life or serious harm. If this is the case, the information should be acted upon forthwith and entered into the intelligence management system as soon as possible afterward.

All the risk that officers take to obtain information and all the risks that citizens take to provide law enforcement with information are wasted if the agency does not have in place an effective system to, first, capture and process the information and, second, to exploit the subsequent intelligence products.

7.21   Failure to Submit Information

A problem often encountered in law enforcement occurs when the recipient of a piece of information has a vested interest in acting upon it. For example, the narcotics officer who in the process of investigating the supply of drugs receives from the person they are interviewing information about the location of drugs being sold by another offender. The narcotics officer takes this piece of information and carries out a search at the aforesaid premises, without the information being entered into the intelligence management system, before it is exploited. While the benefits of such a move may seem obvious to the narcotics officer—they obtain the successful recovery of more drugs—they fail to see any potentially negative consequences of their action. This method of operating is often self-perpetuating and the officer uses the information gained to satisfy their needs and their agenda with almost a willful blindness to the potentially greater needs of the agency. This is a fundamentally flawed way of operating and has the potential to create a number of problems:

- The information is not shared, or shared only to a limited extent, with other members of the agency who may have a more pressing interest in it.
- Investigations are carried out that may not meet the priorities set by the senior management team, thus resources are wasted.
- An intelligence management system establishes checks and balances in relation to any information submitted into it. These include checks in relation to civil liberty issues, issues pertaining to fair trial rights, and the prevention of illegal searches and arrests. These are all ignored.
- The intelligence management system also ensures steps are taken to minimize inappropriate or corrupt behavior. These are negated by such actions.
- Measures in place to protect the origin of that information are often ignored or disregarded. Circumventing such safeguards can lead to serious harm including the loss of life.
- Officers are enabled in the pursuit of personal agendas and prejudicial investigations result.

Officers, in such circumstances, will raise many arguments as to why they should not be allowed to act upon receipt of the information without the information being entered and processed. These arguments include the following:

- The fact is the submitting officer is the one most likely to be told to investigate the matter once it goes through the system. So why bother with processing the information?

- The submitting officer is the one best equipped to act on the information as he knows exactly what it says and the context in which it was received.
- Entering the information into the system creates additional and unnecessary work—time better spent doing real work!
- The processing of the information will create an unnecessary time delay. The bad guys will get away.
- Other members will get to see the information, thus creating a security risk.
- The submitting officer got the information, so she should get the credit for exploiting it.

None of these arguments stand up to any degree of examination. There may be notions of truth in some of these excuses, but more often than not, it is about the officers continuing to pursue their personal agendas.

7.22 Owning Intelligence

A somewhat thorny issue that often arises in intelligence management is that of ownership of the intelligence. There are various schools of thought in relation to this, and it is an enigma that is not easily answered in a definitive way. As a general rule, the agency "owns" the intelligence, and it is for the intelligence manager to decide what should be done with it. However, under certain circumstances, those involved in gathering the information should have a high degree of input into what happens to it, particularly where misuse of it may jeopardize an operation. When it can be argued that ownership of an intelligence product is ceded by an agency is when it passes that product to another agency. Although the initiating agency may place restrictions on how that product can be used, enforcing such restrictions is all but impossible.

7.23 Policy, Procedures, and Guidance

No intelligence management system can function properly without good policies and comprehensive procedures. The terms "policy" and "procedure" are often used interchangeably, again creating confusion among users. Throw in the term "guidance" and it makes for a broken system. Understanding the difference in each is important if the agency is to avoid being left vulnerable to corruption, poor performance, and public criticism. To begin, it is important to note that the law, be it federal, state, or local statute and any attendant documents, cannot be surpassed by policy or procedures. While this may seem obvious, it is surprising how many law enforcement policies are in conflict with legislation, normally because the policy has been written by someone who has not been trained in writing policies and procedures.

- A policy is a statement of an agency's intentions to discharge its obligations to the public in regard to a particular business area. It states an intention to carry out certain functions and provides parameters with regard to those functions. Policy establishes limits to action. They will of necessity be public documents, authorized by the Chief, and normally be brief in nature.
- Procedures outline a method of performing an act or a manner of proceeding on a course of action. They differ from policy in that they direct a member how to act in a particular situation and how a specific task should be performed. Procedures must be comprehensive in nature and explain to the reader what they should do in the vast majority of circumstances they are likely to meet. Procedures are constructed from the knowledge of individuals operating in the business area. Formalizing this knowledge means that good practice is identified and perpetuated long after such individuals have left the agency. In procedures, this knowledge is set out in a structured format agreed upon by senior management and goes a long way to eliminating mistakes that have been made in the past. One of the unfortunate aspects that occur in relation to procedures is that the reason why a particular procedure was put in place is often forgotten with the passage of time. Those currently involved then mistakenly believe that it is all right to deviate from or change that procedure without realizing that they are removing a measure that was put in place to achieve a certain goal or to prevent a risk that would potentially materialize. Procedures should be linked to an agency's discipline regulations, so that members who deviate from them without cause can be held fully accountable and face consequences for their actions. However, procedures can be deviated from, but any member doing so must be held fully accountable for their actions and be expected to justify why they have done so. To protect covert methodology, procedures should be protected from public availability. Where the interests of justice require disclosing part of a procedure document, the irrelevant content should be removed. Carelessness, in this respect by one agency, compromises the methodology for other agencies.
- Guidance. Care should be taken if an agency is formally issuing guidance, particularly if that agency does not have good policies and comprehensive procedures. Guidance is not a substitute for either

policy or procedure, and members will often justify their lack of adherence to guidance with statements such as "It is only *guidance!*" Guidance implies that actions are optional.

While space here limits the amount of discussion that can be had in relation to policy, procedures, and guidance, the following points should be considered:

- Good policy and comprehensive procedures are essential for effective intelligence management.
- Policy and procedures should be written only by a member trained in writing them; they are not easy to write well. Good spelling and grammar are important, and the use of unambiguous terminology is essential.
- National and/or regional procedures provide greater resilience for an agency than stand-alone procedures. The sharing of knowledge and good practice among agencies means that the procedures are much more likely to stand up to outside scrutiny than something that is limited to one agency.
- When it comes to the depth of content, procedures should drill down into the specifics of how each task should be carried out. For example, if an agency's procedures for managing human sources are only 10 or 12 pages, more has been omitted than included, and mistakes will undoubtedly follow as a result.

7.24   Memorandum of Understanding

A memorandum of understanding (MoU) is a document that records the common intent of two or more parties where the parties do *not* wish to assume legally binding obligations. An MoU should only be used to state the understanding of each party in relation to what has been agreed between them, without creating any obligation on either party. In essence, it is a gentleman's agreement.

There are likely to be many circumstances where an LEA has to draw up an MoU with another agency or body to facilitate either the gathering of information or the sharing of intelligence products. Although not legally binding, care needs to be taken in constructing such documents. A standardized format ensures that all critical aspects are captured:

- *Introduction.* This section helps the reader understand the memorandum content. It states the agencies/bodies involved and describes why the document is necessary. It should not include the mechanisms used to reach agreement and reference to historic events relating to the memorandum should be kept to a minimum.

- *Purpose.* This section should be a concise statement of whom and what will be affected by the memorandum.
- *Scope.* This section outlines what will be included and what will not be covered in the memorandum.
- *Definitions.* This section provides definitions for any technical aspects or jargon used in the agreement. It is important that such definitions provide clarity for the signatories thus reducing the potential for conflict at a later stage.
- *Procedures.* This section outlines the circumstances under which the memorandum will come into play and the functions that each party to the memorandum will be required to perform to discharge the named responsibilities. This section should include and provide clarity surrounding any financial obligations arising.
- *Oversight and review.* This section should provide details of the oversight arrangement to ensure the ongoing functionality and provide the date on which it should be reviewed. A maximum period of one year should elapse before any memorandum is reviewed.

An MoU should be signed and dated by all the relevant parties.

7.25   Service-Level Agreements

A "service-level agreement" (SLA) is a negotiated agreement between two parties, where one is the customer and the other is the service provider. SLAs provide a common understanding about services, priorities, and responsibilities. SLAs should be well defined and not drawn up in an ad hoc fashion. SLAs include the following:

- The service being provided
- The standards of service
- Applicable timescales
- The responsibilities of both parties
- Provisions for legal and regulatory compliance
- How disputes will be resolved
- Confidentiality provisions

The Intelligence Unit should have SLAs with other units within their agency. Such agreements improve the standards of service, reduce ambiguity, and help avoid unrealistic expectations of behavior. Furthermore, SLAs improve accountability and provide methods for resolving conflicts.

7.26 Checklists and Aide-Memoire

The fallibility of human memory is well documented. Regardless of the nature of the task being undertaken, structures should be put in place to mitigate the risk of important matters being overlooked and harm resulting. Checklists are a simple cost-effective method of ensuring things are not forgotten or overlooked. They will be of particular use to members who are not working with intelligence-related material on a daily basis. Given the life-threatening nature of some of the activities relating to intelligence management, they are well worth taking the time to construct. While in the first instance it may appear that such checklists are useful only to those new to the role, overconfidence and familiarity often create a situation where even the most experienced officers forget a critical point. Electronic checklists are often developed within software, with the added benefit that they can restrict further progress until all matters have been attended to.

7.27 Entities

Entities are a core part of any intelligence system. An entity is defined as "a unique element that when inputted into the intelligence repository falls within an identified category of, person, geographic location or item." In short, an entity is a uniquely identified person, place, or thing.

Entities will always fall within one of a limited number of specified categories, as identified by the agency's intelligence management procedures. The following are suggested categories:

- Person
- Geographic location
- Means of transport
- Means of communication
- Article
- Organization
- Event

The number of categories should be kept limited but will by default be subdivided; for example, a type of boat being used by drug smugglers will fall into the shipping subdivision of the means of transport category. Such divisions make for easier access to specific material and are helpful in searching for material.

When a unique element is inputted to the intelligence repository and if it does not preexist in the repository, a new "entity" will have to be created by the inputting officer, while if it already exists, it should be linked to the new intelligence. All possible steps must be taken to avoid the creation of duplicate entities. For example, the name "Peirce Dooley" is obtained by Detective Roddick, from a member of the public, as being a suspect in a recent robbery. When Detective Roddick obtains this information, she should check to see if Pierce Dooley already exists as an entity within the intelligence repository. If Dooley does exist as an entity, then the new information should be linked to that entity at the earliest opportunity. If "Dooley" does not already exist as an entity, then a new entity will need to be created within the repository by the inputting officer. Associating material to an entity should be done at the time of information submission, if possible by the submitting officer, or as close to it as possible to accurately link the material to the *correct* entity and avoid *duplication*. In the preceding example, it is best if Detective Roddick can positively identify Dooley at time of information submission. However, Roddick may not have the prerequisite access level to the intelligence repository to see if Dooley already exists there as an entity, in which case, Dooley will be linked, or a new entity created, as the information is processed to intelligence in the Intelligence Unit.

Entities will be linked to each other based on the content of the intelligence product in which they appear; for example, where a suspect is mentioned in an intelligence report as buying a new car, the person is an entity who is now linked to the vehicle that is obviously a transport entity. All entities will have a URN within the repository. In this case, the system will have a URN for the person, and the new car will be given a URN when it is created as an entity (note, this URN is not the license plate!).

The data content of an entity will vary according to entity category and is likely to evolve over time, so any software used must be capable of accommodating such development. For example, the agency may decide to add "body piercings" to a person entity, and the software must be able to accommodate this additional data field. Furthermore, any media associated with that entity should form part of the entity; for example, a person entity may well include a number of photographs or videos. While such media may be accessed in a number of different ways when searching the repository, access from the entity screen should involve no more than one click.

With each entity category, there will be different aspects to bear in mind including the number of subcategories that may be decided upon and the detail to be recorded against each entity. The following provide some ideas in respect of the aforementioned different entity categories.

- *Persons.* A person entity will be built upon the person's name, and while this may appear simple at first glance, there is more to it than may initially be obvious. Name entities must be able to accommodate nicknames, aliases, and the spelling of ethnically diverse names. Other data likely to be found in the entity screen include details of their social security number, offender reference number, passport details, driving license, family members, employment history, places frequented, and so on. A common flaw often found with data fields in relation to people is inflexibility born out of stereotyping and a lack of understanding of the diverse nature of the human race. A common error is the ticking of a box as to whether a person is male or female, thus ignoring the transgendered community. Another problem is ticking boxes to select one of a limited number of ethnic backgrounds. For example, one box is ticked for everyone from the Indian subcontinent labeled as "Indian." Furthermore, the tick boxes rarely allow for anyone of mixed race. Not only do such system flaws create problems for those using the intelligence, but they are also based in prejudice and racism.

- *Geographic locations.* Geographic locations will include housing and commercial premises, streets, towns, parcel lots, and so on. Data fields for geographic locations are likely to include official address; ZIP codes/post codes; type of structure; the use to which it is put; the number of stories, access, and egress details; ownership and occupancy details; and contact details for both. Where possible, all geographic locations should be geocoded before entry into the repository. Geocoding is the process of associating geographic coordinates (often expressed as latitude and longitude) to a location. With geocoding, the location can be integrated with mapping and used in geographic information systems. While this initially takes time, it provides significant long-term benefits. Problems that can arise in adding geographic entities include distinguishing between ambiguous addresses such as 74 Green Street and 74 West Green Street and the geocoding of new addresses for streets that have not yet been added to the relevant geographic information system database. Care must be taken with some geographic areas as the name by which they have been referred is akin to a nickname—locals often have names for places that bear little resemblance to the official naming. These parochial names should be included in a specific data field.

- *Article.* An article can be anything, whether tangible or not. It is for the officer creating the entity to decide as to what should fall into this category or what might be better placed in one of the other categories. For example, a computer is an item, but it can also be used as a means of communication with all the attendant data that follows forming that function. Fortunately, modern search engines mitigate errors in categorizing entities within the repository. Items are likely to include such things as weapons, narcotics, and monetary instruments. When recording such entities, the more comprehensive the details inputted, the greater the benefits in the longer term. For example, when recording a new type of illicit drug, details recorded should include its chemical composition, any precursor chemicals used in its manufacture, and the various street names by which it is known. Often this is not done because of the assumption that everyone already has that knowledge.

- *Means of transport.* This type of entity will include all the obvious means of transport, including cars, buses, aircraft, trains, and shipping. When it comes to transporting illicit materials, this type of entity expands to include everything from submarines to container shipping and cargo planes to microlight aircraft. As with other entities, details of the specifics need to be included when creating the entity and regularly updated. Intelligence staff should query submitting officers with respect to details, when they are not provided.
- *Means of communication.* Communication was once relatively simple: there were letters, telegrams, telephones, and radios and that was about it. Then technology exploded with the advent of the Internet and mobile cellular phones and is exponentially increasing as developers seek to combine the potential of both. Taking advantage of the opportunities, criminals and terrorists have been quick to use new methods of communication including such things as Skype, instant messaging, Facebook, and many other Internet-based technologies. While intercepting such communications presents difficulties, the greatest difficulty is not knowing what is being used and how it is being used. Intelligence staff should be quick to disseminate emerging methodology to other agencies, even if the specifics of who is using them are omitted for operational reasons.
- *Organization.* Organizations will include both criminal gangs and legitimate organizations. Where a person is associated with an organization, they should be linked to it. Where it is a criminal organization, details should include a description of the goals of that organization, political links if any exist, admission criteria, and identifying markings for members such as tattoos.
- *Event.* Events include crimes committed and noncriminal events such as political rallies, demonstrations, and entertainment. Events may or may not be recorded as criminal occurrences for the simple reason they may never have been reported—for example, a major drug importation by a criminal gang. If such events are not recorded as intelligence, failure to find them when further intelligence is obtained can skew the interpretation of that intelligence. While many of these events will have importance in themselves, they are also significant markers that other happenings can be tied to and can be useful in clarifying dates and locations—for example, "It was the day after the anti-capitalist rally" or "They met at the U2 concert in Vancouver."

This is not intended as a definitive list of entities, but agencies are cautioned against increasing the list ad infinitum. Furthermore, the content suggested here for each entity is very limited and is intended only as a starting position. An effective computerized repository will have many data fields already identified and the opportunity to insert more should be available. Computerized systems must also have the facility to "match and merge" duplicate entities.

It is the responsibility of the member identifying a new entity to obtain the maximum amount of detail that it is reasonably practical to do in relation to that entity. For example, if a source handler is provided with the name of a new drug dealer, he should attempt to fully identify the person with details such as age, addresses, vehicles used, and enter a description into the relevant data fields. To maintain data standards, Intelligence Unit staff should challenge where this is not being done.

7.28 Separating Collection from Investigation

There can be significant benefits to separating members involved in the collecting role from those involved the investigating role; that is, the collector of information is not responsible for completing the investigation but merely assists in providing intelligence for the investigator. For example, having handlers whose sole role is to manage human sources or officers dedicated to undercover operations and intercepting communications. While this option may only be possible in larger agencies, separating collection from investigation has a number of advantages:

- The needs of the agency are served as opposed to the needs of an investigator or an investigation.
- The role of collection is professionalized with significantly greater levels of production and lower levels of corruption.
- There is distance between the origin of the intelligence and the judicial process reducing the chances of exposure of the origin of the intelligence.
- Intelligence is provided to the agency on a continuous basis against a potentially wide range of topics as identified by management.
- As such collection units manage information coming from many different places, they are more likely to interlink various threads that would otherwise be missed and to identify emerging problems. When it comes to human source management, they can task different sources to address the same problem, therefore maximizing the amount of intelligence obtained.

- Such units provide greater flexibility in that collection can easily move from one topic to another. This reduces human resource issues such as transferring staff to collect information when a new problem emerges.

Dedicated collection teams are an extremely effective means of enhancing an agency's intelligence capability. They have been standard practice in the military and intelligence agencies for a long time. Dedicated human source units are the standard method of managing human sources throughout the United Kingdom with other countries such as Australia, Canada, and many European counties following suit. The United Kingdom, Australia, and Canada have created specialized units that proactively recruit and develop human sources to provide high-level intelligence on organized crime and terrorism.*

7.29   Reviewing and Purging

Things change and new information becomes available, some of which will clearly identify that intelligence that has previously been reposited is wrong. It is important that the intelligence management system has processes to ensure that entries are kept current and that erroneous intelligence that has been entered is corrected. While it should be impossible to change an original intelligence report if the material in it is wrong, a mechanism is needed to ensure that the correct material is now entered into the repository. Furthermore, it is important to link the new intelligence to that previously received. This provides explanation to future readers and can help prove the integrity of the system. One way corrections can be done is by submitting an officer's comment on the new intelligence report and cross-referencing it to the incorrect report by inclusion of its URN. In some cases, on receipt of corrected intelligence, it may be necessary for an intelligence officer to take time to examine what, if any, actions have been previously carried out as a result of the intelligence, which is now believed to be wrong. Such a situation may have ramifications for cases yet before the courts or having already gone to trial, the direction of ongoing investigations, or the evaluation of a human source who is still being used.

Part of an effective intelligence management system is the ability of an agency to review material that has been previously submitted. Arguably the most important part of this reviewing element is the ability to remove details that have been lawfully collected in relation to a person, but the retention of those details can no longer be justified. In creating the intelligence management system, part of the function of the Intelligence Unit is to examine every piece of information that is submitted to see if it has worth as intelligence. The first

---

* At the time of writing, there is only one such unit in the entire United States that the author is aware of.

safeguard for the agency and for the privacy of individuals is this examination. If a piece of submitted information is deemed of "no intelligence value," it is not reposited as intelligence but still remains held in the information-submission process for a preidentified period in case events should dictate it now has value. If after that period of time it still has not worth, it can be purged from the submission system. A simple example is shown in the following:

> Cesar Martinez from Jonestown is stopped by a Clarkesville police officer late at night, outside a warehouse complex, in Clarkesville. He says he is waiting to meet up with a new girlfriend. Clarkesville police have no record of Martinez.

> Clarkesville police forward the details of the stop to Jonestown police.

> If Martinez **is not** known to be involved in crime Jonestown police should purge the information submission after an identified period.

> (Suggested retention—maximum 1 year)

> If Martinez **is** known to be involved in crime Jonestown police should complete an intelligence report and forward a copy to Clarkesville police who then enter it in their intelligence repository.

Reviewing and purging intelligence held within the intelligence repository should be conducted regularly to ensure that it is relevant, accurate, and fulfills the original, legitimate aims for which it was collected and retained. However, it is not easy to get reviewing and purging processes right. Any intelligence that has been retained in the system but has not been reviewed for a significant period of time should be reviewed and validated before it is disseminated for action. Review and purging should take place against identified criteria including the following:

- The seriousness of the criminality involved. The more serious the criminality a person is linked to, the less likely an agency is to purge that intelligence. Ironically, it is exactly this type of material that is likely to unjustifiably cause a person most harm if it is wrong but creates the greatest risk to others if it is right but purged. Examples of this type of intelligence include involvement in terrorism or child abuse. The balance should tend toward keeping the material.
- Similarly, consideration as to who the person is and the social roles that they are involved in. The nature of a person's life may pose a greater risk to the public, for example, when a schoolteacher is named as being involved in sexual offenses against children, there will be a major dilemma. Given his position, there is an increased risk to children if it is true, but if it is wrong the teacher's career will potentially be destroyed because of flawed intelligence. Of significance here will be the results of any investigation, which begs the questions, "was the

report investigated?" and if not "why not?" With such a serious allegation, the balance will tend toward keeping the intelligence regardless of whether or not anything has been done to confirm or refute it.

- The expectancy in reporting. The fact that there exists only one piece of intelligence in relation to a person would tend to indicate the intelligence is inaccurate. The expectation would be that if they are involved in criminality, more intelligence would have been submitted over a period of time. In such cases, the tendency would be to purge the person from the system. However, given the nature of some types of crime or the type of person involved, there may be a very low expectation with regard to further intelligence. This will normally be the case when the person is isolated from the agency's normal sphere of investigation or because of the numerically low occurrence of offending. For example, if intelligence states that a senior judge is corrupt, there is likely to be very limited access to reporting on that judge. A key element here in the decision-making process is the reliability of the origin of the intelligence report.
- The quality of reporting will always pay a significant part in the decision to purge or not. One report from a highly trusted origin carries significant weight and will probably sway the balance that the intelligence is not purged.
- The quantity of reporting, even if originating from various untested origins, will probably sway the balance toward retention.
- The utility, accuracy, and completeness of the reporting will all be indicators as to whether purging should take place. Do not allow the repository to become cluttered with junk. As the author Arthur Conan Doyle comments, "Depend upon it, there comes a time when for every addition of knowledge you forget something that you knew before. It is of the highest importance, therefore, not to have useless facts elbowing out the useful ones."
- If the origin of material is found to have been malicious in their reporting, all materials should be reviewed immediately and the balance will sway toward purging it all.

Timescales for review and the criteria for purging must be included in the agency's procedures. Where there is doubt, the details should be passed to a higher rank for a decision. If necessary, advice should be sought from the agency's legal advisor. Where there has been significant debate, the reasons for retention should be recorded on a policy log embedded in the intelligence report. Such a document makes it clear to any future reader that the content needs to be treated with caution.

Purging a person's identity from the intelligence repository can be difficult depending on how well the software has been constructed. Care must be taken that the removal of someone's name does not remove relevant intelligence about others, to which that person was linked. If one imagines a web, will removing the spider also remove the web and all the flies caught in that web?

One of the primary functions of law enforcement is protecting the community or as it is sometimes referred to as "community safety." To protect the community from future harm, it is necessary to maintain an intelligence picture of those individuals who are assessed as being likely to harm the community in the future. Retaining such records poses some problems for law enforcement as the individual or for that matter a group may not currently be involved in any specific criminal action or conspiracy. However, using professional judgment, law enforcement officers may assess the individual or group as having the potential to pose a threat to the community, albeit that this threat is future based. This threat may be related to future ordinary criminal activity as would be readily recognized by any layperson or it may be nonspecific in nature as is likely to be encountered in dealing with subversive groups. The assumption that criminals are continually engaged in some form of criminal activity is an oversimplification of the nature of criminal behavior. There may be significant downtime in their activities. Similarly, with subversive groups, a significant amount of their time may be spent in lawful activities, while at the same time the potential for the group to cause serious harm is nurtured and developed. While at all times law enforcement must be able to justify why they are gathering intelligence of an individual or group, the professionalism of those involved in such intelligence matters must be recognized. To ignore the capabilities and expertise of intelligence professionals and to completely mistrust their intentions is a somewhat naive if not prejudicial standpoint. Law enforcement encounters criminality every hour of every day, and for the most part, they are well capable of identifying who poses a threat to community safety and taking appropriate steps to counter that threat. To be most effective, one of the measures they need to take is to build up a comprehensive intelligence picture of an individual or group. This includes monitoring their movements, actions, and associates and maintaining an up-to-date picture of their activities. Failure to do so leaves law enforcement well behind the game when the person or group returns to criminality as opposed to being in a position to potentially see the threat developing. The public needs to recognize that the rationale for keeping intelligence on any person or group who poses a potential threat is community safety. The fact may be that a person may not have even committed a crime before law enforcement gathered intelligence, but that there exist indicators and there is intelligence to say they might pose a threat establishes a compelling argument to maintain intelligence on them for as long as they continue to pose a threat to the community. With that said, law enforcement must always be able to demonstrate the existence of a connection between the individual or group and potential criminality and that such a belief must be reasonable and justifiable.

7.30   Intelligence Advisory

An "intelligence advisory" is an intelligence product, disseminated in written form, from an intelligence manager (the initiator) to another party (the recipient) that provides notice with regard to existing or predicted events. The intelligence advisory signifies the transference of responsibility from the initiator to the recipient to decide what action, if any, to take in regard to the intelligence contained therein.

Even though the recipient may or may not have requested the intelligence, the agency creating the product is assigning the responsibility for deciding what they now need to do about the intelligence to the recipient, in effect saying, "We have obtained this intelligence and we are passing it to the people who are responsible to do something about that intelligence. We have done our job in getting the intelligence. It is now up to you."

Before proceeding to examine this type of intelligence product, let us consider the following example:

Consider a narcotics unit working for Alpha Police Department engaged in handling human sources. A human source overhears information about a bank robbery that is due to take place the following week at the Money Bank located in a neighboring city where Beta Police Department has responsibility. [For simplicity, we will take it that the informant will obtain no further information about this robbery.] We now consider a number of points as to what Alpha Police Department should do with this information:

The obvious point first: the information is submitted by the receiving officer, using the agency's information submission process for human sources. The information is processed, grading it with regard to the past reliability of the human source and with regard to the specific piece of information. An intelligence report is created and placed in the intelligence repository. The Intelligence Manager is notified of the existence of the intelligence report and the need for action to be taken. The Intelligence Manager peruses the content of the report and creates a form of words suitable for the content of the intelligence advisory. The intelligence advisory is then forwarded to the party who has responsibility for dealing with the content of that advisory. That person takes whatever action they deem appropriate and submits a return to the intelligence unit detailing the action taken.

A number of features pertain to an intelligence advisory:

- Issuing an intelligence advisory should be done with thought and care. They should not be used to "cover the initiating party's ass," or as an excuse to do nothing further. There is significant temptation within intelligence creators to pass intelligence on regardless of whether or not it is of any actual use to the recipient. The danger in this is that the recipient becomes complacent about an advisory's content, as it is so similar to what they have heard time and time again. Human failings creep in and a scenario develops akin to "the boy who cried wolf." This is particularly relevant in relation to more general advisories relating to terrorism. Receiving agencies are unable to sustain the level of response they may feel is appropriate and when nothing has happened for the fourth or fifth time any subsequent advisory loses its credibility.

- An advisory may or may not contain recommendations as to how to respond to the contents. Such recommendations exist merely to be of assistance to the recipient in deciding a suitable course of action. They do not remove any responsibility from the recipient nor place the initiator under any greater liability.

- An advisory will always be in written form and forwarded against receipt. In cases where the content needs an urgent response, a verbal briefing may be given before the issue of the written advisory. However, care must be taken that the content of both advisories is the same. Written correspondence is much less likely to be altered or misquoted as it is communicated from one party to another. With modern technology, it is also significantly easier to prove when a written document was compiled, issued, and received than with verbal correspondence.

- Given that advisories will often contain threats of harm that may occur, it is imperative that there exists within the initiating agency a full audit trail relating to any intelligence advisory, linking it back to the initial information and forwarding to the person receiving the advisory. The receiving agency should have an audit trail of who received the advisory, when they received it, in what way it was handled, and by whom it was handled. Failure to have these audit trails can have serious ramifications for an agency should an event be "allowed" to occur, which could have been prevented had an advisory been properly dealt with when the information became available to law enforcement. In addition, if LEAs have system tested such scenarios (see Section 3.11), the chance of such information being overlooked is significantly reduced, therefore lessening the chances of harm.

- An advisory should not give any indication as to the origin of the content and should be issued only by the Intelligence Unit and not by the originators of the intelligence. Even when the intelligence actually originates within the Intelligence Unit, there should be no indication of the nature of the origin of the intelligence content. Placing such detail in the advisory jeopardizes the origin of the intelligence and has the potential to subjectively influence the recipient in their decision of how to handle the advisory.

- The agency must have a fast-track procedure for acting on urgent intelligence. Normally information will be passed to the Intelligence Unit for assessment and a decision on any action to be taken. Where it is necessary to act without delay, the senior officer on duty must take the necessary action and forward the details to the Intelligence Unit as soon as it is practical to do so.

7.31 Deconfliction

There is a real risk of investigations within an agency overlapping with other investigations or operations, either within that agency or with neighboring agencies. This has the potential to compromise one or both of the investigations/operations and in the most serious of circumstances lead to death or serious harm. Deconfliction is the process that is used to determine whether multiple investigations/operations are being carried out against the same person or crime and then to provide notification to each involved party of the shared interest. The process seeks to minimize conflict between the agencies that are involved and maximize the effectiveness of any investigation. Deconfliction may also be used to detect where a person is operating as a human source for more than one agency. There are two factors that must be in place for effective deconfliction:

1. There must be a trusted party that can hold details of all ongoing investigations/operations.
2. All other parties must use the deconfliction process.

With regard to deconflicting human sources, the most effective way to do this is to have a regional human source management software solution where deconfliction can be done automatically.

7.32 Performance Metrics

Performance metrics, also known as "performance indicators," are an essential aspect of most modern law enforcement management and a necessary part of effective intelligence management. Managers need to be able to quantify what is being achieved, and even though when it comes to intelligence management, this is not always easy. Most metrics in law enforcement are quantitative in their nature but given that some intelligence-based activities remain covert, it can be difficult to be specific to what has been achieved. For example, if an undercover officer penetrates an anarchist group intent on causing damage to property in a major city and the intelligence gained from her allows police to thwart the intended activities, how can that success be measured? Some would suggest counting the number of intelligence reports she submitted in relation to the activity, but is this a realistic guide?

Where executive action is taken, seizures made, and arrests effected, it would outwardly appear to be very easy to quantify the success, but to which piece of intelligence or to which resource does one attribute that success if the end result has been because of the combined efforts of many different strands in the intelligence system? Good intelligence-based operations are rarely due to the efforts of one person but are most often the result of an effective intelligence management system working in harmony with the rest of the agency.

That said, all those involved must come up with effective metrics. Some of the easiest ones to use are as follows:

- Stating the results of executive action. For example, a human source provided details that led to the arrest of two persons and the recovery of stolen jewelry worth $100,000.
- Stating the number of intelligence reports submitted against the identified intelligence need. For example, an undercover operation has led to the submission of 49 intelligence reports this month in relation to the trafficking of heroin, an agreed priority requirement.
- Stating the number of actionable intelligence reports submitted against an identified intelligence need. The term "actionable" is intended to convey where the actioning party needs to make minimal effort to achieve the desired result. For example, there are 100 g of methamphetamine at 50 Lakeside Drive, Anytown. They are there now. All the actioning party needs to do is get a warrant and kick in a door! Another interesting side to this metric is to see how many pieces of actionable intelligence are given to a party and how many they actually respond to. Analysis of results in some police departments showed that as little as 10% of actionable intelligence was being actioned by those to whom it was given.
- Stating the number of specific intelligence requests that are answered. For example, where there has been a homicide, and a human source is tasked with trying to identify the perpetrator.

These are just some ideas that are proven to add value to intelligence management and have been instrumental in proving the worth of the intelligence function. There are many out there who would deride intelligence management as an effective and legitimate law enforcement tool—it is nice to have the figures to prove them wrong!

7.33   Information Technology

The effective use of information technology is an essential part of any intelligence management system. Agencies cannot effectively gather and manage intelligence without the use of information technology. The next part of this chapter examines why information technology is needed and discusses some of the potential problems associated with it. Most of the section focuses on computers as they are at the core of what is required and most people know what a computer is and what it can do even if they have no idea how it does it. However, as technology evolves, so does the meaning of the words used and difficulties arise in delineating between one type of device and another. The descriptions used here are intended to provide clarity of meaning and not a technological reference.

- *Computer.* The term used is intended to include a PC, namely, those typically found in homes, Macs (computers made by the Apple company), laptops, netbooks,* and computers that are attached to a network.
- *Tablets.* A tablet is the generic name for a mobile computer that is larger than a mobile phone but similar in style and generally operated through a touch screen.
- *Cellular telephone.* This is often referred to as a "cell" or a "mobile." Essentially, it is a portable phone used to make and receive calls and to send and receive text messages.
- *Handheld device.* Use of the term "handheld device" is intended to convey significantly greater functionality than may be found in a basic cellular telephone. Handheld devices such as a "Blackberry" or "iPhone" have huge and ever-increasing functionality including mobile applications (apps), photograph, video and audio recording, and Internet access.
- *Network.* A network is a group of computers that are interconnected and that allows the sharing of functionality and information.
- *Server.* A server is a computer program that serves the requests of other clients. These clients either run on the same computer or connect through a network. Servers provide essential services across the networks of large organizations. The separation of servers within an agency forms a part of IT security.
- *Records management system (RMS).* An RMS is "an agency-wide system that provides for the storage, retrieval, retention, manipulation, archiving, and viewing of information, records, documents, or files pertaining to law enforcement operations" (LEITSC 2009).
- *Database.* A database is an organized collection of data, stored in digital form, and maintained in a way that supports the agency's

---

* The smaller version of a laptop, so small that anyone more than 40 years of age cannot read the screen, even at arm's length!

requirements for that data. A database should be managed to agreed levels of quality in terms of accuracy, availability, and usability with all data being entered in line with agreed protocols.

- *Digital media.* Digital media is any type of information capable of being stored in the computer, including data, voice, and video. A page is not considered digital media but scan the page and the product of the scanning is a form of digital media
- *Metadata.* This is data that sit "underneath" the data you can see on a computer screen. It is also referred to as metacontent and can be defined as data providing information about one or more aspects of the data, such as follows:
  - Means of creation of the data
  - Purpose of the data
  - Time and date of creation
  - Creator or author of data

The only thing at this stage that an intelligence practitioner really needs to know about metadata is that it exists and that if you send an electronic copy of the data the metacontent is likely to go with it. This has, in the past, caused compromise both to assets and to prosecution cases. (Metadata and its use in open source collection are discussed in Chapter 9.)

- *Commercially available off-the-shelf (COTS).* This term is widely used in the commercial sector and advocated as a solution in literature issued by the U.S. and other governments. The term "commercially available off-the-shelf" refers to an item that is already available in the commercial marketplace as opposed to developing an in-house or one-off solution. COTS software products have the potential to offer significant savings in terms of maintenance and development and may well be easier to procure under government contract.

7.34   Need for Computers

To all intents and purposes, the primary function of a computer is that of labor-saving. There is nothing that a computer can do that a person could not do if they were given adequate time, and there is much that people can do that computers still cannot do. However, people have limited time available, and a computer can do in milliseconds what it would take a person many years to achieve. Time costs money and computers save time. Intelligence management involves working with huge amounts of material and finding links between various pieces. Quite simply, law enforcement cannot afford to pay for the time it would take people to do what is required. Additionally, the material requiring processing is only of worth if it can be processed quickly and people cannot do this. Computers do many tasks more cost-effectively and quicker than people. As McDowell (2009:225) observes,

> Apart from "creative thinking" there is no aspect of the intelligence process that cannot be assisted or facilitated by the appropriate use of suitable computer applications.

Furthermore, computerized systems go a long way to ensuring adherence to standards and procedures and holding agency members accountable for their actions. Peterson (2011), commenting on the use of computerized systems, notes,

> ...appropriately constructed databases are the key to maintaining a criminal intelligence system that is in compliance with regulations and guidelines, allows data to be easily retrieved, supports analysis and allows for automatic audit trailing of access to and dissemination from its files.

Cost and time savings are not the only benefits of a computerized intelligence management system. Purpose-built software will do the following:

- Significantly reduce errors. People are far more likely to make mistakes than a computer. Good software recognizes errors as a person enters them and can force correction, thus reducing the chances of data corruption.
- Provide for rapid and thorough searching using different search types with varying degrees of complexity.
- Create conformity in intelligence products. The software dictates how records will be completed disallowing the tendency that people have to create their version of how records should look.
- Provides a secure and fully auditable system for retaining intelligence. Computerization helps to manage many concerns surrounding intelligence. Problems relating to document security, privacy, and corruption are all more effectively managed using a computerized system.
- Allow for the instantaneous access to records by those who need it, regardless of geographic separation from where it was created. A paper record is useless if it is 500 miles and a flight away.

7.35   Failures in Computerized Systems

Poor computerized systems are all too common in law enforcement and unfortunately no more so than in intelligence management. Ratcliffe and the U.S. Department of Justice Office of Community Oriented Policing Services (2007) highlight the problem:

Technical problems seem to plague every police department. The rapidity with which technology advances always appears to leave many aspects of policing operating in a proverbial dark age. Nowhere is this more apparent than in crime analysis and intelligence, both areas that make significant technological demands.

It is far from unusual to find that an agency has spent a considerable amount of money on what they were led to believe would be a solution for intelligence management within their agency, only to find it does not work the way they thought it would. Understanding why this happens means the mistakes can be avoided.

- What is done is done and cannot be undone. Many agencies have wasted millions on software that will not do the work it was intended to do and then quite willingly spend as much again trying to fix it. When the problems are pointed out, the reaction is often, "We have got this and can't afford anything else." At the back of such comments is often someone not willing to admit fault for the initial decision and fails to take any account of the amount of resources being wasted in continuing with the flawed software. Additionally, there is what is often referred to as the "sunk cost fallacy," a position where having spent so much, those involved feel forced to continue, regardless of future cost. It is irrational behavior that results in the continuing waste of resources. Such decisions are flawed, because the amount of money already spent is actually irrelevant to the decision being made, namely, what should be done now. Cut your losses and start again.
- Not having an intelligence management system in place. If the agency does not have a purpose-built intelligence system, then how can they expect to find software that assists in the management of that system? Far too often, agencies buy software without putting their own house in order before looking for a product to help them. Conversely, an architect does not draw plans for a building without knowing all the products they can potentially use in the construction. It begs the question as to how an agency can design an intelligence management system if they do not know the software functionality that is available. An agency needs to be fully aware of what software solutions are out there when creating the plan for its intelligence management system.
- Beware the Chief. Seduced by "snake oil" salespeople, senior management rarely have an in-depth understanding of intelligence, yet they are often targeted by software companies offering solutions to problems real or imagined. These managers are provided with slick multimedia demonstrations of the product from people who can talk the talk all followed by wine and canapés! Sales staff are doing a job and their job is to sell product. Many of the products are good, but only those doing the business on a daily basis can evaluate any

product and access its suitability within an agency. Only such practitioners can ask the pertinent questions and see potential pitfalls.
Such assessment must involve qualified IT staff as intelligence practitioners rarely have sufficient knowledge of technical matters.

- Practitioners often need solutions relatively quickly, but the business
  processes to get what is needed are perceived as being too slow and
  overly bureaucratic with the processes of scoping and procurement
  taking excessively long periods of time.
- IT departments in charge! Perhaps the most damaging problem for
  practitioners is the procurement of IT solutions by the IT department with little or no consultation with those who will be using the
  software. Born out of arrogance, this attitude wastes millions each
  year for LEAs in terms of poor functionality and the compromise
  of data.

A common belief among some in law enforcement is that as long as
information is held somewhere in a law enforcement computer, then software
can be built and used that will find and extract that information. This belief
is misguided for a number of reasons:

- The cost and technical difficulties of building software that will
  search across all computers within an agency is both technically
  challenging and likely to represent poor value for the money when
  compared to beginning again with a purpose-built solution.
- Many computers used by law enforcement stand alone and are
  unconnected to the Web. They have been kept that way for security
  reasons and do not have sufficient internal security to prevent unauthorized access if connected. If connected to a network, the lack of
  internal security leaves them vulnerable to attack.
- If and when a search engine is placed across such disparate computers,
  the quality of data found is of questionable worth. This raw material
  is not intelligence, because it has not been previously processed. Once
  it has been located in the raw state, the information-to-intelligence
  process has to begin. Once processed, it then has to be entered into an
  intelligence repository. An easier solution is to enter the information
  into the process directly upon receipt, as a matter of course.

7.36 Records Management Systems

Many agencies will be inclined to use their existing records management system (RMS) for intelligence management, the main driver for this being costs.
While it is tempting to keep this paragraph short and say "Don't do it"; it is

unfair not to give some of the reasons behind that sentiment. Existing RMSs should not be used for intelligence for reasons that include the following:

- The myth that law enforcement requires only one software solution to meet all their needs. This usually leads to software that meets no one's needs.
- RMSs are rarely configured for the intelligence function and thus it becomes increasingly difficult to achieve the desired functionality. They have not been designed to deal with the processes involved in intelligence management and therefore it will always be a case of the ugly stepsister trying to fit into Cinderella's slipper. For many of the developing companies, intelligence has just been an add-on or "of course it can do that." "It fits. It fits!" Well, actually, no, it does not. The amount of time wasted in trying to hobble something together and the ongoing costs of ineffective inputting means the agency ends up paying far more for a much poorer result.
- RMSs are significantly more vulnerable to freedom of information (FOI) requests, the argument being made that law enforcement is publicly accountable and that the RMS forms part of public records. From a practical standpoint, members dealing with FOI requests rarely have any understanding of intelligence sensitivities, and the intelligence can too easily be inadvertently released.
- Records in an RMS are interconnected, making it extremely difficult to protect sensitive material from being inappropriately accessed.
- Too often there is insufficient security in the RMS with numerous IT staff having ready access to the servers. This "back door" type of access means that information can be taken without anyone who does not have expert knowledge knowing it is gone. This creates the risk of a major compromise. Furthermore, many agencies subcontract IT work to outside aspects of government or to the private sector, escalating this risk. A separate intelligence system means the number of IT staff required to have access is less and they can be appropriately vetted.
- An RMS is likely to be only one of many computerized solutions already being used within the agency. The users of these are all likely to be equally as hesitant about using the RMS, because it cannot supply them with what they need. The choice is then whether to develop software to integrate all these dysfunctional processes or start again. Linking such diverse technology is likely to be costly, and it will often be cheaper and easier to transfer data from those systems to a new software solution.

- The identity of specialized officers needs to be protected and steps need to be taken to prevent their personal details from becoming public knowledge. The very nature of an RMS means that it is readily available, on a daily basis, to all members of that agency. The number of users and the ease of access to the RMS make penetration more likely. This can create a real threat to officer safety.
- In the United States, using an RMS to store intelligence along with all the other agency records is contrary to government guidance contained in 28 CFR 23 (U.S. Bureau of Justice Assistance 1998).
- An RMS may lack an audit facility of sufficient standard that is required to ensure integrity in the intelligence management function.

7.37   Essential Aspects of Intelligence Software

Some of the features for software for managing intelligence include the following:

- Must be purpose-built. Given that significant amounts of intelligence products that are likely to fall into the need-to-know category, enabling too many members to be in a position to access that intelligence through an "attack" on the computer creates an unacceptable risk. Where a purpose-built intelligence repository is created, IT staff with access to the software should have a sufficient level of vetting to match the content of the intelligence repository.
- Must have a number of "access levels." Access levels enable intelligence of varying degrees of sensitivity to be stored in a way that only those with access to that level are permitted to see it. In lay terms, consider each level as a separate floor in a building. The higher up the building you go, the more you are allowed to see. Those on floor one can see only the content of floor one; those on floor two can see the content of floor two and also see floor one. Access to floor three grants the privilege of seeing what is on floors three, two, and one. And so on. The more sophisticated the agency, the greater the number of access levels they will require to operate securely.
- Access levels should protect entire content. The access level must protect the entire content of an intelligence product. For example, consider the situation where a sensitive report states that Tomas Ankeny is involved in a terrorism plot and has purchased a number of weapons for use in that attack. There may be no other report on Tomas Ankeny within the intelligence repository. If the intelligence report merits being held at access level 9 in the repository, then Ankeny's name and address and so

on should be visible only to those with level 9 access. If Ankeny's name appears at all levels of the repository, even though it is detached from the intelligence content, the investigation may still be compromised by an overzealous officer who happens to have come across it.

- The capability should exist where an officer can see intelligence he has submitted regardless of level, but not have access to other intelligence at any other level. For example, Detective Garcia submits intelligence that is entered at access level 5; his normal access level is 2. He should be able to read the intelligence *he* submitted, including the report that sits at level 5, but no other intelligence at level 5, provided that additional comments have not been added in the Intelligence Unit that Garcia should not be aware off.
- Comprehensive searching across the intelligence management system must be available and should include all standard search types such as keyword, Google type searches, multiple and linked queries, include and exclude functionality, synonym and sounds-like querying, and so on.

There are a number of rules that constitute good practice in relation to data contained in any database. These principles should be applied to all aspects of the computerized system for intelligence management:

- Data from multiple supply processes should be integrated to enable a central view across the entire database.
- The agency should continually strive to improve data quality by providing consistent instructions on completing entries and by fixing erroneous material.
- The content should be presented in a consistent manner that can be readily utilized by the intelligence customers.
- The content should be structured in such a way that it delivers high performance with respect to queries, regardless of the complexity of the query.
- Content in the database should never be capable of being overwritten or deleted except where there is a legal requirement to do so and then a record should be maintained of who removed it.
- There should be a comprehensive record of the history of all entries.

7.38   What Computers Will Not Do

The American writer Sidney J. Harris warned, "The real danger is not that computers will begin to think like men, but that men will begin to think like computers." Unfortunately, there is a growing trend for many involved in intelligence management to look to computers for a solution to provide all the answers. For some it is as if a computer is viewed as an "all seeing eye," which only has to be asked what to find and it will produce the answers. What this has done is not as bad as Harris articulates with men thinking like computers; it is worse: they have become subservient to them.

A major problem for law enforcement and intelligence agencies is the belief that computer software can collect information of the nature and depth that is required to prevent crime and to protect national security. Programs developed for use in intelligence, no matter how sophisticated they may appear, cannot replace traditional intelligence gathering methods.

Computers cannot process information into intelligence; this process requires a person's input. Computer programming has yet to reach the level of sophistication that can replace the judgment of a trained intelligence professional. Furthermore, computers cannot ensure that information is submitted for processing as and when it should be. This can only be achieved by adequate training of officers and the enforcement of the relevant procedures by line management.

7.39 Emerging Technologies

Technology is developing at such a relentless rate that it is all but impossible to write with authority in its regard. However, what can be noted is that the rapidity in its development impacts intelligence management in two main ways:

1. Criminals will seek to use emerging technologies to aid them in the commission of crime or to develop new crimes. The use of technology such as Voice Over Internet Protocol makes intercepting communications significantly more difficult for law enforcement, while Internet fraud is fast becoming more lucrative than the drug trade, with significantly less chance of being caught and a shorter sentence if one is caught. It is difficult for most LEAs to keep up with the nature of these emerging technologies, let alone have staff sufficiently trained and equipped to investigate them. Gathering intelligence against such criminality is also extremely difficult, as much of it is carried out in different jurisdictions and in places where no one but the criminal needs to be. What those involved in intelligence need to keep in mind is, first, the requirement to keep searching for indications of new technologies being used either to facilitate crime or as emerging crimes. Second, the

intelligence professional involved may not have sufficient professional knowledge in this field to obtain the maximum amount of intelligence on the nature and use of the particular technology, in which case, a subject matter expert should be used. Third, while many information-gathering techniques will not be as suitable for dealing with this type of crime, many others will work just as effectively. In addition, there is arguably a substantially greater need for good quality intelligence both on the technology the criminals are using and on the crimes being committed.

2. Technology used in gathering and managing information is advancing rapidly. There are a vast number of gadgets and software programs, each of which claim to be invaluable to those involved in intelligence, and each competing for a market share of the limited law enforcement budget. It is very easy for law enforcement to waste money when it comes to this technology for a number of reasons. First, some of the technology is highly specialized and likely to be used only a limited number of times. Despite how amazing the technology may be, smaller agencies simply cannot justify the expenditure. Second, as with any purchase, it is very much, "buyer beware!" It is easy for sales staff to claim that a product does something, but nothing should be purchased without thorough examination of the product against identified operational requirements that have been prepared in detail by those who will be using the technology and then fully documented. Third, consideration must be given to the likely life span of the technology. If the technology is not being kept up to date as part of a maintenance agreement with the provider, the life span of the product and lifetime costs should be considered before purchase. Fourth, consideration should always be given to sharing the cost of the purchase among partner agencies. Not only is this good housekeeping but also it is the most effective use of taxpayer's money.

7.40   Freedom of Information Exemption

All documents, materials and information, and intelligence contained in an intelligence management system whether computerized or not should be exempt from release under any Freedom of Information Act or other similar legislation. The fact that the intelligence management system sits outside the agency's RMS makes this significantly easier to achieve both from a legal standpoint and from a practical perspective.

7.41   Taking Shape

Having set out to build an effective intelligence management system using integrated IT, the basic structures of what is required should now be taking shape. Figure 7.4 illustrates the various components of an integrated intelligence management system. Each of the boxes on the left illustrates a separate but integrated software module for the collection of information. The information gathered is processed within the Intelligence Unit (illustrated left of center) without any requirement for it to change from electronic format. Where an intelligence product is created, it is lodged electronically within the repository (right of center), from where it can be dissimilated either to other parts of the agency or to other agencies (far right). The software used by the analyst (below) should not retain any data, and any product created by an analyst must be forwarded through the Intelligence Unit. (In effect, it is most likely that the analyst will be a member of the Intelligence Unit.) Each area

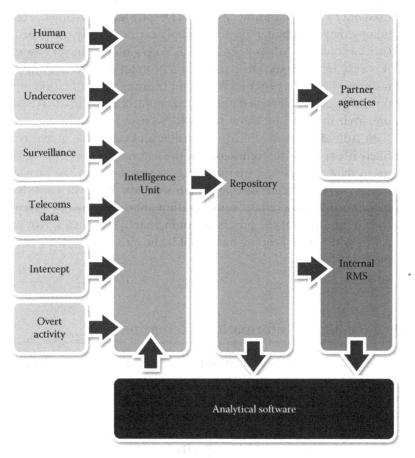

Figure 7.4 An example of a computerized intelligence management system.

of the system is access protected by user-defined roles; in short, if a member does not have the user entitlement to see into an area, access will be denied. There may be benefits facilitating analytical access to the various collection modules, but this must be given serious consideration particularly when it comes to the more sensitive business areas; a balance must be established between potential benefits and security risks.

When it comes to access to the various modules for information collection, the access granted to Intelligence Unit staff needs careful consideration. Table 7.1 illustrates the suggested access that is granted to staff in relation to a covert module, while Table 7.2 illustrates the access to information collected through traditional overt methods of collection.

There are also likely to be a number of other databases that the Intelligence Unit staff will require access to. These may include a database containing information relating to firearms or prisoners, details of numbers collected through automatic license plate readers, or other similar databases. There must always be policies for why any member can access such data, procedures mandating how that data is to be accessed, and an appropriate audit trail of when they did.

Finally, the more information that can be initially captured and transmitted electronically, the greater potential there is for financial savings for the agency, provided each computer used can communicate with the main system. Agencies should strive to be in a position where all staff can submit information for intelligence purposes electronically with very limited, if any,

Table 7.1 Intelligence Unit Access to "Covert Management" Software

Human Source Operational Management Software	
Access denied	Access permitted
Identity	
Application and authorization	
Contact notes	
Rewards	Information submitted
Policy log	
Risk management strategy	
Enhanced profile	

Table 7.2 Intelligence Unit Access to "Overt" Submission Software

Overt Operational Management Software	
Access denied	Access permitted
No restriction	Identity of person originating information
	Information submitted
	Any rewards sought or given

need for hard copy. Web-based software programs should be installed on all of the in-car terminals that staff use, or on the mobile devices they carry, so that they directly input using the agency's information submission.

7.42   The Bottom Line

When it comes to considering IT solutions, these are key factors:

1. Intelligence management is only effective if it is computerized.
2. An agency should not try to "self-build" an IT solution.
3. An agency should not use its RMS.
4. An agency should get an independent professional assessment of the security of any solution used.
5. An agency should be cautious of software companies that say they can build a solution from scratch. If the agency is going down this route, the requirements and specifications must be spelled out to the "Nth" degree.

7.43   Protective Markings

There are two fundamental aspects regarding any intelligence-related-document—*protection of it* and *access to it*. If the protection is not at a high enough level, then it can lead to serious, even fatal, consequences. If the protection is too high, then the people who need it cannot get access to it with equally grave consequences. Getting the balance between these competing agendas is not easy. A tool established by governments in most countries is that of "protective marking." Protective markings are a standardized set of protection grades that are allotted to documents to ensure that only those allowed to have access to the contents of that document do so. Protective markings are used to help protect information from intentional or inadvertent release to unauthorized readers. The primary use of protective markings has always been in the arena of national security with protective marking being used as an indication as to what the government has decided must be protected from wider readership and to what extent it must be protected. As the name protective marking implies, the balance is weighted toward protecting the content from being seen with the level of protection correlating to the amount of harm that might be done should the document be compromised. This is often referred to as the "harm test." Recognizing that government bodies including law enforcement must share information, the protective markings are also intended to provide assurances that the shared content will continue to be protected to agreed standards, irrespective of format or the way in which it has been shared.

With each protective marking comes an agreed set of criteria that identifies what should be kept at that level and a set of standards that explains how that document must be stored and accessed, as well as how it should be transported and often the level of clearance needed to read it. These guidelines are usually comprehensive in their nature, and while easily accepted and achieved within the culture of intelligence agencies, they often do not mesh well with the law enforcement culture. For a body of people who spend their days enforcing laws, cops do not take well to being told what they cannot do and resent when regulations are rigidly applied; however, when it comes to material that is marked secret and above, it is only by enforcing such regimes that the necessary standards of protection can be maintained. A problem that is regularly encountered in law enforcement is the downgrading of protective marking, because it is seen as too difficult or too expensive to meet the standards that have been set by government. Examples of this include the storage of the names of human sources, details of members of the public who have put their lives in danger to provide information, and details pertaining to protected witnesses, all of which are often managed way below the suggested standards set by the protective marking. If the national guidance in many jurisdictions is examined, it can be seen that such details meet the criteria for storage at secret levels or above, yet law enforcement continues to store such details locked in desks or in cupboards that would not keep a child from candy.

There is not always a smooth transition from the application of protective markings from the national security arena to the law enforcement context. Introducing their use or ensuring appropriate use normally requires a member who has real understanding of the theory and is not hesitant in enforcing the rules. The general principles relating to protective markings are as follows:

- Protective markings should be agreed on at national levels and are in place for every government agency.
- Protective markings should provide a standard term for each marking limited in length and preferably one word.
- Protective markings within one nation should correlate with markings in other nations, where information is likely to be exchanged between nations.
- Protective markings should not be confused with the repository access levels used within an agency. However, within that agency, there should be a table showing equivalence between access levels and national protective markings.
- Protective markings can have a number of descriptors where necessary. (Such descriptors are likely to include "commercial," "staff," "medical," etc.)
- Protective markings can bear national caveats such as "U.K. eyes" only.

- Only the originator or designated owner can protectively mark an asset. Any change to the protective marking requires the originator or designated owner's permission. When protectively marking a document, it should be assessed against the criteria for each protective marking. Applying too high a protective marking can inhibit legitimate access, while applying too low a protective marking may lead to the compromise of it.
- Where a large number of similarly marked documents are stored together, the aggregated impact may necessitate a higher protective marking and/or additional control measures.
- A file should be marked to reflect the highest protective marking of any of the contents within it.
- All documents should be clearly marked with their level of protection.
- Protectively marked documents are intended for use within government agencies. Care must always be taken when sharing material outside government, as there may be limited redress should the recipient choose to make it public. However, there are always people within the private sector who will need to see sensitive documents, either because they are providing support services to law enforcement or because their role requires them to have access to such material: for example, the security manager at a major airport may have to see very sensitive intelligence about a potential attack in order to make appropriate changes to security.

There are a number of common problems in protective marking:

- Members do not understand the meaning of the markings and/or pay only lip service to their meaning.
- Members deliberately over-mark documents to avoid sharing information.
- Members deliberately under-mark documents to avoid the constraints appropriate marking would merit.
- Intelligence agencies fail to understand law enforcement obligations with regard to acting on shared information. For example, an intelligence agency may mark details of a threat of an attack on a property as "top secret" and then share it with law enforcement, expecting the LEA not do anything, not realizing the agency is legally obliged to act.
- LEAs failing to understand sensitivity of intelligence and the methodology employed by intelligence agencies. A cavalier approach to the rules leaves intelligence agencies reluctant to share. This often occurs when law enforcement intelligence staff brief out intelligence to senior management who do not recognize the sensitivities required in handling it.

- Failure of IT specialists within agencies to ensure that computer systems provided meet the requirements of protective markings. There is little excuse for this, given the availability of such things as encrypted databases and so on.

It is of benefit to look at the protective markings that are found in a number of countries, both from the perspective of comparing how some countries address protective marking and because of the transnational aspect of terrorism and organized crime.

As can be seen from Table 7.3, there is a standardization of terminology across the top three markings—top secret, secret, and confidential, although there can be variance within these nations with regard to what each term actually means. As general guidance, however, they work well when exchanging documents on a transnational basis. Where things become more complicated, it is in the lower markings with some nations adding extra ones and having different terms for those markings. This causes complications for law enforcement and is based on the fact that most LEAs were not often involved in national security work. This situation has obviously changed with law enforcement frequently being involved with national security work and the increasing need to exchange documents between law enforcement and intelligence agencies. Furthermore, there has been a desire on the part of law enforcement to raise their own standards regarding protective marking and the need to create uniformity when exchanging law enforcement intelligence with other LEAs.

There is a clear need, at least on a national basis, to have a protective marking scheme that allows the exchange of national security material between

Table 7.3   Comparison of International Protective Markings

United Kingdom	United States	Canada[a]	European Union	AUS/NZ	NATO
Top secret	Top secret	Top secret	Top secret	Top secret	Top secret
Secret	Secret	Secret	Secret	Secret	Secret
Confidential	Confidential	Confidential	Confidential	Confidential	Confidential
Restricted			Restricted	Restricted	Restricted
Protect[b]	Controlled unclassified information	Controlled unclassified information	European Council		
Not protectively marked					Unclassified

[a] Canadian law enforcement uses levels protected "A," "B," and "C," which are intended to correlate with national security markings.

[b] While it is recognized that the theory expounded here is the same as that used in the construction of the Titanic, it should not cloud one's judgment of it. The theory for building the Titanic was sound; the flaw in its application was relying on only one safeguard and overconfidence in it!

government bodies, including law enforcement. Most countries have this. Where problems often arise is with law enforcement generated material and the lack of standardization with regard to sharing material. Recognizing that there was a significant problem in the United States, President Bush (2008) issued a presidential memorandum that attempted to address the situation with regard to protective marking. In it, a new category of protective marking is created, namely, "controlled unclassified information" defined as,

> a categorical designation that refers to unclassified information that does not meet the standards for National Security Classification under Executive Order 12958, as amended, but is (i) pertinent to the national interests of the United States or to the important interests of entities outside the Federal Government, and (ii) under law or policy requires protection from unauthorized disclosure, special handling safeguards, or prescribed limits on exchange or dissemination.

This was, at least in part, an attempt to create some form of standardization. However, this order was revoked in November 2010 by President Obama (2010) under Executive Order 13556. Overcoming difficulties around protective markings led Gray and Slade (2008) to comment "The reality that U.S. intelligence agencies do not share information well should come as no surprise—it is both the direct and unintended consequence of policy-maker action." Continuing, they accurately sum up the problems that are not restricted to the United States but are all too common elsewhere:

> ... perhaps the most significant factor impeding the sharing of intelligence between various agencies, particularly those at the state and local levels of government, is security classification policy. These policies, and their resulting practices, hobble sharing in two ways: first, the over-classification of material prevents wide dissemination and second, the lack of provisions for state and local officials to obtain security clearances prevents them from accessing information that is classified. Over-classification can be attributed to a particular institutional attribute of intelligence collection agencies—the primacy of protecting their intelligence sources and methods.

Regardless of the problems that may exist, the bottom line is that it is the responsibility of all intelligence staff to have a sound knowledge of protective markings and how they are applied within their jurisdiction.

7.44 Protective Security

Protective security refers to the process of keeping the agency's assets and information safe from all threats. The agency should regularly assess and manage the risks posed by all potential adversarial groups or individuals.

When an agency is investigating organized crime and terrorism, the agency should employ counterintelligence techniques to understand the strength of the intelligence-gathering capacity of those organizations and the threat they pose to security. Appropriate mitigation can be put in place only if one is aware of the nature and extent of the threat posed.

The following are some of the potential adversarial elements that are likely to pose a risk to the intelligence system of any agency:

- Criminals.
- Terrorists.
- Computer hackers either working as individuals* or as part of an organized group.
- Anarchist groups. The interlinking of protest groups and various groups of hackers has led to a number of high-profile compromises.
- Media/press. Always chasing stories of one sort or another, the unscrupulous journalist will seek out ways to obtain anything to do with intelligence.

An agency's security can be compromised by means of stealth. What appears to be either innocent or lawful behavior is used to obtain the desired information. Two common forms of such stealth attacks are as follows:

1. *Elicitation.* We all like to talk. Far too often, we fail to recognize how much information we actually are passing out if the person is skillful enough to pick up on it. Given that an individual who is inside an agency will have regular contact with many different members of that agency, it is not difficult for them to pick up substantial amounts of information.

2. *Legislative inquiry.* FOI legislation can be used to obtain information that in itself may appear innocuous but when combined with the material obtained from other such requests has the potential to create compromise. Such structure FOI requests are often referred to as "mosaic attacks." Similar circumstances can occur with disclosure during trial with law enforcement failing to recognize the nature of material that has previously been disclosed in other cases. These threats are at their highest when law enforcement is working against a highly sophisticated and structured group.

---

* Such an individual is often the spotty faced adolescent who spends his days and nights in his bedroom, with his parents mistakenly believing he is using his computer for what most teenage boys do, namely, watching porn! Unfortunately, what the kid has been doing is hacking into the computers of the Pentagon or some similar government establishment and the feds are now knocking at the front door.

Establishing an effective protection regime can only be done by using a trained person working to agreed standards. In smaller agencies, it will probably be necessary to seek outside advice, as it is unlikely anyone in the agency will have the necessary level of skill to carry out an effective review.

There are three elements in regard to security, and all three must be addressed by those with sufficient expertise to address the threat:

- Information communications technology
- Staff
- Physical

7.45   Information Communications Technology Security

There should be no doubt with regard to the need for agencies to use computers and other technical equipment with regard to the management of intelligence. However, with the significant benefits come significant risks. When using a computerized system or systems in the management of intelligence, they need to be set up and structured to meet the level of threat that is posed and to manage the risk should that threat become a reality. Rarely is the level of expertise found within an agency to thoroughly and objectively evaluate the security of an IT system. It is well worth the money to have it done professionally. Only someone working in IT security on a daily basis is likely to have sufficient knowledge to evaluate the security given the potential level of threat directed against it. Accreditation under any relevant government scheme, with regard to the security, should be a set objective. Some simple points that must be considered include the following:

- Who has back-end access to the computer? Who are the IT people? How many are there? Are they vetted to an appropriate level?
- How strict is the agency's policy around logins? How often are passwords changed?
- Is all data encrypted?
- Who has print privileges and/or access with memory devices? The numbers should be very low.
- Are all actions fully auditable?

7.46   Personnel Security

The "insider" threat poses perhaps the most likely of all risks to seriously threaten the security of an intelligence management system. People are notoriously hard to predict and unfortunately management often creates the circumstances where it is easy for staff to compromise a system's security. In some circumstances, poor managers create motive for security breaches. Furnham and Taylor (2004) spent nearly 300 pages examining the "dark side" of employee behavior. In building any intelligence management system, the bottom line is to build a system assuming those involved will go bad. If the system is built in this way, the agency minimizes the chances of staff going bad, minimizes the damage they can do if they go bad, and creates mechanisms to readily identify that harm is being done. Some simple points around staff security include the following:

- Are staff vetted? How often is their vetting checked or renewed? Are vettings done to a sufficiently high level, given the member's access?
- How are staff selected for sensitive posts? How many staff are rotated through those posts and how often?
- How well are the personal activities of staff monitored? Are there confidential mechanisms in place to report suspicions?
- How often does the agency assess the amount of harm one individual could do either by the virtue of the posts they are in or by how their career path has exposed them to sensitive material?

Often law enforcement members fail to identify the risk posed by support staff such as cleaners. Human nature makes such individuals seem all but invisible, yet their potential to compromise security is significant. All too often, they are allowed to come and go into sensitive areas as they please; the only authority being needed is that they are carrying a vacuum cleaner! Similarly, security staff often have a significant amount of latitude to move about a building late at night or in the early hours of the morning. Given that law enforcement generally fails miserably in regard to maintaining security standards, opportunities are often rife. Here again, the agency must look objectively at the risk such individuals pose and mitigate those risks.

7.47   Physical Security

Physical security addresses the risks of material being compromised because there are insufficient physical barriers to prevent such compromises. Mechanisms to physically protect sensitive material include the following:

- Secure cabinets
- Alarmed rooms
- Security policies and training
- Asset tagging of important items so that they activate an alarm when removed form a specific area, such as the type of alert that is used to prevent goods being stolen from shops.

- Secure rooms that can be used for sensitive discussions. Such rooms are protected to the highest standards and have counter-eavesdropping defenses employed.
- Establishing a clear desk policy. A clear desk policy is a set of rules regarding what can be left out in an office when no one is present or when a member of staff leaves his desk for a prolonged period of time. Without drilling down into the whys and wherefores of the policy, the bottom line is that if an office has a clear desk policy, a criminal should be able to walk into that office and get *nothing* that could help them in any way. It means nothing is left on the desks, nothing on the walls, and everything locked down tight.
- Nominating a person with agency-wide responsibilities for security.

Effective physical security benefits from an asset-centered approach, with the highest level of protection focused where the asset rests and then proceeding progressively outward through various layers that end at the perimeter of the law enforcement facility. Security should be designed to identify physical assets, the threats posed to them, and the vulnerabilities that exist with steps then being taken to prioritize and minimize the risks.

7.48 Compartmentalization

As far as practically possible, the various parts of the intelligence management process should be compartmentalized to minimize the amount of harm any one breach can cause. Those with access to one specialized compartment should not generally have access to another. For example, an officer having access to the details of the entire agency's human sources should not also have access to the numbers of all the telephones that are being intercepted. Similarly, an officer with access to all drug intelligence will not normally have access to all terrorism-related intelligence. The intelligence manager may have access to all the intelligence but will not have access to the specifics of the operation from which that intelligence originated. The use of intelligence compartments limits the amount of damage that any one person or one breach of security can do.*

All security breaches, regardless of nature, should be recorded and investigated to establish the cause of the breach and what circumstances facilitated it.

---

* While this is not considered an "official" protective marking it is used to facilitate the exchange of sensitive information with nongovernmental bodies such as the industry and the private sector.

7.49   Business Continuity

A key element of protective security is a business continuity plan. This type of plan manages the risk of a potential catastrophic event occurring. In the intelligence world, such events would include a major fire at the headquarters building that holds the computerized system; a natural disaster, which creates a prolonged power outage; the compromise of a large number of details pertaining to human sources; and so on. Anticipating such disastrous occurrences means the agency is not totally wrong-footed when they do occur (and they will!). Business continuity plans will include various control measures such as all computerized records being backed up on a regular basis with no greater time period than a week elapsing between each backup and the copy being stored securely in an alternative location. Additionally, the agency should have emergency accommodation from which they can set up and run the software from the copy. It is not unusual for agencies to have backed up material only to find that they have nowhere to access it from and no way of doing it.

In creating a business continuity plan, consideration should be given to staff matters. It is not unusual for one individual to make himself indispensable to the agency. The staff are the only one with access codes to a certain cupboard or the only one who knows where certain material is. Then he goes and gets hit by a bus and the agency is wrong-footed. Business continuity planning should identify key individuals and make sure that the associated risks are addressed.

Business continuity planning should be appropriate to the size of the agency and the nature of the work in which they are engaged. Planning should address both the management of the immediate circumstances and mechanisms to recover from them.

7.50   Taking Shape

Processes for all aspects of the intelligence management system should now be taking shape and addressing the day-to-day requirements of the system. While there will always be variations and unusual circumstances, the following steps summarize what needs to be achieved:

1. Information enters an agency in one of three ways:
   a. It is deliberately sought out and collected.
   b. It is collected as a result of agency activities.
   c. It is submitted by another agency or statutory body.
2. Information will be processed into intelligence within the Intelligence Unit.

3. Intelligence will be shared within the agency in two ways:
   a. Authorized access to the repository.
   b. Mandated exchange—that is, where procedures dictate that a party be informed of the intelligence.
4. Information or intelligence will be passed to another agency in one of two ways:
   a. Where information relating to another agency is deemed to have no intelligence value to the receiving agency, the information should be passed in raw form to the agency that may have an interest. A statement should be attached stating something akin to "This has no intelligence value to us." Implicit in the transference of the information will be the fact that if it has value to the originating agency, they will be subsequently notified.
   b. Intelligence products will be passed to other agencies through an agreed mechanism. Where it is not obvious why the material is of intelligence value, an explanation should be included.

7.51   Audit

Once the system is created, the work does not finish. There must be regular audits of the system:

- To ensure that the system is still working effectively
- To identify what needs change to maximize performance
- To identify possible security breaches
- To identify wrongdoing or abuse within the processes
- To identify additional training requirements

Each process should be audited with particular reference to "high-risk" areas such as human source management and undercover work, both of which are vulnerable to life-threatening issues and corruption. Audits should be carried out on a routine basis, by someone who is as independent from the process as possible. Audits should range in scope from simple checking that forms have been completed to comprehensive checking of all the records relating to a particular operation or investigation. Effective auditing is more likely to identify faults while they are still manageable; left unattended, they are likely to spiral out of control. Where wrongdoing is identified, corrective and potentially punitive action must be taken or others will view these transgressions as being acceptable behavior.

7.52 Conclusion

The more sophisticated an intelligence management system is, the greater complexity it can deal with. A major concern for decision-makers is their desire for certainty of facts before making a decision. The very nature of law enforcement means that certainty is rarely present. The greater amount of intelligence that is available does not make for absolute certainty, but it is better to have a greater understanding based on a variety of intelligence than being certain, yet at the same time, wrong. A comprehensive intelligence management system will also help in identifying relevant gaps in knowledge. This allows the decision-maker to factor in necessary precautions to compensate for the possible options that these gaps create. The reader should now have a good idea as to the extent of effort required to set up an effective intelligence management system. We now progress to look at a more specialized area of intelligence management analysis.

References

Bush, G.W. (President) (2008) Memorandum for the heads of executive departments and agencies. May 7, 2008. Available at: http://www.fas.org/sgp/bush/cui .html (accessed August 2012).

Cooper, J.R. (2005) *Curing Analytical Pathologies: Pathways to Improved Intelligence Analysis.* Available at: https://www.cia.gov/library/center-for-the-study-of-intelligence/csi-publications/books-and-monographs/curing-analytic-pathologies-pathways-to-improved-intelligence-analysis-1/analytic_pathologies_report.pdf (accessed September 2012).

Furnham, A. and Taylor, J. (2004) *The Dark Side of Behaviour at Work: Understanding Employees Leaving, Thieving and Deceiving.* Basingstoke: Palgrave MacMillan.

Gray, D.H. and Slade, C. (2008) Applying the intelligence cycle model to counter-terrorism. Intelligence for homeland security. *European Journal of Scientific Research* 24(4) 498–519.

Hammer, M. and Champy, J. (1993) *Reengineering the Corporation: A Manifesto for Business Revolution.* New York: Harper Collins Publishers Inc.

International Standards Organization. (2005) *Quality Management Systems: Fundamentals and Vocabulary ISO 9000:2005.* Geneva: International Standards Organization.

International Standards Organization. (2008) *Quality Management Systems: Requirements. ISO 9001:2008.* Geneva: International Standards organization.

Law Enforcement Information Technology Standards Council (LEITSC). (2009) *Standard Functional Specifications for Law Enforcement Records Management Systems (RMS), Version II.* Washington, DC: Bureau of Justice Assistance, Office of Justice Programs.

MacPherson, W. (Sir William of Cluny) (1999) *The Stephen Lawrence Inquiry: Report of an Inquiry.* London: Her Majesty's Stationary Office.

McDowell, D. (2009) *Strategic Intelligence: A Handbook for Practitioners, Managers, and Users*. Lanham, MD: Scarecrow Press Inc.

Obama, B. (President) (2010) Controlled Unclassified Information Executive Order 13556 of November 4, 2010. Available at: http://www.whitehouse.gov/the-press-office/2010/11/04/executive-order-controlled-unclassified-information (accessed December 2012).

O'Shea, T.C. and Nicholls, K. (2003) *Crime Analysis in America; Findings and Recommendations*. Washington, DC: U.S. Department of Justice. Office of Community Oriented Policing Services.

Peterson, M.B. (2011) Collating and evaluating data. In: Wright, R., Morehouse, B., Peterson, M.B. and Palmieri, L. Eds. *Criminal Intelligence for the 21st Century: A Guide for Intelligence Professionals*. Sacramento, CA; Richmond, VA: Law Enforcement Intelligence Units (LEIU); International Association of Law Enforcement Intelligence Analysts (IALEIA).

Ratcliffe, J.H. and U.S. Department of Justice Office of Community Oriented Policing Services. (2007) *Integrated Intelligence and Crime Analysis: Enhanced Information Management for Law Enforcement Leaders*. Washington, DC: Police Foundation.

U.S. Bureau of Justice Assistance. (1998) 28 CFR Part 23 Criminal Intelligence Systems Operating Policies Executive Order 12291. *Policy Clarification*. Available at: https://www.iir.com/28CFR_Program/28CFR_Resources/Executive_Order/ (accessed December 2012).

Analysis 8

It was always the pigs who put forward the resolutions. The other animals understood how to vote, but could never think of any resolutions of their own.

George Orwell, *Animal Farm*

8.1 Introduction

Some may be curious about the quote at the commencement of this chapter; others may be offended (once they work out who it is referring to!). And although it is intended to provoke thought, it is certainly not intended to cause offense. So before all the analysts realize they are "the pigs" referred to in the quote, we begin with an explanation for including it. For many years, and within many different law enforcement agencies (LEAs), analysts have been at the forefront of introducing and driving forward the whole concept of using intelligence in a law enforcement context. Perhaps it is because of this leadership that it is understandable why analysis and analysts have come to be almost synonymous with intelligence management. However, the idea that "analysis" is the "be all and end all" of intelligence management is flawed. Although analysis is an integral part of intelligence management, it is only one part of a complex system. If it is allowed to take precedence over every other part of the system, or if too much value is placed on it, then it can even be detrimental to the overall intelligence management system. Nothing here is intended to blame analysts, on a personal level, for the situation. In fact, most of the blame, if there is blame to be had, once again links back to the overreliance law enforcement has placed on the practices of the intelligence community, when developing intelligence management for use in a law enforcement context. If the allegation is to be made that law enforcement intelligence management focuses too heavily on "analysis," then it is necessary to identify evidence as to how this might have happened. There are many pointers:

- Many definitions of intelligence have a heavy emphasis on analysis, and although at least part of this has to do with the arguably poor definitions of intelligence that exist combined with an equally poor understanding of what analysis is, there has been little effort to move away from using the term "analysis" within definitions. This perpetuates its perceived dominant position in intelligence.

- Analysts are articulate and used to committing material to paper, whereas many others involved in intelligence management have tended toward a culture of committing as little to paper as possible. Hardly surprising then that those who are writing stuff down increase their prominence in the field whether intentionally or not.
- Analyst theory is not considered secret and is openly taught at many education establishments, while many of the other aspects of intelligence management are at least sensitive if not heading well toward secret. This, combined with the fact that many involved in other disciplines of intelligence management are often overly secretive about what they do and how they do it, creates a situation where material on analysis is open to a much wider audience. Furthermore, the less-sensitive nature of analytical techniques means that codes of practice and procedural guidance have been more widely developed and are available in the public domain. A significant number of theoretical papers, books, and other texts on analysis dominate the literature available on intelligence management with little else available in regard to other aspects of intelligence management.
- The widespread use of analysis in the commercial sector serves to heighten awareness of analysis as a discipline.
- In some cases, senior police managers have had very limited knowledge of intelligence and, when looking to develop concepts such as CompStat or intelligence-led policing, have knee-jerked into hiring an analyst believing the analyst to be a solution to their intelligence deficit. This problem is recognized by the U.K.'s Association of Chief Police Officers (2005:61) "Managers often make the fundamental mistake of using analysts' skills inappropriately. It is the manager's responsibility, however, to take ownership of the production of the intelligence products by the efficient use of analysts."
- Unfortunately, as with any aspect of human behavior, there are a few analysts who have seized the opportunity created by a lack of knowledge to press the importance of their role beyond its actual function.

Hanging in there with the pig analogy, one of the biggest mistakes in law enforcement's attitude to analysis is that many agencies have decided to separate the "pigs" into different breeds—the intelligence analyst and the crime analyst, a matter we will return to later. One would wonder if this was a strategic "divide and conquer" move!

To draw to a close this introduction, the problem lies not with the analyst but with how law enforcement understands analysis. Just as in Orwell's *Animal Farm*, where it was all the animals that created the circumstances where the pigs took control, it is all of law enforcement that has created the situation where the role of analyst needs to be reconsidered if the huge potential they offer is to be recognized and used effectively.

This chapter is divided into four main sections. The first section focuses on the role of the analyst and the functioning of that role within intelligence management. The second section addresses some of the benefits of the effective use of an analyst. The third section examines the methods used in analysis, and the chapter finishes with a summary of some of the products that an analyst is likely to be involved in producing.

8.2   Limitations

This chapter is limited in its scope. It is not intended to teach an analyst how to carry out his role. As has already been stated, there is a plethora of literature available that addresses the function of an analyst. What is intended is to educate those involved with intelligence but unfamiliar with the analyst's role to gain a better or more accurate understanding of that role. In addition, the chapter will hopefully remove some of the misconceptions around the role of analysis in intelligence management in the law enforcement context.

Standardization of language in any profession is a key to better understanding. Highlighting the profession's lack of a "common language," the International Association of Crime Analysts (IACA) comments,

> Mutually agreed-upon definitions provide consistent analysis, which, in turn, allows for valid and reliable analytical results (2011:1)

and continue:

> By clarifying and standardizing the core ideas and jargon prevalent within the crime analysis profession, the IACA seeks to promote understanding, enhance communication, and advance knowledge among police practitioners. (2011:7)

Throughout this chapter, where it is possible, the definitions used will be those proffered by the various international bodies that represent the analyst profession.*

8.3   Misconceptions

In attempting to identify the role of analysis and analysts within the context of law enforcement intelligence management, it is important to identify and deal with some of the misconceptions that currently exist. First, an

---

* It is unfortunate that all too often these international bodies cannot find common definitions.

analyst isn't "that cute girl that is really good at charts and stuff." There is an all-too-common attitude held by many involved in law enforcement that all an analyst is present for is to create pretty charts or to tidy up a visual presentation for the "real intelligence officers." Acknowledging that being a cute girl does not preclude anyone from becoming an analyst,* the inference in the comment quoted is that those attributes accurately describe the total role of the analyst. This mind-set shows ignorance on the part of the holder as to the significant benefits a trained analyst can be to an LEA. Preparing charts is undoubtedly part of an analyst's role, but it is the knowledge that is used to create such charts and the use that those charts, and similar products, can be put to that is so valuable to law enforcement. Second, the belief by some sworn officers that nonsworn analysts cannot be trusted is, at best, unfortunate.† Such a belief has at least partly its origins in the fact that most police officers sign up for a lifetime career in the police, whereas it is perceived that civilian analysts will leave after a much shorter period of time and take "all the secrets" with them. Although understandable, on some levels, this mind-set is disingenuous. Many civilian analysts leave law enforcement, not through any disloyalty, but because their skill set is not recognized within law enforcement and is insufficiently remunerated. Third, there is a false belief that the role of analysis is the same in law enforcement as it is in intelligence agencies. Much of law enforcement is about tactical response to problems that are being encountered, whereas analysis in the role of intelligence agencies is much more likely to revolve around long-term strategic considerations. For example, a law enforcement analyst is likely to find herself advising a police investigator on the structure of a drug gang, whereas the analyst working in an intelligence agency works on the impact on his government of a change of government in a third-world regime. The two roles require different approaches and work to different timescales. Having noted the differences, it needs to be recognized that when it comes to terrorism, there is likely to be a much closer alignment of working practices. Finally, the belief that police officers have a better sense of what is occurring than the analyst, because the officer is on the ground and involved in what is happening while the analyst bases their knowledge of what is occurring only through what lands on their desk is, for the most part, inaccurate. Both parties, the analyst and the officer, have potentially different viewpoints of any given situation, but this should not be viewed in a negative light. Although the officer may be intimately involved in events and gain significant personal knowledge that is unavailable to the analyst, such intimate involvement may cloud the officer's ability to view events in the objective way that the analyst can, because the

---

* In fact, the author knows several cute analysts!
† At worst, it is deeply offensive!

analyst is detached from them. A strength for law enforcement is in making use of both viewpoints.

Moving to the specifics of intelligence management, of significant concern should be the fact that many involved in the collection of information for intelligence have little or no understanding of what the role of an analyst is and how an analyst can assist them, nor do they know what their responsibilities are with regard to gathering information to assist the analyst. The main causes of the lack of understanding between analyst and collector are the following:

- Lack of any input by analysts when collectors of whatever ilk are being trained and vice versa. This leads to a lack of understanding of each other's role that gravitates into internecine rivalries.
- Analyst's positions not being sufficiently connected to the collectors, both from a physical perspective and from an inclusivity perspective. Often analysts and collectors are located in geographically separate locations. This creates a physical separation that exacerbates the view that the analyst is not included within the collectors' "team."
- Lack of structures within the agency that encourage and facilitate intelligence requirements that the analyst has being easily shared with those in a position to collect information.
- Prejudice and petty animosities that are allowed by supervisors to perpetuate ad infinitum. As in any job within law enforcement, there are ongoing conflicts that revolve around differences in the various groups.
- Disparate pay scales between a police officer and a civilian analyst.
- Lack of promotion opportunities for analysts.

At the end of the day, such divisions distract from the function of the analyst, namely that of assisting officers in investigating crime. As Osborne and Wernicke (2003:1) articulate,

The objective of most crime analysis is to find meaningful information in vast amounts of data and disseminate this information to officers and investigators in the field to assist in their efforts to apprehend criminals and suppress criminal activity.

Officers and analysts are on the same side; it just may not seem that way sometimes.

8.4   Visualization: Nice Charts and Things!

Although creating nice charts is far from the entirety of an analyst's role, their ability to create visual representations of data should not be minimized. In most investigations, there will be a huge amount of material that is impossible for any person to hold in their working memory for any length of time. Everyone will be familiar with the phrase "a picture paints a thousand words," and this can be very true in intelligence management. Creating visual representations of such material allows members to view it not only in its entirety but also from many different perspectives. Analysts have in their toolbox many different ways to produce visual representations of material. Analysis helps us to overcome the failings in the ability of our short-term or working memory; we can hold only so much information there and for a limited time. A proven technique for coping with the limitation of working memory is getting the material down on paper in some simplified form that shows the main constituents and how they relate to each other.

Not only can analysts present material in a different format for a customer to view it, but they can also enable viewing of that material in a different way from the customer's normal perspective. One of the essential skills of an analyst is to view the world from "a different doorway" than that of the customer and so enable different thought processes.

There are many different ways of viewing material and many options open to analysts in respect to the way they can present it in a visual format. The analyst should strive to create the most effective product that enables the customer to see what may be difficult to comprehend if not viewed in an enlightening manner. In addition, the analyst may have to present material in a way that can overcome the recipient's already held but incorrect interpretation of events. Visualization is a powerful tool. Various visualization options are useful for many different aspects of law enforcement:

- Representation of evidence to support testimony in court.
- Representation of various options to assist management decision-making. Law enforcement managers often have to make decisions about how events may play out in the future. With a myriad of potential outcomes, analysis adds appropriate statements of probability to the various outcomes, thus enabling decision-makers to make better-informed decisions.
- Providing investigative support—for example, showing event timelines and connections between involved parties.
- Integration of crime/event data with mapping tools. Technology has evolved enormously over the past number of years and continues to evolve. The ability to overlay events with maps means that law enforcement can view their area of responsibility and what is occurring there on a computer screen. Few in law enforcement have the knowledge or time to keep themselves up-to-date with the technology, yet the skills the analyst brings to the table readily integrate with the technology.

8.5   Adding Value

A central theme that runs through analysis work is one of adding value. Regardless of the type of material that the analyst begins with—be it statistical data, information, or intelligence—the product that is produced post analysis will have had something added to it by the analyst to make it of greater worth to the customer. It is the role of the analyst to combine and contextualize so that the end result, an intelligence product, can give decision-makers a better picture of what is occurring. This may be a synopsis of the prevailing criminal environment or a specific aspect of an investigation. Nearly every modern policing strategy, from problem-oriented policing to CompStat and intelligence-led policing, benefits from analytical input; some are all but meaningless without such an input.

Analysis is a way of reducing the ambiguity in many highly ambiguous situations that law enforcement managers encounter. Analysis helps remove some of the doubts and can provide clarity around key points, enabling greater understanding of situations for both investigators and decision-makers. The skills that analysts bring to a situation enable them to identify previously unnoticed patterns and connections, and their methodical approach can often eliminate incorrect perceptions. The analyst can also identify emerging trends and areas of high interest to law enforcement, enabling an agency to adopt a more proactive approach. If the analyst is used correctly, he will be able to create an accurate picture of what is occurring together with suitable background information that can help in identifying the underlying causes of a problem.

8.6   Integrated Analysis

There is a belief that there are two separate roles for an analyst in law enforcement:

1. Crime analyst
2. Intelligence analyst

Boba (2005:6), a leading proponent of analysis, describes crime analysis as a "systematic study of crime and disorder problems as well as other police-related issues, including sociodemographic, spatial, and temporal factors, to assist the police in criminal apprehension, crime and disorder reduction, crime prevention, and evaluation."

Johnston (2005), writing on analysis within the intelligence community, describes intelligence analysis as "the application of individual and collective cognitive methods to weigh data and test hypotheses within a secret sociocultural context."

The International Association of Law Enforcement Intelligence Analysts (IALEIA 2011) defines crime analysis as "The application of analytical methods and products to raw data to produce intelligence within the criminal justice field," but provides no definition for intelligence analysis.

Looking objectively at the role of an analyst in law enforcement, it is hard to see why there should be any division in the analyst's role but easy to see maybe why such divisions have occurred:

- A lack of real understanding of what intelligence is and how it should be used.
- Reluctance to allow nonsworn members access to "intelligence."
- The prevalence of the CompStat policing "model" and its overreliance on statistical data created a need for analysts to study the figures and report findings.
- The origins of intelligence analysis from within the Intelligence Community, where there is no data available that can be compared to that used by crime analysts.

The studying of crime data and intelligence are both vital components in analysis, but in law enforcement, one without the other creates half a picture, as Ratcliffe and the U.S. Department of Justice Office of Community Oriented Policing Services (2007) point out:

Generally speaking, intelligence analysis involves the development of critical and substantive products that support law enforcement decision-making efforts that are centered on organized criminal activity. Crime analysis, on the other hand, involves the use of various geographical and sociodemographic information, in combination with spatial techniques, to analyze, prevent, and solve crime and disorder problems. Both disciplines are essential to law enforcement operations, but their ability to provide greater analytical and investigative support has been hindered by the lack of integration between the two units due to various issues, such as departmental policies, the police culture, and a lack of leadership.

The differences between crime analysis and intelligence analysis become readily apparent in the products each produces. The question can often arise: "Is there is a difference between analytical products and intelligence products?" If there is a difference, then: "What demarks that difference?" "Should all analytical products automatically be considered as intelligence products?" Although these questions may at first sight appear to be somewhat splitting hairs and resorting once again to a semantic argument, on further consideration one can see that the questions all actually stem from the original debate with regard to the differences between information and intelligence. As Osborne (2006) remarks, "The technical ability to make maps and generate statistics is not analysis. Often agencies confuse the two."

When an analyst creates a product based solely on statistical data, it should be considered as an analytical product. When an analyst combines statistical data with other information and/or other intelligence products, an intelligence product will result. Even if analysts add their interpretation, if the product uses only statistical data when it is being created, it remains an analytical product. The following examples may explain the differences:

An analyst takes statistical data from the agency's records management system pertaining to the number of street robberies (muggings) occurring within the agency's geographic area of responsibility and plots these on a map. The product shows the areas where most robberies occur. The technique used by the analyst is geographic analysis, and the product created would often be referred to as a "hot spot" map. As this product contains no additional input other than statistical data, it is an analytical product. Even if the analyst creates many products showing the problem on different dates and these products show the evolving nature of the robbery problem, they all remain analytical products. Furthermore, even if the analyst adds interpretation—"I think robberies will continue to increase in area X"—the product remains an analytical product as that interpretation is based solely on statistical data.

An analyst takes statistical data from the agency's records management system pertaining to the number of street robberies occurring within the agency's geographic area of responsibility and plots these on a map, thus creating the aforementioned analytical product the "hot spot" map. The analyst combines this analytical product with many intelligence reports that state that drug addicts are getting the money for drugs from street robberies and creates a problem profile for management regarding the street robberies. This problem profile is an intelligence product.

An analyst takes statistical data from the agency's records management system pertaining to the number of street robberies occurring within the agency's geographic area of responsibility and plots these on a map, thus creating the aforementioned analytical product, the "hot spot" map. The analyst then carries out some open source research and finds that drug clinics in the area are reporting a rise in heroin use. When the analyst takes that information and combines it with the original analytical product and using her professional judgment creates a correlation between the robberies and the increased drug use, her report is an intelligence product.

Understanding the difference between analytical products and intelligence products becomes clearer if one always returns to the definition of "intelligence"—information and process equals intelligence. When an analytical product is created and the information/data used is not subjected to the process, it is merely the same information presented in a different way, be it overlaid on maps showing hot spots or charts showing monthly trends. Even if the analyst adds her opinion as to what is happening, it still remains an analytical product. With an intelligence product, there is always value added through the processing. As Peterson (2005) points out, "crime analysis is statistical and incident based," and she recognizes the idea of its usefulness: "... inferences may be drawn and recommendations made based on crime data." However, she also points out the problems with the lack of understanding of the differences between it and intelligence-based analysis: "Confusion about the distinction between crime analysis data and intelligence data interferes with proper analysis and data handling in the police environment."

If we are to have a more complete picture of the difference between analytical products and intelligence products, the following points should be noted:

- As stand-alone products, analytical products have worth. Just because something is based solely on statistical data does not mean it does not have value, and sometimes significant value, but it does mean the receiver of that product must take cognizance of the nature of that material. If the agency has responsibility for motor vehicle offenses and traffic collisions, then analytical products may well have significant worth in assisting the decision maker. However, management needs to know what they are getting as all too often, law enforcement management make erroneous decisions, believing that they are using intelligence, when in reality they are using statistics.
- By their very nature, analytical products often omit a significant amount of information that if included, would totally change the interpretation of events.
- If analysts are being used only to create analytical products, they are being wasted as a resource. Many analysts are all too aware that the products they are being asked to create fall short of what they could create, were they to be given access to the intelligence that is available.
- An agency should decide as a matter of policy whether or not to store analytical products in the intelligence repository. All intelligence products created by an analyst should be stored in the repository.

Assigning a level of protective marking to intelligence products can cause problems for an analyst. If intelligence of a more general nature forms part of an analyst's product that also contains intelligence carrying a higher protective marking, the whole product will automatically be assigned that higher protective marking, thus reducing the permitted readership. If the sensitive content is removed, it may change how the product is likely to be interpreted.

Another problem to be overcome in analysis in regard to sensitive documents is addressing the question as to what level an analyst should have access to within the intelligence repository. In smaller agencies, this is likely to be less of a problem, because they may only have one analyst. In these cases, there is little within the intelligence repository that the analyst will not be able to access if the agency wishes to make full use of the analyst's skills. In large agencies, this problem is likely to be more pronounced, with specialized areas likely to have their own analyst and where intelligence is compartmentalized to a greater degree. When it comes to an analyst preparing strategic and tactical assessments for individual districts, the analyst always has to take cognizance of the fact that though he has had access to intelligence, he may well not be able to include that intelligence in the assessment because of the likely distribution of such documents. At the same time, the analyst cannot leave out material that may alter the area commander's decisions. Furthermore, there are likely to be times that analyst does not have access to certain material, and though he submits his assessment in good faith, it is inaccurate. When building an intelligence management system, an agency must build in safeguards to address these types of circumstances.

The crime/intelligence divide creates problems for law enforcement. LEAs that have only crime analysts know what crimes are occurring, where they are occurring, and the impact they are having but often lack a detailed understanding of *why* particular crimes are occurring, *who* is involved, and the strengths and weaknesses of those involved. Agencies that have only intelligence analysts have insight into the perpetrators, their background, and their strengths and weaknesses but limited insight into how the criminality is manifested and the impact it is having.

The reason why the division between crime and intelligence analysis has been allowed to continue is hard to say, yet it does perpetuate, unfortunately within the majority of agencies. O'Shea and Nicholls (2003) in their report for the U.S. Department of Justice's Community Oriented Policing Service commented:

> Police have improved greatly their capacity to store, access, and disseminate data. However, the fact remains: according to our findings, crime analysts continue to "count" crime far more effectively than they "analyze" it.
> If the ultimate aim is to be able to collect more data, access it more easily, and count it better, then we have arrived. If, however, the aim is to "analyze" the data through using more sophisticated methodologies, that is, making the best use of the analytic tools available to solve community problems, then we clearly have not arrived. In the end, the substance of tactical output that crime analysis units currently produce is remarkably similar to what was produced twenty years ago.

It is questionable whether or not things have improved since 2003 or whether analysis in law enforcement in any other jurisdiction would emerge with more favorable comments.

It is hardly surprising, when there is such a division of roles, that some agencies have purchased one software solution for those involved in crime analysis and a different solution for those involved in intelligence analysis and that neither solution can "talk" to the other solution. Aside from the obvious financial waste involved, such circumstances create real problems in integrating analysis.

Analysts themselves must at least accept some responsibility for the continuance of the two camps. It is impossible to say how much of a contributing factor to this unhealthy divide is perpetuated by the fact that the two main professional bodies for analysts, the IACA and the IALEIA highlight the difference in their titles.

A common term found in the Intelligence Community is that of *all-source analysis,* and as the term implies, it is about the analysis of material, regardless of where it has originated. Although integrating information from multiple origins can be a challenge, it is difficult to deny that the preference of most decision-makers is to make a decision based on all the information that is available, as opposed to just part of it.

Integrated analysis links information with intelligence so that agencies are able to see the complete picture of the environment that they are operating in. Combining the two allows the agency to develop the most effective strategies to combat the problems that are present. Integrating crime and intelligence analysis should be the goal of all agencies. That is not to say that there are not some occasions in larger agencies when the nature of the unit or section that an analyst is working in means that the impact of crime data will have little, if any, significance. For example, if an analyst is involved in an investigation into a terrorist organization, there may well be very limited data available but a huge amount of intelligence.

Integrating analysis allows an agency's managers to be more effective in deciding where to deploy resources, as they are able to compare and contrast existing and emerging problems and make decisions based on all the knowledge available. At a tactical level, existing criminal activity can be compared to traffic enforcement, public order problems, and resources distributed based on the identified priorities. At the strategic level, the agency is able to adopt a much more proactive and problem-oriented approach, because it knows what is likely to happen in the future and the steps it and partner agencies need to take to combat the potential threats.

8.7   Facilitating Integrated Analysis

Care must be taken with data, information, and intelligence collected by any LEA. Such material is collected according to the culture and expectations prevalent within that agency. Aside from the distortion caused by unreported crimes, unfortunately there can be the willful distortion of crime figures, as everyone in an agency is likely to be under pressure to keep such figures down. Offenses such as burglary may be recorded as vandalism or assaults minimized so that they disappear off the radar. Poor data quality can also create distortions when it comes to analysis. Similar problems can arise in intelligence management with poor data quality and existing or emerging problems not being reported on, not for lack of their existence but because of gaps in the collection coverage. Coverage problems are likely to be exacerbated where collectors have a vested interested in collecting a certain type of information, normally that which will further their own investigations.

The nature of their work means that analysts will often identify gaps in intelligence. Analysts should be involved in identifying the intelligence requirements for collectors, using their insight into what is needed as opposed to being merely the passive recipients of intelligence reports from which they are then expected to develop other products, despite already knowing the picture will be incomplete. When it comes to the analysis of intelligence, the primary purpose of the analyst is to make sense of the material and to provide greater understanding for the end users. Analysts know what they need to do this, should be able to ask for it, and where possible, get it.

Problems can arise when an analyst is kept distant from an investigation, either physically located in another building or excluded from all discussions about the investigation, save for when the investigator wants something done. Whether this is done deliberately or just happens will vary from agency to agency and investigation to investigation. Analysts can make significant contributions to an investigation, and where resources allow, should be fully integrated into the team. An analyst should have as close access as possible to the original material as their task requires and as security permits.

8.8 Analyzing

One of the key aspects that the trained analyst brings to the table is a way of thinking. The way that we as people view anything is normally a prisoner of our life history; our behavior is a combination of instinct tempered by any skills we may have been exposed to along the way. Few of us have actually had training in how to think objectively about a subject. Many analysts have been "trained" in different ways of viewing any matter: how to break it down into component parts and examine each of these parts. Winston Churchill remarked, "True genius resides in the capacity for evaluation of uncertain, hazardous, and conflicting information." So, much of law enforcement intelligence management involves uncertain, hazardous, and conflicting information that the skills of the analyst to make sense of such material can prove extremely valuable to an agency.

An experienced analyst has the training and skills to identify patterns and anomalies that would go unnoticed to the untrained eye. They can bring disjointed material together to identify the bigger picture and use such material to predict what is likely to happen in the future with regard to a particular problem.

Analysis is a fundamental part of intelligence management, and as such, it is necessary to explore what "analysis" is in the context of intelligence management and what it is not. In addition, because there is so much confusion, admitted or not, around the term analysis, this will require both semantic and contextual discussion. First, we will begin by looking at the conventional meaning of the word, thereby identifying the key elements when it comes to its contextual use.

Analysis is the process of breaking a complex topic or substance into smaller parts to gain a better understanding of it. It involves the separation of material into its constituent parts for individual study, the interpretation of those parts, and then the synthesis of the separate elements to form a coherent picture. Analysis involves reasoning and logical deduction.

In an intelligence management context, we can consider analysis as a process of identifying the components of any criminal activity, determining their relationship, and then synthesizing these separate components to form a coherent picture of what is happening and what may happen in the future. Being able to do this is fundamental to the role of the analyst. With the advances in technology, the preparation of many intelligence products that once required additional training and skills can now be carried out with limited knowledge and good software. Analysts need to be able to analyze!

It should be noted that much of what is produced through analysis will be based on "uncertain" and "conflicting" material. Analysts are often trying to complete a jigsaw with many of the parts missing and no box lid to show them what is meant to be there. Harris, Maxfield, Holladay, Godfrey, and United States Law Enforcement Assistance Administration Enforcement Program Division (1976:30), in their definition of analysis highlight the potential for error or ambiguity: "Analysis is that activity whereby meaning actual or *suggested* is derived through organizing and systematically examining diverse information" (author's italics). When material is analyzed, it will often only suggest what is happening or what will happen; it is not fact and should not be taken as such. An analyst should always give an indication of how strong the suggestion is, but the recipient must take cognizance of the potential for it being erroneous. Analysis is the driving force behind products known as "strategic assessments" and "tactical assessments" discussed later in the chapter.

8.9   Common Terms Used in Analysis

Without delving into the "how to" of analysis, there are some useful phrases and terms that follow:

- "A *premise* is a previous statement serving as a basis or an argument." A "premise" in inference development is used to identify facts or pieces of information that go together to make a particular point. Premises are the first and key stage in the true process of data analysis.
- An *inference* is a statement that describes what the analyst thinks is happening. In any criminal investigation, the objective of analysis is to find an explanation of what the intelligence means. This explanation is known as an "inference." An inference is drawn from premises. A common mistake is to develop an inference and then look for premises to support it. An inference can be of limited value to a decision-maker without some estimate of its probable truth.
- There are four types of inferences:
  - *Hypothesis.* A hypothesis is "a tentative explanation, a theory that requires additional information for confirmation or rejection" (IALEIA 2011).
  - *Prediction.* A prediction is, as the word infers, an inference about something that will happen in the future.
  - *Estimation.* An estimation is an inference made about the whole from the sample that is available. Estimations are usually quantitative in nature. Many in law enforcement will be familiar with estimations of the profits drug gangs are making or the number of members of a subversive organization.
  - *Conclusion.* A conclusion is an explanation that is well supported by the available material including related hypotheses, predictions, and/or estimations. At the time of presenting, a conclusion will give all the appearances that it is likely to be confirmed.
- *Quantitative analysis* is a technique that seeks to explain behavior using measurements and mathematical and statistical modeling. In the intelligence context, it is about analyzing data using mathematics to predict or explain events. The aim of quantitative analysis is to use the data that is available and seek to give a precise measurement to explain what has occurred. Using this method, the analyst remains detached from the subject matter relying on the methodology to produce results. At best, it rarely provides a full picture and it is a difficult technique to use in the intelligence arena, because the volume of data is simply not available to come to any defendable conclusion. Given that much of what requires to be analyzed involves

human behavior and lies within the social and behavioral sciences, such analysis becomes extremely difficult.

- *Qualitative analysis* relies on the judgment and experience of the person carrying out the analysis. It is about using information that cannot be quantified. With qualitative analysis, the aim is to provide a complete picture of what is occurring. With this method, the analyst may have only a vague idea of what she is looking for, with the nature of the research evolving as time progresses. In this, the analyst becomes an essential element in the process, driving it forward and using her skill and knowledge to interpret events. Qualitative research is about finding meaning. Given the nature of the intelligence business and the difficulties that present themselves in attempting to find a way in which to quantify much of the data and information available, it is hardly surprising that qualitative analysis is used most often. The obvious problem with this method is the potential for overreliance on the analyst carrying out the work. It makes the assumption that she has the aptitude, training skills, and motivation to do the job. Having said that qualitative and quantitative analysis both have their place, they should not be viewed as competing with each other. The reality of the intelligence business is that rarely is there sufficient accurate data to even contemplate using only quantitative analysis.

8.10 What Makes Analysis Easier?

The following are some factors that make it easier for an analyst to produce better reporting:

- *More and better intelligence.* The more good intelligence an analyst has, the less they have to rely on more dubious material such as that coming from the Internet.
- *Accuracy.* Accuracy in reporting is important, and accuracy in evaluation is equally important. Poorly evaluated intelligence can distort the analyst's view.
- *Timely intelligence.* Like everyone in law enforcement, analysts work to a time scale. If it is taking days or weeks for a piece of intelligence to reach the analyst, then they cannot be expected to function effectively.
- *Access.* Analysts need access to intelligence at as high a level as security permits and to as much intelligence for them to complete their task as security permits.
- *Intelligence originating from knowledgeable insiders.* Good human sources provide details of the organization's activities and how they are thinking.

8.11 Drawing Conclusions

It will often fall to an analyst to draw conclusions from the intelligence that is available at any given time. A problem for the analyst is that it is not always easy to draw conclusions where there is limited or conflicting intelligence. Where analysis takes place and all the intelligence points to one conclusion, the intelligence is said to be "convergent." In such circumstances, it is relatively easy for an analyst to state what he believes will occur. However, some intelligence reports may be completely at odds with other intelligence reports, and in such circumstances, the intelligence is said to be "conflicting." Even when one argument based on the intelligence has been evaluated, and is of a higher grade, it is incumbent on the analyst to draw attention to the conflict in reporting. Having said that, analysts must make their decision based on the weight of the intelligence they hold at that given time. Perhaps one of the most difficult situations is where one set of intelligence reporting outwardly appears to be in conflict with another, but the two potential outcomes are not mutually exclusive. In these circumstances, the intelligence reporting is said to be "divergent." The situation is exacerbated where both sets of intelligence come from equally reliable origins. In analyzing intelligence reports, the analyst must keep an open mind to potential outcomes for both sets of intelligence, taking care not to favor one over the other. The temptation will be to feel obliged to side with one, without considering the notion that they may both be correct. We are often limited by the scope of our experience and imagination.

Although the analyst will always strive to make accurate predictions of potential outcomes, the reality is that the outcome will not be as predicted. This occurs for many reasons. First, action taken by law enforcement as a result of the analyst's predictions changes the actions of the criminal. For example, the analyst predicts that anarchist groups will infiltrate a civil rights demonstration, but publicity before the demo of a high police presence deters the anarchist groups. Second, although the overall thrust of the prediction is correct, some of the details are wrong. For example, the analyst predicts a sharp rise in high-value metal thefts citing the potential for copper theft from electrical engineers, yet what occurs is the theft of lead from the roofs of buildings. The prediction of metal thefts is correct, but location and metal type was incorrect. Third, the criminal changes his mind of his own volition. The analyst is, in many cases, trying to predict human behavior and trying to guess what the criminal will do. Attempting to predict future behavior with any degree of accuracy is notoriously difficult. Jeffrey Cooper, quoting a Central Intelligence Agency (CIA) analyst, writes, "getting inside the other guy's head" can only be conjectural because, in most cases, even the "other guy" doesn't know exactly why he's doing what he's doing (Cooper 2005:20).

8.12 Analyst Reporting

Without examining in detail how analysts should structure their reports, there are a few points that will be of interest to all involved in intelligence:

- An analyst can provide significant assistance in law enforcement operations and investigations and should be an integral part of every major investigation.
- Products produced by the analyst must be accurate, evidence based, and objective. They should be created using critical thinking and analytical judgment. The analyst must be able to fully explain any deduction made in a report. The key strengths that analysts brings to an investigation are the thorough nature of their exploration of the material they have examined and the unique skill set they can apply to such material.
- The "data source" for included material must be clearly attributed. IALEIA (2011) comments on data source attribution to the effect that "Every intelligence product shall clearly distinguish which contents are public domain or general unclassified information, which information is restricted or classified, and which contents are the judgments or opinions of analysts and/or other professionals." Failure to do so damages the credibility of the product and can cause breaches in security. Care must be taken with any analyst product to avoid wider readership than was permitted for the content that was used to create it. Where material from open sources is used and has not be previously been processed into an intelligence report or other intelligence product, it should be referenced using Harvard referencing or similar.
- Analytical products should reflect all relevant data available through whatever sources and means available even if it is contradictory.
- Analysis must be produced in a timely manner. An analyst should attempt to identify patterns as they emerge; fully analyze them establishing the who, what, when, where, how, and why factors; and then disseminate their findings as soon as possible.
- Delivery to the customer should be in time for it to be useful for decision-making. Timeliness includes not only the amount of time required to deliver the product but also the usefulness to the customer at a given moment.
- The scope of a product is the level of details contained in the product. It makes clear the extent and nature of the research involved. The scope should be clearly identified by the customer if they have requested a product. Where an analyst self-generates a product, details of the scope should be included in the document.

- Any written report must be clear and concise. It should be written in the third person, avoid jargon, and be limited in the number of acronyms used, with each explained the first time it is used. Spelling and grammar must be correct, as people are very quick to pick up on such errors, and unfair as it may be, these damage their view of the credibility of the report.* Furthermore, when names or terms are spelled incorrectly, it can cause genuine confusion. Use plain language and avoid words the reader may have difficulty understanding. A report should flow with one point moving logically into the next. Reports should be as short as possible or they won't be read. Time is always limited. Diagrams should be as simple as possible, and if possible, the use of mathematical theory avoided. A significant number of potential readers will not have the necessary grasp of mathematical theory to understand correctly what is being conveyed. When using statistical data, figures should be rounded up to the nearest whole.

- Analysts must be aware of and take care to avoid the many potential cognitive distortions they can fall prey to. Heurer (1999) in his excellent book on the psychology involved in analysis highlights many of these potential traps.

8.13   Products

There are many different techniques an analyst can use and many different products they can create. The use of analytical techniques is fundamental to the development of many intelligence products. The specifics of the situation will determine the number and combination of analytical techniques and products that will be used by the analyst to create a report. The customer should always discuss requirements with an analyst and to discuss how they want the ultimate product to look. As discussed earlier, there are essentially two categories of product that an analyst can create.

Figure 8.1 shows the flow in the creation of "analytical products" created using agency data without any intelligence input. Such products are often used in the mistaken belief that they are intelligence products. Aside from a

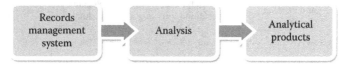

Figure 8.1 Creating analytical products.

* With the exception of this book, as the author's ability to spell is legendary!

lack of understanding of intelligence, this often happens because an agency is "data rich" but "intelligence poor." Creating lots of charts and diagrams can create the illusion that the agency knows what is happening on the ground. This situation is not the fault of the analysts; they can only work with the material they are given.

Figure 8.2 shows the flow in the creation of intelligence products. As can be seen, these are created using a combination of data, intelligence, and research. Further research by the analyst may or may not be necessary but is often included as it can provide useful background material. The analyst can also create intelligence products without any recourse to data produced from the agency's records management system.

As shown in Figure 8.3, all intelligence products created by the analyst should be lodged in the repository and linked to the relevant entities.

There are many products that an analyst can produce, and although it is not the intention here to give an in-depth explanation of each and every

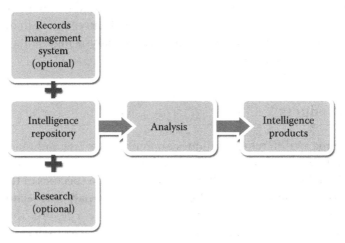

Figure 8.2 Creating intelligence products.

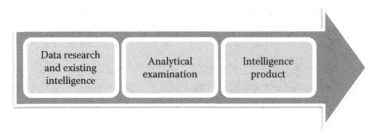

Figure 8.3 Intelligence products—from analyst to repository.

product, it is important for people involved in intelligence management to have a good understanding of the types of product available and how they may benefit from using these products. It is fair to say that quite a few who are involved in various aspects of intelligence management have very limited understanding of what an analyst is capable of producing. In preparing many of the products discussed below, the analyst has to answer many questions. As the analyst is not involved in collection, it is up to those involved in collection to provide the answers. The questions shown below are typical of those that members involved in managing human sources should be asking of those sources.

8.14 Gap Analysis

No matter what type of product an analyst is preparing, in the vast majority of cases, what will become apparent to them are the gaps in intelligence—in other words, what is not known or what is missing in the matter at hand. In identifying intelligence gaps, the analyst must subject the nature of these gaps to scrutiny. There are many points to be established with regard to any intelligence gap:

- How big is it? The amount of intelligence that is missing needs to be quantified in relation to what is known.
- How important is it? The importance of the missing intelligence needs to be quantified in relation to the potential impact it could have on the overall picture.
- How soon is it needed? It is necessary to establish timescales and priorities for intelligence collection. Resources are limited and some intelligence is needed more urgently than other intelligence.
- Why is the gap there? An intelligence gap may exist for many reasons, including the need for that intelligence, its not being identified to collectors, a failure to collect information from which intelligence can be developed, the lack of collection capacity for that type of intelligence, or a breakdown in the intelligence management system. The cause of the gap must be identified before it can be rectified.

8.15 Problem Profiles

The IALEIA standards document (2011) states that a problem profile "identifies established and emerging crimes or incidents for the purpose of preventing or deterring further crime." Problem profiles provide intelligence customers with a greater understanding of new and existing problems and/ or potential threats that they are facing. In addition, they provide the locations that are of interest and an indication as to any relevant time factors. Problem profiles have their roots in Herman Goldstein's concept of problem-oriented policing (1990). Establishing the nature of the problem is the first step in identifying what can be done about it and should open up many ways to counteract the problem, including investigative opportunities, the potential crime prevention initiatives, and problem-solving partnerships. Problem profiles can provide justification for law enforcement in taking action that may engage privacy rights or be viewed by some as controversial. The fact that a problem is clearly articulated and recorded provides evidence that subsequent police action was not carried out in an arbitrary or capricious manner. When a problem profile is presented, a course of action relating to that profile should also be decided, and where necessary, the problem should be reviewed on an identified timescale.

When a problem profile is requested, the following should be included by the requesting customer:

- The timescale for the profile to be completed.
- Authority to access the material required if this is not already in place. The analyst may have clearance to a material up to a certain level but finds that significant relevant material is held at a higher level. If access to such material is not forthcoming, the analyst should highlight the omission in the profile.
- Where there is limited existing material, a plan for the collection of new material should be agreed between the requester and the analyst.
- The depth and breadth of the profile. With most subjects, research avenues can be limitless and the customer must provide clarity as to what use the profile is intended for. With experienced analysts, this may be self-evident given they are likely to know the customer's role and therefore what they are likely to require—a profile for the Chief is more likely to be a strategic overview, whereas the product requested by an investigator is more likely to examine the specifics of the problem. However, it pays to check before commencing the work.
- The key elements the profile is expected to address and what elements or aspects to concentrate on.
- The way in which the customer wants the material to be presented whether as a formal presentation or a written report. Although there is no fixed method of presenting details of a problem to the customers, there should always be a comprehensive written report that can be reposited in the intelligence repository.

A problem profile should do the following:

- Provide a clear picture of the problem from an intelligence perspective, and if necessary, include crime data.
- Identify any gaps in intelligence that exist relating to the problem.
- When relating to strategic matters, facilitate the senior management team to identify police priorities.
- When relating to tactical matters, facilitate the investigator to identify investigative strategies.
- Be protectively marked in accordance with the relevant protective marking scheme and stored accordingly. It should be noted that the whole problem profile must be marked based on the highest protectively marked content held within it. In other words, if there is "Secret" material in the profile, then the entire profile will be marked "Secret." Recognizing that this can cause dissemination problems, consideration may be given to having an "appendix," with the sensitive material referenced in the profile. Significant care must be paid to how it is referenced within the profile.
- Contain details of both the author and the person requesting the profile, the date it was prepared, and the reasons why it was prepared.

When it comes to creating a problem profile, the starting place is normally the answers to six questions and these starting points are then further developed. As iterated earlier, these questions are here more for the benefit of collectors than for an analyst:

1. What is happening?
   a. What is the crime that is being planned or committed?
   b. Has there been an increase in this type of crime?
   c. Is this a new type of event?
   d. Are there political or social connections to the crime?
   e. In what way is the crime likely to change/escalate?
   f. What do we not know about what is occurring?
2. Where is it happening?
   a. What are the exact locations of the crime?
   b. What type of premise or location is involved?
   c. Is the crime confined to a specific police area, or is it more widespread?
   d. Are there numerous locations connected with different aspects of the crime?
   e. Is a geographic progression identifiable?
   f. Are the crime locations linked to where certain victim types are more generally found?

3. When is it happening?
    a.   What days and time of day are the crimes occurring?
    b.   Is there a correlation between the time of the crime and other events?
    c.   Is there an escalation at certain times?
    d.   What is the sequence of events leading up to and after the commission of the crime?
    e.   Are the crimes seasonal or cyclic?
4. Why is it happening?
    a.   Why is it happening?
    b.   Why is there an escalation of this crime type now?
    c.   Why are the particular victims chosen?
    d.   Why do the crimes occur at a particular time?
    e.   Are there social demographic changes as an influencing factor?
    f.   Are other factors influencing events?
5. Who is involved in what is happening?
    a.   Who are the victims?
    b.   Who are the key people involved?
    c.   Who is lending support?
    d.   How are they connected?
    e.   What are their intentions?
    f.   What are their capabilities?
    g.   What are their motives? (This requires more than a superficial answer.)
    h.   What skill sets do they have?
    i.   What are the group dynamics?
6. How are they doing it?
    a.   What is the modus operandi?
    b.   Why is that modus operandi used?
    c.   What equipment is needed for the crime?
    d.   How are items connected with the crime disposed of?

In answering all of these questions, and the many more that will come to mind, the analyst should always base the answers on the evidence available. The question repeated throughout should be, "Where is the evidence to support this?" Failure to link the answers to the evidence creates a profile more likely to be interwoven with conjecture and bias. Furthermore, the profile should clearly identify where there is a lack of intelligence. Filling these intelligence gaps is likely to be one of the most pressing issues in any subsequent action to be taken. In preparing a problem profile, there are many opportunities for the analyst to use diverse methods to present the material gathered. A problem profile will often contain both crime data and intelligence. Many of the tools described in subsequent paragraphs will be of use in preparing a problem profile.

A problem profile may suggest potential strategies to deal with the problem with both potential and negative outcomes of adopting each of the strategies. However, decision as to what is to be done generally lies well outside the remit of an analyst, and care must be taken by the analyst not to overstep the mark.

8.16 Crime Pattern Analysis

Crime pattern analysis is "a process seeking links between crimes and other incidents to reveal similarities and differences to help predict and prevent future criminal activity" (IALEIA 2011). Crime pattern analysis is about finding substantive links between various crimes, potential links that include geographic links, timescales, victim type, or methods used by the perpetrator. In essence, crime pattern analysis seeks to identify a pattern in many isolated incidents and uses the information gained from such analysis to see if collectively further information becomes apparent since when the incidents were considered in isolation. Crime pattern analysis recognizes that the traditional law enforcement approach of an officer being assigned a case and working to solve that case in isolation can often be ineffective, because the officier fails to see linkages to other crimes. Many cases are often the work of a single perpetrator, or there are aspects common to numerous cases such as type of property taken, type of victim, or the location of the crimes. When examined collectively, an analyst can often identify a set of common features, which makes one set of crimes different from what would normally be perceived as similar crimes. The purpose of crime pattern analysis is to use the analyst's findings to inform law enforcement of possible strategies to combat the problem. Crime pattern analysis is greatly enhanced when intelligence reporting is used in conjunction with data analysis. This can give a much clearer picture of what is occurring. Furthermore, crime pattern analysis can help identify gaps in intelligence coverage and provide intelligence collectors with specific questions they should be seeking to answer. For example, the crime pattern analysis may identify a specific modus operandi used in home invasions and the geographical area that they appear to be related to. Human source handlers can then be tasked to ask their sources specific questions relating to the crime pattern.

The IACA (2011) paper on crime pattern definitions identifies seven types of crime pattern:

1. *Series*. A group of similar crimes believed to be committed by the same group or same person. For example, many householders are targeted by a group of bogus builders who identify building work requiring urgent treatment and on receiving advance payment for the work subsequently disappear.

2. *Spree.* A specific type of series where there is a large number of occurrences of the same crime type committed over a very short timeframe. For example, numerous shops in a shopping mall fall victim to the theft of electronic goods all occurring in one afternoon.

3. *Hot prey.* As the name suggests, this relates to the type of victim. A pattern is identified in that all the victims of the particular crime share similar characteristics or are engaged in similar behavior at the time of the incident. For example, lone female shoppers fall victims to carjackers when emerging from a supermarket after purchasing the week's food supplies.

4. *Hot product.* This refers to a particular type of property that is targeted by the criminals. For example, the rising price of copper leads to the theft of electrical cable from substations and builders yards, the intention of the thieves being to resell it as scrap metal.

5. *Hot spot.* A hot spot refers to a location where many similar crimes are committed in proximity to each other. For example, the theft of car radios from parking lots close to the town center. Hot spots are often readily identified by the use of geographic information systems (GISs).

6. *Hot place.* This refers to a location that has seen an escalation in similar crimes over a limited period. For example, the area adjacent to a particular nightclub sees an escalation in assaults, damage to property, and rowdy behavior over the period of a few weeks.

7. *Hot setting.* A hot setting refers to similar crimes being committed at similar types of property. For example, many boatyards have high-value engines stolen over the winter months.

As a crime pattern is normally limited to a specific set of similar crimes exhibited over a limited duration, they can often be dealt with by a tactical response such as an increase in the police presence in an area. It is different from a trend that will usually have a time component, which can be correlated to an increase or decrease in the crime.

8.17 Target Profiles

"A target profile is a person or organization specific report that provides all that is known on the individual or organization that may be useful as the investigation is initiated" (IALEIA 2011). It is important to any investigator to have a greater understanding of the individuals suspected of committing the crimes that are being investigated. A target profile can provide significant benefits regardless of whether the "target" of the investigation is an individual, an unstructured group, or an organized crime gang. Benefits include the following:

- Providing a clear picture of the nature of the target, its identity, its background, and its criminal history.
- Providing clarity with regard to relevant associations.
- When there are many different targets involved, it aids management in deciding which target poses the most significant threat.
- Creating justification for actions with regard to the engagement of the privacy rights of individuals.
- Identifying the nature of the threat the target poses.
- Identifying the strengths and weaknesses of the target group and where it is a group, the group as a whole, and individuals within that group.
- Identifying intelligence gaps pertaining to the target.
- Where the target is a group or organization predicting how that target is likely to behave in the future. By referencing the targets, historic activities and comparing them to their current activities, indications of where they are likely to be heading can be established. Identifying the norms that dictate the activities of its members is likely to give a good indication of how they are likely to behave under a given set of circumstances.

Given the amount of work that can be entailed in preparing target profiles, they will normally be undertaken only where the offenses involved are serious, where the suspect is a prolific offender, or where the target group poses a significant threat to law and order. A target profile should be more than a restatement of the person's criminal history. The profile is intended to add value and understanding to existing knowledge. Key elements in any target profile for an organization are likely to be network analysis for the group as a whole and the social network analysis for the group members. Target profiles should be prepared in a standardized format, protectively marked as appropriate and reposited in the intelligence repository.

8.18 Victim Profile

A victim profile focuses on the traits or circumstances of people who have been victims of a certain type of crime. The idea behind focusing attention on a victim is twofold: first, to see if there is anything that may lead to identifying a perpetrator, and second, as part of a crime prevention strategy—if the agency can identify the type of person that may fall victim, then they can be warned and provided with advice. The concept of victim is not confined to people and may extend to businesses or types of premises.

8.19   Criminal Business Profile

A criminal business profile is a product that details how criminal operations or techniques work, including how victims are chosen, how they are victimized, how proceeds of crime are used, and the strengths and weaknesses in the criminal system (IALEIA 2011). Just as any business analyst will look at a legitimate business to understand how it functions, a criminal business profile subjects the criminal action to the same scrutiny, the main difference being that legitimate businesses are analyzed to make them function better while the criminal business is analyzed to find ways to destroy it. Analysis of a criminal business will include the following:

- What techniques and tools do the criminals use and how is each of these used?
- How are victims or locations selected?
- How are security measures circumvented?
- What specific methods are used to facilitate each aspect of the crime?
- If there are proceeds from the crime, what is the method of their removal from the crime scene and their subsequent disposal? In the case of money, how is that money laundered?
- What techniques are used to frustrate detection?
- What means of communication are used to facilitate the crime?
- What vulnerabilities exist in the criminal enterprise?
- What previous failures have there been in carrying out these activities? For example, "When have their operations failed?" or "When have participants been arrested?"

8.20   Network Analysis

Network analysis can be defined as the "collection and analysis of information that shows relationships among varied individuals suspected of being involved in criminal activity that may provide insight into the criminal operation and which investigative strategies might work best" (IALEIA 2011). It is also referred to as association analysis. Network analysis should not be considered exclusively in terms of the people involved but should also include other aspects of the criminal enterprise connected to those individuals, such as the links the individuals have to other entities, the significance of those links, the roles played by the individuals, and the strengths and weaknesses they create for the organization (ACPO 2008). A network analysis is illustrated in Figure 8.4. The two central components of network analysis are as follows:

1. Nodes. Nodes are entities of any description; people, places, things, etc.
2. Links. Links describe the relationship between the nodes.

At the strategic level, network analysis provides a detailed understanding of the scale and seriousness of the criminality emanating from an organization, whereas at a tactical level, it can identify investigative options and opportunities to disrupt the functioning of the group. Network analysis often results in the production of graphic representations of the network, but there are limitations in regard to how much information can be represented and the potential altering of the overall chart by the addition of new or conflicting material. Furthermore, the more nodes that are added, the more difficult it becomes to actually see what is there. In preparing such network analysis, the problem with being overloaded with material is real as is the problem that a dearth of material in regard to a key node can distort the analysis. Network analysis often highlights gaps in the intelligence and can give a strong indication as to where intelligence coverage needs to be increased.

There are four concepts that are important features in a network analysis:

1. *Entity.* The type of entity: person, vehicle, place, communications, objects, and organizations.
2. *Relationship.* The nature of the relationship between the nodes: friendship, family, business, and subordinate.

Figure 8.4 Simple network analysis. (Reprinted with permission from Visual Analytics Inc., MD.)

3. *Directionality.* This relates to the flow of information within the network and provides indications as to how it functions.
4. *Strength.* The strength of a link is an objective judgment based on the material available.

In theory, creating a network analysis is a relatively simple process:

- Identify the entities to be analyzed.
- Gather the background intelligence available on these entities.
- Define the objective of the analysis.
- Clarify the scope of the analysis.
- Agree on the timescale.
- Use a network analysis tool to visually map out the network.

In practice, it is never quite as simple as the first thing identified will fill the gaps in the intelligence as is needed!

8.21 Social Network Analysis

Social network analysis examines the relationships between people. In a social network analysis, the nodes in the network are people, while the links show the relationships between those people. The term social network analysis was first coined by Barnes (1954), when he hypothesized that social life is a "total network" of relations made up of "a set of points, some of which are joined by lines." Much of the more contemporary material on social network analysis can be traced back to the work of Stanley Milgram (1967) in his research on how people are connected. This research led to the famous phrase, "six degrees of separation," which refers to the notion that any one person living in the world can be connected by shared relationships to any other person in six steps.

Using mathematical formulae contained within specialized software, social network analysis can determine values for each relationship, allowing an analyst to categorize different categories of "centrality" within a network. Analyzing centrality is basically a way to identify who is at the center of the network. Depending on the criteria used, an analysis may lead to different people being located at the center. There are three main types of centrality:

- *Degree centrality* is determined by both the number of direct connections that a person has and where each of those connections leads to. The leader of a gang is likely to have a high degree centrality. This is shown in Figure 8.5.

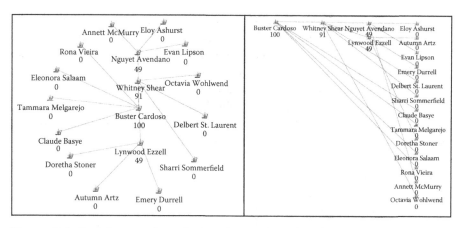

Figure 8.5 Social network analysis—degree centrality. (Reprinted with permission from Visual Analytics Inc., MD.)

- *Betweenness centrality* measures the degree to which people are located between other important people. In other words, for "A" to get to "C," he needs to go through "B." People with high "betweenness" have a powerful role in the network. If they can be eliminated, the network may be severely damaged or dispersed altogether. In the analogy above, take away "B" and it means there is no connection between "A" and "C"—the network is destroyed.
- *Closeness centrality* focuses on those people with the shortest path to all the others. The pattern of their direct and indirect ties allows them quicker access than anyone else in the network. Their position allows them to monitor the network's information flow. Such people make great human sources.

Understanding networks and their participants provides insight into the various roles within that network and can identify who are the leaders, movers, and shakers; who is isolated; and where clusters with shared agendas have formed. All this is useful to those investigating the group; it allows those at the core of the network to be targeted for prosecution and identifies those on the periphery who may be more willing to become a source.

Social network analysis recognizes that relationships are important and maps both formal and informal links. This assists in understanding the group dynamics. If law enforcement is to combat the activities of a group, it helps to understand what is going on within that group.

The benefits of social networking analysis should be readily apparent to anyone who has worked against organized crime groups. To be of benefit, the technique does not need to have the full degree of rigor an analyst brings. Less-structured networking diagrams can be of use in the debriefing of a human source. Allowing a source to discuss gang structures while at the same time showing them can elicit significant further detail. Furthermore, when "repentant" criminals are being debriefed about their historic involvement, similar benefit can be had in using the technique while in discussions around their old social networks. Where such matters are likely to become more complex, the involvement of an analyst should be considered to at least provide pointers for the members involved, as to what to look for. Some of the questions that likely need to be answered for social networking analysis and may very well answer include the following:

- Who is central in this organization?
- Who do they interact with?
- How often are the interactions?
- What type of interactions are they? Social, business, etc.
- Who initiates the interactions?
- Are there distinct groupings within the organization?
- Are certain members connected to some other members to the exclusion of the others?
- Who connects different groupings within the organization?
- Are the links between people changing in strength or centrality?
- Who could take over the roles of the key people if they were removed?
- Who is on the periphery?
- Does anyone in the group appear to be being excluded by members of the group?
- Is the organization vulnerable to infiltration? And if so, where would be a good place to attempt infiltration?

Carley (2012) has long been a proponent of the idea of what she refers to as "dynamic network analysis." This she describes as varying "…from traditional social network analysis in that it can handle large dynamic multi-mode, multi-link networks with varying levels of uncertainty." She continues that this type of analysis becomes necessary in examining terrorist organizations and similar groups. She writes, "Terrorist organizations have network structures that are distinct from those in typical hierarchical organizations—they are cellular and distributed…. It is even more difficult for us to understand how such networks will evolve, change, adapt and how they can be destabilized." There is no doubt the emergence of international terrorism in its current form and that of transnational criminal groups can make it extremely difficult to establish the exact nature of those involved in a network. Problems include the following:

- Transnational nature of criminality inevitably makes it difficult to have an accurate intelligence picture. Many of those involved may not be identified, and key intelligence may be missing.

- When one central player is removed, they are rapidly replaced with another. However, in reality, while a person may take over a role, he will often not be as good as the person he is replacing, so the strength of the organization is damaged.
- The ability to take action may be limited, especially if a key player is in another jurisdiction. Even if the other jurisdiction can take action and is willing to take action, their timing may be restricted or the level of disruption they can cause may be less than one would desire.
- There may be significant cultural differences in many parts of an organization. Crime brings different people together for a shared reason. The analyst must be careful to take cognizance of ethnic or cultural differences and avoid adopting an ethnocentric viewpoint.
- Many of the current organizations involved in terrorism, and to a lesser extent organized crime, are based on what could be referred to as "loose ties" or, in other words, there is the absence of any strong relationship between the parties involved. This is a marked difference between dealing with organizations such as the mafia, Hell's Angels, or the Irish Republican Army, where there are strong group bonds and those involved go through a formalized membership process.

Having identified a social network, Carley et al. (2003) recommend four types of people to remove to have the best chance of destabilizing a network:

1. The person with the highest degree centrality.
2. The person with the highest betweenness centrality.
3. The person with the highest cognitive load. This refers to the person who has to do the most mental work to keep the organization functioning.
4. The person with the highest task exclusivity. This refers to the person who does vital jobs no one else can do.

As can be seen from this list, if these positions in a network have been identified, then it becomes easier to know who should be targeted. This is a very useful tool in the group analysis stage of the proactive recruitment of a human source (Buckley 2006).

8.22 Spatial Vulnerability

Following on from social network analysis and intrinsically linked to it is the idea of identifying spatial vulnerabilities in a group. A common starting point with regard to any investigation is to identify the members of the criminal organization and their associates. Normally, this may just be presented in a list format with the individual's details and a position in the organization. An old military term for such a list is an "Or-bat," an abbreviation of "order of battalion." Although useful in itself, there are many other ways to use this information. One of these methods is a technique known as spatial vulnerability. As its name implies, it refers to plotting the members of the organization diagrammatically with the intention of identifying weaknesses in that organization. The objective is that if law enforcement can see the vulnerabilities, these can be exploited to destroy the organization. This is similar to social network analysis but with some differences.

The application of spatial vulnerability involves allocating each member of the criminal gang a designated letter. These letters are then plotted on a series of concentric circles with the most ardent members of the gang being more centrally located and those with a less significant involvement being plotted toward the outer circles, in effect producing a target with each gang member located in one of the circles. One of the first benefits that this provides is to allow the senior investigator a much clearer picture of those within that organization who pose the highest threat. These are the individuals whom the investigator will most likely pursue to convict and in an attempt to destroy the organization. One of the most challenging aspects of using this technique is selecting criteria to use in deciding what constitutes one's level of affiliation to the organization and how much strength to award each criterion. What may at first appear to be an obvious indicator of a high degree of affiliation may, after further consideration, be an indicator of vulnerability or dysfunction within the organization. Although indicators of affiliation will vary from organization to organization, some that can be used include the following:

- Length of time affiliated to the organization
- Rank or position within the organization
- Familial attachment
- Cultural-, ethnicity-, faith-, or peer-related affiliation
- Personal "cost" of membership

This technique should not be viewed merely as a way to present material. Before charting the organization's members, if an investigative team takes part in dialogue, it will often reveal different perspectives with regard to the organization that is under investigation. Deciding on the criteria to be used in plotting the organization allows participants to explore the attributes of that organization and the individuals who belong to it. This has the potential to unearth factors that have previously gone unnoticed. These will often be vulnerabilities in the organization or in individual members.

A further extension of this technique can be used in the proactive recruitment of human intelligence sources. The same basic methods are used but with the focus being on identifying an individual within the organization who may be vulnerable when approached by law enforcement and asked to become a human source.

8.23 Market Profile

A market profile is "An assessment that surveys the criminal market around a particular commodity in an area for the purpose of determining how to lessen that market" (IALEIA 2011). Commodities include things such as drugs and stolen goods or services such as contract killing or prostitution. Market profiles need to be continually reviewed and updated as criminal business is often as vulnerable to such factors as supply and demand as in any other business.

A market profile will explain the status of the market and the level of interest in it, the availability of product, and the price one would expect to pay for it. Furthermore, it may make reference to the key individuals or organizations involved, and anything that is likely result from or be connected to the state of the market. For example, reduced supply of a drug may escalate prices and so escalate the number of burglaries or street robberies, as addicts attempt to find the additional money to fund their habit. Legitimate trade can affect the criminal market and such factors should be included in the market profile. For example, a significant rise in the price of scrap metal may increase the theft of metals, such as copper and lead. The production and maintenance of market profiles takes time and should be carried out only where there is a specific strategic or tactical need. Market profiles can be extremely useful for undercover officers in that it can provide them with essential background knowledge for the roles they are undertaking.

8.24 Results Analysis

Results analysis is "an assessment of the effectiveness of police strategies and tactics as used to combat a particular crime problem. It may include suggestions for changes to future policies and strategies" (IALEIA 2011). Results analysis is not about analyzing the performance of staff. It is about identifying what strategies have worked or are working in relation to the identified crime problems. Results analysis will also identify strategies that are not working. It can also be used to identify good practice. Results analysis can be a useful tool when dealing with partner agencies. Being aware of what is being achieved and what is not may give a strong indication as to where the issue lies in dealing with the crime problem.

Results analysis is a relatively new technique, and while it was initially designed to assess law enforcement response to crime problems, it can be used to identify what is working and what is not working in relation to intelligence collection. All too often, covert information-gathering operations are allowed to continue ad infinitum, without any objective assessment of the results they are achieving. Having an analyst study the productivity of sources can indicate how effectively they are being managed and the amount of intelligence that results. In a similar vein, analyzing the amount of intelligence resulting from prolonged surveillance operations can give management a clearer picture of the costs and benefits. Another potential area for this type of analysis is assessing the accuracy of intelligence when compared with the results achieved from it. Although there may be limited statistical data to make comparisons, comparing what intelligence indicated and what the result of executive action was is another way of checking that the intelligence management system is producing the results it should.

8.25   Communication Analysis

Sometimes referred to as "telephone record analysis" or "toll analysis," communication analysis can be defined as "The analysis of records pertaining to communications." Such records will include those relating to communications via telephone, e-mail, pager, text messaging, etc. It should be noted that this type of analysis will in most jurisdictions involve details only of the existence of the communication; the devices involved; the registered owners/subscribers of those devices; and the date, time, and duration of the communication. What was contained in those communications will often require a significantly higher level of authority and much greater justification than is required for the communications records mentioned.

Communications analysis is widely used in law enforcement and can provide useful results. There are two main types of analysis used in relation to these records:

1. *Quantitative analysis*. This type of analysis looks at the date, times, frequency, and duration of calls and attempts to establish patterns in the calling.
2. *Association analysis*. This type of analysis uses link diagrams to try and identify the purpose of the calls and the relationship between the parties involved.

Communications analysis can assist in investigations in many ways:

- It can provide the name of the subscriber.
- Taking the lead from a suspect's phone, new associates can be identified.

- Patterns of calling may identify the hierarchy within an organization.
- Duration of calls may indicate the nature of a relationship, as may the timing of calls.
- The location of a caller can be identified when using a mobile phone.
- Bank details can be obtained, depending on how the phone was bought and the calls are being paid for.
- The type of phone being used may indicate whether or not it is to be used for illegal activities. Most people like to have a good quality handset, and with the handset is associated a certain amount of social status or "bling" value. Someone using a very cheap phone may well indicate intent to use it for a very limited period and then "chuck" it. This is a possible indicator that it is being used for a criminal purpose. Figures 8.6 and 8.7 show two ways in which telephone analysis can be presented.

Communications analysis can provide justification for and will be a vital step in obtaining warranty to intercept the content of a communications device.

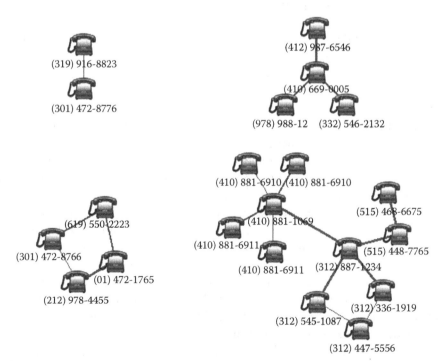

Figure 8.6 Telephone records analysis—connections. (Reprinted with permission from Visual Analytics Inc., MD.)

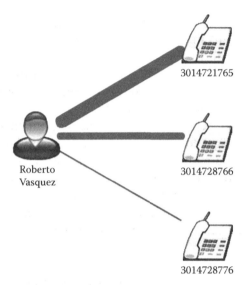

Figure 8.7 Telephone record analysis indicating "weight" of traffic. (Reprinted with permission from Visual Analytics Inc., MD.)

8.26 Financial Analysis

IALIEA (2011) defines financial analysis as "A review and analysis of financial data to ascertain the presence of criminal activity. It can include bank record analysis, net worth analysis, financial profiles, source and application of funds, financial statement analysis, and/or bank secrecy record analysis. It can also show destinations of proceeds of crime and support prosecutions." Financial analysis of a person's accounts or those of a criminal organization or of the movement of money involved in a particular crime can provide valuable leads both for investigators and for intelligence purposes. Understanding how a person manages and controls their money provides valuable insight into how they think and may give indications as to concerns they have or the level of trust they have for some of their associates. Furthermore, as many crimes are motivated by money, it is useful to understand the amounts of money involved and where any vulnerability exists in relation to the related financial transactions. Crime, just like any other business, can suffer from cash-flow problems. Financial analysis is a highly specialized activity and should normally be undertaken only by someone trained in forensic accounting or as a financial investigator, as only someone with this level of understanding is likely to be able to correctly interpret events. Figure 8.8 shows the linking of financial transactions to various other entities.

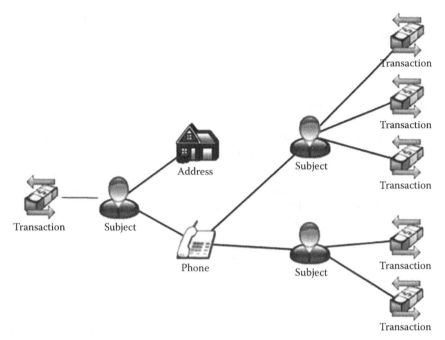

Figure 8.8 Financial analysis. (Reprinted with permission from Visual Analytics Inc., MD.)

8.27   Event Flow Charts

An event flow chart shows a sequence of events so that the times of occurrence and the relationships among the events may be made clearer. It is a useful tool to help understand the lead up to a particular occurrence. In complex investigations, the early preparation of an event flow chart can highlight investigative leads and opportunities for intelligence gathering. Event flow charts can assist in developing a greater understanding of the methodology of a criminal organization. Where criminals repeatedly use the same modus operandi, having prepared event flow charts of previous events enables the potential identification of the buildup for future events. Such indicators can act as a type of early warning system. Although in theory it would be possible to have software that indicates such a buildup, the sophistication required is unlikely to be found in many agencies. However, those members working against specific targets and having had the benefit of seeing an event flow chart of previous events may, in their daily course of duties, spot a similar buildup. Many members that work in intelligence on a daily basis often identify buildups in activity from hostile groups citing their intuition as to why they believe an event may occur. Event flow charts can often put substance behind such beliefs. Furthermore, if a pattern is identified in such charts, it can make officers more likely to see a similar pattern as it emerges in the future.

8.28   "Geo" Stuff

There are many different and often interrelated products that an analyst can create using mapping as a central element. LEAs are often restricted to a designated geographical area to define their responsibilities. Although this has many practical benefits, it must be remembered that criminals are rarely bound by such geographical constraints, and law enforcement should take cognizance of this factor, especially when using geographic based products that are limited to their geographic area of responsibility. Particularly with agencies covering smaller geographic areas, it is always of benefit to extend any such products to surrounding areas.

Geographical material can be presented in many different ways, but if the agency does not have some sort of electronic GIS, it is not going to be able to carry out these techniques. A GIS is a set of computer-based tools designed to capture, store, manipulate, analyze, manage, and present all types of geographical data. In short, a GIS merges maps with the data that allows the user to create anything from a simple point map to a three-dimensional visualization of relevant data. If one imagines pinning a note to a map, the pin indicates the location, and the note tells you what happened there. So it is with a GIS; the pin is replaced by a symbol and the note by a database table directly accessed through the symbol, Different symbols can indicate different types of events. An important part of intelligence management is ensuring that any address or location is geocoded (see Chapter 7), so that it can later be viewed using GIS technology. Another benefit of GISs is their use of digital orthophotography. Digital orthophotography involves combining an aerial photographic image with the geometric qualities of a map, and the ability to combine these two aspects makes understanding of the geography involved significantly easier (See Figure 8.9). In a GIS, the data that is attached is separated by type and by what are often referred to as "themes." For example, burglaries would be one type of data and robberies another, whereas "public order offenses" may constitute a theme but contain a variety of offenses. The idea is that one data type or theme can be laid over another to give a more detailed or more specific picture.

With the huge advances that are being made in relation to electronic media, the potential benefits in combining technologies increases almost on a daily basis. Geotagging is one such benefit. Geotagging is the process of adding geographical identification metadata to various media. For example, when a person snaps a picture on her mobile phone, embedded in the image is the location, date, and time it was taken. Uploading of such material into

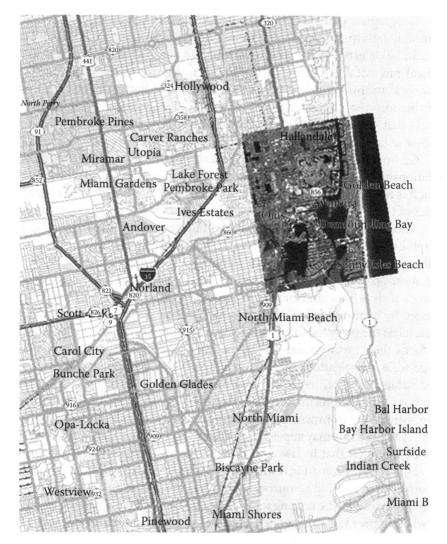

Figure 8.9 Orthophotography. (Reprinted with permission from Visual Analytics Inc., MD.)

a GIS can provide real-time visual images, and the information is recorded for future analysis.

Terms such as geographic mapping, geospatial analysis, and geographic analysis have all become synonymous with analysis involving GISs, with each term being recognized by some, and a different one being used by others. The nuances in meaning are relatively easily overlooked by the lay reader. Geographical mapping is concerned with analyzing the spatial patterns of crimes committed by numerous offenders over a period of time and is often used to identify such things as crime "hot spots."

Geographic analysis can be defined as "An evaluation of the locations of criminal activity or criminals to determine whether future criminal activity can be deterred or interdicted through forecasting activity based on historical raw data" (IALEIA 2011). However, the use of the term "historical raw data" in this definition is questionable. If only data is involved, then the "evaluation" that is created may well be flawed. Having said that, there is no doubt that such analysis can provide useful indicators of the likelihood and nature of criminal activity or public order problems in a particular area.

Geospatial analysis looks at the locations where crimes occur and the relationship that those places have to one another, working on the principle that it is not only important where a crime takes place but also the characteristics of those locations.

Another technique that can be used in association with mapping is geographic profiling (GP). Rossmo (2000:1) defines GP as "an investigative methodology that uses the locations of a connected series of crimes to determine the most probable area of offender residence." GP is typically used in serial crimes such as rape and murder to provide assistance to a criminal investigation. By relating the believed movements of an offender to a geographical area, it has the potential to provide to investigators with an indication of where to focus their investigation. GP helps investigators prioritize information in large-scale investigations by looking at an offender's geographical tendencies and habits. This technique is based on the underlying principle that crime locations provide information regarding the victim and the offender's interaction with the environment and may indicate the offender's familiarity with the area. Although this may appear to be exclusively an investigative tool, it should not be forgotten that in law enforcement, the vast majority of intelligence is all about progressing an investigation. GP can provide indication as to where information-gathering resources should be deployed to further an investigation. For example, the tasking for human sources living in a particular area, as to whether they know someone who also lives in that area and matches a particular profile, may produce results. In a different application, this type of product can be useful in understanding the lifestyle of the target of an investigation.

8.29   Demographic/Social Trend Analysis

Demographic/social trends analysis is defined as "An examination of the nature of demographic changes and their impact on criminality, the community, and law enforcement" (IALEIA 2011). Its purpose is to identify how factors such as unemployment, homelessness, and changing populations within an area are likely to impact crime and disorder in an area. Many LEAs police areas where sociodemographic factors play a huge part in the level and nature of criminality. Sociodemographic information includes characteristics of individuals and groups such as sex, race, income, age, and education. Changing populations make a real difference, especially where there is conflict between different minority groups. Where factors such as immigration bring about change in who holds the position of dominant group, problems such as increased public order problems and "turf wars" have the potential to occur. Similarly, an influx of a particular group may lead to the emergence of a particular type of crime.

Tasking intelligence collectors to provide intelligence in relation to demographic changes ongoing in neighborhoods may be of little immediate tactical use but can prove to be valuable at a strategic level. Collectors need to be specifically tasked to get this type of intelligence, as they rarely think that such material is of use, as it provides no immediate practical benefit to them. When social data and intelligence are analyzed, they can provide a valuable input to inform and influence local policymaking in crime prevention strategies such as "crime prevention through environmental design."* Creating products such as a sociodemographic analysis is one more way that intelligence can inform the wider law enforcement family.

8.30   Risk-Related Products

A task that may often fall to the analyst is the preparation of risk-related products. Unfortunately, many involved in law enforcement have limited real knowledge of the various aspects of risk management. It is common to find terms such as risk analysis, threat assessment, and risk management all used interchangeably. Furthermore, people often describe risk in terms of low, medium, and high expressions of risk that are meaningless. The International Standards Organization (ISO 2009) provides clear guidance on the most effective methods for the management of risk. They detail the vocabulary that should be used and explain how any risk must be expressed in terms of the likelihood of its occurring and the consequences should it occur. One of the strengths of the International Standards is that they advocate a degree of flexibility to meet the specific circumstances or the context in which they are used. The Standards explain the process in many stages: first, identifying the nature of the risk and evaluating it in terms of likelihood and probability, thus producing an inherent risk document; second, selecting appropriate control measures to mitigate the risk followed; third, by a reevaluation that produces the residual risk document. It is on the basis of the values contained in the residual risk document that the subsequent

---

* Crime prevention through environmental design is a multidisciplinary approach to deterring criminal behavior through environmental design. See: Ray, C. J. (1971). *Crime Prevention through Environmental Design*. Beverly Hills, CA: Sage Publications.

course of action is decided. Although predating the International Standards Organization guidance, Buckley (2007) provides a comprehensive description of the structures necessary to manage risk in covert policing using the same methods as outlined in the International Standards Organization document. Furthermore, the methods outlined for covert policing can be easily adapted to meet the needs of any law enforcement circumstances, including public order and the threat posed by terrorism. Many LEAs leave themselves vulnerable because of the lack of adequate risk management. This deficit is particularly prevalent in covert law enforcement with the limited amount that is written with regard to risk, often amounting to all but meaningless drivel.

8.31   Key Terms

To have effective risk management structures, there are many key terms that need to be understood and used consistently. The following terms have specific relevance in the law enforcement environment:

- Risk is defined as "Effect of uncertainty on objectives" (ISO 31000:9). A risk is an event that leads to consequences. Both the event and the consequences must be included in the statement of the risk. An example of a risk statement is "There is a risk that a person my slip on the wet floor and fall causing themselves injury." The event is the "slipping and falling" and the consequences are the "injury."
- *Risk assessment.* This is the process of identifying and quantifying the risks in terms of likelihood (probability) and impact (consequences) that are present under a given set of circumstances.
- *Likelihood.* Also known by the term "probability"; this is the chance of the event happening.
- *Impact.* Also known by the term "consequences"; this is the harm that is caused if the event occurs.
- *Risk management.* This refers to what is done to manage the risk. Risk can be managed in one of four ways:
  - *Retain:* The agency accepts the risk.
  - *Avoid:* The risk is unacceptable under the circumstances, and the action that is creating the risk is avoided or terminated.
  - *Threat:* Control measures are put in place to lower the likelihood or impact or both.
  - *Transfer:* The impact of the risk is transferred to a third party. (Think of car insurance—if you crash, someone else pays.)
- *Control measures.* These are specific steps taken to mitigate each identified risk.

- *Victim.* This refers to who will suffer as a result of the event and can refer to a person or a location.
- *Threat agent.* Also referred to as the threat actor, this is the person or thing that will cause the event. This will include criminals, organizations, or natural events such as weather.
- *Vulnerability.* How vulnerable is the potential victim?
- *Capability.* What is the threat agent capable of doing?
- *Intention.* What are the intentions of the threat agent?
- *Victim attractiveness.* Out of all the other potential victims, why this one?

8.32   Risk-Related Analytical Products

There are many products that an analyst can prepare in relation to risk. It should be stressed that unless the analyst has been properly trained in risk management and the agency has agreed procedures for managing risk, including values for likelihood and impact, anything produced is of questionable value and open to whatever interpretation a reader of the product wants to make. The analyst should always seek assistance from those with the most up-to-date and accurate material in preparing any of these products.

8.33   Threat Assessment

A threat assessment is an assessment of the threat posed by a criminal or terrorist presence within a jurisdiction. The assessment focuses on the criminal's or terrorist's capability and willingness to carry out the threat, either now or in the future. This product is likely to include the suspects involved, their ideology, their modus operandi, logistical considerations, and details of those who provide support. The threat posed by any entity can be viewed as:

$$\text{Threat} = \text{Intention} + \text{Capability}$$

Table 8.1 provides examples of values for threat. Although such values do not replace a properly authored threat document, they can be of significant practical use, for example, in briefing senior managers or in the briefing of staff who may have to face the threat. The level of threat should not be confused with likelihood of risk. The two are different with threat being one element used in evaluating the likelihood of an event. A person may have the intention and capability to mount an attack, but the security surrounding the potential victim may be so high as to prevent such an attack ever happening. The lack of specific intelligence with regard to a potential threat does not

Table 8.1   Example of Threat Values

Threat Values	
Very low	On the evidence available, the threat posed by this agent is assessed as being very limited.
Low	On the evidence available, the threat posed by this agent is assessed as being limited.
Medium	On the evidence available, the threat posed by this agent is assessed as being credible.
High	On the evidence available, the threat posed by this agent is assessed as being substantial.
Very high	On the evidence available, the threat posed by this agent is assessed as being severe.

mean that no threat exists. Too often, agencies will comment that there is no intelligence to suggest a threat, all the time failing to acknowledge that any objective assessment of the person or group involved and the given circumstances would suggest that a threat exists. Lack of specific intelligence may just be a result of poor coverage on the agency's part.

8.34   Vulnerability Assessment

A vulnerability assessment is an assessment of the potential vulnerability of a specific victim, be it a person or a location. This assessment is based on the nature of the victim and identifies potential weaknesses that leave the victim vulnerable to attack. With a person, it may include just a study of his pattern of life; but with a location, it will require a survey by a person trained in countering the threat that the potential victim will be exposed to. This may be a crime prevention officer or a counterterrorism security officer. Such a survey will include the victim's ability to withstand an attack. Of relevance will also be the proximity of the potential victim to the threat agent.

Table 8.2 shows values that may be used in a vulnerability assessment. As can be seen when Tables 8.1 and 8.2 are compared, there is an association between the values for suggested for threat and the values suggested for vulnerability.

8.35   Risk Assessment

Sometimes referred to as "risk analysis," a risk assessment for a particular set of circumstances may contain many risks. For example, there are likely to be between 15 and 20 separate risks in any standard undercover operation. Each of these must be assessed and values stated for the likelihood and

Table 8.2   Example of Vulnerability Values

Vulnerability Values	
Very low	On the evidence available, the vulnerability of this potential victim is assessed as being very limited.
Low	On the evidence available, the vulnerability of this potential victim is assessed as being limited.
Medium	On the evidence available, the vulnerability of this potential victim is assessed as being credible.
High	On the evidence available, the vulnerability of this potential victim is assessed as being substantial.
Very high	On the evidence available, the vulnerability of this potential victim is assessed as being severe.

Table 8.3 Example of Likelihood for Terrorist Attack on an Identified Site

Likelihood (Probability)	
Grading	Meaning
Very low	There is no evidence to indicate the likelihood of such an event at this site, and under the existing circumstances, it is assessed that the event is unlikely to occur within the relevant period.
Low	On the evidence available and under the existing circumstances, it is assessed that such an event is less than likely to occur than occur at this site within the relevant period.
Medium	On the evidence available and under the existing circumstances, it is assessed that the circumstances exist where the event may occur at this site within the relevant period.
High	On the evidence available and under the existing circumstances, it is assessed that the event is more likely to occur than not at this site within the relevant period.
Very high	On the evidence available and under the existing circumstances, it is assessed that the event will almost certainly occur at this site within the relevant period.

impact for each separate risk. Once each of these risks has been quantified, then decisions have to be made as to how each risk will be managed. Table 8.3 provides examples for values of the likelihood of an attack occurring at a site of potential interest to terrorists.

Table 8.4 shows how the values for likelihood are derived. An additional factor that of "attractiveness" is added. This factor recognizes that terrorists are likely to give considerable thought into picking a victim that will provide the maximum benefit to their cause. With this factor added, the formula for arriving at likelihood can be written as follows:

$$\text{Likelihood} = \text{Threat} + \text{Vulnerability} + \text{Attractiveness}$$

Table 8.4   Assessing Likelihood of Terrorist Attack on an Identified Site

		Factors Affecting Likelihood of Terrorist Attack
Threat	Intention	Is there intelligence to suggest that this business or site has been specifically targeted? Is there intelligence to indicate that similar sites have been targeted? Has the relevant terrorist grouping publicly expressed threats in relation to similar businesses?
	Capability	Does the relevant terrorist grouping have the organizational capability to carry out such an attack? Do they have the necessary equipment?
Vulnerability	Security	How good is the protective security pertaining to the business? What gaps are there? How easily can these be identified?
	Predictability	How predictable is behavior at the business? Are patterns of behavior likely to make the business more susceptible to attack or likely to negate existing security measures?
Attractiveness	Criticality	Does the site or part of the site form a critical part of the business? If it is, is this likely to be readily identified? How long would it take to recover from an incident?
	Prestige	Is the site or business of a prestigious nature and as such make it more likely to be attacked? Are there likely to be mass casualties?

Table 8.5 provides examples of values for the impact caused by a terrorist attack at such a site. The four different areas of impact recognize that there is more than one type of consequence after an attack; for example, if an electrical substation is blown up, there may be no injuries, but other fallout may be huge.

Table 8.6 provides impact values for risks in covert operations. As can be seen, the methodology is similar, though the values and areas of impact have changed.

For the most part, LEAs are extremely poor at dealing with risk (Buckley 2007). Understanding is limited, yet knowledge, all too often, is readily assumed. The tables outlined above provide an indication of how different values can be attributed in different areas in the management of risk. Each table only provides an abbreviated version of a specific value. Full explanation of each value and details of how they have been derived should be contained in the agency's procedures for risk management. Other factors that must be considered are the timescales for a potential event. If the timing of a potential event is imminent, then action must be taken rapidly. Timescales,

Table 8.5   Examples of Impact Values for Terrorist Attack

	Impact (Consequences)			
Grading	Harm to Life	Public Confidence	Economic Harm	Public Disruption
Very low	No loss of life. No or limited injury	Public concerns raised on a local basis for a limited period	Limited financial loss confined to the site	Local disruption for a limited period
Low	Loss of life <10 and attendant casualty levels	Public concern raised on a regional basis for a prolonged period	Significant financial loss confined to the site potentially leading to bankruptcy or closure	Significant disruption on a local basis for a prolonged period
Medium	Substantial loss of life (11–100) and attendant casualty levels	Concern raised on a national basis for a limited period	Significant loss over a prolonged period and/or impacting on the financial well-being of similar businesses in the immediate geographical area	Significant disruption on a regional basis
High	Severe loss of life (101–1000) and attendant casualty levels	Widespread, long-term public concern and outrage	Long-term damage to the financial well-being of the similar businesses throughout the region potentially leading to bankruptcy/closure	Significant disruption for a limited period throughout the country
Very high	Massive loss of life (>1000) and attendant casualty levels	Significant and long-term life-changing behavior by persons not directly affected by the event	Long-term damage to the financial well-being of the similar businesses throughout the country leading to bankruptcy/closure	Significant disruption for a prolonged period throughout the country

where relevant, should be included in a risk document. And as a final comment on risk, the use of numbers instead of words is not appropriate in a law enforcement context. There are simply no statistics to back up mathematical values, and using figures in these circumstances is done for all the wrong reasons.

Table 8.6   Examples of Impact Values in Covert Operations

		Impact (Covert Operations)		
Grading	Harm to Life	Agency Reputation	Economic Harm	Operational Compromise
Very low	Distress to individual	Embarrassment at local level	Less than $1000	Minimal exposure of operational methodology
Low	Minor injury	Significant embarrassment at local level	Less than $10,000	Exposure that is prejudicial to the investigation of crime
Medium	Injury requiring hospital treatment	Embarrassment at regional or national level	Less than $10,000	Causes damage to operational effectiveness
High	Significant or lasting injury	Significant damage to agency reputation	Less than $1,000,000	Causes significant damage to operational effectiveness and/or impacts on national security
Very high	Death	Irreparable damage to agency reputation	Greater than $1,000,000	Causes exceptionally grave: damage to operational effectiveness and harm to national security

8.36   Briefing Products

Part and parcel of both gathering and using intelligence requires that members of the agency know what to look for and what to gather information on. Preparing briefing products to keep staff informed is a task that often falls, rightly or wrongly, to the analyst. Inevitably, it is the presentational skills of analysts that often makes them the right candidate for this role. If a briefing document is professionally produced, it is more likely to be read. Briefing documents can take on a variety of forms, but increasingly these are being produced in electronic format, as they are quicker to distribute, unlikely to be removed from the agency, allow greater accountability with regard to whether they have been read by a member, and are cheaper to produce. Many agencies now provide briefing documents for smartphones, although there are some security implications around doing so. Regardless of the format, briefing documents should do the following:

- Avoid jargon and inappropriate language.
- Be produced on a regular basis.
- Be updated or removed whenever the content is no longer valid.
- Be authorized by the intelligence manager.
- Have different distribution groups as dictated by the content.

- Use a variety of media if possible including both videos and photographs. People like variety and are more likely to pay attention to something novel.

Intelligence briefing is explored further in Chapter 11.

8.37 Strategic and Tactical Assessments

Strategic and tactical assessments are an everyday part of the analyst's day. They "are completed to assess the impact of a crime group or a criminal activity on a jurisdiction, now or in the future" (IALEIA 2011). The idea behind assessments is basically taking a look at what is happening now and making a prediction as to what is likely to happen or what might happen in the future based on what is known and verified, believed but can't be verified, and unknown. An assessment of the likelihood of the event occurring is also included as this provides a clearer picture to the decision-maker. Given that the analyst will have as clear a picture of what is occurring or what might occur including suggestions as to how to combat the problem may be included in an assessment, but this will normally be at the choice of the customer.

Strategic assessments are an overview of the current issues affecting an agency, and the issues that are likely to affect the agency in the foreseeable future. Strategic assessments should be a collaborative effort and report as to the effectiveness of the existing measures being deployed. Following the preparation of a strategic assessment, an analyst will be guided by two criteria that will point the analyst toward the outcome. The first criterion is what has happened in the past. When it comes to how people behave, the best indicator of their future behavior is how they have behaved in the past. In analyzing the past, the analyst will be able to identify key elements of the problem that is under scrutiny. The second criterion is the indicators that point toward what will most likely happen in the future. For example, a Chief of Police is concerned that there may be an escalation of theft of metal to be sold for scrap and commissions a strategic study of the problem. The analyst will consider all the information he has about previous scrap metal thefts—where they occurred, when they occurred—and attempt to identify any peaks in the related crime pattern and potential causes for those peaks. These can be considered as falling under the first criterion. From this research, the analysis concludes that metal thefts increase once the scrap metal reaches a certain monetary threshold—for example, $10 per kilo—and that the first place targeted by the thieves are yards belonging to electrical contractors. The analyst can then set indicators that will point to a potentially escalating problem—the second criterion. In this case, it will be the open-market price threshold that is reached, and there has been a reported burglary at an electrical contractor's yard where copper wire was stolen. It is reasonable to predict that this type of crime will increase, and therefore the correct move for the Chief is to deploy additional resources to meet the problem. The underlying drive behind strategic assessments can be shown by examining the dialogue between a Chief and an analyst.

Chief: Tell me what is happening in my area and tell me what is going to happen.
Analyst: Intelligence says this is happening and based on that that I assess that this will happen.
Chief: Can you suggest any strategies that might help?

Tactical assessments inform decision-makers in regard to what is happening with specific problems and are mainly aimed at the short- to mid-term. They will often revolve around specific crime groups or crime types. The underlying drive behind strategic assessments can be shown by examining the dialogue between a district commander and an analyst.

Commander: Tell me what is happening about this specific problem.
Analyst: Intelligence says this is happening and based on that that I assess that this will happen.
Commander: Can you any suggest anything that we can do?

In the United Kingdom, strategic assessments and tactical assessments are key documents in developing policing plans using the National Intelligence Model (NIM) (ACPO 2005). This NIM is intended to guide every police service in respect of the implementation of intelligence-led policing. Working under the model, strategic assessments inform the planning process and are developed for regional, service-wide, and district levels on a yearly basis being reviewed at six monthly intervals. Tactical assessments address shorter term issues for a district, a police service, or a region and inform tactical planning meetings that are held on a monthly or bimonthly basis.

8.38   Analyst Reporting

A report from an analyst may use just one or many different products and can include maps, charts, and images. A narrative should always accompany these types of products explaining the relevance of each and providing an overall commentary on the subject being addressed.

8.39   Assisting Covert Activities

Those involved in covert operations have traditionally been reluctant to allow access by an analyst to the planning and execution of such operations. This probably has its roots in the fact that many analysts were unsworn and the belief that they had nothing to contribute. Many of the products listed above can be of significant value in planning and executing covert operations. If this was the only reason to allow an analyst access, it would be more than enough. However, analysts have more to give in the way they have been trained to think. A properly trained analyst will bring a different perspective to such operations: a different way of looking at them and a different way of thinking about them. A team is likely to be stronger with the involvement of analysts.

8.40   Technology

Arguably a commentary on analysis without some discussion in relation to technology would be incomplete. In the interests of completeness, a few comments are provided:

- The array of potential software available is massive. There are many "commercial off-the-shelf" products out there. If the rest of the agency's intelligence management system is properly constructed, it will make it a lot easier getting analytical software to work effectively. If the agency is paper based for many of its intelligence functions, then what will be needed is to hire a typist*—the analyst will need one!
- The capabilities of new technology are growing exponentially, with software now able to do at the touch of a button, what once required the efforts of a trained analyst over a prolonged period. Keeping technology up-to-date saves money.
- As with all technology, people don't take the time to understand how it works, and therefore many features go unused. The technology is there, and some of it is pretty damned amazing—use it.
- Technology is a tool, and like any other tool, it depends on the skill of the person using it. Much of what is out there needs specialized understanding of not only how to use it but also what to use it for. Investing in training for analysts is essential if they are to realize the full potential of the new technology.
- Make sure that analysts are involved in purchasing new technology. They know what it needs to do and can see past the pretty pictures that leave the rest of us oohing and aahing!

---

* For those of you that are confused by this comment: In the olden times, typists were people who were hired to work at primitive print machines, taking written words, entering them into the machine, and producing a document in a more legible format. Typists are believed to have become extinct toward the end of the twentieth century. This was rather unfortunate, because they did liven up Christmas parties.

8.41   Conclusion

This chapter has addressed the role of the analyst in law enforcement. It advocates that there should be no separation between crime and intelligence analysis and that having an integrated function is the most productive and effective route for an agency to follow. Furthermore, analysts should be tasked to carry out the functions for which they are trained and not placed where their skills are not fully used such as in performing general intelligence-related functions. The analyst forms a vital part of the intelligence management system, and their role provides significant assistance to the agency as a whole. As Evans (2008:123) remarks, "Good analysts provide the information necessary to proactively tackle problems. They help manage risk, provide justification for why things are done (and more importantly, why other things are not done) and can help generate audit trails that facilitate accountability and oversight." Analysts are skilled professionals and should be facilitated in performing the role they are trained for.

Unfortunately, because of the heavy bias that is often attached to the fact that an analyst is likely to be nonsworn and the preeminence of rank based structures within law enforcement, the input of an analyst is often given limited attention. Using a specialist and then not listening to them is akin to going to the doctor and then ignoring what they tell you!

References

Association of Chief Police Officers (ACPO). (2005) *Guidance on the National Intelligence Mode.* U.K: Centre for Policing Excellence (Centrex).

Association of Chief Police Officers (ACPO). (2008) Practical advice on analysis. National Police Improvement Agency (NPIA). Available at http://www.acpo .police.uk/documents/crime/2008/200804CRIPAA01.pdf (accessed November 2012).

Barnes, J.A. (1954) Class and committee in a Norwegian island parish. *Human Relations* 7 P39–P58.

Boba, R. (2005) *Crime Analysis and Crime Mapping.* California: Sage Publications.

Buckley, J. (2006) *The Human Source Management System: The Use of Psychology in the Management of Human Intelligence Sources.* London: HSM Publishing.

Buckley, J. (2007) *Invest Now or Pay Later: The Management of Risk in Covert Law Enforcement.* London: HSM Publishing.

Carley, K.M. (2012) Dynamic network analysis. In: Breiger, R. and Carley, K.M. Eds. *The Summary of the NRC Workshop on Social Network Modelling and Analysis.* National Research Council. Available at http://stiet.cms.si.umich.edu/sites/ stiet.cms.si.umich.edu/files/archivedHTML/researchseminar/Winter%202003/ DNA.pdf (accessed July 2012).

Carley, K.M., Dombroski, M., Tsvetovat, M., Reminga, J. and Kamneva, N. (2003) Destabilizing dynamic covert networks. In: *Proceedings of the 8th International*

Command and Control Research and Technology Symposium. Conference held at the National Defense War College, Washington, DC. Evidence Based Research, Track 3, Electronic Publication, Vienna, VA.

Cooper, J.R. (2005) *Curing Analytical Pathologies: Pathways to Improved Intelligence Analysis*. Washington: Centre for the Study of Intelligence. Available at https://www.cia.gov/library/center-for-the-study-of-intelligence/csi-publications/books-and-monographs/curing-analytic-pathologies-pathways-to-improved-intelligence-analysis-1/analytic_pathologies_report.pdf (accessed September 2012).

Evans, R.M. (2008) Cultural paradigms and change: A model for analysis. In: Harfield, C., MacVean, A., Grieve, J.G.D. and Philips, D. Eds. *The Handbook of Intelligent Policing: Consilience, Crime Control and Community Safety*, pp. 105–120. Oxford: Oxford University Press.

Goldstein, H. (1990) *Problem-Oriented Policing*. New York: McGraw-Hill.

Harris, D.R., Maxfield, M.G., Hollady, G., Godfrey, E.D. and United States. Law Enforcement Assistance Administration Enforcement Program Division. (1976) *Basic Elements of Intelligence*. Washington, DC: Law Enforcement Assistance Administration, U.S. Dept. Of Justice.

Heurer, R.J. (1999) *Psychology of Intelligence Analysis*. Washington, DC: Centre for Intelligence Study. Available at https://www.cia.gov/library/center-for-the-study-of-intelligence/csi-publications/books-and-monographs/psychology-of-intelligence-analysis/PsychofIntelNew.pdf (accessed August 2012).

International Association of Crime Analysts (IACA). (2011) Crime pattern definitions for tactical analysis (STM Committee white paper 2011-01). Overland Park, Kansas. Available at http://www.iaca.net/Publications/Whitepapers/iacawp_2011_01_crime_patterns.pdf (accessed December 2012).

International Association of Law Enforcement Intelligence Analysts (IALEIA). (2011) *Law Enforcement Analytical Standards*. 2nd ed. Global Justice Information Sharing Initiative. Available at http://it.ojp.gov/documents/law_enforcement_analytic_standards.pdf (accessed November 2012).

International Standards Organization. (2009) *ISO 31000:2009 Risk Management– Principles and Guidelines*. Geneva: International Standards Organization.

Johnston, R. (2005) *Analytic Culture in the US Intelligence Community: An Ethnographic Study*. Washington, DC: Center for the Study of Intelligence, Central Intelligence Agency. Available at https://www.cia.gov/library/center-for-the-study-of-intelligence/csi-publications/books-and-monographs/analytic-culture-in-the-u-s-intelligence-community/chapter_1.htm (accessed July 2012).

Milgram, S. (May 1967) The small world problem. *Psychology Today* 1(1) P60–P67.

Osborne, D. (2006) *Out of Bounds: Innovation and Change in Law Enforcement Intelligence Analysis*. Washington, DC: Joint Military Intelligence College.

Osborne, D. and Wernicke, S. (2003) *Introduction to Crime Analysis: Basic Resources for Criminal Justice Practice*. New York: Haworth Press.

O'Shea, T.C. and Nicholls, K. (2003) *Crime Analysis in America Findings and Recommendations*. Washington, DC: U.S. Department of Justice. Office of Community Oriented Policing Services.

Peterson, M. (2005) *Intelligence-Led Policing: The New Intelligence Architecture*. Washington, DC: US Department of Justice, Bureau of Justice Assistance.

Ratcliffe, J.H. and U.S. Department of Justice Office of Community Oriented
      Policing Services. (2007) *Integrated Intelligence and Crime Analysis: Enhanced
      Information Management for Law Enforcement Leaders*. Washington, DC: Police
      Foundation.
Rossmo, K. (2000) *Geographic Profiling*. Boca Raton, FL: CRC Press.

Intelligence Originating from Traditional Law Enforcement Activities

9

> Everything we hear is an opinion, not a fact. Everything we see is a perspective, not the truth.
>
> **Marcus Aurelius**

9.1 Introduction

Much of the work of law enforcement lies outside the world of intelligence. Law enforcement agencies (LEAs) are expected to provide various services. Most LEAs will use extensive resources in the traditional aspects of law enforcement including overt patrolling, responding to calls for assistance, and carrying out investigative functions. These functions constitute the public perception of law enforcement and, in the minds of most citizens, will fall into two categories: the uniformed officer and the detective/investigator. These can be thought of as the "traditional" law enforcement roles, seen by the public through regular coverage in both factual and fictional television programs, and in movies. The use of the term "traditional" is not intended to have any derogatory connotation, nor is it intended to suggest an outmoded way of behaving. It is used here to suggest continuity in the nature of the work being undertaken: namely, protecting the community and catching the bad guys—the stuff cops have been doing for years. Historically, the roles of the uniformed officer and the detective are, for the most part, not normally associated with intelligence collection, except for the occasional portrayal of a detective having a street-level informant, as it is so realistically portrayed in the old television series *Starsky and Hutch*. Unfortunately, while most agencies have progressed away from this limited perspective, there still remain a few where anything to do with intelligence is viewed as something akin to an extraterrestrial life form. As already discussed, the purpose of intelligence is to support the more traditional aspects of law enforcement, but in turn it is incumbent upon the traditional aspects of law enforcement to support the intelligence function. This chapter explores the various ways in which traditional law enforcement activities can reap huge amounts of information that can be considered for intelligence purposes. It will highlight some of the problems that occur when a systematic approach is not used, and how an agency can be left vulnerable if processes are not designed to capture the information in a structured way.

9.2   Gathering

As this section is being written, the author is watching a squirrel run around the bottom of a tree, gathering morsels of food, some of which it eats, but with the majority of it the squirrel ascends the tree and disappears into a hole, emerging a short time later minus the food. It is as if somewhere in the squirrel's little mind the message is firmly lodged: "I need some of this food now, but I am going to need more of it later, so I will store it away while I can." There is often a lesson readily available, if we take the time to learn it.

Those involved in traditional aspects of law enforcement often don't see the benefits of putting something away that may be of use later, especially when it comes to intelligence. This attitude can come about for a number of reasons including the following:

- *Lack of knowledge.* Very few agencies provide any training to staff in relation to intelligence management. It is regarded as something they don't really need to know, or if they do, they will pick it up as they go along. Training with regard to the nature of intelligence and how to submit information for consideration as intelligence should be delivered to staff in their initial training. Where an agency wants to professionalize its intelligence function, training needs to be delivered to all staff likely to be in a position to gather information. Such training should include an overview of the agency's intelligence management system, information submissions, and the role of the Intelligence Unit. The training should stress the overall benefits to the agency that intelligence can provide and the benefits to individual members. The training should establish the Intelligence Unit as a first point of contact for all intelligence-related matters.
- *Lack of a means to facilitate information submission.* Few agencies provide a user-friendly mechanism to submit information for intelligence purposes. Unless a user-friendly mechanism is in place, staff will take the easier option and not submit the information. The agency must effectively capture the information that members obtain. Capturing information of potential use extends beyond having an effective submission process. The agency must encourage staff to continually look for opportunities to obtain more information. For example, rather than just interviewing a suspect for the crime under investigation, the opportunity should be taken for further conversation with that suspect about other unrelated activities that they may know about.

- *Expectations of behavior.* The agency should have clear policies and procedures instructing staff with regard to what should be submitted. Compliance with instructions should be monitored by supervisors, with acknowledgement of compliance and consequences for noncompliance.
- *Clear direction from intelligence staff.* If members are expected to submit information, then Intelligence Unit staff should regularly brief them as to the nature of the information that is desired and encourage them to go out and get it.
- *Lack of effective IT.* The disjointed nature of many of the IT systems found in LEAs means that staff may enter information into one software program, but because this isn't connected to the intelligence software, the material has either to be double-keyed or is lost.

The remainder of this chapter will address the ways in which those involved in traditional law enforcement will encounter various opportunities to submit information of potential use for intelligence purposes.

9.3   Stop-Checks and Observations

Perhaps the simplest origin for information that can be of use for intelligence purposes is the observation of a patrol officer or where a patrol officer stops and checks the identity of a person. Patrol officers spend huge amounts of time in high-crime areas. They regularly observe persons of interest and often have cause to stop and check people behaving suspiciously in an area or committing some minor transgression of the law. These observations and stop-checks provide a rich hunting ground for information to add to the intelligence picture. Information obtained from observations and stop-checks will include the following:

- *New associations.* For example, a known criminal is stopped for running a red light and in his vehicle is a new associate. Details of this new associate should be submitted as it may fill gaps in an intelligence picture.
- *New vehicles.* For example, a police officer who is driving past a known criminal's house may observe them getting into a new vehicle. Submitting the license plate of the vehicle and its description may later prove of value to a surveillance team.
- *New locations.* For example, a known criminal may be observed away from his usual place of business or entering an unusual location, and both these factors may help further an investigation.

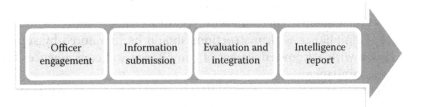

Figure 9.1 Stop-check or observation intelligence repositing.

All these pieces of information taken on their own may seem to be of little worth, but they may prove to be vital pieces for an investigation. It should always be remembered that any investigation is like a jigsaw puzzle: once all the pieces are in the right place, the picture becomes obvious. When submitting these details, the submitting member should include the date, time, and location of the occurrence and whether the identity of the person was confirmed or merely "believed to be" the person in question. Sometimes a cop's eyesight isn't as good as he believes it to be! An inaccurate report can distort the intelligence picture. Submitting such information should always be done on a standard information submission and be processed as illustrated in Figure 9.1. If, during a stop-check, the person being checked volunteers information, this should be treated as information coming from a member of the public and an additional information submission used to protect that person's identity. While it may be quicker to submit the information using one submission, at a later stage, this has the potential to compromise the person through circumstances such as disclosure.

9.4 Information from "Members of the Public"

Citizens provide huge amounts of information that can be useful in adding to the intelligence picture. Citizens come into contact with the police for a variety of reasons and under a variety of circumstances. An agency needs to have clarity with regard to how information from a citizen is to be handled: when it has the potential to be used for intelligence purposes. Buckley (2009) provides guidance as to how an agency should categorize information received from citizens. By creating two distinct categories of individual, the agency is able to direct staff toward the correct reporting mechanism. The two categories here are somewhat adapted to meet the needs of numerous jurisdictions:

1. *Registered "Human Source."* This is a person whom the agency has registered as a result of legislation or under their procedures for such individuals as meeting the criteria for such registration. The

assumption is then made that the person will be managed in accordance with the agency's procedures for human sources, and any information obtained from the source will be submitted according to the mechanism for human sources.

2. *Members of the Public (MoPs).* Any person who provides law enforcement with information and is not a member of the agency or a registered human source for that agency is considered to be an MoP and managed accordingly. Information from MoPs is submitted through one standardized mechanism, regardless of who they are or their motive in passing information. It should be noted that, where a person provides a statement of evidence, they will primarily be regarded as a witness, but any additional information they provide outside the evidential chain should be treated as coming from an MoP. The fact that someone is designated as a MoP is only to facilitate the submission of information for intelligence purposes. It does not affect any right they have for their identity to remain confidential, nor does it infer any lesser obligation on the agency to discharge its responsibilities in keeping that person safe from any harm that may result from their assistance.

MoPs will most often fall into a number of generalized groupings, all of which are likely to come into contact with law enforcement in different ways, and have different motives for passing information to police. The groups will include the following:

- Victims of crime.
- Witnesses to crime.
- Suspects of crime.
- Community representatives. Specific care needs to be taken with some community representatives, as they may well have hidden agendas and ulterior motives for passing information to law enforcement.
- Neighborhood watch volunteers. While the majority of people taking part in neighborhood watch programs are genuine, care must be taken that some involved do not use the scheme to spread malicious gossip or exploit their connection with law enforcement to act as vigilantes.
- Prisoners in jails.
- Businesspeople.

The agency must have a way of capturing the identifying details of all MoPs who provide information and of monitoring the circumstances under which that information was provided. Accepting anonymous information has significant risks and is of arguably limited use. Monitoring

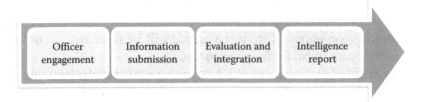

Figure 9.2 Member of the public intelligence repositing.

someone who provides information on a "regular" basis has a number of advantages, the first of these being that it allows the agency to identify any person who should be registered as a human source and so provide a greater amount of information. It allows the agency to identify those individuals who, although providing information, in doing so create a risk for the agency. Finally, it helps mitigate the risk of an agency member using the supply of information to mask a corrupt relationship in which they are engaged. Figure 9.2 shows the repositing of information from a member of the public.

9.5   Outcasts and Those Living on the Periphery

The very nature of the modern society means that there are always those who live on the periphery of society or are de facto viewed as outcasts of that society. Where living such a life by choice or circumstance, these people often fall well below the radar of those within society yet are the very type of person to come into regular contact with law enforcement. The nature of their lifestyle means that many of these types are viewed as having little to contribute, yet these people can, if treated appropriately, provide valuable information. They see what is going on in the streets they inhabit and often overhear much. Furthermore, they can offer insights into worlds that are all but impossible for law enforcement to penetrate effectively. For example, prostitutes will often be able to supply information with regard to clients they perceive as being a threat to others because of unusual, violent, or deviant behavior that lies outside of their normal experience; street people will often be able to report unusual behavior, which is often carried out right in front of them, as they become all but invisible to "normal" people. Those working with people on the periphery of society can also provide valuable information, as they see a lot that is going on and often have the trust of the people they are working with. Building relationships with such workers can pay dividends with regard to information gathering. Of particular value is their ability to spot changing trends in the use of particular drugs and the reasons for such shifts; intelligence that can be useful from a strategic or problem-solving perspective.

9.6 Trading Minor Violations

In most jurisdictions, an officer identifying minor offenses such as traffic violations or public order transgressions has the discretion to pursue the matter further or to let it rest, with action such as advice and warning. It is not unusual for MoPs to volunteer information, either in the hope that they will not be prosecuted or in gratitude for an officer using their discretion not to prosecute. This is another valuable origin of information for law enforcement. Where an officer receives information and at the same time decides not to pursue a prosecution, this must be recorded on the information submission, regardless of whether the officer perceives the two occurrences as being directly connected or not. Recording these facts ensures that the officer is protected from allegations of perverting the course of justice, and those evaluating the information have a better understanding of how it has been obtained and why it may have been provided. Information received in such a manner should be submitted using the standard submission for information received from MoPs.

9.7 Interviews of Persons in Law Enforcement Custody

Sometimes referred to as "cell interventions" or "intelligence interviews," these are de facto conversations with someone in custody, for the purposes of gathering information that may be of use for intelligence purposes. Working on the arguably somewhat prejudiced principle that if a person has been involved in one crime the chances are they may know about other crimes, and combining this with the facts that the officer has a good opportunity for dialogue and the person may have an incentive to talk, intelligence interviews can be very productive. The underlying principle of such interviews is that they are "in confidence." Generally speaking, an event should be considered an intelligence interview only when it takes place within the confines of a law enforcement establishment. This is because structures and procedures for any information-gathering process will be situation specific. There are a number of factors to be considered with regard to such interviews:

- *Legality.* Attention must be paid to the legality of any such interview. Generally speaking, the person cannot be detained for a further period to conduct such an interview if they should lawfully have been released following the investigation of the crime for which they were detained. The interview should not focus on any crime to which the interviewee was involved, as this would engage numerous legal constraints.

- *Motivation.* Those carrying out such an interview should have an awareness of human motivation and what is likely to motivate the person to give truthful information. Much of the success of such an interview will depend on how the interviewee has been treated since detention.
- *Process.* The information-submission process must ensure that the interviewee's identity can be kept separate from the information submitted. This is to protect her, should the intelligence gained be exploited at a later stage. People will normally give information only if they can be protected.
- *Recording.* The recording of such interviews, either using audio or video, should not take place where such material can be obtained either through disclosure or freedom of information. It would not be the first time such confidential interviews appeared on YouTube. People will only give information if they can be protected!

9.8   Stop Snitching

The "stop snitching" campaign has its origins in Baltimore and has caused significant harm in the United States to the ability of law enforcement to collect evidence and intelligence from citizens, particularly from minority or "hard-to-reach" communities.* Without delving too much into the history of the campaign, it can be said to be motivated by a number of factors, including the following:

- Mistrust of the police.
- Perceived racism of the police.
- A so-called "code of honor" among criminals not to betray their own, regardless of the cost.
- The failure of police to protect those who provide evidence or information. Lack of adequate witness protection is a widespread problem particularly in the United States.†

---

* For more information on "snitching" see U.S. Department of Justice Office of Community Oriented Policing (2009). The Stop Snitching Phenomenon: Breaking the Code of Silence.
† Witness protection is a bit more than $20 and a ride to the bus depot!

- The perception of the police being against, or at war, with a particular community; this perception often being promoted by the criminals living within that community.
- A sense of injustice that minor offenders are being "snitched on" and prosecuted, while the "kingpins" do the snitching and are allowed to walk free.

Although this is far from a comprehensive list of reasons why the campaign has been successful, there is a lot that law enforcement can do to overcome it, as it can do with any "hard-to-reach community."

- Effective community policing. The agency needs to get "good" officers on the ground, into the communities, and let those officers build trust. Psychology says, "if we trust someone, we are more likely to give them information." Far too often, community policing has been allowed to become a dumping ground for those officers who don't want to work or are unsuitable for any type of work. Community officers are the agency's public face and what they say and do impacts how the community reacts. Furthermore, care must be taken not to allow some overzealous detectives to undermine the investment these officers have made.
- Law enforcement needs to put in place structures to protect those who provide information. Far too often, a person gives information and within days their identity becomes known and their role as a "confidential" informant is widely reported throughout their community. This begs the question, where is the confidentiality? Why would anyone in their right mind give information?
- Police commanders should publicize the necessity for the community to assist law enforcement, highlighting the parasitic nature of crime gangs and emphasizing the close working relationships that law enforcement has with community and faith leaders. Again, this makes the assumption that the legwork has been done and such relationships are in place and that law enforcement is not perceived as being racist or prejudiced against one community or one group.
- No law enforcement officer should be allowed to use the terms "snitch" or "rat" or any such derogatory term. All this does add credibility to the campaign. The use of such language by journalists, lawyers, or whoever should be challenged by law enforcement, just as they would challenge the use of any other inappropriate language. Citizens should be continually praised for having the courage to come forward and provide information that helps their community.
- Exploit circumstances. Whenever an incident of a particular nature arouses community outrage, law enforcement must grab the opportunity to gather information about the incident and to build

relationships that increase the likelihood of obtaining information in the future. While some may critique this from an ethical standpoint, the reality is that law enforcement must take every opportunity that arises to build bridges with these types of community. It is better that some good comes out of a tragedy than nothing at all.

9.9   Suspicious Activity

They say "the road to hell is paved with good intentions," but very often, the paving is laid by those in a rush to get a path down, regardless of where it goes. Unfortunately, this is very much the case in relation to suspicious activity and how law enforcement receives information relating to it. To understand where the problems lie and how to overcome them, it is necessary to look at history. Suspicious activity "reports" originated as a mechanism to allow financial institutions to report banking transactions that they thought had the potential to be connected to money laundering to law enforcement. Given the huge amounts of money connected to criminality and the difficulties criminals had in legitimizing that money, many jurisdictions introduced legislation to force banks to report what the bank believed to be "suspicious" transactions. In reality, much of the legislation affixed a set amount, over which a report had to be made to the legal authority. Although much of this legislation was aimed at organized crime and narcotics, its use in combatting terrorism has long been recognized as a tool. And for the most part, this worked well. Large amounts of information were gained, and the banks continue to pass "suspicious activity reports" to law enforcement. As financial investigation is a highly specialized arena, such reporting had little, if any, impact on the average law enforcement officer.

This type of reporting was extended in some jurisdictions to the pharmaceutical industry with the intention of placing it under some form of obligation, moral or statutory, to report suspicious activity around the procurement of precursor chemicals for illicit drug manufacturing. This too had a degree of success, but because of the nature of the business area, there were significantly fewer reports. Given that such reports were likely to be limited in number and specialized in nature, this type of reporting had no real relevance for the average officer.

After 9/11, when the threat of terrorism escalated in many countries, a number of programs were instituted between law enforcement and the private sector to enable private sector professionals to relate to law enforcement behavior that they, in their professional opinion, deemed to be suspicious. A key aspect of these programs was the recognition of major gaps in law enforcement knowledge that could be filled in by industry professionals.

For example, two men photographing an electrical substation may look a bit odd to a cop, but when the industry professional adds the fact that without the substation the neighboring city of one million people would be blacked out, then the activity takes on a much greater degree of importance. Another example of information that industry could provide was how certain items could be subverted in their use to aid terrorism. Many pharmacists would be aware of the potential use of hydrogen peroxide for making explosives, but law enforcement, even if they had recognized this potential use, would have had very limited knowledge of how widely available it was and of the many different formats it could be found in. This created the potential for a professional to approach law enforcement and say, "Look, this happened, and I think it is strange" and for law enforcement not to see the significance in it. While these types of examples show the gap in law enforcement knowledge, the reverse of this was occurring within industry. Some industry professionals were unaware of the use that terrorists were seeking to make of apparently mundane items. For example, the farm supplier who sells tons of fertilizer every day without realizing that terrorists are using it to make bombs, or the hair dresser who thinks hydrogen peroxide is only for bleaching hair. Outreach programs to sectors of the private community provided professionals with awareness and encouraged them to use their professional knowledge to identify suspicious activity and advise law enforcement of it. Because of the natural connection between the professional element and the type of information being exchanged, the information was often of substantial worth.

In most jurisdictions, these professional exchanges remain the norm, and agency staff understand their role, and the agency processes can readily deal with them. However, this is not the situation in some countries, and primarily in the United States, where the idea of reporting suspicious activity has become confused. The reason for discussing the U.S. situation is twofold. First, to identify how and why problems such as this have the potential to develop in any intelligence management scenario if things are not properly thought through, and second, to attempt to provide clarity for those who may need it in regard to dealing with suspicious activity, whether in the United States or elsewhere.

In designing any process, there are a number of problems that regularly occur such as the following:

- A process that deals with similar circumstances already exists, so people think it will do. They see the similarities but don't pay sufficient attention to the differences. Because the process wasn't designed to deal with what it is now being asked to do, it fails. This situation occurs through lack of attention to detail or an inability to think things through to every potential conclusion.

- Those being asked to develop a new process do not have the capability to develop original ideas to meet the new circumstances. They revert to what they know and build a process that is limited by their experience and knowledge and lack of creativity.
- The belief that words don't matter. If you are attempting to describe something, or instruct another in a concept, there must be clarity in language. Any ambiguity in terminology creates potential for misunderstanding, and failure of the process becomes inevitable. Using words that are readily recognized and identified as meaning something else will be interpreted as having the same meaning in the new context. If we are going to describe something, we need to choose the language we will be speaking.
- The desire to solve all the problems in one go or to catch all potential scenarios with one sweep of the pen. Rather than developing a number of processes, what happens is that one process is created that the designers think capable of dealing with everything. In reality, they create something that is overly complicated and confusing for many and won't work efficiently. Consider if highway planners said, "We shall just build a road and everyone can travel on it." This may seem like a solution, but in reality you either have to make rules for all the potential users, or you have the potential for pandemonium. A single highway will work sometimes, where there is limited use, but having recognized the potential for failure, planners put in pedestrian walkways, cycle tracks, motorways, interstate highways, etc., all with the expectation of specific usage and restrictions.

We now move on to look at what has occurred with suspicious activity reporting in the United States and identify some of the problems. Before doing so, it is necessary to recognize the significant benefit in having a national document to address what is a national problem. The fact that it is a national scheme should imply that it is fundamentally sound and that it should result in more effective sharing and a greater opportunity to join what could be "distant dots" to find something meaningful. The definition of suspicious activity contained in Information Sharing Environment (ISE) Functional Standard for Suspicious Activity Reporting (2009) is as follows:

Observed behaviour reasonably indicative of pre-operational planning related to terrorism or other criminal activity.

A suspicious activity report is the documentation that follows this observed behavior.

This all seems very easily understood, until one starts to drill down into it and attempts to identify pitfalls. The first thing that should be asked in any process design is "What is this process intended to achieve?" And if one is honest about it, suspicious activity reporting, in the context for which this guidance was created, is not about crime but about terrorism. The primary desire is that information relating to what might be terrorism is not missed, regardless of the origin of the information or the geographic region it emanates from. To understand suspicious activity reporting in the present context, one must return to history and the legacy of 9/11. The drivers for suspicious activity reporting revolve around the need to identify the dots, so that they can be joined up to prevent an attack. Using the terminology "suspicious activity reports," hijacked from the process relating to money laundering (and pharmaceuticals), was a flawed option, because neither what is desired nor the methods to achieve the goal are the same as with money laundering. The inclusion of suspicious activity relating to crime does nothing but detract from what should be a clear end goal. Because of the disparate nature of terrorism, the limited warning signals there are likely to be, and the serious consequences of it, nothing should distract law enforcement's efforts to bring together all intelligence relating to it.

Another problem relates to the failure to recognize what suspicious activity reporting is seeking to achieve in the "information to intelligence to dissemination" process. An LEA needs to have in place processes to deal with the submission of information, regardless of the origin of the information or the content of that information. What some believe suspicious activity reporting will achieve is some sort of new mechanism for collecting information; it isn't. It is about where the intelligence derived from collected information is disseminated to.

Focusing solely on terrorism, what needs to be achieved if the dots are to be recognized, shared and then joined, the agency needs to have in place the following measures:

- Staff training. Many in law enforcement have a very limited knowledge of terrorism, and the knowledge they do have is obtained from the media. Staff need to be trained to recognize what could be terrorist activity. Specific training needs to be delivered to frontline officers, as they are the ones likely to be responding to incidents that have been reported as suspicious by citizens. Such training cannot be delivered in a couple of hours or by handing out pamphlets. For frontline officers, there are likely to be two aspects to a report of suspicious activity: "investigative" and "intelligence." Two examples may help in understanding. In the first example, "The security staff at a major port reported details to police of a car that seems to be travelling erratically in the area. They are concerned that it may be someone scouting the area. Police investigate the call and find it is a couple from out of town who are genuinely lost. The investigation is closed with no need for an information submission. In the second example, The couple can offer no credible excuse for their behavior, but there is no reason or lawful basis to detain them further. In this case rather than just writing the incident off, the officer recognizes the potential of preparation for a terrorist attack and submits an information submission to the Intelligence Unit who look at the incident from an intelligence perspective and then reposit an intelligence report. It may never be clear as to why the couple were at the port. It may be crime or terrorist related or the couple may just be in some illicit relationship. Nevertheless, law enforcement have investigated as best as they can, and the intelligence report (a "dot") is now where it can potentially be linked with other dots.

- Officers need to be able to evaluate a situation, and if they have identified it may be terrorist related, they need to be able to move to not only resolve the incident but also submit the information for intelligence purposes.
- Supervisors need to check that the officer responding to the report of suspicious activity (an incident) or the member receiving the information (where no overt response was required) has done all that needs to be done at her level. The nature of the incident will dictate the level of response that is adequate. The supervisor should confirm if there is information potentially of use for intelligence purposes that an information submission has been submitted.
- The agency needs standardized information-submission mechanisms. Those outlined in Chapter 6 are sufficient to deal with any situation relating to activity that may be terrorism related.
- Staff in the Intelligence Unit will have sufficient knowledge of terrorist-related matters to evaluate the information, reposit an intelligence report, and disseminate that report to the customers who need it. In repositing the intelligence report, the Intelligence Unit will link it to any entities and can add their knowledge and research to provide explanation and context prior to dissemination. The intelligence report will be available to the agency if required at a future time and can be used to identify potential threats and accordingly direct local resources.

Anything that might be terrorist related is dealt with in the same way. If staff are made aware of what may be terrorist-related activities, and the agency has an adequate intelligence management system, then all that is required on a national basis is a clear pathway for the agency to disseminate the intelligence to a centralized agency. There is no need for any other guidance, framework, terminology, etc., because all it does is add confusion.

Brinner (2011:187) highlights another problem that occurs: that of seeing what we expect to see. He comments, "When we don't acknowledge the ambiguity of SARs we run the risk of assigning them too much credibility. …we see plenty of suspicious activity around our critical facilities simply because that is where we have invested our resources to look." This problem has its basis in "confirmation bias" (Nickerson 1998) and occurs because our minds will perceive what we program them to focus upon. If we are told some one is bad, we will look to see their faults; if we are told a house is haunted, we will seek out indicators that it is so. Unfortunately, in the case of suspected terrorist activity, this leads us to the situation where we are much more likely to get erroneous reporting.

If suspicious activity is reported at the time of the occurrence and there are sufficient resources to respond to that report, then this obviously has the potential to defray concerns that could be generated from many such reports. What may outwardly appear to be some sort of nefarious activity may be nothing more than someone lost or a couple having a clandestine liaison. However, when a response to the activity has not been possible or has gleaned no additional information, it will fall to the Intelligence Unit to make an assessment of what has occurred. This should be done in a step-by-step approach shown in Figure 9.3.

Having worked through the process, the Intelligence Unit may decide that additional warnings need to be given to local commanders or the premises where the activity occurred or that there may be a need for a full investigation. Alternatively, the Intelligence Unit may decide that the activity should be logged in an intelligence report in the intelligence repository for future reference, or shared with other agencies. Sharing such reporting has become

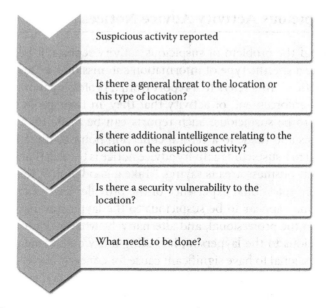

Figure 9.3 Suspicious activity reporting at a location.

a cornerstone of counterterrorism efforts with regard to protecting potential terrorist targets, as what may appear innocuous at one location may provide indicators of a potentially greater threat if repeated at similar locations.

To provide a clearer picture to the end user of such reporting, Brinner (ibid) suggests adding graded commentary to this type of report. In ascending order, indicative of the level of seriousness with which the report should be viewed, comments similar to those suggested can be added:

1. Assessed as not threat-related
2. Minimal suspicion generated
3. Behavior that is atypical or unusual for the location
4. Strong indications of behavior consistent with a threat posed, including where there has been aggressive testing of security
5. Strong indicators of activity that converge with a credible specific threat to that location or a general threat to similar locations

While the lowest grading in the commentary suggests the clear impression that the activity in question is assessed as not posing a threat, it may still be worth recording simply because of the nature of the location where the activity took place. These types of comments can be included on an intelligence report under a heading such as "submitting officer's comment," thus making it clear where the remarks have come from and separating them from the body of the text.

9.10 Suspicious Activity Advice Notices

To get around the problem of suspicious activity reports, it becomes necessary to create a specific type of information submission—a "suspicious activity advice notice." This refers to a report from a professional or a professional body, to law enforcement, of activity that they, in their professional assessment, deem to be suspicious. Such reports can be made on a voluntary or statutory basis and made to a central collection point or directly to an LEA. Fundamental to a suspicious activity advice notice is the fact that a professional in the relevant business area is saying, "Take a good look at this; I think it is strange." The professional experience of the provider carries credible worth. That which may appear to be suspicious to the layperson may be a regular occurrence to the professional, and alternatively, what may not be the slightest bit suspicious to the layperson, including a law enforcement officer, may cause a professional to have significant cause for concern. It is the opinion of a professional, when added to the information, that directs the information be given significant consideration, when it comes to dictating how law enforcement should respond. When a suspicious activity advice notice is received, the fact that it is such should be clearly labeled in the heading of the information submission to draw to the reader's attention the necessity to give it appropriate consideration. The subject line of the submission should also clearly indicate the nature of the potential activity, for example terrorism or drugs.

When suspicious activity advice notices are made, they are not inevitably the subject of in-depth investigation. Many reports relating to financial transactions or relating to suspected drug activity will not be pursued because of resourcing issues and the volume of reporting.* Someone within the agency has to make a decision as to whether or not to pursue the matter further. When an agency receives such an advice notice, it should be recorded on an information submission and processed through the system in the normal manner. Inevitably, some of these will be actionable and others will be recorded for record purposes only.

Where a suspicious activity advice notice is made as a result of a legal obligation, it should be processed as information coming from an institution even if the report is made by a named person on behalf of that institution. Where suspicious activity is given by a professional who is under no legal obligation to do so, the information should be processed in the same way as any information coming from an MoP. This enables the agency to mitigate risks to that individual or in regard to the material being shared. (See issues relating to Data Protection in Section 4.13 of Chapter 4.) Generally speaking, in such circumstances, the person's business address will be recorded as opposed to their personal address.

While this creation of a separate category of submission may seem like additional effort, if the mess had not been created in the first place, it would not be necessary. In effect, regardless of how the receipt of such information is dealt with, there is likely to be little difference in processing through the receiving agency, as the information-submission mechanisms for all types of submissions are very similar. The difference comes in what should be done with the information when it is processed. An information submission labeled as being a suspicious activity advice notice should be subjected to objective analysis and a decision made as to whether or not a warning should be issued, to whom it should be issued, and the nature of that warning.

9.11   Intelligence Nuisances

Unfortunately, the world is beset by the mad, the bad, and the sad and more often than not, some of these end up providing law enforcement with information, some on a regular basis. With all such individuals, there exist serious

---

* In the United States, the Financial Crimes Enforcement Network (FinCEN) controls more than 150 million reports filed under the Bank Secrecy Act and similar laws.

risks, and any effective intelligence management system must be constructed in such a way that these risks are mitigated. When it comes to citizens providing information, there are, broadly speaking, three types of individuals who need special attention. Acknowledging that it is an extremely simplistic stance to take, but to make it easier to remember, we will refer to these three types as the mad, the bad, and the sad.

1. *The "mad."* Unfortunately, there are many individuals within society who have mental health issues. The very nature of their health problems means that they are likely to be drawn to create fanciful stories and then share these stories with law enforcement, particularly a uniformed officer who they are more likely to have contact with. Often, the information they will provide has an air of plausibility about it gleaned from television or from chat in the local community. These individuals create two main risks. First, if the evaluation of the information is not carried out properly, then the potential exists for false information to be included, thus distorting the intelligence picture. Second, and of much greater importance, is the risk that the individuals create to their own safety. Many such individuals will live on the fringes of society, where many from the criminal fraternity also reside. The risk to the safety of such persons and their inability to manage that risk to themselves should always be considered in law enforcement encounters. Law enforcement should be extremely circumspect in dealing with these people and, in the vast majority of circumstances, actively discourage this passage of information.

2. *The "bad."* Many people have a huge incentive to corrupt the intelligence management system. Criminals will use their knowledge of intelligence gathering processes to their own ends. Such attacks, for attacks they are, will include placing false information in the system, knowing it must be disclosed later in subsequent legal proceedings; the corruption of officers; and building a legend for themselves that they are working for law enforcement as a source, and therefore everything they do is for law enforcement and causing harm to other people they have a grievance against. There are so many problems with such individuals, not the least being that some of the information they will give will be very accurate. Taking information from such a person is very risky and should only be done using well-established processes that highlight the risks and with effective risk-management strategies. It needs continual monitoring or both the receiving officer/s and the agency will be harmed, and the bad guy will walk from charges.

3. *The "sad."* There are many people in this world who are lonely, and the face of a police officer may be the only friendly face they encounter. And if the police officer is any good at all, the friendly face will be

accompanied by two big ears that are willing to listen. Unfortunately, this creates a set of circumstances where the person realizes that the police officer pays more attention and spends more time if there is something of law enforcement interest to hear. This leads to them inventing material. Although no malice may be in their actions, the result is still the same; law enforcement ends up with a pile of material of questionable worth at best.

An agency must have a process in place to identify such intelligence nuisances and label them according to the risk they present. The risk section of the information submission should always be completed when processing information they have provided. If their motives are considered to be "hostile," they should be labeled as such. Only a member of an identified rank should be able to label or remove the identifier that a person is an intelligence nuisance. Great care must be taken with grading the information received from intelligence nuisances and in taking action based on any intelligence product created from information they have provided.

9.12 Crime-Stoppers

In many jurisdictions, there are mechanisms in place where a person can give information about crime to a neutral party, and that information is then passed to law enforcement. Many such programs operate under the label of "crime-stoppers" or something similar. They are very effective in gathering information and act in the role of honest broker between citizens with information and the law enforcement community. It could be interpreted as an indictment on law enforcement and their inability to obtain sufficient trust from citizens that an intermediary is necessary, while at the same time, the ability of crime-stoppers to pay rewards for the information cannot be overlooked as a motivating factor. Regardless of the motivation for people contacting crime-stoppers, as opposed to passing information directly to LEAs, law enforcement needs appropriate structures in place to process the information as it is received into intelligence, and then where the option exists, to disseminate the intelligence product. Crime-stoppers usually establish a specific point of contact with relevant LEAs, and the Intelligence Unit is the most appropriate contact point as they have the professionalism to process the information provided. On receiving the information from crime-stoppers, the Intelligence Unit will process the information as they would any other piece of information, and where appropriate, create an intelligence report and reposit it accordingly. On receipt at the agency, the first step will be to transfer the crime-stoppers information onto the relevant information submission. The Intelligence Unit must ensure that when action is taken as a result of crime-stoppers' information, that crime-stoppers are notified of the result of that action. There are a number of problems with crime-stoppers' information:

- The way in which the information is received from the citizen means that there are often significant gaps in the content.
- Information passed can often be little more than rumor or speculation on the part of the caller.
- The nature of the program means it is very vulnerable to malicious reporting.
- The program is particularly vulnerable to "intelligence nuisances."
- Highly valuable information is often passed but can be overlooked by law enforcement because of the way in which it has originated.
- It can be extremely difficult for law enforcement to follow up where clarity is needed.

Accepting the limitations of this type of information, it is an effective aid to law enforcement, and many of the problems can be minimized by an effective information-to-intelligence process.

9.13   Instant Messaging and Web-Based Options

In an attempt to maximize the amount of information law enforcement receives and to explore potential options, some LEAs have introduced mechanisms where MoPs can submit information anonymously via smartphone applications or via a website. This method of submitting information is likely to have a significant appeal to younger people for whom this type of communication is the everyday norm. Although agencies should always be applauded in attempts to maximize the information flow, these types of information gathering mechanisms are limited in what they can achieve. The fact that the information is anonymous means that in many jurisdictions, very limited, if any, executive action can be taken using the information provided. The mechanisms can be used to deliberately submit erroneous information with the deliberate intention of confusing investigators or to disrupt the flow of an investigation. Furthermore, information can be submitted that is intended to be disclosed in a court case to undermine the credibility of a witness or to introduce doubt in the minds of the jurors. Depending on the volume of material that is submitted, staff can become diverted from dealing with more productive tasks, merely to deal with what is, at best low-grade intelligence. Having said all that, occasionally there will be information provided that is of real worth.

9.14   Telecommunications Information

A huge amount of information can be obtained from the telecommunications industry, whether in regard to fixed line telephones or mobile cellular phones. This will include the following:

- Calls made
- Calls received
- Number of calls made to each party
- Duration of calls
- Sequencing of calls
- Geo-positioning of mobile phone regardless if a call is made or not
- Number of texts and similar messages made and to whom
- Number of texts and similar messages received and from whom

Obtaining such information from the service providers will in most jurisdictions require some form of legal authority. Furthermore, the way in which the provider returns the information to law enforcement can make a huge difference with regard to the amount of effort that has to be used to process the information. The most practical format for the entire process of requesting and receiving the information is for the whole process to be done electronically. This saves significant time for both parties.

On receipt of the information, the officer receiving it may submit it in its raw form as a list of names, numbers, dates, etc. However, where there is a major investigation being undertaken, the analytical examination of the information is highly recommended. An analyst has many options with regard to presenting the information, drawing conclusions, and gaining deeper meaning from the raw information. Repositing telecommunications products is shown in Figure 9.4.

9.15   Interrogating Cellular Telephones

The forensic examination of a cellular telephone can recover huge amounts of useful information including all that is contained in the directory, calls made

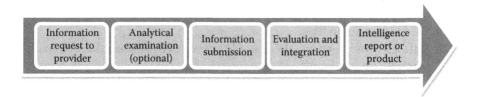

Figure 9.4 Telecommunications intelligence repositing.

and received, and the content of instant messages sent from and received by the phone. These can all provide valuable intelligence. While technology is readily available to grab all this information in all but the blink of an eye, there are real problems with some agencies exploiting the technology without any regard for the privacy rights of the citizen. All that this is likely to lead to is prescriptive legislation that makes it inordinately difficult to obtain this information in a practical manner. Where there is no legislation with regard to this type of activity, law enforcement should put in place procedures that address privacy concerns and ensure that there is lawful justification for the action. When reviewing the material obtained, intelligence staff should take the opportunity to integrate numbers with known persons and attach any nicknames used to existing entities. The nature of phone usage means that nicknames and abbreviations will be in common usage. When reviewing the content of instant messages, it must be borne in mind that the context in which they have been received will have significant bearing on their meaning, and they may be of limited worth if examined in isolation. The covert interrogation of a cellular phone provides the same information as overt interrogation, with the added benefit of the target being unaware law enforcement now has it.

9.16　Interrogating Computers

During many investigations the forensic examination of computers can take place and while the primary intention may be one of evidence gathering, the examination can yield huge amounts of information of use for intelligence. Computers will in this regard include PCs, Macs, tablets, etc. Such information will include the following:

- E-mail addresses and content.
- Contacts. If the user has a program such as Microsoft Outlook installed, there will be a list of names addresses and other information from the contact list.
- Documents.
- Websites visited.
- Travel details.
- Finance details.
- Video and audio files.
- Lifestyle information. How people spend their time on the web may say a lot about them!*

---

* Especially, the amount and type of porn or other questionable material they have been looking at.

9.17 Agency Records

As already referred to in Chapter 7, most LEAs will have other computerized systems to assist them in their business. These are likely to include the following:

- A records management system (RMS) for the recording of incidents reported to them. This database may also provide criminal records, the results of searches, records pertaining to investigations, arrest, and custody records.
- Computer-aided dispatch (CAD) software for directing response.
- Case management software to assist officers in preparing investigative files.

Unfortunately, standards of data entry in many agencies are often limited in terms of quality, depth, and scope. Those entering such material often do so with limited regard for anyone else who may want to access it at a later time. That said, there can be huge amounts of information in various IT systems, some of which may be useful for intelligence purposes.

These systems also contain a lot of information that is not of sufficient worth to merit investing the time to convert it to intelligence. There are three potential sets of circumstances relating to information contained in the agency's records:

1. Information of sufficient intelligence value to merit immediate conversion into intelligence. The information may be of significant importance in its own right or it may have limited value as a standalone piece of intelligence, but it is of worth in addressing the agency's priorities. Examples of these will include the following:
   a. The arrest of Thomas Stanes for the murder of a gang member. Stanes was found near the scene, but there is insufficient evidence to charge him. This is important intelligence in its own right—namely, that Stanes is a suspected murderer.
   b. Sid Johnson is arrested for a minor assault. The investigating officer obtains his address. Johnson is a major player in an organized drug network and the address is a new one. This is important intelligence, because Johnson is directly linked to an agency priority.
2. Information of insufficient intelligence worth at present. Law enforcement officers attend many incidents and expend a considerable amount of time on response-type investigations where they will collect information while resolving the incident or investigating the crime. Much of this information will not help address the agency's priorities. Much of it is likely to be low-level/background-type

information: for example, a new address or a new vehicle for a minor criminal. As it does not relate to the agency's priorities, converting this information into intelligence is likely to be a waste of time. One of the biggest problems agencies have is dealing with an overabundance of potential intelligence. An example of this scenario follows:

a. James Chatama is a minor criminal with two convictions for theft and drug possession. He is involved in a road traffic collision, and the investigating officer records in the RMS Chatama's address, contact details, and the names of the passengers in his car. At the time of the collision, nothing was known about Chatama other than the minor convictions and his association with other criminal types. He was not of interest in relation to any agency priority. Updating Chatama's details in the intelligence repository would expend more time than it would provide benefit.

3. Information that becomes of intelligence worth. This refers to information that, while not believed important at the time of recording, becomes important later. An example may be beneficial in illustrating this

a. Following on from the example given in point 2; six months later Chatama's name appears on an intelligence report naming him as a violent extremist. The information contained in the RMS is now of intelligence value and the agency needs the capacity to search across its databases to pull out all such information and process it into intelligence.

To maximize the benefit an agency can obtain from the information within its current databases, the following measures should be in place:

- All staff should be aware of the agency's expectation that they will submit information likely to be of use for intelligence purposes.
- Part of the routine daily duties of Intelligence Unit staff should be to peruse the systems used for routine law enforcement duties and extract information that they assess to be of use for intelligence purposes. This is in some ways a belt-and-braces approach, as those using such systems should know when this type of information should be submitted for intelligence purposes. The majority of the material extracted will be of use in providing background intelligence with regard to people or investigations. Some information may, when combined with existing intelligence, be of significant investigative or operational importance.
- The Intelligence Unit must have in place the capacity to search across all the agency's records in a single action. Material contained in these databases can be accessed through the use of a search engine designed

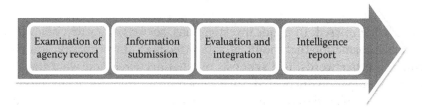

Figure 9.5 Agency record intelligence repositing.

to sit over a number of databases. Having this search capability is useful, particularly when one knows what one is looking for. The sophistication of such search engines continues to improve rapidly and the speed with which they can find a relevant entry far surpasses any manual search. There will be some limitations to this, in that it will be unlikely to have direct access to Internal Affairs records and potentially the records relating to victims of sexual assault or child abuse. Alternative arrangements should be in place should access to such records be necessary.

Information from the agency's management systems should always be submitted using standardized information submissions, so that the origin of the information is clearly identifiable. If a unique reference number for the original information has been generated on that software, the number should be included in the information submission. Repositing from agency records is shown in Figure 9.5.

9.18   Information from Investigations

It is a clear responsibility of the officer-in-charge of any investigation to ensure that any information gleaned during the course of that investigation, whether relevant to that investigation or not, and which may have intelligence value, is submitted to the Intelligence Unit. This rule applies regardless of the size or complexity of the investigation. Many investigations unearth what can be very valuable intelligence, but this is never submitted to the Intelligence Unit for processing. This is often because the officer's priorities rest with the investigation and they can see no additional personal benefit in submitting the information they have obtained. Contained in an agency's procedures for intelligence should be an onus on an investigator to submit any information they obtain that may be of use for intelligence. Investigators may be all too ready to accept intelligence when it benefits them but do not share the same enthusiasm when it comes to returning the favor. Although adopting a belt-and-braces approach and to some extent duplicating effort, when a major investigation is taking place, it can be very beneficial to have Intelligence Unit staff regularly debriefing those involved to avoid intelligence being missed. In major investigations, such as a murder, one valuable piece of information that should be submitted is an "investigation summary," which in other words, is a synopsis of what occurred and what the subsequent investigation uncovered. Such a document can be linked to the entities involved and placed in the intelligence repository for the future benefit of all.

Where a person who has been "turned" from criminality is intending to give evidence against their old associates, there will often be a huge amount of material that has potential intelligence value. Those involved in interviewing such a person for evidential purposes should also bear in mind the potential to use the material provided for intelligence purposes. Furthermore, there is likely to be a lot of material that is unsuitable, for whatever reason, to use as evidence, but that is nevertheless of value in producing intelligence. Where this type of information is produced, it should be submitted using an information-submission form for a member of the public. However, once that person has entered a protected persons/witness protection program, care must be taken that his new identity is not inadvertently linked to his old identity. It is for this reason that information coming from a protected person within a protection program is submitted through the officers providing the protection, and anonymized accordingly.

9.19   Financial Information

Information about a person's financial activities can provide substantial material of intelligence value. It will always have to be obtained with proper authorization and through whatever official channels exist between banks and law enforcement. The type of material that is of worth will include:

- Account statements
- Transfers between accounts
- Joint accounts
- Business accounts
- Credit checks
- Records of money in all its forms
- Transnational and/or offshore banking

Interest in a person's finances should not be limited to normal banking. There are numerous different ways that criminals can move and store money. Dealing with financial intelligence is a job for someone that has had training in the role, as the layperson really has no idea of the complexities involved. In addition, if the agency has the benefit of analysts with training in financial investigation, they can add significant worth by using their skills to bring clarity to the financial picture. Those gathering information originating elsewhere should always be open to identifying such material as bank names and locations, account numbers, and indications of the modus operandi of the suspects in relation to finance.

9.20   Forensic Information

A potential avenue for information that is often overlooked is information that emanates from forensic laboratories. The main work of forensics is undoubtedly evidential in its nature. However, there are numerous aspects of this work that can be used to fill in gaps in an intelligence picture. Most law enforcement officers are unfamiliar with the science involved in forensics, and in many cases overwhelmed by the technical aspects of it, and most forensic scientists have little, if any, experience in relation to intelligence management. There is often a disconnect between these two aspects of law enforcement. With emerging technologies, such as enhanced fingerprinting techniques, facial recognition, and other aspects of biometrics, the potential for greater amounts of information to be obtained from forensic science is significant. However, unless there is communication between the two camps, it is unlikely that the full potential can be recognized. Only through open dialogue can each side start to see potential areas for development. Some areas where valuable information should be exchanged include the following:

- *Fingerprint identification.* In most jurisdictions a fingerprint expert will not confirm identification unless there is a fixed number of points of similarity. The balance for this figure is rightly set on the high side. However, in many cases, the expert can identify an individual with fewer similarities. While the identification may not be sufficient to meet the evidential standards, this information is of real worth from an intelligence perspective. With any aspect of biometric identification, similar circumstances are likely to occur. In short, the scientist "knows" this person has done this crime; they just can't prove it. This is as reliable as any other piece of intelligence we are likely to receive.
- *Criminal processes.* Many aspects of criminality involve a criminal manufacturing process. Examples of this will include the manufacture of narcotics, homemade explosives, and weaponry. Science can create a vivid picture of how these criminal operations are carried out including the raw components, the necessary equipment, and manufacturing timelines. All these details can help develop tactics to combat these problems and interdict the perpetrators. All are of intelligence value.

- *Ballistic history.* Many weapons will be used in different incidents. Having a full history of the weapon and its use, particularly when subjected to analytical techniques, can provide valuable intelligence including potential supply routes for illicit weaponry.
- Intelligence collectors will often encounter information that makes little or no sense to them. A source may be reporting some sort of unusual activity on the part of a criminal, which has no obvious meaning; for example, an attempt to procure some item. Consultation with a scientist may well provide insight as to what this item can be used for. Scientists are likely to look at such an item from an entirely different perspective and while they may not initially recognize the potential use, they can provide a suitable range of questions to put to the source to help further the investigation. Bringing the source of the information and the scientist into face-to-face discussion should be given real consideration.

Information from forensic laboratories should be submitted to the LEA either directly or though the agency's liaison officer using the agency's standardized information-submission mechanism. Intelligence managers should be in regular contact with laboratory staff to build relationships and identify mutual benefits.

9.21   Open Source Information

Open source information can be defined as "information that is available to the general public." When it comes to their intelligence capability, some LEAs place significant reliance on the open source collection of information. A few agencies rely almost exclusively on this type of information to supplement their agency's records and to provide an intelligence picture. If this is the only option an agency has, then it is unfortunate, because, while there is much to be gleaned from open source collection, there are significant limitations. Open source information is often confused with "closed source" material—for example, records, etc., that are not available to the public and have to be accessed by a legal process.

To gain a greater understanding of the origins of open source information and its worth, it is necessary to return to the factors that have influenced information collection in the past. A significant number of the techniques that law enforcement now use in intelligence management have their origins in the various intelligence agencies that worked against threats posed to national security. There was a time when there was value to be had from any piece of information that could be obtained from closed regimes; that which was broadcast on local television and reported in local papers was of intelligence interest. For example, the price of potatoes in one of the Soviet republics and attendant public disquiet may have had an impact on how the Russian government would react at international talks with the West. As such, local press coverage of such an event had intelligence value. In addressing the existing threats to national security, such information may still have intelligence value. However, such types of information are unlikely to have any practical use to an LEA.

One of the oft-stated attractions with open source information is the perception that it can be done easily, with limited, if any, accountability, and with no real risks. Probably the only "truth" contained in this is that the person articulating it is adopting a "risk averse" approach to intelligence gathering.

Beginning with the lack of a need for accountability, an assumption often made by law enforcement is that because information about an individual is readily accessible, an LEA is entitled to seek out that information and retain it. This is incorrect. Citizens have the right to privacy. As already articulated in Chapter 4, the "State" should not be enquiring into any citizen's privacy without due cause. The argument will often be made that if a person is placing material about his life on the Internet, then it is available for all to see. While acknowledging the fact that the material is there for anyone to see, the fact that the government goes looking for it raises privacy issues. This conflict revolves around the concept of anonymity. In essence, a person goes about his life as one of billions on this planet, with no one, especially the "State," taking any interest in them. Once the government casts its all-seeing eye upon that citizen and begins to look at that citizen, anonymity is lost and privacy considerations evoked. In countries, such as the United Kingdom, that have incorporated the European Convention on Human Rights into their legislation, such a search engages Article 8, "private life" issues, and must meet the threshold for interference as set out in the Convention. In the United States, the collection of such information without appropriate authority is, at best, questionable. The intelligence gained from such a search must meet the "criminal predicate" requirement before it can be retained. There would appear to be little point in searching for something that cannot be used. Any open source searching in regard to a specified individual or individuals should have authorization from an officer of appropriate rank, prior to the commencement of that search.

Moving on to the aspect of the ease with which open source material can be collected, what is beyond doubt is that the Internet contains vast amounts of information including significant amounts of personal data. Law enforcement is hungry for information, and software is easily available to reap information from the Internet. The temptation is to use this available software to harvest information from the Internet.

However, a few words of caution are needed here:

- Much of the information harvested will need to be sorted to establish its worth. Depending on the type of search that has been done, the amount of information obtained can be enormous. (Entering the author's name in Google returned over three million hits!*) Someone has to sort through this to obtain that which is of value. Uploading this volume of material into the intelligence repository without processing merely clogs the system with rubbish, while processing it all would take a huge amount of time.
- When first viewed, software that performs such searches can appear extremely impressive, particularly to those unfamiliar with intelligence management. Software companies are highly skilled at selling their wares. Many of the products do what they say they do, but still are of limited worth, because the bottom line is that a lot of what is out there is simply not worth any effort to get it.
- It is easy to be deluded that volume equals quality. Many of us with limited computer savvy are easily impressed when someone brings back our name and address from the Internet, when we believed it wasn't there.
- Much of the software available is designed to search across an agency's own computer databases to ensure that all data are brought together. If an LEA has its business processes in order in the first place, this should be unnecessary, as there should be a very limited number of databases being used for law enforcement work. Normally, this will mean two—the RMS that records all ordinary police duties including dispatch, arrests, and incidents, and the intelligence repository.
- Those involved in processing open source material have to be particularly aware of the possibility of misinformation. Many groups are all too aware of the activities of law enforcement in relation to gleaning information from the web and often populate sites with disinformation. As McDowell (2009:203) points out, "Data generally available on the Internet is there because individuals and agencies want it to be in the public domain." This begs the question, "If the person wants others to see it, what is the true value of it?" When examining open source material, one must always bear in mind the likelihood that the bad guys are deliberately trying to deceive or mislead.
- Much open source material is gleaned from social media, journalism, and the ever-increasing number of blogs on the Internet. This

---

* The vast majority of these had absolutely no linkage to the author and perhaps 10 would have provided anything of "intelligence value" had one be interested. That said, the author does lead an extremely dull and boring life!

makes it very difficult to correctly identify who placed the material there and where they obtained it from.

- Most LEAs have limited capability in examining websites that are not written in their native language.
- Often, it appears that open source information can be gathered with limited risk to the agency involved and at a limited cost to an agency. On first viewing, all one needs is someone trained to do it and a computer with Internet access, and the belief is that one will obtain good intelligence. However, when one explores further, there do exist risks and the costs may be significant when one examines the end product. First, many law enforcement officers search the Internet for information without being trained in the role and without having sufficient understanding of the dangers that the Internet poses. They have little understanding of how the Internet works and that their journey from site to site is not done without leaving a trace; they are under the mistaken belief that their visits are anonymous. Unfamiliar with the constructs of the Internet, they fail to realize that as soon as their computer hits a site, that site is reacting to their address and deciding how to react to that approach. Not only does this mean that the information obtained may be exactly what the hostile party wants law enforcement to hear but also that the hostile site has now recorded an address on which to mount a retaliatory strike. Given the sophistication of many hackers and the often-limited defensive capabilities of law enforcement IT, this is not a good way for an agency to expose itself. Going online is dangerous unless it is done by professionals. For those uninitiated into the world of the Internet, when you visit a site, the typical message you leave behind is illustrated in Table 9.1: The Internet Protocol (IP) address is unique. The "ISP" is your Internet service provider. The website that you have just visited had an IP locator and has grabbed your Internet address and knows where to find you. To quote the Defense Advanced Research Projects Agency (DARPA) IP Specification (1981), "A name indicates what we seek.

Table 9.1 An Example of Material Obtained by an IP Locator

Hello, visitor from: Bedford, United Kingdom

Your Country Code: GB

Your IP State: Bedfordshire

Your IP Address: 11.222.333.44

Your Hostname: 7xx88x99.bb.sky.com

Your ISP: Sun Broadband

Your Organization: Sun Broadband

An address indicates where it is. A route indicates how to get there." If the site is hostile, they now know where to direct their resources in an attack. This is the threat on the web in its most simplistic form.

- In relation to the costs involved, there are a number of factors to consider:
    - The Internet is an easy place for someone to get lost in! Open source intelligence gathering requires an inordinate amount of self-discipline on behalf of the researcher. It is very easy to be diverted from the target of the research in pursuit of information that appears to have a link to the target and then to follow a second link, then to a third and a fourth and a gradual move away from the target of the research. Before too long, an inordinate amount of time has elapsed, and the researcher is so far off what they started searching for as to be on another planet! While initial steps are easily accounted for, as the search moves further and further out, the links become increasingly more tenuous until they become a waste of resources. Inevitably, the agency is sitting with a pile of information that requires processing yet is of little intelligence use. This is the nature of the Internet, and researchers need to be aware of its vagaries and the ease with which anyone can become ensnared. Researches need to have clear parameters with regard to their area of focus, what they are to obtain, and where to draw the line in the search.
    - The cost of setting up a covert search capability with attendant computer history linked to that address can be sizeable.
    - Training open source researchers is not without significant cost if the role is to be performed effectively.
    - If the researcher compromises personal details, the dangers of a cyber attack on one's personal life may be severe, depending on the group under investigation.

A fundamental part of open source searching relates to the examination of what is commonly referred to as "social media." Over the past decade, there has been a fundamental change in the way many people communicate. One aspect of the change in communication has been the use of social media such as Facebook, foursquare, Twitter, and many other similar Internet-based sites. We have discussed the potential issues around the legality of law enforcement monitoring these types of exchanges, when the focus of the examination is based on a specific person's correspondence. Each jurisdiction is likely to have differing attitudes toward intercepting or harvesting this type of information. Social media can provide massive amounts of valuable information, but accessing people's accounts, whether in the public domain or not, engages their rights to privacy and may in some jurisdictions require some form of authorization.

Open source material can provide historical and cultural insight and it can be useful for identifying the ideologies of various subversive, criminal, or terrorist groups. Where a new group has emerged, and in particular, where it has its origins in a minority ethnic or national group, open source research can provide a good starting point in understanding the background of those who are involved. Of course, the limitations of such research must be acknowledged and the potential for cultural or national stereotyping recognized.

9.22   Open Source: Non-IT Related

Long before the days of the Internet, there were and still are other places where information can be obtained from, and it is sometimes surprising how much can be obtained.

- *Newspapers.* Particular attention should be paid to local newspapers, as some suspects may be involved in sport or community activities that are being reported in the local press. Not only can this be somewhere to obtain details of lifestyle, but it can also disclose new relationships or clarify the nature of a relationship previously identified. And in some cases, if you get lucky, you also get a full face, up-to-date photograph of the person of interest. Newspapers also provide an idea as to the depth of public concern in regard to various policing problems. This type of information may well be of use to an analyst in preparing an intelligence product such as a problem profile.
- *Television and radio.* From a law enforcement perspective, the most beneficial programming is likely to be local newscasts.
- *Libraries.* For analysts seeking greater understanding of a particular subject, libraries are generally a cost-free resource, and given the cost of textbooks, this can lead to significant savings.
- *Academic papers.* By their very nature, academic papers should have gone through a relatively high degree of scrutiny before publication. They can be useful in providing research information in relation to a particular problem such as prostitution, human trafficking, or illicit drug use.
- *Publications from voluntary bodies.* Many nongovernmental bodies and voluntary groups publish reports and pamphlets on various issues of concern to them. Although such information may not be of the highest quality in terms of accuracy or content, it can provide valuable insight.

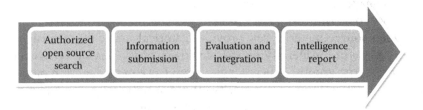

Figure 9.6 Open source intelligence repositing.

- *Industry publications.* Trade journals can provide valuable information about new technological developments that may be used by
  criminals or have a potential use for criminals. Furthermore, many
  trade organizations such as retailers have investigative bodies that
  carry out studies aimed at thwarting crimes such as thefts from
  shops. These results are then published. Because of the resources
  available to such bodies and the specialized nature of their research,
  they often know more about these crimes than do law enforcement
  officers.

If any article or publication is used in compiling any intelligence product, it should be fully referenced in the content of that product using the
Harvard referencing system or an equivalent. This means that the original
material from which the intelligence product was derived will be available
at a future date. Where such a publication is of high relevance to the content
of the intelligence product, a copy of it should be attached to the intelligence
product. If using a computerized intelligence repository, a copy should be
scanned into that repository.

Open source collection is a really effective method of collecting information that can be used for intelligence. It is amazing what people put out
there, whether they know it or not. This information is there for the taking by law enforcement, provided that a person is properly trained in how
to access it safely and the agency has structures in place to address privacy
issues. Figure 9.6 shows open source intelligence repositing.

9.23   Commercial Vendors of Information

Often referred to as data aggregators, there are many commercial vendors of
information: companies that will do the research and provide the information for a fee. Although such companies can provide significant amounts of
information, the following should be borne in mind:

- Security. Is the company a reputable company and can they be trusted by the LEA not to compromise either through negligence or malice the details of what law enforcement has requested?
- Is the company gathering the information lawfully?
- Furthermore, using a third party to collect information does not negate the need for there to be legality on the part of the agency with regard to interfering with a person's privacy.
- Does the fee the company charge represent value for money?

9.24 Dissemination of Open Source Intelligence

While care must be taken around the dissemination of any intelligence report or product, some involved in intelligence believe that information obtained through open sources can be disseminated without any further consideration. What this fails to recognize is that it is no longer information that is being disseminated but intelligence that has been created for a law enforcement purpose. It is not just raw information; it is information that has gone through a process and has had value added to it. Dissemination without thought shows a basic lack of understanding of the difference between information and intelligence. It is not that such intelligence cannot be shared in some format, it is merely that what is shared, how it is shared, and to whom it is shared must all be considered first.

9.25 Closed Source Information

Significant amounts of information that may be of use in progressing an investigation or establishing a more complete intelligence picture of a suspect are located in "official" government databases. In addition, there is likely to be significant information in other closed databases. While law enforcement may desire this information, there can be difficulties in obtaining it lawfully. We will refer to such information as "closed source information."

Closed source information can be defined as "information relating to a person that is held in either a government or privately managed database or records system and is not available through open inquiry." This definition is intended to have a broad meaning. In short, if information is not meant to be openly available to the public, then it will fall into this definition. Examples will include banking records, benefits records, medical records, vehicle ownership details, insurance records, travel documents, etc.

The majority of countries now have strict privacy laws relating to the disclosing of records they hold pertaining to an individual. These include legislation to make it a criminal offense to ask for or to disclose any personal information to an unauthorized person. Law enforcement officers often fail to be aware of the exact nature of the legislation and work on a premise that if they are asking for such material in pursuit of an investigation, then their action and the person giving them the material are both acting lawfully. This is at best a misguided approach. In many jurisdictions for law enforcement to obtain such information lawfully, there needs to be in place a written agreement or memorandum of understanding—between the agency and other government body, or between the agency and the private body—as to how such information will be exchanged. Even if this is not a legal requirement, the agency should put in place such a process. This negates the risk of infringement on an individual's privacy and the risk of an officer obtaining the information for personal benefit. Such a process should include the following:

- A written agreement between the LEA and the other body as to how such information will be requested and received and to ensure legal compliance, if relevant. Such an agreement should include how the agency will handle that material appropriately and that the other body will not disclose to the individual that it has been requested.
- The agreement should establish specific points of contact for information requests and exchanges.
- The agreement should include a period in which the request should be answered and the facility to have it completed expeditiously, if necessary.
- The request for information should be in writing and authorized by a suitable rank from within the agency.
- Prior to authorizing any such application, the authorizing officer should be satisfied that the information is necessary in pursuit of a lawful investigation. These details should be in writing on the application. For security reasons it may be necessary to redact some of these details prior to submission to the body holding the information.

It is recognized that whether an information option is regarded as open or closed may vary within a particular jurisdiction; what must be noted by staff enquiring is how that information may be obtained lawfully, meeting privacy or human rights obligations. The agency must provide clarity in regard to such considerations and make clear in procedures how such information is to be obtained.

Many bodies are under a statutory obligation to disclose certain information to law enforcement. While this information is disclosed primarily to enable law enforcement to identify if further investigation is required, such

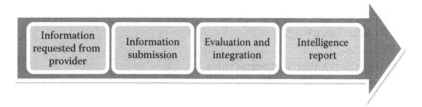

Figure 9.7 Closed source intelligence repositing.

information, while insufficient to merit an investigation, in itself may be of use for intelligence purposes (see Section 9.10).

Closed source information can be very useful and because of its origin, it is more often than not of high quality in terms of accuracy and the reliability of the origin. On receipt of the information, it should be submitted to the Intelligence Unit for evaluation and integration by a trained officer. If an intelligence report is created, the information in its original form should be preserved, attached to an information submission. Repositing closed source intelligence is shown in Figure 9.7.

9.26   Closed Source Options

There are numerous closed source options for obtaining information. Each Intelligence Unit should maintain a checklist of the options that are available to them and the method used to obtain such information from that party. As there may well exist certain sensitivities with regard to the sharing of information with law enforcement, and notwithstanding concerns over the safety of an individual or company that assists law enforcement in this way, it may be of benefit that the Intelligence Unit acts as a specific point of contact for the agency for both intelligence and investigative inquiries. For example, a detective investigating drugs trafficking requiring evidential disclosure from a bank may in such circumstances have to go through the agency's Intelligence Unit to obtain this as opposed to making their own approach to the relevant bank. This has the added advantage of maintaining a solid and controlled relationship with parties that law enforcement may need to "go the extra mile" in some later investigation.

Whether or not material is deemed to be closed or not will vary from jurisdiction to jurisdiction, with some information being a matter of public record in one place and not in another. Below are examples from an exhaustive list of "closed source" options:

- Vehicle licensing departments.
- Driver's license departments.

- Passport details.
- Public utility companies—electricity, gas, water, telephone, etc.
- Weapons licensing.
- Banks.
- Currency transaction companies.
- Credit-check agencies.
- Insurance companies.
- Airlines.
- Travel agents.
- Car rental agencies.
- Taxi companies.
- Real estate agents.
- Universities and schools. Particular care should be taken with such bodies as they are often regarded as a place of safety by those in authority and because inquiries may involve those who have not attained the age of adulthood.
- Mail and parcel delivery companies. It should be borne in mind that many companies have legislation regarding interference with the mail.

9.27 Public Order Reporting

Before beginning to discuss the use of intelligence in regard to public order, it must be acknowledged that it is the duty of law enforcement to facilitate, and indeed protect, those taking part in legitimate protest. Such protests are protected human rights, and are based on legal frameworks that ensure free speech and freedom of assembly. Balancing these rights with the need for public safety and the need to prevent unlawful activities can be extremely difficult, particularly when potentially unlawful acts are likely to escalate to more than nuisance level—for example, people sitting in the road or chaining themselves to railings. One of the first considerations for law enforcement is whether or not it is legitimate to collect information in relation to what is intended to be a legitimate process. It can be argued that gathering information about such protests already engages the various rights and affects the privacy of those taking part. The contrary argument can be made: gathering such information is necessary to ensure that the protest can take place safely, without it being subverted by those with criminal intent. The rationale for using information-gathering techniques, in particular covert techniques, should be documented and authorization obtained at an appropriate level within the agency.

Intelligence with regard to public order situations can prove of substantial worth to those charged with policing such events. Whether the intelligence is collected using human sources, undercover officers or technical means, all intelligence can bring different perspectives to what is happening or likely to happen. Generally speaking, the use of undercover officers and human sources will be most effective if there is prior warning of the event. In effect, it is often a human source that will be in a position to provide forewarning of possible trouble, especially when the problems are likely to emanate from what is a legitimate event or lawful process. However, if there is no prior warning of a public order situation, and provided the agency has suitable structures in place, intelligence can still be obtained through technical means and from the deployment of human sources. In regard to the use of sources in such circumstances, it is necessary to have instantaneous access to details of which sources could be deployed and the ability to task them at short notice. Many agencies do not have such a capability.

One of the most important aspects of intelligence is that relating to the tactics that demonstrators/protestors intend to use during their time of protest. While this type of intelligence may vary from protest to protest, similar tactics are used by some groups more than once. Generally speaking, the more criminal the intent of a group is, the more likely they are to have structure to what they plan, and the greater benefit there is for law enforcement to know it ahead of time.

The Internet and social media are being used increasingly by protest groups. Using such technology causes problems for law enforcement but also offers opportunities. Using technology such as geographic Internet searching allows law enforcement to see what is occurring in cyberspace relating to a particular geographic area. Just as using a camera to pan an area allows one to observe what is happening in that area, this type of technology allows the user to "see" what is occurring in the cyber world. Not only does an agency need the technology to capture this information, but it also needs a process to ensure that it gets from point of capture into the Intelligence Unit. Although in essence such a process will be similar to any other information, there will also be the necessity to transmit it instantly to the operational commanders responsible for the protest. What makes many of the features of public order intelligence unique is the rapidity with which the information is presented to law enforcement and exploited by them—in many cases it will be almost instantaneous. This is obviously of significant benefit when deploying both overt and covert resources.

The potential use of intelligence relating to public order is not limited to protest. Many public events have the potential to deteriorate into a hostile situation, and many such events have been used as an excuse for criminal activities. Examples of this include the hooliganism associated with English soccer and similar incidents associated with some music events.

After a public order disturbance, human sources should be debriefed to ascertain if they know the identities of any persons who took part in criminal behavior. These debriefings can be augmented by showing the sources photographs of the perpetrators and asking them to identify those they know.

9.28   Information Received from Another Agency

If things are working as they should, an agency should be receiving significant amounts of both intelligence and information from other LEAs,
intelligence organizations, and other governmental bodies. The agency
needs to capture this material and process it into their system. The
Intelligence Unit should act as a specific point of contact for receiving
and managing this type of material, regardless of the origin. Where an
agency has more than one Intelligence Unit, one of them should be nominated to receive the material. Care should always be taken to ensure that
the handling constraints that are attached to the material are met. Where
this cannot be achieved, the intelligence manager should notify the
agency that has provided the material. Repositing information received
from another agency is shown in Figure 9.8. Even if the other agency has
forwarded an "intelligence report," it is still reposited in this way.

9.29   Gathering Intelligence in Prisons

Prisons provide an environment in which the effective management of intelligence is not only critical to the smooth running of the prison itself but also
of potentially vast importance to the wider law enforcement community.
Prisons are both a microcosm reflecting the reality of what occurs outside
and in many ways a totally unreal world in that the vast majority of those
incarcerated will be of interest from an intelligence perspective. Any prison
intelligence system needs to address two central themes:

- Intelligence to support the proper running of the individual prison
  and the wider penal system
- Intelligence to assist law enforcement operating outside the confines
  of a prison

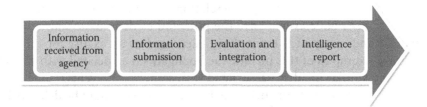

Figure 9.8 Other agency information repositing.

It is only through consideration of both these themes that the maximum benefits for citizens, and in some cases inmates, can be obtained. Although it may appear to be obvious, we will begin by examining the benefits of having an intelligence system in place within a prison:

- Prisons can function properly only if the rules that are put in place for the management of that establishment are adhered to. Prisoners will try to subvert those rules. It is important for prison management to know how and why the rules are being subverted; whether it is the supply of contraband or sexual assaults on fellow inmates, effective intelligence gathering will provide the how, what, where, and when it is happening and who is involved. This will assist in preventing such activities.
- Prisons hold many people with violent dispositions. The potential for violence to occur is huge, with both other prisoners and prison guards being the victims. While violence may, in many cases, be a spontaneous reaction to events, other violent acts will be planned with expert precision. Knowledge of these events puts management in a much stronger position with regard to preventing them.
- Corruption involving guards is a very real problem in many prisons. While recognizing that the prison environment and regular exposure to certain offenders can put individual guards under significant pressure, many officers slip into corruption for personal benefits. Acts of corruption will be broad in spectrum and are likely to include the smuggling of fairly innocuous pieces of contraband into the prison, taking messages out of the prison for the benefit of inmates, and sexual assaults on prisoners. Again, intelligence provides the details of where this is occurring.
- Gangs are prevalent in many prisons. In order for the prison to be effectively managed, prison staff must know all they can about these gangs.

Just as there is a need for intelligence to be shared between LEAs those involved in managing prisons need to create structures where intelligence can be shared between prison establishments. Prisoners move from one prison to another and it makes sense that what is known about them follows them. This, of course, assumes a degree of structure within each prison to collect information and process it properly into intelligence.

When it comes to benefiting the wider law enforcement community, there is a huge amount of intelligence that can be obtained from prisons:

- Movements and discharges of prisoners. While this type of information can seem of little use on its own, when linked to other intelligence it can help complete an intelligence picture.

- Communications including telephone contacts. Many criminals continue their criminal activity even though in custody. To do so, they have to communicate with the outside world. All communications have the potential to be of intelligence value.
- Prison visitors. It can take considerable effort to visit someone in prison. Generally speaking, people have much better things to do. Examining details of who visits a prisoner and the frequency of those visits can provide intelligence in regard to the strength and potential nature of relationships. Where a person would have been expected to visit a prisoner but doesn't may also be of intelligence value when it comes to understanding the group dynamics or personal relationships within that group.
- Relationships that begin in prison or grow in prison can make for strong bonds because of the shared experiences. Sharing adverse experiences can create loyalties than would normally occur in the outside world. Who a person has served time with is of intelligence value.
- Radicalization. There have been suspicions for many years that the radicalization of people often takes place in prisons. Given that many law enforcement officers involved in counterterrorism have no real understanding of the workings of a prison or prison life, assistance from intelligence staff within the prison is essential to understand what occurs and how it occurs. Failings in intelligence systems mean that prison officers don't have a good understanding of the concept of radicalization and what is of intelligence value, and collectors on the law enforcement side often don't ask the right questions (Walsh 2011). Prison staff needs training in how to spot indicators that radicalization is taking place and law enforcement need to engage effectively with prison staff to encourage the sharing of intelligence where radicalization is suspected.
- Gang details. There is a lot of intelligence in relation to gangs that is likely to become available in prisons. Where the person is likely to continue their criminal involvement with the gang upon release, this intelligence is likely to be of use to law enforcement as soon as the person hits the streets.
- Disclosures/confessions. People talk in jail; there is little else to do. While often much of what is said is casual bragging, there is still much that is likely to be true. Structures should be in place to identify opportunities to use such conversations either to gather intelligence or to gather evidence. Where it is proposed to use the confessions of one prisoner to another in evidence, rigid control measures must be in place as soon as any related investigation begins. These must address the safety of the assisting prisoner and ensure the integrity of the evidence they are collecting. When the information they obtained is to be used purely for intelligence purposes, it too must be treated with suspicion and subject to added scrutiny.

Law enforcement also needs to share intelligence with prisons. Just as what occurs in prisons may impact on the outside world, events outside the prison may have an impact on those inside. Intelligence obtained by law enforcement but having the potential to affect the effective running of the prison is likely to include the following:

- Threats to the life of an inmate. If an individual has fallen out with someone on the outside, it does not mean that they are safe when they are inside. In fact, it may mean they are more vulnerable as the bad guys know where to find that individual anytime. Given the reluctance of many to go into the protective custody side of a prison, the individual is often left exposed to any threat. It is imperative that where law enforcement identifies a threat to any person in custody, the nature of that threat is shared with the prison in order that the prison can take whatever measures it deems necessary.
- Communications between the prison and the outside world. Law enforcement will often become aware of illicit communications both into and out of the prison. The way in which these communications are taking place should be shared with the prison, although as always consideration must be given to the prevailing circumstances, including the potential harm to the prison and the potential harm to any law enforcement investigation.
- Corrupt officers. Often through investigation of crime groups on the outside law enforcement will be in receipt of intelligence regarding the identity of corrupt prison staff. These details should be passed to an appropriate person within the prison management.

Law enforcement needs to give careful consideration before undertaking any form of covert operation within a prison, particularly that of deploying a human source. Prisons are a different environment than the real world: the rules are not the same, and issues around safety for all involved need to be well documented. Consideration may also have to be given to the fact that a prison cell may be legally interpreted as being a person's home and, therefore, privacy issues come into play.

9.30 Automated Vehicle License Plate Readers

Automated vehicle plate readers read the license plate/vehicle registration number of a motor vehicle as the vehicle passes a fixed camera. Everything that the camera sees is recorded and the number of the vehicle entered automatically into a database. While the primary functions of such cameras are crime detection and prevention, they can have significant potential as an intelligence gathering tool. First, if the vehicle is of interest to a surveillance team, then the vehicle number can be entered into the system and as soon as the vehicle passes a camera, an alert is triggered, indicating the vehicle's whereabouts at that time. This method can also be used if it is desired to intercept the vehicle in an attempt to arrest the driver. Second, if a vehicle's details are entered into the system, it is possible to chart where and when the vehicle has passed any camera on the network over a fixed period. Clearly, when this information is analyzed, it can provide intelligence. Obvious as it may seem, it must be borne in mind that the fact that a vehicle was at a certain location, at a certain time, does not necessarily mean the person of interest was driving it.

While this type of software application will require a separate database, that database should be linked electronically to information submission software to facilitate submissions into the intelligence system without the need for the double-keying of data.

In implementing automated readers, the agency needs to have in place procedures relating to all aspects of the functioning of the system, including addressing these specific issues:

- Data obtained should be kept in its own database or in a partitioned area of an existing database in which that data is separated from all other law enforcement data. It should remain there, untouched by anyone, unless access to that data can be lawfully justified. Lawful justification will include access for either the furtherance of an investigation or for intelligence purposes.
- There must be an authorization process for the access. The reason for access should be justified in writing and carried out only by authorized members.
- A period of retention for the data should be stated. Nevertheless, as no member will have access to the data, save for where there exists lawful justification for access, there is no reason why the data cannot be retained for a more prolonged period than if law enforcement had unfettered access to it. While the data is secure in the database, no privacy issue is raised as the vehicle's movements lie undiscovered, and de facto the owner remains anonymous. When access is sought, the privacy issue becomes relevant, but will be addressed through the access process. Having said that, retaining the data any longer than one year becomes difficult to justify. Destroying it any sooner would be foolish, as many offenses/ events do not come to light for considerable periods after they have happened.
- Other LEAs should have access to the data, provided they can fulfill the lawful justification criteria and agree in writing to use it only for

lawful purposes. There must always be a written request for access to the data.

- The contents of the database should remain private and exempt from any public access. Exemptions for the database should be sought relating to freedom-of-information legislation. This information is collected and retained to assist LEAs in discharging their legal obligations, and for no other reason. Unfortunately, there are some in law enforcement who believe that any record in a law enforcement system is up for grabs by the media or anyone else who asks. "Freedom of information" legislation is intended to ensure transparency in relation to the actions of government agencies. It was never intended to compromise the privacy of the public. The public have a right to expect that their privacy should not be compromised purely because they have had contact with law enforcement or because they have driven past a camera! Disclosing such details flies in the face of the privacy obligations discussed in Chapter 4.

9.31   Conclusion

Traditional or overt law enforcement creates numerous opportunities to produce large amounts of good quality intelligence. However, more intelligence is probably missed than collected, because agencies do not have the necessary structures in place. Members of an agency need a minimum amount of training to make them aware of what intelligence is and how they can assist in the collection of intelligence. The ideal place for this training is as part of an agency's initial training program for new entrants. Regular briefings by Intelligence Unit staff should heighten interest and update members on the type of information that is of current interest to the Intelligence Unit. Where an agency wishes to increase its collection capability, training for all existing staff will be required. Those supervising investigators need to check that information gleaned from investigations is submitted to the Intelligence Unit for consideration as intelligence. An effective intelligence system benefits the entire agency, and it is incumbent upon all members to support the collection of information to fuel that system.

References

Brinner, R. (2011) Suspicious activity reporting: Shifting the analytical paradigm. In: Wright, R., Morehouse, B., Peterson, M.B. and Palmieri, L. Eds. *Criminal Intelligence for the 21st Century—A Guide for Intelligence Professionals*, P184–191 Sacramento, CA: Law Enforcement Intelligence Units (LEIU) and Richmond: International Association of Law Enforcement Intelligence Analysts (IALEIA).

Buckley J. (2009) Managing information from the public. In: Billingsley, R. Ed. *Covert Human Intelligence Sources: The Unlovely Face of Police Work*, P97–P108. England: Waterside Press.

Defense Advanced Research Projects Agency (DARPA) (1981) *RFC 791, Internet Protocol—DARPA Internet Program Protocol Specification*. Arlington, Virginia: Defense Advanced Research Projects Agency. Available at: http://www.ietf.org/rfc/rfc791.txt (accessed December 2012).

Information Sharing Environment (ISE) (2009) *Information Sharing Environment. Functional Standard (FS) for Suspicious Activity Reporting (SAR) Version 1.5* Available at: http://www.ise.gov/sites/default/files/ISE-FS-200_ISE-SAR_Functional_Standard_V1_5_Issued_2009.pdf (accessed December 2012).

McDowell, D. (2009) *Strategic Intelligence: A Handbook for Practitioners, Managers, and Users*. Lantham MD: Scarecrow Press.

Nickerson, R.S. (1998) Confirmation bias: A ubiquitous phenomenon in many guises. *Review of General Psychology (Educational Publishing Foundation)* 2(2) P175–P220.

U.S. Department of Justice Office. Office of Community Oriented Policing. (2009) *The Stop Snitching Phenomenon: Breaking the Code of Silence*. Washington, DC: U.S. Department of Justice. Office of Community Oriented Policing.

Walsh, P.F. (2011) *Intelligence and Intelligence Analysis*. New York and London: Routledge.

Intelligence from Covert Operations

10

Human affairs are so obscure and various that nothing can be clearly known.

Desiderius Erasmus

10.1 Introduction

If we are to have a good understanding of how an intelligence management system will work effectively, we need a rudimentary understanding of each of the processes that will contribute intelligence to that system, what that process can contribute, and the limitations of those processes. For reasons previously discussed in Chapter 9, many in law enforcement are of the mistaken belief that all the intelligence they will need will come from their records management system and open sources such as the Internet. This is a fallacy. Criminal gangs and terrorist groups are not going to post their operational plans for criminality on the Internet and no matter how sophisticated a search engine is available or how elaborate the analysis is of the material that is found, if a law enforcement agency (LEA) wants to know what criminals are doing, it must use covert means to obtain that information. As Brinner (2011) comments,

> Obtaining bona fide threat intelligence requires clandestine or surreptitious means—human and technical sources—because there is no other way to gain access to it and learn what would otherwise remain hidden.

Such operations involve considerable effort. Criminals are going to put as many obstacles in place as they can to prevent law enforcement from penetrating their organizations and finding out their intentions. The more sophisticated and better established the gang, the greater the number of hurdles that law enforcement will have to jump over to get to the information that is desired. Johnson (2007:2), when discussing intelligence gathering in a national security context, details the lengths that those involved may need to go to in order to obtain the desired information:

> The hidden information must be ferreted out of encoded communications or stolen from safes and vaults, locked offices, guarded military and intelligence installations, and other denied areas—a potentially dangerous task involving the penetration of an enemy's camp and its concentric circles of defense.

In this chapter, space does not allow for providing a comprehensive guide as to how each of these types of operations should be managed. The sections that follow concentrate on the structures necessary to get the information originating from covert operations to where it needs to go, so that it can be used for intelligence purposes.

10.2 Covert Operations in an Integrated Intelligence Management System

Before progressing any further, it is necessary to address a few ground rules. Those with any level of experience in law enforcement will be aware of the problems that can exist within the covert aspects of law enforcement, but if we are to build an integrated intelligence management system, one where everything joins up and works in tandem, then many of these problems will have to be confronted:

- The information gathered belongs to the agency. Members do not have any right to withhold any information from the agency. All information needs to be submitted to the Intelligence Unit for processing into intelligence. The dangers of withholding such information are so high that any member not submitting information obtained through a covert operation may be regarded as being perilously close to, or engaged in, corrupt behavior. Such activity begs the following question: Why are they not submitting the information? Answers given rarely satisfy any objective assessment.
- Software for different types of covert operations should, as far as practically possible, be interlinked, and this software should be linked seamlessly to the intelligence repository. The amount of resources wasted in activities such as double keying can be astronomical if the two are not linked together.
- Under no circumstances should an agency's records management system contain details of any covert operation or covert asset. They are simply not secure enough for such records.
- Intelligence from covert operations is essential if the agency is to have any real understanding of what the criminals are doing. It cannot be replaced. Obtaining the information and exploiting the subsequent intelligence can carry with it substantial risk including loss of life. Covert operations should be carried out only by properly trained and accredited members, adhering to comprehensive agency policies and supported by adequate resources. Far too many agencies think that these are the activities any "detective" can do.

- Material of covert origins is not intelligence purely because of its origin. The all-too-common view that it is intelligence is wrong. It remains as information until it has been processed.
- Care must always be taken that compromise of an intelligence product coming from a covert asset does not lead to compromise of that asset. The structures advocated in this book have been designed to significantly reduce the chance of this happening.

In the following sections addressing intelligence gathering using various covert methods, a list is provided of records that are essential for conducting such operations. Setting aside the fact that the agency should have such records in place to ensure good governance, they are necessary to ensure that a maximum amount of good-quality intelligence is produced. Without these controls, information that is obtained is not shared, time is wasted in gathering information that is of little use to anyone, or information cannot be exploited, because it has not been obtained lawfully. The agency also runs the risk of exposing methodology because of the lack of sufficient controls. The assumption is made that in all the cases mentioned the records will be contained in a purpose-built computerized system.

10.3 Compartmentalizing Operations

For the most part, records pertaining to each type of covert activity should be kept separately from other types of records. This is simply a matter of security to protect the origin of material and the methods used in collection. Although the staff who regularly take part in one form of covert activity will probably have at least a working knowledge of the other covert methods, there remains the need to protect a considerable amount of what activities the agency is involved in. It all comes down to the "right to know" and "need to know" principles. Acknowledging the principle of keeping such activities separate, many of these types of operations will be carried out in tandem and be integrally linked to each other, as part of a larger scale investigation. In such cases, there will be a need for staff to have a greater awareness of what is taking place. For example, an undercover officer being introduced to a criminal gang by a human source must know the identity of that source and the associated risks to him. In a similar vein, officers carrying out surveillance may well need to know that one of those taking part is a source.

In constructing the management processes for these types of operations, there must be the facility for central oversight at an appropriate level of all such activities. This is necessary not only to ensure that everything works cohesively but also to ensure "deconfliction." There is a high potential for different members of one agency to carry out operations that are likely to conflict with the activities of other members in the same agency, particularly if it is a large agency. Where there are many small agencies working in the same geographical area or against similar targets, the potential for "blue on blue" is through the roof unless some tried and trusted method of deconfliction is in place. If such structures are not in place, then the potential for serious consequences should not be underestimated. All too often, investigations are compromised, but more tragically blue-on-blue engagements lead to the death of an officer at the hands of another officer.

10.4 Policy and Procedures for Covert Operations

For each type of covert activity, the agency should have in place a policy that states the techniques that may be used and the specific procedures that detail how those techniques will be used. The policy is a public statement and will of necessity contain little, if any, of the methodology used. On the other hand, procedures must be broad in their nature and of sufficient detail that any member taking part in such an operation knows exactly what they are expected to do under any given set of circumstances. This type of work is fraught with danger, and staff needs clear instruction regarding how they should behave. The belief that this can be detailed in 10 or 12 pages is wrong; the degree of detail that needs to be included simply won't fit in such a limited text. If that is all there is in the agency's procedures, there are huge gaps, and the agency is well on the path to potentially serious problems.

10.5 Surveillance

Covertly monitoring the activities of a suspect can produce significant amounts of intelligence and is often a valuable technique to successfully exploit limited intelligence that has been obtained from another origin. This section discusses the use of all forms of surveillance except the interception of communications and the placing of "listening" devices in buildings or vehicles.

For many agencies, surveillance is used only to augment existing intelligence and to achieve operational goals. For example, the agency has intelligence to indicate that Leo Hernandez intends to obtain a quantity of methamphetamine from an unknown dealer on an identified day. Surveillance is deployed on Hernandez with the objective of following him to the location where the drugs are to be bought and then arresting both parties. This is a perfectly legitimate use of surveillance, but it is far from the only goal that surveillance can achieve. Surveillance is a very powerful intelligence gathering tool, if it is used properly. First, the objectives of the surveillance have to be clearly identified, with boundaries set by the investigating officer, clearly stating how aggressively the team should pursue the surveillance. If it is a long-term target, then the threshold where potential compromise is worth the benefit is likely to be very high, and the team should minimize that risk by terminating the surveillance if compromise is likely. However, if the potential gain on a given day increases, then the potential benefit to be had will justify the higher risk of the surveillance being detected. Second, the surveillance team needs to be briefed as to the nature of the targets they are likely to be following. This will include any potential threat they pose to the surveillance team and the target's knowledge of surveillance techniques. The surveillance team must be kept updated continually about any new intelligence that may affect the safety of the officers involved. All too often, an initial briefing is given, but there is limited updating over the course of the investigation. Third, the surveillance team needs to be aware of what information is likely to be of potential intelligence value. The team needs to be told what they are looking for. Often with surveillance teams, the situation occurs where the team sees something but overlooks its importance; as Sir Arthur Conan Doyle states, "You see, but you do not observe." Fourth, there must be a mechanism to capture information and an individual who is responsible for submitting the information to the Intelligence Unit.

10.6   Essential Records for Surveillance

If the surveillance function is to become a fully integrated part of an effective intelligence management system, there are a number of records that should be contained within the surveillance file for each operation:

- *Application.* An application for surveillance should detail the nature of the investigation, address privacy issues, and detail the risks associated in carrying out that operation. It should detail the methods to be used for surveillance, including the use of any technical devices. The application should be completed by the requesting officer in consultation with a trained surveillance officer. It should be submitted through line management for authorization by a person of appropriate rank who has sufficient knowledge to make a balanced judgment as to whether or not the surveillance should take place.
- *Authorization.* The authorization for surveillance will include any parameters that the authorizing officer deems necessary and dates for the duration of the authorization.
- *Review.* The progress of the operation should be reviewed on a regular basis to ensure that it is achieving the agreed goals and that

resources are not being wasted. In shorter term operations, the limited duration of the operations may limit the need for review, but in longer term operations reviews should be done on a monthly basis.

- *Cancellation.* There must be a formalized cancellation of the surveillance, at which point a record should be made of the costs of the operation and what has been gained from it.
- *Policy decision log.* This is a record of all strategic decisions made in relation to the surveillance operation.
- *Surveillance log.* This is a centralized record of what occurs each time a target is placed under surveillance. A new surveillance log should be kept for each time surveillance commences on the target. The log should include the names of each member taking part in the surveillance, including the team leader and the name of the log keeper. The team members should certify the veracity of the log at the termination of each surveillance run. At the termination of each surveillance run, the team should be debriefed to ascertain anything they may have noted of intelligence value. This should be included in the surveillance log.
- *Personal records.* Each member may have personal notes to record events during each surveillance run. A new record should be used for each run, and these should be appended to the surveillance file with the original being kept securely and a copy being scanned into the electronic surveillance file.
- *A surveillance debriefing report.* This is a summary of the day's events during a surveillance operation. If during the day there is a significant break in the surveillance, separate debriefing reports should be prepared for each time period. The surveillance debriefing report is completed from the surveillance log by a surveillance officer. The debriefing report should not contain details of any surveillance operator other than the completing officer.
- *Information submission mechanism.* An information submission is prepared from the surveillance debriefing report, normally by the investigating officer. The information submission needs to include all of the information that is of potential intelligence value. This is then submitted to the Intelligence Unit.
- *Financial management.* A comprehensive record of the cost of the surveillance should be kept. This should include man-hours used and any expenses incurred.
- *Technical equipment inventory.* Each surveillance file should include a record of any technical equipment used.
- *Performance management tools.* As with all aspects of law enforcement, a set of performance metrics must be agreed upon and performance records need to be kept.

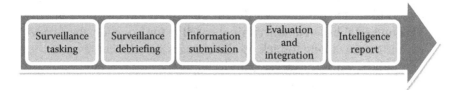

Figure 10.1 Intelligence repositing from surveillance operations.

- *Centralized recording.* All surveillance records should be centrally retrievable. Any additional records or electronic media that are kept elsewhere should be logged in and linked to the original surveillance file.

Figure 10.1 illustrates intelligence repositing from surveillance operations.

10.7 Covert Searching

Many agencies carry out covert searches. Covert searches will include those carried out on such targets as vehicles, garbage bins, and buildings, both occupied and commercial. Such searches are a form of surveillance and are best dealt with through the mechanisms that the agency has in place for surveillance. These will include having a section dealing with covert searching in the surveillance procedures, using the surveillance record-keeping software and officers who have had appropriate training. In most jurisdictions this type of operation will require some level of authorization, and in many jurisdictions it will require a warrant issued by a court. The agency must also have mechanisms in place to deal with any material of an evidential nature that is seized at the time or of which a visual record has been made, for example, photographs of a weapons cache in situ.

10.8 Lifestyle Surveillance

"Lifestyle" surveillance is, as the name implies, surveillance carried out on an individual to identify features of their lifestyle. This type of surveillance can be carried out for a number of reasons:

- *To establish a baseline.* When a person is likely to be under surveillance for a considerable period of time, it is necessary to establish what normal behavior is for them. Those carrying out the surveillance will become familiar with the target's normal behavior and mannerisms while that individual is not engaged in criminal activity. Such behavior is likely to change when the person engages in criminal activity. Having established a noncriminal baseline for behavior, the surveillance team is likely to pick up the changes in behavior, even if they are subtle, when the target is undertaking criminal behavior.

- *To establish a pattern of life.* A fundamental part of knowing a target is establishing what their "normal" daily activities are. For many career criminals each day may initially appear haphazard, but prolonged surveillance can establish patterns in their lifestyle. Knowing such patterns can pay dividends when the target has to be located on short notice. Such patterns may not always be obvious, and the use of an analyst to chart the activities can reveal much.

- *Proactive recruitment of human sources.* Surveillance can tell a lot about a person, and such information can be extremely useful in the proactive recruitment of human sources (Buckley 2006). Where a person is being targeted for recruitment as a human source, the surveillance team should be briefed by the recruiting officer as to the type of material that is required, because it may be different from what the surveillance team normally regards as being of value.

Some involved in law enforcement balk at carrying out such surveillance, believing that because such activity is not in the scope of the immediate investigation of a criminality, it is unlawful and/or unproductive. This is rarely the case. Investigations into serious crime can require a huge amount of preparation and investment in resources. To satisfy the legal requirements, clear explanation must be given linking the lifestyle surveillance to the accomplishment of investigative goals and showing the necessity of such preliminary activities.

10.9   Surveillance Equipment

By the time this book is published, there is likely to be some new gadget that assists in carrying out surveillance. As technology advances at what appears to be a relentless rate, it is all but impossible to give clear guidance on what should be done with each and every device that can assist in surveillance. Although this is not the place to discuss what is available, some points are worth noting:

- *Legality.* As a general rule, if a device is interfering with a citizen's rights, then there is going to be a requirement for a lawful basis to use it and an authority to grant such activity. It stands to reason that law enforcement should not be allowed to use a camera to watch a person's house or to track a vehicle without some level of authorization. Setting an appropriate level of authorization can be difficult. However, if it is left to lawyers, the bets are on that it will benefit the criminals. If the option remains available, it is much better if law enforcement is proactive in setting credible standards to protect citizens' rights while at the same time allowing it to protect citizens by carrying out its role successfully.

- *Restricting use.* Many technological breakthroughs can be of enormous benefit to law enforcement; however, such benefits far too often fail to be fully realized, because there is a lack of restriction into when and where the technology is used. A lot of the equipment should be used only in major investigations. With each use of equipment comes the risk that its availability becomes known to the criminals, rendering it defunct. It is simply not worth running this risk for some relatively minor investigation.
- Technology can be compromised, because officers have failed to deal with court disclosure effectively, and the capability of the technology is then revealed to the defense. An agency should take all possible measures to protect the existence and functionality of such equipment in the disclosure process. If the item is compromised, it is not compromised just to that agency but to all law enforcement.
- Unfortunately, technology is all too often exposed through some "fly on the wall" type police documentary and as a direct result of the self-aggrandizement of the officer involved.
- *Controlling purchase and use.* Boys like toys. There can be a huge temptation to purchase equipment that is not really needed (especially if it is coming from federal or grant funding.) Much of the technology involved in surveillance is expensive. Agencies need to take care with regard to what is purchased and control how it is used. Too often equipment is bought with little thought given to the value that will be made of it. Purchase of any such equipment may well be justified, but managers should be able to see how it will be used and the benefits that will ensue prior to purchase. There is little point in buying something that will, after the initial thrill, be left to lie in a cupboard until it becomes obsolete.
- In a similar vein, all too often equipment is "lost," because no record is kept within the agency of who has it and where it is.* Purchase of surveillance equipment should be done centrally within an agency, against agreed criteria, and there should be a central record of who has any piece of surveillance equipment at any time.

---

* Although the benefits may appear obvious and the harm minimal, the surveillance team's new Nikon is not meant to be used to record the family holiday in Disneyland.

- Agencies should work together to pool resources, thus saving in purchasing equipment that lies unused when it could be of use to others.

Where surveillance is carried out using technical equipment, either as the whole of an operation (such as with a static camera) or in support of a surveillance team, the information gleaned from that equipment should be submitted in the same manner as the submission of any other information obtained from surveillance.

10.10 Human Sources

Human sources are an essential part of gathering intelligence. Should an agency for whatever reason choose not to use them, they are depriving themselves of not only the information that the sources can themselves provide but also opportunities to create other information gathering opportunities, such as identifying the right locations for listening devices and surveillance leads. Having said that, human sources bring with them significant problems, the least of which being evaluating the information they produce and then using it safely. To begin with, it is necessary to emphasize what is meant by a human source:

A human source is defined as "a person who has been deliberately recruited and is managed to collect information to satisfy an intelligence requirement" (Reid and Buckley 2005).

Different jurisdictions have different terminology for a person fulfilling this role. In the United Kingdom, the term mandated in law is a "covert human intelligence source (CHIS)," which may appear a somewhat cumbersome and obtuse term, until one reads the legislative definition and gets a true understanding of what cumbersome and obtuse means.* With the exception of the Federal Bureau of Investigation, the term human source is not

---

* A person is a CHIS if

    a. He establishes or maintains a personal or other relationship with a person for the covert purpose of facilitating the doing of anything falling within paragraph (b) or (c).

    b. He covertly uses such a relationship to obtain information or to provide access to any information to another person.

    c. He covertly discloses information obtained by the use of such a relationship or as a consequence of the existence of such a relationship.

    A relationship is established or maintained for a covert purpose if and only if it is conducted in a manner that is calculated to ensure that one of the parties to the relationship is unaware of the purpose.

    A relationship is used covertly and information obtained is disclosed covertly if and only if the relationship is used or the information is disclosed in a manner that is calculated to ensure that one of the parties to the relationship is unaware of the use or disclosure in question.

commonly used within law enforcement in the United States. The preferred term in the United States is "confidential informant." Acknowledging that the common parlance for a human source is the word informant, the decision to use the term human source is based on a number of factors.

- Many law enforcement officers are inclined to refer to human sources by derogatory terms such as "rat," "tout," or "snitch." Such terminology is not only unprofessional but also counterproductive, as it damages the credibility of the person providing the information. Even terms like informant carry with them negative connotations.
- The term, "confidential informant," widely used in the United States has numerous interpretations, many of which do nothing but confuse both laypeople and professionals alike. This confusion leads to many problems, including a failure to adequately protect individuals who have given information, miscarriages of justice and failed prosecutions, and officers becoming involved in corrupt relationships. In short, the situation with regard to the use of the term, "confidential informants," and arguably the methods used in their management are a mess (Brown 2010; Natapoff 2009).
- For those unfamiliar with or inexperienced in managing human sources, there is often the misguided belief that they are in some way very different from other people in terms of their motives and their behavior, whereas in reality what drives their behavior is akin to what drives the behavior of any other human. The use of the word human is intended to emphasize the similarities, as opposed to informant, which has so many negative stereotypes attached to it.

Despite all the problems with human sources, they may be the only way to obtain certain information and, as such, they are a necessary component of any effective intelligence gathering strategy. However, care must always be taken when acting upon intelligence that originates solely from a human source, where it is impossible to corroborate that intelligence—that is not to say "don't do it," rather "if you are doing it be careful."

10.11   Maximizing the Information from Human Sources

Unfortunately, many involved in human source management have limited knowledge of how to manage a human source effectively and few have had training in the skills necessary to obtain the maximum amount of information from them. Those involved in source management will already be starting to disagree with this, but answering a few simple questions may help focus the mind: How much training have you had in managing human sources? How much of that training was devoted to psychology? How much of that training was devoted to interview skills tailored to the source environment? The reason why human sources are managed is to get information from them. Without specific training, all we are getting if we are lucky is a combination of what the sources can remember to tell us that day and how much of that they want to tell us. Despite the fantastic potential of the well of information that human sources provide, few in law enforcement know how to tap that well of anything close to its true potential.

There are many problems that are specific with regard to obtaining information from human sources. These problems are related to the source, to the handler (the officer managing the source), and to the agency. Buckley (2006) provides an in-depth examination of many of the problems associated with human source management* and how to overcome them. Some of them are provided here by way of example:

- Depending on how many people the information has passed through before getting to the source, much can be lost or distorted, just as in a game of "whisper down the lane." Effective debriefing by handlers can reduce but not eliminate this distortion.
- Sources lie. At least in part due to the fact that some law enforcement officers have a very limited knowledge of what drives human behavior, they create circumstances where it encourages deceit from the source. Good management of a source creates circumstances where the source is motivated not to lie.
- Sources say what they think we want to hear. Often either with an eagerness to please or because of potential rewards, sources will tell their handlers what the source thinks will please the handler. Misperception of events and self deceit add further to the potential for distortion of the information
- Sources get little or no training for their role, so they often don't have any more than their "street-smarts" to identify what might be useful information. The properly trained and developed source knows exactly what the handler wants and goes out of their way to get it.
- Handlers are not trained by their agency in effective interviewing skills to elicit truthful information. Such interview training needs to be designed specifically for use in the source arena. Handlers don't

---

* *The Human Source Management System: The Use of Psychology in Managing Human Intelligence Sources* (Buckley 2006) provides a step-by-step guide with regard to many of the aspects of controlling human sources, including proactive recruitment and effective handling.

ask the source the right sort of questions to access the source's memories that are at a subconscious level.

- Handlers think they can remember all the information a source gives them during a debriefing. They can't, and a significant amount of the information that the source has provided never gets recorded.
- Handlers are not provided with specific intelligence requirements prior to each meeting they have with a source. It is left to the handler to decide what to ask the source or worse left to the source to decide what to report. The intelligence manager should continually be providing the handler with questions to be answered by the source. These questions should include further development or clarification of the information that the source has previously provided.
- The agency fails to put into place structures where the right sources can be proactively tasked against the desired targets. The agency should know what sources can report on what targets. Developing an enhanced profile of the source at the commencement of a relationship, and continuously developing this as the relationship progresses, means that the agency is continually aware of what a source can report on. Serious thought needs to go into how such structures operate and how requirements are passed to handlers.
- Much of what a source tells a handler can get lost in translation. Handlers don't listen effectively and interpret events from an ethnocentric perspective. A simple test for this is to ask oneself if you handed a source an intelligence report would he recognize the content as originating from them or would the meaning have become so distorted as to be unrecognizable? Moreover, there is always the problem with handlers putting their spin on what the source is saying or influencing the source to report in a particular manner. As Noble (2009:20) says in his excellent paper on human sources, "While a source might provide incorrect reporting or outright lie, a collector can just as easily misquote the source, fail to make note of something critical, or even misrepresent a source's information for personal reasons. It is important for all concerned to recognize that the HUMINT process can be led astray by the collector as well as the source."
- Where and how sources and handlers meet creates circumstances that are not conducive to effective communication. Both parties are normally on guard and under stress. This leads to misinterpretation errors and omissions in the information obtained. Audio recording of source debriefings should be favorably considered.
- Supervisors, intelligence officers, and anyone else with the power to alter the information submitted prior to it being reposited as an intelligence report can potentially distort the source when reporting. Finished intelligence products should be reviewed by the handler

to ensure that what is reposited conveys the spirit and substance of what the source originally said. The temptation to alter what a source has reported always exists if that report doesn't fit with the current intelligence picture or with a manager's view of that picture.

- Handlers fail to follow through with the source and accept part of the story, failing to consider if the source has sufficient access to the criminals to provide the level of information the source has provided; that is, is it coming firsthand, secondhand, etc.? Handlers need to question the sources to ascertain the reasons behind them knowing only part of a story when everything they have said suggests they should know more.

10.12   Proactive Tasking of Human Sources

Sources should be clear with regard to what they are reporting on and to what specific information the agency is involved in gathering. Sources should be clearly tasked* by their handlers, so they don't waste time and effort seeking out information that is not of interest. Tasking sources is, in essence, providing them with "intelligence requirements," though this may often involve considerable guile on the part of the handler in order not to educate the source as to the nature of the investigation. Figure 10.2 illustrates intelligence repositing from a human source.

10.13   Source Self-Reporting

A major problem in managing intelligence revolves around self-reporting: that is, when a source is reporting activities in which they have been present

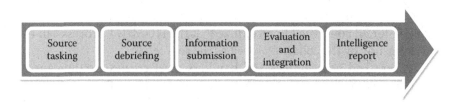

Figure 10.2 Intelligence repositing from human sources.

---

* Unfortunately, in some jurisdictions, such as Canada, the tasking of a human source creates legal complications, a problem that can originate from poorly written legislation based on misconceptions of the nature of human source management and/or poor interpretation of the legislation by agencies or the courts.

or in which they have been involved. The two main aspects of this can be summed up as follows:

1. *Legality.* Where does the source sit from a legal perspective if they are admitting criminality or something that is arguably criminal? For example, if a source is present when an armed robbery is discussed, where does he stand from a legal perspective? Such matters will always occur and will be case specific and jurisdiction specific.

2. *Reporting problems.* For the sake of illustration, let us make the assumption that the source has done nothing unlawful, but has been present at a meeting where the robbery was discussed by three associates. Completing the information submission is easy because of the full account of the meeting between the source and his three associates that have been given by the source to the handler. However, when it comes to completing an intelligence report, a number of questions jump out. The first one of these being, do we include the source's name in the intelligence report? This question is not easily answered, as we have to consider that this document may end up being disclosed to defense counsel should the three be arrested for carrying out the robbery. If the source's name is not there, it may look strange to the bad guys. Second, he has nothing to do with this robbery, so why is it lawful to enter his name into an intelligence repository? The answer to this is probably "yes legally this is correct but …" with the but being that we may not totally believe him when he said he played no part. Third, including the source's details in the report may start to raise his profile; then other police may start to pursue the source, while the handlers are trying to keep his profile low and not bring him under too much notice. These are just some of the issues to which there are no definitive answers. Experience and a bit of thought will dictate what should be done on most occasions. If a source is being managed properly, then the agency should be doing its utmost to keep his identity safe while maximizing the intelligence produced. Far too often, LEAs treat sources as "one-hit wonders" as opposed to longer term investments.

10.14   Problems in the Evaluation of Source Reporting

An intelligence manager is in a position to see that a particular source report is in some way flawed because he receives information originating from many different places. This should be brought to the attention of the handler's supervisor. Handlers often become "attached" to their sources and can be blind to deception. Where it becomes apparent to an intelligence officer that the reliability of a human source is becoming questionable, consultation should take place where it is practical to do so with those officers involved in managing the source. There is potential for significant damage to be done to an agency if such matters are not addressed and the human source is allowed to continue in an unreliable manner commonly referred to as "yanking the officer's chain."

10.15   Community-Oriented Information from Sources

As discussed in Chapter 2, an agency should adopt an integrated approach to policing with the agency's intelligence management system providing products to support as many different aspects of the agency's work as possible. One type of information that can be readily overlooked by those involved in strategic decision-making is that relating to the communities from which significant volumes of crime originate. These host communities are often areas that have low-income residents with all the attendant social problems. The low-income nature of these areas can often be exacerbated by the presence of large numbers of recently arrived, diverse ethnic groups, which in itself can lead to social strife.

A major problem in policing is to obtain accurate information about what is occurring in these areas and what issues are of real concern to the residents. Police managers often listen to so-called or self-nominated community representatives who are more intent on promoting their own agenda rather than truly representing their community's concerns or problems. The benefit of accessing information supplied by sources operating in that community is that it is more likely to be an accurate reflection of what is occurring and what is of concern to residents. This makes the assumption that the source is being properly managed and that each piece of information is properly evaluated.

Many officers involved in investigating crime in these areas, particularly where their remit is serious crime, fail to obtain information relating to less-serious crime or underlying social causes of crime. Although it is understandable that this occurs, it is indicative that a more holistic approach is not prevalent within the agency. Common flaws include the following:

- The officer managing the source within the area is too busy getting information about her investigation to ask questions about other crimes or social issues.
- The officer managing the source has insufficient knowledge of the area in general terms to effectively question the source.
- Management has little idea of the type of information that could help it and even less of an idea that the agency has resources in place that can directly and accurately obtain such information.

- Analysts have failed to request the specific information they require to form a true picture of what is occurring.

Sources within a community should be tasked to report on the following:

- Underlying social issues
- Tensions between various groups within the community
- Persons perceived by the community as being involved in antisocial behavior/quality-of-life issues
- Any gangs or groups involved in the area and the ringleaders of any such gangs or groups
- Meeting places, hangouts, and so on, used by perpetrators
- Identification of perpetrators involved in minor crimes, although care must always be taken in overt action against such persons that the source is not exposed
- The accuracy of views articulated by pressure groups/community representatives in relation to what is the reality within the community
- Community concerns and views on particular crime types
- The perception of law enforcement within the community and of any actions taken by it within that community
- Potential solutions to problems within the community

Information obtained in this way allows the senior management team to make much better educated decisions about how to police the area. Where an agency uses this type of approach and all involved are bought into the process, it is a clear indicator that an integrated intelligence-led approach to policing is being used effectively.

10.16 Buy Bust Operations

"Buy bust" is a technique that is often used by those involved in narcotics operations. At its worst, it involves sending a source to buy drugs in order to verify that there are drugs at a particular location and as soon as the drugs have been purchased, the investigators bust the dealer. Short of putting a large neon sign on the source's head that reads "informant," it is hard to think of a more obvious way to identify someone who is assisting law enforcement. Although the example given may illustrate the crudest use of the technique, this exploitation of human sources unnecessarily places the source's life in danger and adds little to combat the greater drugs threat. Often there is little, if anything, of an intelligence nature submitted, and the detective moves from bust to bust with no thought of using the source to gain a more comprehensive intelligence picture, one where operations can be carried out to combat the supply at a much higher level. Adding to this problem is the fact that, because no time is invested in building a relationship with the source, the knowledge that the source has in her head is never extracted and submitted for intelligence purposes. Such operations are fraught with danger to the source, the officers involved, and the agency and are generally of little benefit to an overall counter-drug strategy. If these types of operation are commonplace within an agency, and the agency wants to maximize the quality and quantity of intelligence it is receiving, then there needs to be a fundamental change in the way it allows sources to be managed.

10.17   Essential Records for Managing Human Sources

There are a number of records that are essential for the management of a human source to ensure effective management and a greater productivity from that source. Furthermore, such records ensure legislative compliance and should specifically address privacy issues.

- *Recruiting.* As soon as an officer begins the recruitment of any person as a human source, agency records should be commenced with details of that individual being submitted to a central point within the agency. The primary purpose of this is the early clarification as to identify whether or not that person is currently, or has ever been previously, registered as a human source and to deal with whatever matters arise from such an event. When a large number of agencies are working in a similar geographical area, a centralized clearing house for all the agencies is highly recommended. This may also help to identify if the person is already the subject of another investigation/operation.
- *Application.* An application to formally register and use the source should be submitted by a handler through a supervisor to an appropriate rank who has sufficient authority to say the following on behalf of the agency: "It is OK to use this person as a registered source." Applications should detail the nature of the investigation and how the use of that source will further the investigation or investigations in general. The application should address privacy issues and detail the risks associated with the management of that source.
- *Authorization.* The authorization will include any parameters set by the authorizing officer and include the date and time of commencement of the authorization and the date and time of termination.
- *Review.* At a specified time, there should be a mandatory review of the authorization to ensure the source is achieving what was expected.

Too often sources are kept "on the books" simply because no one takes them "off the books."

- *Cancellation.* Cancellation is the formal notification that for whatever reason the source is no longer being used as a source. In most cases, the source should be informed.
- *"Enhanced profile".* This is a comprehensive list of all the sources' associates and places frequented, their lifestyle, and skills created to maximize the potential for tasking and to facilitate agency-wide deployments.
- *Criminal participation authorization.* This is a formal authorization for the source to engage in a criminal act on behalf of the agency. This can be used only if the jurisdiction has legislation that permits this. Too often such conduct is allowed to continue with the handlers just turning a blind eye to criminality, because it is providing benefit to them in the form of information.
- *Policy-decision log.* All decisions relating to the management of a source should be recorded in such a way that all those involved in the management can see them.
- *Finance management.* All financial transactions relating to a source should be recorded in the source file.
- *Contact report.* A contact report contains details of everything that occurs during a contact with a source, including all the information they provide and everything pertaining to their welfare.
- *Information submission.* This will follow the style of all other agency intelligence submissions, although there may be some variances to accommodate the nature of source management. It will still be called an intelligence submission, and all four sections will be present. The information submission should allow for both "source comment," that is, what the source's take is on the information, and any comment from the handler who is submitting it.
- *Intelligence report.* The agency's standard intelligence report should be used for all source reporting.
- *Performance metrics.* Measuring performance for both sources and the officers managing them can be difficult. Care must be taken to avoid performance being measured solely in terms of quantity of information received, and consideration should always be given to the quality of that information. Performance indicators are likely to include a number of intelligence reports addressing intelligence requirements, the number and nature of persons arrested as a result of the information provided, and details of any goods recovered. Cognizance should always be taken of the number of intelligence reports from the source on which executive action was taken but that failed to produce the expected results.

10.18 Undercover Operations

The term "undercover operations" includes a number of different types of operations; the primary factor being that a sworn officer assumes another role for the purposes of furthering an investigation or gathering information on a suspect or suspects. Examples of undercover operations include the following:

- *Decoy operations.* This is where an officer poses as a decoy to draw a suspect into a situation where he may be apprehended. Decoy operations are often used in the investigation of sex attacks with a female officer being "exposed" as a potential victim in an area where such previous attacks have occurred and in the investigation of prostitution offenses where female officers pose as prostitutes in an area where there is a problem of "curb crawling" by male motorists.
- *Test purchase operations.* These are operations usually found in narcotics investigations, where an officer buys illicit commodities from a suspect to gather evidence of them dealing in the commodity. The undercover role is usually of a very limited duration, and the evidence gained may be used directly or to gain corroboration of human source information to aid in obtaining a search warrant.
- *Infiltration operation.* These are the mainstay of undercover work and involve one or more officers infiltrating a criminal group or building a relationship with an identified suspect with the intent to gather incriminating evidence or information that is used for the furtherance of a criminal investigation. Infiltration operations will last from a number of weeks to many years.
- *Natural cover operations.* This type of operation involves an officer assuming a false identity for the purposes of proactively recruiting a person to be a human source.
- *Covert Internet investigation.* This type of operation is carried out over the Internet with the vast majority, if not all, of the transactions being carried out in cyberspace. These types of operations are often used to identify pedophiles exchanging pornography via the Internet, to gain evidence against those using chat rooms to procure young individuals for sexual purposes, and to investigate those involved in computer hacking.

10.19 Intelligence Gathering in Undercover Operations

An all too common failing in undercover operations is that of adopting a purely evidence-focused attitude. Although in most cases the gaining of evidence to convict offenders will be paramount, this is no excuse to miss the

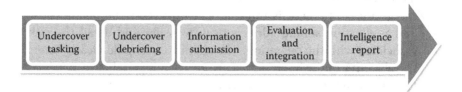

Figure 10.3 Intelligence repositing from undercover operations.

opportunity to gain huge amounts of information that will have intelligence value. Failure to maximize the intelligence output comes about for many reasons, but primarily it is because the mind-set of those involved is not focused on intelligence, and the structures are not in place within the agency to capture the intelligence. When an undercover officer is being debriefed by her "cover officer," the cover officer, or in some cases an investigating officer, will take statements for evidential purposes, ensuring that all possible evidence is captured, but it is following this that an extensive debrief should take place to capture information for intelligence purposes. Much of the material that an undercover officer gathers consciously and subconsciously will be unrelated to the case under investigation, but it will have significance for other investigations or provide insight into the dynamics of the group under investigation and/or the methods used in that type of criminality. All this needs to be captured and submitted for processing. As the undercover officer may be living the criminal life on a daily basis, she will become blind to the extent of the knowledge they have that others in law enforcement don't. The debriefing process should be carried out thoroughly to elicit this knowledge by delving into the nuances of the people involved, their personalities, and their thought processes. It is all too rare that law enforcement gets such an insight, and the opportunity must be seized when it is there. Figure 10.3 illustrates intelligence repositing from undercover operations.

10.20 Essential Records for Undercover Operations

The following records are required for undercover operations. The structure of the records will need to be tailored for each different type of undercover operation:

- *Application.* An application to carry out an undercover operation should be submitted by a supervisor to an appropriate rank who has sufficient authority to authorize such an operation. Given the potential high risk to which the officer may be exposed, this may require a high rank within the organization. Applications should detail the nature of the investigation, how the undercover officer will infiltrate the group, and how this infiltration will further the investigation. The application should address privacy issues and detail the risks associated with the operation. The application should clearly state if the objective of the operation is primarily evidential in its nature or for intelligence purposes, but neither precludes the other.

- *Authorization.* The authorization will include any parameters set by the authorizing officer and include the date and time of commencement of the authorization and the date and time of termination.
- *Review.* At a specified time, there should be a mandatory review of the authorization to ensure that the operation is achieving what was expected. The deployment of an undercover officer creates significant risks for that officer and should be prolonged only as long as it is necessary. Furthermore, the cost of such an operation is likely to be significant and needs continuous monitoring.
- *Cancellation.* Cancellation is the formal notification that the operation has been terminated.
- *Undercover profile.* This is a comprehensive list of the undercover officer's appearance, traits, and skills created to enable the effective deployment of that officer. The profile will also contain details of all previous deployments, the legends used in those scenarios, and details of all parties they encountered during those operations.
- *Criminal participation authorization.* This is a formal authorization for an undercover officer to engage in a criminal act on behalf of the agency. This can be used only if the jurisdiction has legislation that permits this type of activity by an officer.
- *A formalized briefing document.* This document details all the information that was given to the undercover officer prior to the commencement of the operation. This is particularly relevant where the objective of the operation is to obtain a confession from a suspect. Withholding critical information from the undercover officer about the offense ensures that when they obtain it from the suspect, the only alternative way to hear intimate details of the crime is from the perpetrator.
- *Policy decision log.* All decisions relating to the management of the undercover officer should be recorded in such a way that all those who need to see them can. Sometimes, there will be an operational need to exclude the undercover officer from access to some decisions, as knowledge of those decisions may have an impact on the neutrality of their evidence.
- *Finance management.* All financial transactions relating to the operation should be recorded in the undercover file.
- *Undercover officers' meeting report.* The undercover officer should complete comprehensive records after every meeting/interaction

with the target or targets. These notes should contain details of everything that occurs during the interactions.

- *Statements of evidence.* When material of an evidentiary nature is obtained during a meeting with a target, the undercover cover officer should prepare statements of evidence as soon as practically possible. These should be linked to the undercover officer's contact report for that meeting in question.
- *Cover officer contact report.* The cover officer should complete a written record of each and every contact she has with the undercover officer. Such a report should contain details of what was discussed, the tasks given to the officer, and any matters pertaining to the undercover officer's welfare.
- *Transcriptions of audio recordings.* When audio recordings are made of meetings, the facility should exist to include the original digital audio and the transcriptions in the electronic file for the operation.
- *Information submission.* This will follow the style of all other agency intelligence submissions, although there may be some variances to accommodate the nature of undercover work. All four sections will be present. The information submission should allow for both undercover officer comment, that is, what her take is on the information, and any comment from the submitting member. Comments by the undercover officer are likely to have significant value, as the officer may well have intimate knowledge of the emotions and thought processes of the group that she has penetrated.
- *Intelligence report.* The agency's standard intelligence report should be used for all undercover reporting.
- *Performance metrics.* Measuring performance for undercover officers can be extremely difficult. The nature of their work means that a huge amount of time is invested in merely building relationships with the target and her associates. However, this does not mean that it is impossible to find an agreed set of performance metrics to chart the worth of the operation.

10.21   Interception of Communications

To carry out their activities, criminals have to communicate with each other. They do so in many different ways. When it comes to intercepting communication, there are two simple aspects for the members of law enforcement to bear in mind:

1. If you don't already know what can or can't be intercepted, chances are you don't really need to.

2. If you find out that criminals are communicating with each other in
   a particular way, the details of how they are doing it must be submitted for intelligence purposes.

Criminals are all too well aware of the capabilities of law enforcement to
intercept communications and will always seek new ways to communicate
securely. The difficulty for law enforcement is identifying how the criminals
are communicating and then to find ways to intercept those communications
without the criminals realizing that law enforcement teams have the capability. The logic in the two points made at the beginning should be apparent: law
enforcement needs to know what the bad guys are doing, but we don't want
them to know we know.

One of the key problems with regard to interception is legislation. In
many cases, the laws allowing interception simply cannot keep pace with the
way in which technology is evolving. This can leave law enforcement out on a
limb with regard to the legality of some types of interception and what they
need to do to intercept communication. Although this is ultimately a failing
on the part of the lawmakers, input from law enforcement is often disjointed
and lacking in sufficient depth to convince the lawmakers of the need for
better legislation.

10.22   Intercepting Telephone Calls

The idea and capability of intercepting telephone calls has been around for
a considerable period of time and the majority of criminals are careful with
what they say when calling. However, this does not mean that intercepting
calls is not an effective tool for law enforcement, from both evidential and
intelligence perspectives. Advances in technology and the increased use of
mobile technology present to law enforcement both additional challenges
and additional opportunities. Mobile telephones now transmit much more
than words exchanged between the calling parties, not the least of which is
the geographic location of the parties at the time of the call. All members
involved in intercepting communication need comprehensive training if the
maximum amount of intelligence is to be obtained from such a technology.
Although voice recognition technology can now positively identify a caller,
this facility is not always available, and a common error remains in attrib-
uting the caller identity as being that of the known phone owner. It should
never be assumed that a person using a phone is its owner. Another common mistake is ignoring information because it doesn't relate directly at that
time to a specific crime. Huge amounts of valuable intelligence with respect
to targets are lost because those transcribing the material don't have a clear
understanding of how useful snippets of information can be in building a

clear intelligence picture of the targets, their group, the group dynamics, and the methods they are using.

10.23 Listening Devices

As long as people talk, listening devices will be of value to law enforcement. They can produce huge amounts of high-quality intelligence. The technical quality and capability of such devices has increased enormously over the past several years. Setting aside any further technical discussions or discussions regarding operational deployment, as they are outside the scope of this book, we move to discussing taking information from such devices and the problems with converting that information into intelligence. The first issue to deal with is ensuring that the information obtained is as precise as possible, and this comes down to accurate transcription.

One of the main problems with regard to transcription from listening devices is the lack of understanding about the nature and composition of communication. It is the responsibility of the agency to provide training to staff involved in transcribing the intercepted product. Huge amounts of material are lost or misinterpreted because of the lack of understanding about how people communicate. There are a number of common problems:

- *Language.* Anyone involved in transcription must be fluent in the language being spoken by the targets. If the transcriber is not fluent, the risk of misinterpretation is high.
- *Dialect.* Your English is not my English. Although this book is written in English, there are undoubtedly words that a reader from the United States may interpret differently from a reader in the United Kingdom. For example, in the United Kingdom, "pants" are what you wear under your trousers, but Americans understand pants to be something you wear as an outer garment.* Unless the transcriber is familiar with the dialect spoken, words are likely to be misinterpreted. If there is doubt, this should be indicated in brackets in the transcription.
- *Slang.* Speech is often peppered with slang. Slang comprises informal words and expressions that are not considered to be a formal part of the speaker's language or dialect. They are commonly used in social, as opposed to formal, settings and often used euphemistically. Slang words are often linked to peer groups, and as such their meaning may be lost on anyone who is unfamiliar with that group. Factors

---

* You wear pants as an outer garment only if you are Superman!

such as age and social background may make it more difficult for the transcriber to contextualize the words correctly. Again, this should be highlighted in the transcription so the member examining the transcript will know to give the term further scrutiny.

- *Code words.* Most criminals use code words to describe illicit commodities or criminal activities. Those transcribing intercepts should be provided with a lexicon of potential code words by the officer managing the operation. The transcriber should seek to add to this lexicon when they encounter a word that obviously has an alternative meaning. Once such code words are identified, they should always be submitted in an intelligence report so the knowledge is not lost for future investigations.
- *"Trigger" words.* Transcribing can be a boring and arduous task and one to which the mind often dulls. Trigger words are words that when heard immediately spark interest: for example, gun, bomb, and meth are all likely to cause the listener to retune in to the conversation. Trigger words have both advantages and disadvantages. First, where the entire product is not being transcribed they may become all that the transcriber listens for, which is obviously too likely to lead to other potentially valuable material being missed. Second, they can be very useful when supplied by the investigator, particularly if they are words not often of specific interest. If there are certain words that have specific value to an investigation, consideration should be given to providing the transcriber with them. These may include names of particular persons of interest.
- *Vocalics.* The word, "vocalic," refers to anything that is spoken and heard except for words. Vocalics includes the following:
  - *Tone and pitch.* This refers to how the voice sounds. Saying something with a different tone or pitch can change the meaning of what is said.
  - *Volume.* This refers to how loud the speaker's voice is at the time the words are spoken. A raised voice can be a sign that the words have importance or that the person has authority. Alternatively, in the context of criminality lowered volume may well be a sign that what is being discussed is of a clandestine nature.
  - *Speed of speech.* The speed of someone's speech can indicate many things that may be important, such as nervousness of the speaker or that the matter under discussion is of pressing significance.
  - *Emotional characterizations.* This refers to the emotional expressions that are contained within the speech or those that precede or follow the speech, such as laughing or crying. Such characterizations can entirely change the meaning of words. If these are not included in the transcription, then they can create the wrong meaning.

Table 10.1 An Illustration of the Components of Communication

Words spoken	10%
Vocalics (the way they are spoken)	40%
Nonverbal accompaniment	50%

– *Minimal encouragers.* Sounds such as "uh-uh," "uh-huh," and "um" are common parts of communication and are designed to maintain the conversation. They are uttered by a listener to encourage the speaker to continue or by a speaker asking permission to continue to speak. With each utterance, there is normally confirming eye contact. This eye contact will more often than not be unavailable even if there is video as such movements are very subtle. Human nature dictates that the transcriber is likely to adopt the easiest route by omitting such encouragers and thereby losing the meaning they conveyed.

Table 10.1 gives an indication as to the composition of communication. As can be seen, the words spoken comprise a very small part of the meaning that is intended. Given the nature of listening devices, the potential for misinterpretation is significant even if all the words are clearly heard. However, such circumstances rarely occur, with targets talking over the top of each other and other noises interfering with the recording quality. As a rule of thumb, the transcript of a conversation should read like the script for a play including the actions.

Regardless of the nature of the intercept device, be it located in a house or a vehicle, be it the interception of telephone calls or the interception of instant messaging, cognizance must always be taken of what is missing in the communication.

Although, as already stated, listening devices can produce significant amounts of intelligence, like everything in intelligence management, they bring with them their own problems and challenges. For many LEAs they will simply not be an option because of resourcing issues. For others, such work will be carried out on their behalf by a third-party agency. If this is the case, the third party needs continuous comprehensive briefing in relation to the operation and what the requirements are.

10.24 Live Monitoring

When an operation is in place, it may be necessary to continually monitor a listening device with the monitoring officer making the decision as to when to record. This places significant responsibility on such officers, as the

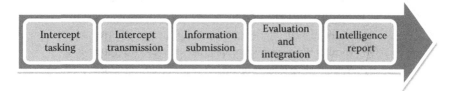

Figure 10.4 Intelligence repositing from interception operations.

chances of missing the start of something of value is considerable. However, recording hours and hours of useless drivel to be transcribed later is also counterproductive. One way of managing both these risks is to record the material as it is being monitored and then have the member immediately certify that there is nothing of worth in it and mark it "Not for transcription." Another risk of live monitoring occurs when what is heard dictates immediate action. In these circumstances, it comes down to the experience of the member involved and the preparations made in advance by the agency to deal with anticipated situations. There will always be the risk that the member mishears or misinterprets what has been said. If all practical steps are in place beforehand, then errors can simply be put down to the cost of doing business. Figure 10.4 illustrates intelligence repositing from interception operations.

Similar types of forms as are present for other types of covert operation will be necessary for interception regardless of the type of interception taking place. A standardized, four-part information submission will always be used to input the information gleaned.

10.25   Covert Internet Investigation

Covert Internet investigations are investigations that are carried out over the Internet. These are generally highly specialized in their nature while being very similar to undercover operations. From a technical perspective, the nature of the investigation brings with it many similar problems and opportunities that arise in obtaining open source information. Although the how to of carrying out such an operation is always limited by the need-to-know principles, there are a number of factors that should be borne in mind:

- All such operations should be properly authorized with regard to intrusion into the privacy of any person.
- Similar records should be kept as those for an undercover operation.
- Means must be put in place to maximize the amount of intelligence that is gained. Such operations are likely to be directed against highly specialized types of criminality, for which the opportunities for

law enforcement to gain better insight into that type of criminality are rare.

- Care should be taken to ensure that intelligence gained from such operations is disseminated to law enforcement partners who are likely to be investigating similar crimes. The assumption should not be made that they already have the intelligence.

10.26   General Observations Regarding Covert Operations

There are a number of general observations that can be made in relation to covert operations and how they can impact intelligence management:

- *Material acquisitions.* It is not unusual for materials of various sorts to be obtained during covert operations. For example, a source may bring a copy of a finance ledger he has obtained that details money laundering, or an undercover officer may bring a sample of a drug that is being marketed. When material is obtained, there is likely to be a potential conflict as to whether or not that material constitutes evidence or if it has been obtained for intelligence purposes. There are no hard and fast rules, and each situation will have to be judged on the individual circumstances. Although legal constraints will obviously be a significant part of the decision-making process, the potential for compromising an asset or an operation must also be factored in.
- *Evidence and intelligence.* Just because material is included in a statement of evidence does not mean it does not have value for intelligence purposes. Statements should be read through and anything of intelligence value extracted from them.
- *Protecting the origin.* The origin of the intelligence should not be included on any intelligence product. Intelligence products should be capable of being linked back to the origin through a unique reference number embedded in each product.
- *No dissemination.* There will be times when the intelligence product from covert assets cannot be disseminated or will be subject to extremely limited dissemination to protect the asset or operation. Such restrictions are justifiable, but an explanation must be given in writing on the initial submission.
- *Review.* Where intelligence from a covert asset has been reposited at a high level in the repository, or is not being disseminated at the time of entry to protect an asset or an operation, it should be reviewed after an identified period to see if it can be further disseminated or the repositing level lowered.

- *Operational names and code names.* A fundamental part of any covert activity is secrecy. There is significant benefit to allotting a name to all covert operations. Operational names mean that an operation can be discussed while lowering the chances that someone accidentally overhears the discussion and understands what the conversation specifically refers to. Furthermore, it means that different aspects of an operation can be brought together under one banner. Operational names should use appropriate language, as they may later be disclosed in court. They should not include anything that references the nature of the investigation and are better if they use words that are unlikely to appear elsewhere. Examples of operational names would include "Erasmus" or "Tenderlake." Operational names should be used only once. When it comes to a human source, it may be more appropriate to allocate a code name, sometimes referred to as a pseudonym. Code names should include a forename and surname, and any reference made to that source is by means of the code-name as opposed to their real name. For example, a person with the real name Michael Brown is referred to by the code name of "Chris Wheeler." All those involved in his management know his real name but never use it, and his real name is not included in any document except his initial registration document.

10.27 Conclusion

Many users of intelligence accord greater credence to reports that are generated from covert operations, and although this is understandable, given the effort that is often involved in obtaining such intelligence, it should always be based on an objective assessment. One of the key benefits of anonymizing all intelligence reports is to reduce the chances of such prejudices creeping in.

Covert operations carry with them many inherent risks and should not be undertaken lightly. Unfortunately, each year people die because such operations are carried out by people who do not have the training to carry them out and are working in systems that are ineffective. And sometimes, people die regardless of the fact that officers have the training and are working in good systems; such is the nature of the business. Huge volumes of high-grade intelligence can be produced from covert operations, and where an agency has the resources and the need to carry out such operations, they should be considered. In many cases, a failure to take such opportunities will reflect poorly on the agency concerned. At all times, the Chief must be in a position to justify the use of such techniques and be able to articulate their benefit.

Having looked at the different ways intelligence may be obtained, we now progress to how that intelligence can be exploited.

References

Brinner, R. (2011) Suspicious activity reporting: Shifting the analytical paradigm. In: Wright, R., Morehouse, B., Peterson, M.B., and Palmieri, L. *Criminal Intelligence for the 21st Century: A Guide for Intelligence Professionals.* Sacramento, CA: Law Enforcement Intelligence Units (LEIU) and Richmond: International Association of Law Enforcement Intelligence Analysts (IALEIA).

Brown, E. (2010) *Snitch: Informants, Cooperators, and the Corruption of Justice.* New York: Public Affairs.

Buckley, J. (2006) *The Human Source Management System: The Use of Psychology in the Management of Human Intelligence Sources.* London: HSM Publishing.

Johnson, L.K. (2007) *Handbook of Intelligence Studies.* London and New York: Routledge.

Natapoff, A. (2009) *Snitching: Criminal Informants and the Erosion of American Justice.* New York: New York University Press.

Noble, G.R. (2009) Diagnosing distortion in source reporting: Lessons for HUMINT reliability from other fields. Dissertation. Department of Intelligence Studies, Mercyhurst College, Erie, PA.

Reid, C. and Buckley, J. (2005) *Human Source Management: A Better Approach to Managing Human Intelligence Sources.* UK: Home Office Police Research Awards. Crown Copyright.

Using Intelligence

11

Intelligence is nothing if not an institutionalized black market in perishable commodities.

John le Carré

11.1   Introduction

If law enforcement is all about "kicking in doors," then the function of intelligence is to tell you which door to kick in, on which day, and if the door is not kicked in on that day, then the intelligence has been wasted! Intelligence is intended for use; however, the term "for use" needs further consideration to ensure that all options are fully exploited. This chapter explores the various ways that intelligence can be used and identifies many problems in using intelligence. The chapter also examines why the "kicking in doors" mind-set exists within law enforcement and shows some of the problems with it.

11.2   Old School Law Enforcement

Old school intelligence exploitation works something akin to this model: "I bust a guy. He wants to cut a deal. He tells me where the next guy is. I bust that guy. He wants to cut a deal. He tells me...." Law enforcement is enforcing the law, offenders are being brought to justice, and the officer is working really hard. Life continues and everyone is happy. Although this may be a somewhat simple explanation of the way "intelligence" was used in crime investigation, there is significant truth in it, and unfortunately, there remain too many who have failed to move forward from this model.

The reality is that using intelligence in this limited way rarely changes the bigger picture. Undoubtedly, offenders are brought to justice and cases are solved, but successes often have limited, if any, long-term effect on crime problems; one street dealer is replaced by the next. There is no progress to making neighborhoods safer for residents, and those operating at the highest levels of criminality are all but immune from the law. Furthermore, this limited method of combatting crime is useless when it comes to terrorism. In addition, whatever intelligence is collected by an officer is used exclusively for the benefit of that officer or at best that officer's unit or section; there is no wider benefit for the agency. If the full worth of intelligence is to be obtained, all the intelligence has to go to one place and be disseminated from that place to the most appropriate consumers. This dissemination must be done in a controlled and timely manner. This function falls to the Intelligence Unit.

11.3   Using Intelligence: The Right to Decide

All available intelligence pertaining to any investigation will be in the possession of the Intelligence Unit. It is the responsibility of the intelligence manager to decide whom that intelligence should be shared with and when it should be shared. Naturally, there will be safeguards built into the intelligence management system to make sure that this function is carried out effectively and to the benefit of the entire agency. When an agency has more than one Intelligence Unit, additional structures will be required to ensure intelligence from the entire agency is considered before dissemination, and the agency will have different mechanisms in place to get intelligence products to identified consumers. Decision-makers must be made aware of the benefits and potential fallout of any course of action they take, so any risks in using the intelligence should accompany the sharing of any intelligence product. It is well within the role of the intelligence manager to suggest different options for the exploitation of the intelligence. Where the intelligence has been gathered through covert activities, it may be prudent to consult those involved in the collection. Not only can this add additional safety measures, but it may also be essential in the further exploitation of the intelligence.

There is natural tension when deciding whether intelligence should be used for either strategic long-term goals or short-term gain; the temptation is often to sacrifice potential future opportunities to obtain immediate results. Investigators often feel pressured to produce short-term results, at the expense of more significant gains, because the significant gains would take time to develop and would only be met in the future. One way of viewing this is to think of how the pressure to win a battle may ultimately compromise the ability to win the war. Unfortunately, this problem continues to plague law enforcement with staff so tied up fighting battles that they lose sight of how to win the war. Nowhere is this more apparent than when narcotics officers are constantly doing street-level drug busts while failing to develop longer-term strategies to deal with the organizers and the supply chains. The reasons why this occurs include the following:

- It often takes little effort to get to a quick result regardless of any risks that may be present. Officers often put their lives on the line for what amounts to a trivial result.

- Law enforcement is often under scrutiny to produce statistical evidence of what they are achieving. The number of prosecutions can superficially make a unit or agency look effective regardless of the lasting effect of such efforts, and few examining such numbers drill down into the details of who is being prosecuted or their level of criminal activity. Ten drug busts or one hundred drug busts—which unit is working harder? It is impossible to say given such limited data, yet it is often such data on which performance is measured. The flaws in the use of such statistical data have not gone unnoticed by all. In a 2011 report on the activities of narcotics units in Mississippi, the following comments were made: "Observed outputs while helpful for measuring the intensity of drug enforcement operations, may not prove at all useful for measuring the broad social outcomes—crime control, reduction of criminal victimization and improvement of our individual collective lives—we desire from law enforcement" (Greene and Allard 2011:31). It is surprising how many fall into the trap of measuring performance through simplistic statistical analysis.
- It is often difficult to quantify the benefits of strategic intelligence, because everyone involved is under pressure to get "results." The temptation is to give something that is quantifiable rather than that which has to be explained in qualitative manner.
- It is often difficult to make senior managers understand the need to hold fire and await a longer-term, hard hitting result, particularly if it involves greater risk. Longer-term benefit often involves greater risk, and a significant number of officers will not take those risks because of concerns for the impact it may have on them personally. In doing so, they disregard the longer-term risk to society as a whole.
- Officers are often motivated by thoughts of personal gain to the detriment of the gains to be had by the agency as a whole. There is no benefit for them working toward a goal where their efforts will not be recognized.

If law enforcement is to be effective in thwarting the activities of criminal organizations, they must attack that organization at all levels and in all ways and not just individuals within that organization. This means operations and investigations must be directed against the organization at both strategic and tactical levels. Learning from ancient Greek history and Hercules' famous battle with the many-headed Hydra of Lerna, when one head was cut off, Hydra merely grew two more, thus the efforts that were made were all in vain. How often does this happen in law enforcement with street-level dealers being removed only to be replaced the same evening by another dealer? Law enforcement must tackle organized crime in such a way as to reduce the chances of the criminal gang merely replacing the foot soldiers time and time again. They need to target all levels of organization and the structure of the organization as a functioning system.

Moving on from the debate about what purpose intelligence should be used for, there are many factors that the Intelligence Unit must be able to deal with when intelligence is to be used:

- Information that may be actionable must move quickly through the system, and the Intelligence Unit must be able to cope with the rapid flow of information to be used as intelligence. The Intelligence Unit must have a robust process where procedures are adhered to, but procedures must also be flexible to meet situations that require expedient action. Where procedures are circumvented explanation as to why will always be expected and must be justifiable.
- Where the Intelligence Unit identifies actionable intelligence, the agency needs the capacity to deploy resources rapidly, if that intelligence requires immediate action. There is little point in obtaining good intelligence if there is no one available to exploit it.
- Where intelligence is to be disseminated and there are risks in exploiting that intelligence, those receiving that intelligence must be made aware of the risks so that they can make an informed decision.
- The financial cost of exploiting intelligence should always be considered. Failure to do so can result in wasting limited resources for little gain.

A common problem is middle managers who bypass the intelligence management system and take action based on the information that has not been properly processed. Because of their position of power, they can direct subordinates to take actions without informing them of the basis for that action. This has the potential to harm any investigation and the agency as a whole. Where this occurs, action needs to be taken toward those officers, as they have the potential to cause serious harm and de facto make the entire intelligence management system all but redundant.

11.4   Dealing with Senior Management

Quoting the author John le Carré again, "a desk is a dangerous place from which to view the world," we highlight one of the difficulties in dealing with management that does not understand intelligence. This quote captures what many intelligence professionals encounter on a regular basis when dealing with law enforcement managers: the perception of an inability to grasp what is really happening out on the streets. This perception creates circumstances where poor decisions are made, but before we continue to address how a lack of awareness of prevailing circumstances can lead to poor decisions, it is important to discuss whether or not this is a reality. There is some truth in the perception that managers, particularly the more senior managers, have become somewhat distant from reality. Their jobs tend to focus more on strategic longer-term decision-making, leaving them with not as much time for dealing with the minutiae. Undoubtedly, one can lose some idea of what is really happening. However, there comes a time when minutiae mean everything and the senior manager must listen to those who have the knowledge. That said, it is down to those with the knowledge to effectively communicate what the manager needs to know.

If a manager will not accept what their staff are telling him, there is every chance that something will go wrong. Such decisions are borne out of arrogance and lead to circumstances where decisions are made on first impressions, partial views, and incomplete information. Of course, when it goes wrong, somebody will have to be held accountable. This is one of the reasons why effective records are so important.

Perhaps the scarcest resource in an agency is a senior decision-maker's attention span, and the little bit available can easily be lost. Briefings for senior managers should be succinct. Where there is a need to drill into detail, the reasons for doing so should first be explained to the manager.

An awareness of the psychology relating to decision-making is beneficial. There is a very large body of literature on both the physical and psychological effects on judgment and decision-making under stress that is relevant to this field. Knowledge of this helps to avoid errors. Intelligence rarely gets to the decision-maker in a way that presents a complete and unambiguous picture of what is occurring. Deciding the best way to exploit intelligence is often fraught with difficulties and includes the following:

- Balancing the benefit of taking executive action against this, the fact that it may lead to the possible compromise of the origin of the intelligence.
- Balancing short-term gain against long-term potential gain. With any piece of intelligence, there are likely to be differences of opinion as to how to exploit the intelligence. The professional intelligence officer will be able to identify and weigh the different options, and these options often need to be explained to the decision-maker, as the decision-maker may not have an understanding of the full ramifications of any action. Such a decision needs to be taken as a result of logical thought and based on the professional consideration of all potential options and their outcomes. Far too often, decisions are based on "This will make me look good now" or "This will take the heat of us now."
- Accepting of short-term pain for long-term gain. It takes strong, ethical leadership to make difficult decisions in regard to not reacting too

soon or in the wrong way, purely because things are not the way one would desire them to be. A Chief may be getting significant public criticism from the press about inaction about low-level drug dealing, whereas at the same time, she is aware that her staff have penetrated the main drug supplier's gang, and a major bust is being developed. Intelligence management is not for the faint of heart; too often, potentially great operations are ruined because of a poor decision made by someone who does not have the resilience to make the right decision.

- Taking risks. Rewards are the result of successful risk-taking. Risk management is about managing risks, not avoiding them. Exploiting intelligence will often involve significant risk. As already mentioned the "risk averse" Chief, who won't let covert operations take place in his area because of the risks involved, exposes his and other communities to much greater risk while fooling only himself into thinking he is being effective.
- Accepting that things will go wrong. Unless we are prepared to accept failure, the tendency will always be to not take action, and if we take action without thought of failure, then we will not be prepared when the failure occurs. In exploiting intelligence, we should always ask the questions "How could this go wrong?" and "What am I going to do if it goes wrong?"

George (1980) offers some techniques that can be adapted to intelligence management–related decisions.

- *Satisficing.* This option was developed by Herbert Simon (1957) and involves selecting the first option that appears to be "good enough" to deal with the situation, as opposed to examining all the potential options available and then deciding which one of them is the best. In short, it is not about looking for the perfect solution; it is about finding one that ticks all of the important boxes. Klein (2001) identified this as a technique often used by experts in deciding what course of action to follow. Klein found that the technique of satisficing was extremely useful under time-limited circumstances. Satisficing works well in covert operations, when what is happening is fluid and continually evolving.
- *Incrementalism.* This is a method of working through a situation by making many small incremental changes as one progresses instead of one large leap. Taking incremental steps allows the decision-maker to see how the situation is evolving as each step is taken. This can be very useful when acting against an organized crime grouping where there is likely to be prolonged engagement. Rather than feeling forced into an all-or-nothing option, the decision-maker directs that

a series of progressive but small steps be taken and the subsequent developments be monitored.

- *Consensus.* The consensus approach involves opting for the decision with which the greatest amount of agreement is likely from those involved. Although undoubtedly there are significant benefits to this method, one always has to be careful that the agreement stems from it being the right decision and not just agreement with the boss.
- *Comparative reasoning.* This technique compares the current situation with previous situations, and a decision is made to follow the path that is less likely to commit the same mistake as has happened before or the solution that offers a similar strategy that led to a previous success. There is a logic to this method, and in many circumstances, it will prove beneficial. However, it assumes that the decision-maker will have the skill and the prior knowledge to relate the current situation to previous ones.

A common error that is often made is in disclosing to elected officials activities within law enforcement that should be kept secret. Although it may be necessary to keep elected officials informed, there is a line that should not be crossed, particularly when it comes to covert methodology or the identities of people assisting law enforcement. As a general rule, intelligence-related matters should not be discussed outside law enforcement. What may be presented as seeking accountability is often little more than idle curiosity.

11.5 Protecting the Origin of Information

A key consideration in actioning any intelligence is the protection of the origin of that intelligence. Regardless of how tenuous a link there may be, there is always a link between where the information came from and the action that has been taken. The amount of effort that has to be expended to disguise this link will be dependent on the sensitivity of the origin and the sophistication of the resources being directed to find it. Protecting the origin of the material is often a legal obligation and should be considered as the most professional approach. An effective intelligence management system will go a long way to protecting where intelligence originated and the methods used to get it.

One way of disguising the origin of information is the use of "red herrings." A red herring is a clue that is intended to be misleading or distracting. For example, where a law enforcement agency (LEA) has specific intelligence about the location of a large quantity of drugs, but LEA the origin of that intelligence needs to be protected, the agency may carry out many other searches at the same time to "muddy the waters" for the criminals. Such searches must always meet the legal requirements, in their own right.

The red herring is merely the coordination of the searches, and this may be sufficient to create the confusion for the criminal.

Consideration must also be given to protecting the origin of the intelligence during any subsequent interviews with suspects. Generally speaking, the more people who know where the intelligence came from, the greater chance there is that it will come out. It is very easy for an interviewer, in the heat of a moment, to let something slip that compromises the origin or the method.

11.6 Community Impact

Keeping the community on the side of law enforcement is extremely important. There is little point in a Chief expending huge amount of resources to have it all come crashing down because of a poorly executed operation. Although sometimes these things happen, whatever can be done to avoid a negative community reaction should be done. Meeting community expectations is not made any easier by the fact that most LEAs serve more than one community and what may be totally acceptable to one community may be met with hostility and suspicion by another. When major intelligence-based operations are planned and time permits, it is useful to carry out a community impact assessment before taking action and identify strategies to mitigate any potential harm being done to community relationships. An effective public relations strategy and contacts with local community leaders are two possible measures that can be taken to avoid negative effect on the relationship with the community. Those working in intelligence should consider the potential fallout from their operations, as failure to do so may leave them bearing the brunt of the blame and being scapegoated if community relationships deteriorate following an operation. In addition, the compounded effect of many similar operations directed against one community may have the same detrimental effect on relationships as one major one. Community concerns should not be allowed to dictate what action law enforcement takes, merely the way in which actions are carried out.

11.7 Briefings

Agency members need to know who the bad guys are and where they are. An easily accomplished and effective method of combatting crime is to point resources in the right direction and tell them when to be there. Generally speaking, the assumption should be made that members will not make much of an effort to get themselves up to speed on what is happening, so intelligence officers must work hard to find the most effective ways of briefing out intelligence. Briefings should be interesting and creative with details being kept to a limited amount so that the recipient is likely to remember them. Members should be held accountable by supervisors if they do not know details that have been shared through intelligence briefings. Members can be briefed in many ways including the following:

- *Display boards.* Some would argue that display boards are a thing of the past, but this belief is easily contradicted by the continuing presence of boards advertising various products. The commercial sector would not use the method if it was not effective. There should be an intelligence display board where officers are paraded, before duty and in the reception area of the Intelligence Unit's office.
- *Computerized briefing pages.* Computerized briefing is one of the most effective ways of sharing intelligence. Computerized briefings are available 24/7, which means that those working unusual shift patterns always have access, regardless of the hour. Computerized briefing limits the access as the member has to log on to read the briefing. It allows a supervisor to see which members of staff have or have not read the briefing. Computers allow for extremely effective methods of presenting material and can include photographs and video. Investing in publishing software and training staff to use it professionalizes the creation of briefing documents and increases the likelihood they will be read and effectively convey the message.
- *Verbal briefings.* Delivery of regular verbal briefings to frontline staff is a fundamental part of the role of an intelligence officer. Briefing staff facilitates questioning and builds relationships with frontline members. Generally speaking, a written record should be kept of the date and time of delivery and include a summary of the key points covered. Such briefings can be carried out as a planned and structured exercise, such as during a training session or on an informal basis just before officers going out on patrol. Verbal briefings should always be tailored to the audience.

There should be a written record of any briefing given by intelligence staff, as this shows accountability and productivity.

11.8   Intelligence for Officer Safety

The term "officer safety" is widely used to refer to the safety of the members of an agency while they are performing their role. Unfortunately for some members, the nature of their role means that the threat to their safety exists both at work and when they are not at work. The term "officer safety" undoubtedly carries with it an emotional element* and goes further than merely seeking to address legislative requirements around workplace safety. Intelligence can make a significant contribution to officer safety:

- It identifies threats made against members in general and against specific members.
- It identifies areas where members are more likely to be in danger.
- It can enable individuals with a history of violence to be "flagged" in the intelligence repository so that officers engaging them can be warned in real time.
- It identifies vehicles associated with crime. These too can be flagged, so that an officer knows what he may encounter before approaching the vehicle.
- It identifies patterns and contributing factors that have previously impacted officer safety. These can then be shared in a "lessons learned" approach. In Northern Ireland, many police officers were killed and injured because the lessons of previous attacks were not taken onboard; officers repeatedly put themselves in danger because they didn't know or had forgotten the lessons of other attacks. People forget! Continuous reinforcement by supervisors, operational training, and intelligence staff is needed to keep such things fresh in the mind.
- It identifies the capabilities of criminals and their intentions with regard to future encounters with law enforcement.

Intelligence relating to officer safety must always be put into a format that enables sharing with the frontline. Failure to do so puts officers in danger. In addition, it is detrimental to internal agency relationships, creating mistrust between frontline officers and those they perceive as having the intelligence. Once such mistrust starts, it has the potential to rapidly take hold and escalate.

11.9 Intelligence for Executive Action

In law enforcement, there will be many times when intelligence can be used as a basis for executive action. Executive action may take place following a prolonged covert operation or because there is a piece of actionable intelligence available. Typical actions will include search and seizure operations

---

* Law enforcement officers knowingly put themselves in danger but have a right to be annoyed if all that could be done to protect them is not being done.

and the arrest of suspects. There are many standard features to bear in mind when taking executive action.

First, the intelligence should have been processed through the intelligence management system before any action is taken. Although there may be occasions when there needs to be an immediate response, these will be far from the norm, and in such cases, intelligence records should be updated as soon as practically possible.

Second, in most instances, the direct outcome of executive action will be a court case, and all parts of the action will feature as part of a prosecution or the defense case. As such, actions must be carried out in the knowledge that what was done will be subjected to judicial examination.

Third, many such operations will be standard in their nature and include limited risk. However, where there are additional risks, these risks should be documented before action is taken, and measures should be put in place to mitigate them. Those taking the action should be thoroughly briefed, particularly where there is the potential for officer safety issues or where the lives of citizens may be put at risk. This may well include briefing those taking part in the executive action with the content of additional intelligence reporting; a simple example of this is where officers are intending to carry out a search of a house, where the occupant is known to have firearms, and especially, if there is intelligence that he is likely to use them. Failure to brief such intelligence to those taking executive action will definitely lean toward negligence, unless there are really unusual circumstances.

Fourth, if an agency's collection processes are working well, there is likely to be more intelligence, on which one could take executive action, than the agency has resources to take such action. It will then fall to those in a position of power to decide which actions are to be taken and which are not. Priority should always be given to those actions that support the agency's intelligence priorities. There should be a mechanism whereby senior management can identify when and how actionable intelligence has been acted on and the result of that action. The agency must also be able to see clearly where action could have been taken but was not. Effective statistical analysis of this material can be of significant benefit in identifying where and how resources are being used effectively or wasted.

Taking executive action is often not without risk, and times will occur when a Chief may not want any covert action, let alone a high-profile intervention taking place in their area. Concerns over the risk of the failure of the operation and the potential fallout for the Chief lead to circumstances where they refuse to let an operation take place within their area. This "not in my area" risk averse approach means that, in many cases, the opportunity to apprehend the criminals is lost and they continue carrying out their activities to the detriment of citizens in that area and elsewhere. Although it can be argued that such a decision is the prerogative of the Chief, in some circumstances, it is an indictment on their suitability for the position they hold. Although they may find many ways to justify their decision, much of it may simply come down to them not wanting a failure to be embarrassing or politically costly. This course of action ignores the existence of the failure to apprehend criminals, but one they can easily brush aside, as it is not a "public" failure.

11.10 Covert Response: Disruption

Covert response refers to action carried out by law enforcement to thwart criminal activity, for which any third party is unaware that law enforcement action has taken place. Covert response is an integral part of intelligence management. There is a huge amount of pressure to protect the methods and origins of information collection. Excessive overt action will inevitably compromise the method being used to collect information, not only jeopardizing any future information but also jeopardizing sensitive techniques and potentially compromising lives. Although the issue of protecting the origin of information and collection methods has been explored earlier, understanding that it may be necessary to respond to intelligence covertly is necessary for all involved. An example of a covert response to intelligence is as follows:

> There is intelligence to say that a drug deal will take place at Lakeshore Parking Lot at 8 p.m. tonight. For whatever reason, law enforcement cannot take executive action but at the same time does not want the deal to take place. To abort the deal, the covert response is to have two police officers in the parking lot at 7:45 PM for 30 minutes in uniform eating donuts and drinking coffee. To the criminal, it looks normal— "lazy, fat cops,"—but out of necessity, the criminal cancels the deal. Objective achieved (and the cops get free coffee and donuts!).

Although this is a very simplistic example, it gives an idea of what is intended by covert response and the sort of thing that can be done. Anything that disrupts criminal activity is a success for law enforcement. Disruption is a very effective way for an agency to combat crime while waiting for the preferred opportunity to take executive action.

11.11 Intelligence to Inform the Public

Although not often considered as a use for intelligence, it can be used to inform the wider public of the reality of events that may be causing them concern. For example, the threat of terrorism has been allowed to loom large in the minds of citizens since 9/11 and given the fact that the whole purpose of terrorism is to terrorize, it can be argued that law enforcement is limited in its response to curbing such fears. Using intelligence, one can give the public a much clearer understanding of what the truth is about terrorism, without having them live their lives in unnecessary fear. Furthermore, all too often, law enforcement allows the "uninformed" to inform citizens as to the nature of the people engaged in terrorism or organized crime. Although painted as "evil" by the media, an objective analysis of the intelligence will often show that this picture is incorrect. The public need to be informed of the reality so that the help they can provide is not compromised because it has been based on hyperbole and prejudice. As the late Italian Magistrate Giovanni Falcone* remarked,

> The men of honor are neither devils nor schizophrenic. They would not kill their mother or father for a few grams of heroin. They are men like us. The tendency in the western world, and particularly in Europe, is to exorcize evil by projecting it onto ethnic groups and forms of behavior which seem different from our own. But if we want to fight the Mafia effectively, we must not transform it into a monster or think of it as an octopus or a cancer. We must recognize that it resembles ourselves.

Similar problems are often encountered in local law enforcement when local news media hype up a particular type of crime, such as attacks on elderly homeowners. By using the analyst to create a problem profile, the Chief can provide the community with an informed account of the extent of the problem, together with possible crime prevention strategies that have been identified from intelligence. The more accurately informed the public are, the greater help they can be in preventing crime.

11.12 Sharing with Non-Law Enforcement Partners

As often been identified by law enforcement and others, policing is not the sole responsibility of the police. In recent years, far greater interest has been shown in joint approaches to deal with social/criminal problems within society. Involvement with such agencies such as social workers and local legislatures may appear obvious, but the contribution that can be made by professionals such as town planners in designing out crime should not be overlooked. Although involvement of these professional bodies and other agencies from the voluntary sector is now often adopted into national or

---

* Giovanni Falcone was murdered by the Italian mafia on May 23, 1992, in Sicily. He had been instrumental in bringing hundreds of mafia members to justice.

regional legislation,* there is often a failure to gather the correct type of intelligence necessary to assist these bodies in solving the problems. This failure is most often because of poor communication between senior management and those in a position to gather such intelligence. Solving this problem requires many steps to be in place:

1. A level of trust has to be present between the LEA and its other partners. This does not mean that the agency will necessarily share sensitive or tactical intelligence with them. What it does mean is that each party must accept the other's professionalism and that material exchanged will be of a truthful basis and not used to manipulate the situation or to press home either party's agenda.

2. There has to be a clearly documented list of what each party wants to know. For example, a town planner may want to know if building housing developments with many cul-de-sacs/no through roads helps reduce crime. They must articulate this clearly and pass it to law enforcement. Community police officers can provide information from their experience, but what also can be done is that human source handlers can ask their sources about the criminal perspective on this. Each viewpoint can be aggregated and analyzed with the analyst providing a comprehensive law enforcement viewpoint in report format, which is then provided to the planners. This makes the assumption that an effective mechanism to convey the intelligence requirement out to the relevant intelligence collectors exists within the agency. The term "relevant" is important. For example, only handlers managing human sources who are likely to be able to provide such information should be tasked. Not all handlers should be tasked, as there is a limit to what they and their sources should be tasked toward. Spurious tasking is in the longer term unproductive.

3. Law enforcement partners must have at least a very basic understanding of the limitations on intelligence products. They must understand that intelligence assessments are not the same as factual reports. Furthermore, any such intelligence assessments shared with partners must bear a caveat that clearly indicates the level of accuracy law enforcement attribute to that intelligence product. This can be given in lay terms such as "This assessment is based on what we would regard as very reliable information" or "This assessment is based on what we would regard as low level reporting." Using such terminology makes it significantly easier for the

---

* For an example of mandatory partnerships between local government and law enforcement, see the United Kingdom's Crime and Disorder Act 1998. http://www.legislation.gov.uk/ukpga/1998/37/contents.

layperson to understand. However, the agency must be in a position to correlate this type of wording directly with its internal assessment methodology.

11.13   Sharing with the Private Sector

Sharing intelligence with the private sector is essential for businesses to be able to put in place adequate crime prevention strategies. How such intelligence is shared will be dependent on the nature of the intelligence and what the intentions are in sharing it. Potential ways to share intelligence include the following:

- General advice given to the business by a crime prevention officer—the officer having been briefed on the intelligence and asked to devise a strategy to combat the threat. In advising the business, the officer makes little if any reference to "intelligence," as doing so may just open a can of worms and lead to a million questions. The crime prevention officer can use wordings such as "We are concerned about a potential rise in this type of crime and would suggest…."
- A warning can be passed by word of mouth to a trusted contact within the business or to a person in power in that business: for example, the chief executive officer or the head of security. There should always be a written law enforcement record of what was said and to whom.
- A formal written warning detailing the threat can be passed to the company. Although this may indicate that the warning is based on intelligence, the origin of that intelligence will not be disclosed, nor is there a need to disclose the exact wording of the intelligence. Law enforcement needs to include sufficient detail to allow the business to take steps to mitigate the threat but no more.

There are three main purposes in sharing intelligence with the private sector:

1. To warn of the threat so that the business can decide their options.
2. To enable the business to make the necessary changes to their security that may deter an attack. Such changes are useful, but they are often maintained only for the length of time in which the threat is on their minds.
3. Where intelligence may fail to prevent an attack, it can provide enough prior warning as to limit the impact of an attack.

In sharing intelligence with the business sector, the member involved should also seek to gain additional information that can point toward a clearer picture of what may or may not occur. Those in business will often be able to add detail or suggest other measures that can be taken to mitigate the risk. Furthermore, they may be able to suggest others who may be affected by the threat, as they have knowledge of the industry. Understandably, law enforcement cannot be expected to recognize every potential victim for some specialized areas of criminality. A simple example of this in relation to the theft of high-value metals—one might realize that electrical companies are an obvious victim for copper theft but fail to recognize the threat to railway companies.

In disseminating any intelligence to the private sector, law enforcement must be wary of providing any competitive advantage to that business or of causing disadvantage to any other business. Although it may not be obvious at first glance, such things can occur and law enforcement needs to be wary in this respect.

Another potential problem that occurs is sharing intelligence with a company that one assumes to be a national company. In the nature of the current business world, many companies are multinational, choosing to operate under many different facades according to their business needs. For example, a U.K. agency may share intelligence with what they believe to be a U.K. company, when in effect it is owned by a parent company based in another country. Although the nature of law enforcement intelligence should mean that the potential for harm to be caused should rarely present itself, it is just one more factor to be considered.

11.14 Intelligence to Develop Crime Prevention Strategies

Continuing the theme of working to prevent crime, intelligence should be used to help develop crime prevention strategies. This approach, while consistent with problem-oriented policing, often fails to recognize its full potential because of a disconnect between those having access to the intelligence and those responsible for developing the strategies. The problem is exacerbated by the inability of those developing crime prevention strategies to "task" intelligence collection to support their role. Furthermore, those involved in collection have limited understanding of crime prevention methods, and those involved in crime prevention have limited knowledge of the breadth of intelligence that can often be obtained. Common uses that intelligence can be put to developing crime prevention strategies include the following:

- Knowledge of the causes of problems can be used to assist in crime prevention through environmental design.

- Knowledge of terrorist capabilities can be used to develop appropriate hostile vehicle mitigation for buildings that are likely to be targets of vehicle-borne bombs.
- Knowledge of the modus operandi of criminals can assist in changing the behavior of potential victims.

11.15 Intelligence to Seize Assets

Many countries have enacted legislation to deal with the proceeds of crime. Proving that a criminal has obtained his assets from can be extremely difficult if the threshold to be met is the standard criminal one of "beyond all reasonable doubt." Meeting this all-but-impossible threshold left the assets of too many criminals untouchable, even when the criminal was convicted of other offenses. To combat the problem, countries lowered the threshold of proof to the same level as has to be met in civil proceedings and made it possible for intelligence to be used in the proceedings.

Using intelligence in court proceedings carries with it many problems, not least of which is the need to protect the origin of the material and/or the method used in its collection. As such, the agency needs to have in place rigorous processes to vet all intelligence that is to be used in proceedings to ensure that a compromise will not occur. Having said that, there is a huge amount of intelligence that can be collected to support such actions and these include the following:

- Details of all assets owned by the person. Items that are often missed are things like high-value jewelery, antiques, art, and vehicles.
- The locations of all properties owned by the person, their family members, or business associates. This should include properties owned outside the jurisdiction.
- Details of any bank or financial institution used by the person, including any accountant.
- Details of how they manage their finances: whether they keep it hidden in cash and or use ledgers or computers to keep records.
- Lifestyle-related intelligence can go to show an abundance of cash. Activities such as lavish holidays, parties, or excessive gambling all show the flow of money.
- Negative intelligence—that is, the intelligence that will refute claims made that the money has been obtained legitimately.

As a side note, the money raised in such investigations should be used to fund further investigations and to increase the agency's intelligence-gathering capacity and not allocated to fill the gaps in some unrelated deficit in the agency's budget. The intention of allocating such money to an agency in this way is to combat crime, not to address poor accounting.

11.16   Intelligence to Support Public Events

Intelligence provided to commanders both before and during public events can be extremely useful. A representative of the Intelligence Unit should attend planning meetings for large public events or any protest where there is likely to be a public order problem. An awareness of what is happening can ensure Intelligence Unit staff are less likely to overlook something that would be of interest to the commander. Intelligence providing forewarning of what may occur at the event will help guide commanders with regard to resourcing levels, thus saving valuable resources. During events, intelligence staff should be readily available to process information that is coming from the event and link it to intelligence that is already in the system. Commanders should be aware that intelligence staff will also have access to intelligence that they cannot reveal, but that which may have an impact on what is happening on the ground. In such circumstances, it is the role of the intelligence manager to brief the commander with the details that can be disclosed.

11.17   Counterintelligence

One use of intelligence is to protect the law enforcement intelligence gathering from attacks from the other side. How organized an adversary is will dictate how pressing the existing need is for law enforcement to have a counterintelligence capability. Generally speaking, the more organized and more resilient a criminal grouping is, the more sophisticated their tactics will be to thwart law enforcement intelligence gathering. Many groups have the capability to at least attempt to penetrate law enforcement with the intention of disrupting enforcement activities. Although there is an obvious threat from terrorist groups and organized crime, law enforcement assets have been compromised in the past by relatively disorganized groupings, exploiting vulnerability in an agency's security. One of the most serious threats posed to law enforcement from this type of activity is the linking of anarchist groups and those involved in computer hacking. Attacks on law enforcement software have resulted in the compromise of intelligence assets. Although it is acknowledged that those perpetrating such events are acting criminally, the question has to be raised as to who was responsible for creating the gap in the agency's security that allowed it to happen. In all probability, there will be many people who were responsible for placing sensitive material on a computer system that was all too easily attacked. Included in such a list are likely to be the officer in charge of intelligence, the head of information technology, and the person who held the purse strings, if they refused to provide the money necessary to equip the agency with software that was of a sufficiently high-security specification.

An agency should continually gather intelligence that identifies how criminals are targeting the agency. This intelligence should be subject to regular analysis to identify the nature and level of any threat posed to the agency or to members of that agency.

One of the biggest threats currently posed to law enforcement is the potential for hacking into computerized systems. This has resulted in many compromises of sensitive material including officers' personal details, intelligence, and, of the most concern, the origins of intelligence, including the true identities of citizens who provided information. There is little that can be said that can excuse those within the agency who create a situation where these breaches are so easily perpetrated, especially when software systems specifically designed to mitigate such risks are readily available—not using such software is negligence.

11.18   Intelligence and Terrorism

One of the problems in using intelligence relating to terrorism is that it is often relatively short on specifics but full of generalities. In using such intelligence, it is hard if not impossible to find the balance. Take, for example, a piece of intelligence that comes to law enforcement from a very reliable origin and states, "Terrorists intend to bomb a New York night club the forthcoming weekend." Law enforcement has many options:

- Warn the public. Nobody goes out, which means that many businesses, and not just nightclubs, are financially damaged.
- Warn all nightclub owners; but what defines a "nightclub"?
- Saturate New York with police in the hope of deterring the attack. How much will this cost?
- Do nothing. Is this an acceptable option?

Regardless of the course of action, the weekend passes without an attack; so what should law enforcement do the following weekend? Maybe the attack was postponed for whatever reason! And the weekend after? Such is the nature of intelligence relating to terrorism and the problems dealing with it. However, the problem shown here is one of management, not intelligence. Managers must make decisions based on what they have available at that time. It is their decision and provided it is done in an objective, accountable way, having consulted appropriate experts and considered all the options, it is a defendable decision.

Sometimes it is difficult to justify throwing resources at counterterrorism. It must be borne in mind that terrorism is about terrorizing; casualties are only an instrument in that game. The longer the terrorist group can force the community to change its behavior, the more effective it is being. Spending money on preventative measures may be money wasted, unless it is soundly based on "effective" risk management—the key word here being "effective." For example, millions of pounds were spent on putting hostile vehicle mitigation along Whitehall Street in London. Many of these buildings may be at risk because they are used by military and government, but the number of deaths that would result from such an attack is minimal. Compare this investment with the expenditure on Trafalgar Square that is situated at one end of Whitehall and has thousands of people in it each day and there is no mitigation of any worth. Situations like this occur because of the misuse of intelligence and a poor understanding of risk management and led to a terrorist success, in that the terrorists have wasted taxpayers' money on something that was not necessary. The government has limited money to spend, and it must be spent effectively. Huge amounts of money are wasted on counterterrorism measures. The questions that need to be asked in deciding the risk are "If I was a terrorist, where could I attack to cause the most harm?" and "How would I do it?" In answering such questions, there may well be intelligence to say that terrorists may like to attack a certain type of target, but that doesn't mean they intend to attack the target. Intelligence is often be used to distort a risk assessment by those who do not understand risk management. This can lead to limited resources being deployed in the wrong place. Furthermore, money wasted on counterterrorism is a victory for terrorists. Where money is spent, it should be based on a rational objective decision based on properly evaluated risks, and not driven by the rhetoric of politicians, the media, or product suppliers. Where there is general intelligence to indicate that a particular type of building or person is likely to be attacked by terrorists, law enforcement should visit all similar potential targets in their area of responsibility, explain the nature of the threat, and provide advice on preventative measures. Such targets will vary according to the nature of the terrorist campaign being waged, but common targets include crowded places, critical national infrastructure, airports, and iconic buildings/tourist attractions.

11.19   Intelligence for National Security

When it comes to national security, the line between what is the remit of law enforcement intelligence gathering and what is the responsibility of intelligence agencies is often vague. In intelligence gathering, there are many areas that law enforcement may encounter, that will potentially have implications for national security. Some of these include the following:

- Anarchist groups engaged in creating public order situations.
- Computer crime, where some hackers are inclined to view it as a sport to see how much damage they can do to others through cyber attacks.
- Animal rights groups and other similar pressure groups whose activities move from legitimate protest to adopt a more subversive or criminal approach.
- Espionage activities. In many countries, it is only law enforcement that can undertake a criminal investigation, even if the activities pertain to national security.

In all these situations, there must be structures in place to develop working relationships with the relevant intelligence agency. In joint investigations or operations, there should be written agreements as to the responsibilities of each party involved. If these do not exist, there is every chance that there will be some sort of a conflict that will damage the task at hand.

11.20   Intelligence to Make Legal Change

Legislation needs to continually evolve if it is to meet the various threats posed to society. Convincing the lawmakers (and the lawyers in their employ) of the need for change can be an arduous process. Quite rightly, they will want evidence as to the need to create a new law or to change an existing one. Intelligence can be used to provide such evidence. Where law enforcement intends to petition for a change in legislation, as much high-quality intelligence should be gathered to support the request. The intelligence needs to stem from reliable origins and be corroborated by other intelligence. It also needs to be well presented in a format so that any layperson can grasp both its meaning and its significance.

11.21   Paralysis by Analysis

Robert Jordan, in *Wheel of Time*, his epic novel of another world, provides advice that is equally applicable to those using intelligence in this world:

Never make a plan without knowing as much as you can of the enemy.
Never be afraid to change your plans when you receive new information.
Never believe you know everything.
Never wait to know everything.
The man who waited to know everything was still in his tent when the enemy burned it over his head.

There can be a tendency to overanalyze problems to a stage where there is always an excuse not to take action. This comes about because those involved want the "best" result or they are waiting for the "perfect" time to strike. Unfortunately, best and perfect may never realistically be on the cards, and law enforcement ends up waiting until they are forced by circumstances to act and then it is often because of unforeseen circumstances. Rather than being proactive in its approach, the agency is forced again into a reactive stance. Intelligence is rarely perfect or complete, and there comes a time in every investigation when action should be taken. If the work has been done, a good enough result will follow.

11.22   Creativity

An element of creativity, when it comes to using intelligence, can add considerable benefit in both the short term and the long term. For example, the U.S. government had intelligence as to where Osama bin Laden was living. Many decisions would have been taken as to how best to exploit this intelligence and the various options that were available together with the associated risks. Where the creativity in planning shows through is with regard to the plan, should the action result in bin Laden's death. The fact that his remains were "buried at sea" shows that the planners came up with a solution that addressed concerns about his grave becoming a shrine, yet still showed respect toward the physical remains. The nature of the burial avoided alienating many who could have been offended by disputes over what to do with the remains. There will be many law enforcement operations where community sensitivities need to be considered. Ofttimes, empathy followed by some creative thinking will produce a better way of exploiting the intelligence when it comes to dealing with community concerns. Creativity also has a role to play when it comes to adding value to the exploitation. For example, many different searches directed against different but linked targets can increase the impact it has on the groups from a psychological perspective and has the added benefit of protecting the origin of the intelligence being exploited. A series of sequential arrests will have a similar effect. Too often, we lose opportunities because we are constrained by our previous experiences and lack of imagination. In operational planning, it is a good technique to "take five for creativity," where 5 minutes is set aside for those present to come up with creative ideas on how to improve the plan.

11.23   Getting It Wrong

The very nature of intelligence means that sometimes we are going to get it wrong and occasionally very wrong! Suck it up princess; it is just the way it goes. If you can't deal with that, then you are in the wrong business.

These may be harsh words, but too many have unrealistic expectations around what intelligence can and cannot achieve. It is not an exact science; in fact much of it is best guess. Using intelligence to piece together what happened in the past is difficult, but using it to see the future all but impossible. If we could see the future with accuracy, we would be picking the lottery numbers and buying a big house in the sun!

Fortunately, most of the time, the resulting harm is minimal, but sometimes it can have fatal consequences. Some of the common ways in which intelligence-related failures occur are the following:

- The original information was wrong. Information is often incomplete and sometimes just wrong.
- The information is not submitted properly because of officer failure or system failure.
- The information-to-intelligence process fails. The information is graded incorrectly, or an analyst misinterprets or overlooks a relevant part.
- The dissemination process fails. The people who needed it didn't get it in time.
- Poor decisions are made based on the intelligence.
- The tactical exploitation of the intelligence fails. For example, surveillance loses the target of the operation.

Cooper (2005) discusses the fact that just because a decision made using intelligence turns out to be wrong does not automatically mean that the process followed in reaching that decision was flawed. "We're not very good at evaluating the quality of intelligence analysis independent of the outcome. We're outcome oriented, rather than process oriented." When a failure results, it is important to consider the nature of the decision separately from the intelligence on which that was based. The fact that intelligence was correct does not mean that decisions made based on it will have been the right ones. Furthermore, if the intelligence is incorrect, it does not necessarily mean that the methods used to collect and process it were incorrect. For example, a human source may have been told one thing that was subsequently submitted, processed, and action put in place. Unbeknownst to all involved, the bad guys changed their intentions at the last minute, and the actions taken by law enforcement became worthless. We can show this further with a real-life example. A human source is told a bomb will be planted at target A. Law enforcement take all possible measures to protect target A. At the last minute, the terrorists change their mind and bomb target B, for which there was no related intelligence. A superficial and prejudiced view would be that law enforcement had intelligence and should have prevented this attack.

Betts (1978) compares and contrasts failure and success in intelligence:

"intelligence failures are not only inevitable, they are natural. And failures are trumpeted while successes often are publicly unknown. Analysts have to accept this as the cost of doing business."

Failures should not be swept under the carpet; instead, they should be subjected to an audit to accurately identify the cause of the failure. Failures are a learning opportunity. Arguably, the most important factor for those involved is that they should not be internalized. Punishing oneself for mistakes is destructive. We all make errors, learn from them, but leave them in the office; your family does not need this sort of baggage brought home.

11.24 An Evolving Picture

Intelligence does not stand still and neither do the targets of an investigation. The circumstances on the ground may change, and what the intelligence tells us about those circumstances may also change. Law enforcement must be willing to change to meet new circumstances. Being held captive by a plan that was created based on what was happening is a sure way to be caught out by the new conditions. One of the greatest frustrations for decision-makers is undoubtedly being told something is reliable one minute and making a decision based on that, only to be told later that the intelligence on which they based their decision has now been superseded by new intelligence. Intelligence officers need to be aware of the difficulties this can create, and they need to take cognizance of the feelings of mistrust that such changes can provoke.

11.25 Feedback

When intelligence is used, the agency should have a mechanism whereby the use of that intelligence, and any results obtained from it can be attributed to the origin of that intelligence. Although this is not always possible and can, at best, be difficult, it is necessary to justify the resources employed in intelligence management. Unfortunately, those in intelligence often hide their light under a bushel, because they are so wrapped up in the "need to know culture," or they are so pressed by getting the next job done. This creates a situation where they do not take the time to record successes. They are then left wrong-footed when someone asks what they have contributed or achieved. More importantly, from an agency perspective, the Chief is left bewildered when she is asked why she spent thousands on informants and has nothing to show for it!

11.26   Conclusion

Intelligence is at the core of modern law enforcement. At a strategic level, intelligence is there to provide the Chief and other decision-makers with the knowledge to make better decisions about the nature and extent of the problem they are facing. At a tactical level, intelligence can be and should be used in many different ways to combat criminal activity. Intelligence that is not of any use to one agency may be of significant use to another, and in such a case, what should be done is sharing. However, sometimes the proper thing to do with intelligence is nothing. Criminals will be there tomorrow, and there is little point in compromising a potentially long-term asset for a short-term gain. Knowing what is best to do with intelligence is not something that one just knows; it is a skill that must be learned and developed. Having gold on one's shoulders may give one the right to make a decision with regard to using intelligence, but it does not give one the knowledge to so.

References

Betts, R.K. (1978) Analysis, war and decision: Why intelligence failures are inevitable. *World Politics* 31(1) 61–89.

Cooper, J.R. (2005) *Curing Analytical Pathologies: Pathways to Improved Intelligence Analysis*. Available at https://www.cia.gov/library/center-for-the-study-of-intelligence/csi-publications/books-and-monographs/curing-analytic-pathologies-pathways-to-improved-intelligence-analysis-1/analytic_pathologies_report.pdf (accessed September 2012).

George, A. (1980) *Presidential Decision-Making in Foreign Policy: The Effective Use of Information and Advice*. Boulder, CO: Westview Press.

Greene, J. and Allard, P. (2011) Numbers game: The vicious cycle of incarceration in Mississippi's criminal justice system. A Justice Strategies Report. Available at: http://www.aclu.org/files/assets/DLRP_MississipppiReport_sm.pdf (accessed July 2012).

Klein, G. (2001) *Sources of Power: How People Make Decisions*. Cambridge: MIT Press.

Simon, H. (1957). A behavioral model of rational choice. In: *Models of Man, Social and Rational: Mathematical Essays on Rational Human Behavior in a Social Setting*, pp. 241–260. New York: Wiley.

Challenges and the Way Ahead

12

There is a deeper pleasure in following truth to the scaffold or the cross, than in joining the multitudinous retinue, and mingling our shouts with theirs, when victorious error celebrates its triumphs.

Horace Mann

12.1 Introduction

Creating an effective intelligence management system brings with it a number of challenges, both internally and externally. Perhaps the mind-set to adopt when commencing such a program of reform can best be understood by answering the question, "How do you eat an elephant?" And the answer—"One piece at a time?"*

An effective intelligence management system will only be of benefit if it is fully integrated into decision-making at all levels of the agency. Generally speaking, people will make better decisions if they have more accurate information at the time the decision is being made. As Walsh articulates, "In order to fully understand how intelligence works in different applications and whether it is working effectively, there is also a need to examine the structure of any intelligence system and how components and processes within that system function" (Walsh 2011, p. 91).

The current situation in which many law enforcement agencies (LEAs) pay lip service to the concept of intelligence-led policing, and others delude themselves that they understand and effectively manage intelligence, will persist until there is an acknowledgment of their lack of true understanding and the subsequent implementation of what is effective.

12.2 Arguments over What Is Best Practice

At the time of writing, 10 years after 9/11 and the many subsequent reminders, the dots still are not anywhere near to being joined up, primarily because many can't tell the difference between a dot and a dash or more specifically

---

* Of course some out there might ask, Why would you want to eat an elephant? When it comes to the intelligence management elephant, if you don't eat it (metaphorically speaking), it has the potential to walk all over you!

457

between information and intelligence. Exacerbating the problem is the fact that if law enforcement intelligence was a country, it would be the country of the blind where there are too many one-eyed kings, each claiming expertise in intelligence, when the real experts are few and far between. There remains significant debate as to what is good practice in all the different components of intelligence management. It is difficult to find agreement, but this shouldn't be used as a reason not to try and identify good practice through research and to share that good practice more widely. Research should be carried out involving both practitioners and academics, with each party bringing its knowledge and experience to the table.

12.3   Standardization of Approach

While the overall success of the U.K. National Intelligence Model (NIM) can be debated, one key element that makes it stand out is that it was mandated across all the U.K. police services. This means that all the agencies are using common language and common methodology. Contemporaneously, with the implementation of the NIM, has been the implementation of a raft of other national guidance on all aspects of covert intelligence gathering methods, legislation, and independent national oversight of the implementation of such. Acknowledging that there remain many problems, U.K. LEAs are well ahead of most other agencies in most respects when it comes to collecting and managing intelligence properly. That said they have been on the receiving end of terrorism for over 40 years, which may tend to focus the collective mind.

If the dots are to be joined, then the methods used to gather intelligence need to be at least similar, if not the same across the jurisdiction. For places like the United States, with its huge population and geographical expanse, this may be limited to statewide standards and a statewide intelligence repository. In Canada, despite its relatively large number of police services and a huge territory, it has already commenced creating a nationwide intelligence database, the Canadian Criminal Intelligence System. While there is a significant way to go with creating national standards for intelligence collection methods, their journey has at least begun. In Europe, despite the huge diversity in legislative frameworks, common guidance is being developed in many areas, with countries sharing best practices across various aspects of law enforcement. Many European countries have national police services that obviously make it easier for national intelligence repositories; how well their intelligence management systems work in adding to these repositories is unclear. New Zealand, having the benefit of one national police service, will always be at an advantage in creating an effective intelligence management system, while the fact that its antipodean cousins in Australia have very few police services joining up those intelligence management systems and methods should be relatively easy.

For intelligence management to be effective, agencies need to work to common standards, develop and share best practices, and intelligence repositories need to be connected so that the contents can be easily searched and readily shared where appropriate.

12.4 Need for Capacity Building

Regardless of how clichéd it may sound, the world really is a small place. With the international nature of business, the ease of travel and communication, crime, and terrorism are well established as transnational enterprises. The disparity in wealth and in cultural, religious, and political beliefs among nations provides a backdrop where crime and terrorism are likely to flourish. The failure of those living in modern countries to have any real understanding of what life is like elsewhere creates unrealistic expectations regarding the strategies that governments in the developing nations should adopt to combat crime. To blame a Colombian farmer for growing coca plants to feed his family is disdainful, when one fails to compare it to the banker who has chosen to sniff coke up his nose at $100 a pop.

Furthermore, there is little point criticizing the problems found in law enforcement in emerging nations, unless we are prepared to invest substantial amounts in developing the capabilities of law enforcement in those countries.

12.5 Keep the Baby: Dump the Bathwater

Many will be familiar with the old adage throwing the baby out with the bathwater, a metaphor explaining the disposing of something good while intending to get rid of something bad. Unfortunately for many, when it comes to intelligence management, they can't tell the difference between baby and bathwater, and in their fear of losing the baby, they keep so much bathwater that the baby drowns. A significant part of managing intelligence is about making decisions about what is worth keeping and what is not worth keeping. Deciding what to keep and what to dump requires the involvement of trained staff. If we return to what many view as the cause of 9/11—namely, the failure to join up dots—the reality is that if we now try to keep all the dots, we have no hope whatsoever of seeing the important dots, because there will be so many dots and so many permutations. The belief that software is now so sophisticated it can cope with almost unlimited amounts of information is just that—a belief with no evidence to back it up. And bad as this is, what is worse is the myth that information can be processed into intelligence by some magical piece of software, although the sales literature of some software development companies would often have us believe otherwise. Many in law enforcement invest all their resources striving to pull information from anywhere and put it into any number of different silos, where the reality is they don't have the means to process it. There is much truth in the commentary by Goan et al. (2006) when they remark, "In recent years it has become clear that our ability to create vast information assets far outstrips our ability to exploit and protect them." The idea that just grabbing everything we can get our hands using computer search engines creates the false impression that we are managing intelligence, whereas in reality, all we are achieving is self-delusion. Law enforcement needs to have a much better understanding of what intelligence is and what it is not and many agencies need to have a long hard look at how much actual "intelligence" there is in their intelligence management system.

Unfortunately, some people remain trapped in the mistaken belief that analyzing their crime statistics constitutes intelligence-led policing, failing to realize that the geography of the problem is not necessarily the geography of the cause. Only when the concept of intelligence management is fully understood will law enforcement reap the benefits that it provides.

12.6   Interagency Working

Any intelligence practitioner who has worked in operations or investigations with other agencies is all too aware of the many difficulties that can arise in such joint ventures. When it comes to working together, the management of intelligence can become a significant hurdle if it is not addressed in the early stages. To have a better understanding of some of the issues that may arise, we discuss three of the most common joint working arrangements:

- Operations/investigations involving only police
- Operations/investigations involving local police and national LEAs
- Operations/investigations involving intelligence agencies

Operations involving a number of local LEAs in some ways are, generally speaking, the easiest to mount, as those involved are likely to know the other members involved, if not personally, they know of them or know them through association. There is also likely to be close cooperation in other aspects of law enforcement. When it comes to working in intelligence matters, the biggest hurdle is often the lack of an adequate structure to facilitate effective intelligence sharing for the duration of an investigation. Within the United States, this problem is particularly pronounced and exacerbated by the fact that many individual agencies do not have effective internal intelligence management structures, let alone the ability to create a structure interface with other agencies. Contradicting the view held by some that all LEAs have the capability to undertake the intelligence function, Martens (2011) writes, "In fact most traditional LEAs lack the depth or resources to properly administer the intelligence function." Once the connectivity and other resourcing issues are overcome, the other problem likely to be encountered is that of competing interests from the management of the individual agencies, potentially driven by political pressures. Such issues, if they are likely to arise, should be dealt with in writing before the commencement of the investigation.

Working with national agencies brings its unique problems, the most fundamental one being as to who has the lead in the investigation. This is not always as easily resolved as it may first appear. Often the national agency will take the lead because it is mandated to do so, or because it is supplying the finance for the investigation. However, a local agency may have already commenced an investigation that has subsequently expanded and for whatever reason now needs involvement from the national agency, either from a support perspective or because of the seriousness of the criminality. The conflict that arises in such situations is common to many nations and leads to significant resentment, expressed in various ways. As Osborne (2006) points out, the situation where "local agencies" do the work and the "federal agencies" take the credit will to lead a situation of mistrust. Unfortunately, whether justified or not, it is a concern that most members who are working with a national agency will have.

In considering joint operations between police and intelligence agencies, the underlying cultures will always be a significant problem. Law enforcement is very much "a can do, will do now" culture that is very much based on getting pursuing investigations and getting quantifiable results, mainly in the form of prosecutions. Conscious of public concerns about privacy while being all too aware that everything they do is likely to be exposed in public sooner or later, law enforcement will always have accountability at the forefront of all they do. Intelligence agencies for the most part work toward longer-term, more strategic goals, often having the luxury of time to plan and consider responses with success rarely a tangible thing. Theirs is very much a culture of secrecy, with every aspect of who they are and what they do being guarded. Such a clash of cultures and goals inevitably leads to conflict and disagreement. Highlighting the often dysfunctional relationship between law enforcement and intelligence agencies (referred to as the intelligence community [IC]), Mike Bayer, Branch Chief of Transnational Criminal Investigations Diplomatic Security Service at the U.S. Department of State, writes,

Out of undue regard for certain concerns Law Enforcement and the IC have repeatedly stymied one another. Law enforcement invokes privacy concerns and investigative case secrecy to protect its information. The IC invokes "sources and methods" to protect its capabilities (Bayer 2007).

The reality of the world today and the threats from terrorism, industrial espionage, and cyber attacks mean that law enforcement and intelligence agencies must work hand in hand. To do so, both must change with law enforcement gaining a greater understanding of methodology involved in longer-term intelligence gathering, and the IC gaining a greater understanding of the constraints and pressures under which law enforcement work. Culturally for both sides, there are real challenges.

Agencies are just reflections of the people in that agency, and those people have often been shaped by people who have long since left. Undoubtedly, in many circumstances, there will be historic problems that make building a working relationship difficult, especially if the problem is recent or indeed ongoing. Relationships between agencies take time to build and can easily be damaged by the proverbial agency idiot.* Using dedicated liaison officers to build and stabilize interagency relationships goes a long way to dealing with many of the problems that occur. Provided that the individual chosen has the necessary personality and abilities, he will be able to smooth over many of the bumps in the road that occur in any relationship and to establish greater productivity as a result.

12.7   Joint Task Forces

The nature of modern law enforcement necessitates many joint investigations involving various agencies, with members being seconded from each of these agencies. These agencies are likely to have different structures and procedures for managing intelligence. This has the potential to cause logistical problems with staff, friction between individual members, and interagency conflict. Problems are likely to include the following:

- *Information submission.* Members may feel compelled or be obligated to submit information they receive when taking part in the task force to their own agency as opposed to the task force where it should go. Information may be submitted to the joint task force but never be forwarded to the agencies of the seconded members. The intelligence is lost to all at the conclusion of the task force.

---

* "Agency idiots" would appear to be mandatory in all jurisdictions. Generally speaking, they can be recognized by the more experienced member within about 20 seconds of the first encounter, although it may take longer to identify the more insidious and harmful ones.

- *Competing agendas.* Despite there normally being an agreed mission for the task force, there are often side agendas relating to the participating agencies. This can lead to the limited task force resources being used to pursue intelligence collection to meet the needs of one agency as opposed to the task force as a whole.
- *Conflict with regard to procedures.* Members may be restricted by their agency in using certain collection methods. This creates the potential for dysfunction within the task force.

Many of these problems can be avoided if someone takes the time at the commencement to write down a set of protocols as to how intelligence will be managed and these are signed off on by the respective Chiefs.

12.8   Fusion Centers

Fusion centers came to the forefront in the United States following the 9/11 attacks. Viewed as being part of the solution to address the perceived disconnect between the private sector, local, state, and tribal law enforcement and the various federal agencies, huge sums of money have been invested in making them a reality. However, there has been substantial criticism of their effectiveness.* Without going into the various arguments as to what they are or are not achieving, it is safe to say that while there remains such disparate views in relation to their function and worth, these centers will be unable to achieve their full potential. There is nothing in the construction of an intelligence management system as suggested here that should conflict with the effective functioning of a fusion center. As illustrated in Figure 12.1, fitting with the concept of an intelligence management system that can be widely replicated, all fusion centers should carry out two functions with the option of a third function as follows:

1. Intelligence fusion and the deconfliction function in relation to complex investigations, covert operations, and covert assets.
2. The exchange of material between law enforcement and the private sector with primary reference being in regard to terrorism prevention.
3. The "hosting" of a regional Intelligence Unit.

Before explaining any of the three functions any further, the key issue that requires addressing is as to whether these centers are to focus exclusively

* See report on Fusion Centers: "United States Senate, Committee on Homeland Security and Governmental Affairs, Permanent Sub-committee on Investigations. Carl Levin, Chairman. Federal Support for and Involvement in State and Local Fusion Centers (2012)" and the associated law enforcement response.

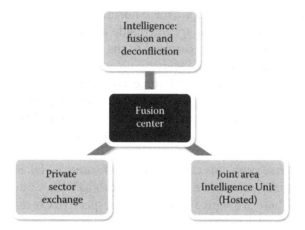

Figure 12.1 A fusion center model.

on terrorism, the function for which the federal government provided the funding, or whether they are to address terrorism and all other criminality, the position to which many have already gravitated. Given that there would be limited other similar structures available for dealing with crime intelligence, the case can clearly be made for adopting an all-crimes approach. Another argument that would point to the same conclusion is that it is increasingly difficult to justify the level of expenditure to address the limited level of terrorism, especially when one contrasts it with the high level of criminality. Regardless of which option is chosen, the three suggested functions can be explained further.

The first function is basically one of joining the dots with the center being used to bring together intelligence from the various agencies within its geographic area of responsibility, in order that the intelligence can be interlinked and analyzed. The need for the greater sharing of intelligence between agencies cannot be denied, and the reluctance of some agencies and officers to share intelligence needs to be addressed. As White (2004) comments, "Despite the police obsession with secrecy, the reasons for not sharing intelligence crashed into the World Trade Center on September 11." A subsidiary function but linked function that a fusion center can perform in support of law enforcement in the geographic area is that of providing a "deconfliction" resource for operations and investigations. Given the nature of fusion centers, this role would seem to rest easily with them, as they have no investigative or operational function and can easily act as an honest broker in dealing with such transactions. When it comes to conflicts that often crop up between agencies over investigations and operations, another way to put it is that fusion centers don't have a dog in that particular fight!

The second function—namely, that of improving the communication with the private sector—should include aspects such as education programs, advice on appropriate risk mitigation to meet the identified threats, and the establishment of point of contact, should law enforcement need industry expertise or opinion.

The third optional function is to host an Intelligence Unit that performs the same role as any other Intelligence Unit, except that it does so for a number of smaller agencies that have insufficient number of staff to justify having a unit of their own. The hosting of such a unit sits well with a fusion center simply because it is likely to be centrally located and have space to hold it. Information collected by each of these smaller agencies is submitted to this Intelligence Unit and the staff there process it into intelligence, storing it in a repository for each agency. They also can disseminate it to the relevant customers. The intelligence is owned and controlled by the relevant Chief and the fusion center has no greater right to access the intelligence than any other agency; the fusion center acts only as host. While the logistics of creating this type of function may initially take some effort, it makes sound operational and economic sense. The arguments over fusion centers, and the problems with some of them, are one of the symptoms related to poor understanding of intelligence management in the law enforcement context.

12.9 People Issues

All too often within agencies, intelligence management is crippled by the internal politics of the agency and what is often euphemistically referred to as "healthy rivalries." These problems can be manifested in many ways: detectives working in one branch snub those in other branches, those in intelligence work viewing their uniform colleagues as lacking in ability or their unsworn colleagues as being untrustworthy, and a reciprocated mistrust between management and staff. These circumstances are nothing new in law enforcement but become more pronounced and are exacerbated by the intelligence context. The "secret" nature of work is often the only spark needed to start the fire. The "need to know" culture in which those involved in intelligence reside becomes resented by colleagues on the outside, and this resentment is often helped on its way by the egos involved. Resentment from those who have attempted selection to intelligence work, but failed, can also fan the flames. Urban myths about what intelligence staff have or have not done in the past just add fuel to the fire and what is left is what can only be described as institutionalized dysfunction.

One can often spot this type of dysfunction within the various units and sub-branches of the intelligence function, with a clamor to see who can be the biggest fish in the pond. In circumstances where knowledge is seen as equating to power, the greater knowledge one has, the greater power one thinks they have, so why would one share that knowledge with anyone else?

In addition, the more one knows, the more indispensable one believes oneself to be, so failing to share intelligence is seen as providing security in one's role.

Get over it! Every member of an agency has a different role to play, regardless of status, rank, or position. No one is more important than anyone else. No role is more important than any other role. If a person is a true professional, others will realize this and those who can't, aren't. Those involved in intelligence are motivated by the same underlying needs and desires that every other person has. They are neither special nor infallible. Internal divisions benefit only the criminals and terrorists.

12.10   Testosterone and Hubris

Fill a room with guys and you will get a pissing contest—crude but true. A huge problem in intelligence management is a lack of diversity when it comes to staff. Without going into the whys and wherefores, the unfortunate reality is that law enforcement remains a male-dominated profession. This does not make for creative thinking. Add a lack of diversity with regard to ethnic background and you have a room full of people thinking with at best, one mind. Give them a few years at the job and you can surely add hubris to the mix. Then what you have is one arrogant mind ... debatably!

In reality, it may not be quite that bad, but there is little doubt that having a team that is diverse in their makeup means it is much more likely to function more effectively than one that is made up of people from similar backgrounds who behave in similar ways.

12.11   Leadership

If an agency is going to make changes into how it gathers, manages, and uses intelligence, then the drive for that change must come from senior management and have the full backing of the Chief. If the drive and the resources are not provided to make such changes, then the agency is just paying lip service to a concept. Intelligence management is like any other aspect of police work; it needs thought, effort, and investment and is continually evolving. Summing up the problems that occur in law enforcement with regard to new ideas, particularly intelligence, Osborne (2006:77) remarks as follows:

> Too often, law enforcement agencies and policymakers praise the new ways of doing business yet do not provide the resources to engage in the processes, including resources. ... Without a redirection of resources, there will be no change. Law enforcement systems themselves resist change, sometimes employing one of the processes in name only, and going on about business as usual.

Leading an LEA is rarely easy, particularly when that agency is dealing with many competing issues. Leaders want and need to know what is happening now and what is likely to happen in the future. An effective intelligence management system can provide Chiefs with a huge amount of what they need to know. How it fits into their agenda* and what they do with that knowledge is their prerogative.

12.12 Training

Intelligence management is a difficult arena in which to work. Many of the skills necessary are part and parcel of everyday law enforcement. However, many others require additional training. Learning is better, easier, quicker, and more cost effective if it is delivered as structured learning. All involved in intelligence management need extensive training and that training must be relevant and realistic to address the problems likely to be encountered in the real world. In recent years, the creation of training environments where no one can be "upset or have their feelings hurt" or where certain words cannot be used or certain topics discussed, these settings are not realistic and therefore the training obtained is not as accurate and structured as it needs to be. Many involved in intelligence gathering will be working in environments that are hostile both from physical and from psychological perspectives. Officers need to be taught skills to meet these threats and assessed to see if they have the resilience to cope under pressure. The place to do this is in the classroom, where a student can "fuck up" in safety and learn from it. All training must be realistic to address what a member is likely to encounter and failure to provide such is negligence on the part of the agency. Competent trainers know what is required; they can explain and justify anything they do in the classroom and should have no concerns about scrutiny.

12.13 Building Expertise

Some LEAs have the benefit of having an individual within their agency who has true expertise in a particular area of intelligence work. These individuals have invested significant time and effort in developing the depth and breadth of their knowledge on a particular subject. While the rest of us went to the bar or the golf course, they put their head into the books and studied to develop their knowledge. Such expertise is a huge asset for any agency, yet the knowledge and worth of many of these individuals may be overlooked by

---

* Chiefs always have an agenda!

their colleagues and managers for various reasons. In volatile situations and during complex operations, overlooking the benefits experts can provide has the potential to cost the agency dearly.

The difference between the behavior of experts and that of others in stressful and evolving situations has been studied at length and has relevance to situations likely to be encountered in exploiting intelligence. Klein (2001) identified that experts can see patterns in events that remain oblivious to the less-experienced person. What is obvious to the experts in an instant may remain totally hidden to another. Experts don't build solutions from scratch at each event. Experts run scripts in their mind that compare the events now occurring with the large volume of events they have previously encountered. They rapidly identify similarities in these events and can correlate with another, enabling them to make a far more rapid decision and one that is sufficient to meet the needs of the circumstances. This process can be so embedded in the mind of an expert that many are unable to explain how and why they have come to the conclusions they have. They do it without conscious thought and with very limited lost from their solution than from what could be later seen as an ideal solution. This degree of expertise is unfortunately limited and can often be overlooked or indeed resented as others fail to understand how the answer has appeared or they feel insecure that they were unable to see the solution the expert has produced. To paraphrase the late Steve Jobs, "Don't employ experts and then tell them what to do!" Agencies should have in place a register of experienced people or experts within their agency that the less-knowledgeable officer can readily turn to when she has a query about an intelligence-related matter.

12.14   Public Issues

"Law enforcement would be a great job but for the public." Everyone involved in law enforcement knows that the public are fickle and when it comes to anything to do with "intelligence," well, then it goes to a whole higher level of "fickleness." Everything to do with intelligence is taken to be code for "secret police" and "citizens disappeared from their beds in the dark of night." And unfortunately for many countries, this was, and in some cases is, the reality of what was understood to be intelligence-related activities by law enforcement. In any modern democracy, the primary task of law enforcement is the protection of citizens, and intelligence is a legitimate tool for law enforcement to use toward that goal. Law enforcement should always have publicly available documents that can inform citizens of the nature of the intelligence work that the agency carries out. Lack of knowledge about intelligence only adds to existing misapprehension and fear within the public that will lead to suspicion and hostility. Most citizens have a lack of any real understanding of the way in which intelligence is gathered and managed. What they see about intelligence activities in which their local LEA is involved conflicts with what they have seen in the movies or on television, where unrealistic expectations have been created and are now not being met.

Very few citizens who are uninvolved in crime know anything about intelligence, but have genuine concerns about its misuse. Those citizens who have the greatest understanding of it are the criminals and their legal representatives, and the terrorists and their political representatives; all have motives to undermine it as a legitimate law enforcement tool. If law enforcement abuses it as a technique and is not proactive in promoting it, then those with the most to gain from diminishing its use will be in a position of ascendency.

What should always be stressed and understood is that criminal investigation and intelligence gathering are not separate functions. The reason that law enforcement has an intelligence function is to prevent or investigate crime and/or to preserve public safety and order. The belief that the law enforcement intelligence function within modern democracies is some Orwellian conspiracy to oppress citizens would be laughable, if it wasn't used by some to hamstring effective law enforcement.

12.15 Dealing with Media

LEAs are public bodies and very much accountable to the citizens they serve. The public has a right to know how their taxes are being spent and to be reassured that law enforcement is not abusing the power that citizens have entrusted them with. The way that the public get its information about law enforcement is through the media. The press, radio, and television all eagerly follow law enforcement activities, looking for anything to fill up column inches or airtime. Intelligence work is a rich picking ground for stories, and as such law enforcement needs to be aware that its activities are being scrutinized with a fine-toothed comb. Law enforcement must be aware of what it releases to the press. If too little is released, then the perception will be that law enforcement is hiding something. If too much is released, then it has the potential to compromise valuable assets. Where executive action has been taken, and that action is as a result of intelligence, no press statement should be made without consultation with the intelligence manager as to what can be released. In addition, the agency should use only trained people to speak with the media. Not only does this reduce the chances of having the agency idiot appear on national television, but it also reduces the chances of that individual compromising the origin of the information and/or sensitive methodology. Compromises such as these can affect not only that agency but also every other agency in the jurisdiction. Far too often, law enforcement members appear on television either in press conferences or on "fly on the wall documentaries" and discuss methodology that there is no need to discuss, other than to satisfy the member's ego. The Australian's have an acronym for such an individual: "FIGJAM" which stands for "I'm good, just ask me!"*

There is no doubt that LEAs need to be proactive in how they inform the public about their use of intelligence gathering and the importance of it—it is after all a form of advertising. Generally speaking, such discussions should not include any mention of specific intelligence gathering techniques that were used. For example, if the police make a number of arrests, and they release a press statement saying it was done as a result of using a "confidential informant," then the criminals are going to start specifically looking for someone. De facto the agency has put a person's life at risk and for what? Why tell the bad guys how we do our business? Any statements about the use of sensitive methodology should be done in general terms. There is a lot that law enforcement can learn from the intelligence community about operation security and learning to keep one's mouth shut. The real professional working in the world of intelligence knows that results will speak for themselves and is left cringing by those who need acclamation for what they have done.

12.16   Transparency

LEAs are not the same as intelligence agencies; they are much more accountable to the citizens they serve. While many aspects of the methodology used in intelligence management need to be kept secret, there is also a need for law enforcement to be transparent in what they are doing and why. This book has made numerous suggestions around building a system that safeguards citizens' rights, and law enforcement should not hesitate in making the public aware of the existence of such structures. If an agency is subject to external oversight or inquiry, it should be proactive in disclosing what can safely be disclosed around procedures structures and training. Far too often, metaphorically speaking, law enforcement shoots itself in the foot by adopting an attitude of withholding everything. Law enforcement should readily give what can be given, readily state what cannot be given and explain why it cannot be given, and if it is forced by the courts to give material the disclosure of which is likely to cause real harm, include with the requested material a comprehensive assessment of that harm that will be caused. Acknowledging that there may, in limited cases, be "hidden agendas" on the part of some inquirers, law enforcement should always seek to build a relationship based

---

* The "F" in the acronym is not a typo. Work it out yourself!

on cooperation and openness. The LEA should have nothing to hide in regard to how it conducts its business.

12.17 Information from Citizens

Citizens will always have a fear associated with giving information to law enforcement, especially if law enforcement does not have in place adequate structures to protect the identity of the citizen from the outset and is not proactive in continuing to protect their identity from becoming public knowledge in any subsequent judicial process. Law enforcement must create structures that will protect citizens who give information and must make citizens aware that such structures exist, to allay their fears and encourage the supply of information.

Specifically, in U.S. law enforcement, there are too many officers who are shoddy in relation to protecting the identities of "confidential informants," with significant number of informants being exposed in the press and in the courts on a daily basis. This situation often arises through lazy police work during an investigation, the presence of a results-based mind-set and a reluctance to make the effort to protect the informant's identity in courts. Mismanagement of human sources in the United States has been well documented (Natapoff 2009; Brown 2010; Greene and Allard 2011; Jones-Brown and Shane 2011), and the current situation causes significant harm to the effectiveness of law enforcement's intelligence capabilities. For the benefit of both law enforcement and the public it serves, the situation needs to be remedied. Some work to remedy this has begun with the introduction of "informant"-related legislation in a number of states.

12.18 Legislation

In every jurisdiction, there will be legislation that affects how law enforcement executes its role. In intelligence management, there is often specific legislation and/or government policy documents that dictate how and why intelligence can be gathered, stored, and shared. In addition, there are often other pieces of legislation that, although off the radar to mainstream law enforcement, can have an impact on intelligence management. Regardless of the nature of the legislation or policy, those involved in intelligence management need to have a sound knowledge of *all* relevant legislation and policy and the impact that it can have on their role. Furthermore, those involved in intelligence management need to be proactive in monitoring forthcoming legislation to ensure that there is no negative impact on their ability to function. When legislative change is needed to ensure effective intelligence management, law enforcement should be vigorous in the pursuit of such change. Given that intelligence management is only a part of their remit, any legislative change for intelligence purposes is likely to be only one of many concerns that a Chiefs has. Professional law enforcement bodies and/ or national working groups, which specialize in intelligence, need to take the lead on behalf of all agencies and their respective Chiefs, setting aside minor differences to present a view that is united from the intelligence professional's perspective.

12.19 Financial Constraints

Often the excuse not to make changes in an agency's intelligence management system is "lack of finance." Law enforcement will always have limited resources, but using intelligence properly makes law enforcement much more cost-effective. Not using intelligence effectively wastes resources and causes harm to the public, sometimes significant harm. There are few LEAs that would not benefit from a review of their intelligence management structures, with such a review providing greater efficiency and significant long-term cost savings. When, as a result of review, a number of agencies pool resources and share in the development of an intelligence management system, planning should include the use of the money from the undoubted cost savings that will be made. These savings should be reinvested to obtain the best software that meets the needs of those involved and so increase and perpetuate the total cost savings over the longer term. Other potential financial benefits of review include reducing the risk of things going wrong, the attendant financial costs in lawsuits, and increased productivity from staff, as frustrations with existing practices are diminished.

12.20 Conclusion

Intelligence management continues to change with some agencies and some countries being further ahead than others. In many ways, intelligence management in the law enforcement context is evolving in the way a new generation emerges from under the shadows of an older generation. This emerging generation has a long path to tread to establish its own terminology, standards, and methods, as opposed to the ones they have been given and relied upon from the previous generation. At the same time, the older generation, those in the IC and the military, have to cope with a changing world where, arguably, the newer generation has more relevance for the majority of citizens. Intelligence management is a major aspect in law enforcement's efforts to combat crime and terrorism and in public safety. However, there still remain too many in law enforcement without a sufficient level of understanding to maximize the potential benefits. Although there remains significant work to do, there is sufficient knowledge and desire among many professionals to remedy the current shortcomings.

Law enforcement's strength has always come from sharing good and bad practices and learning from what other agencies do well and the consequences of others doing something badly. Unfortunately, the failure to learn from the mistakes of others, or to accept that others are doing something in a better way, is still evident in the majority of countries. The writer Douglas Adams said, "Human beings, who are almost unique in having the ability to learn from the experience of others, are also remarkable for their apparent disinclination to do so." And no better examples of this would he find than in law enforcement.

Some may find that they already knew much of what has been contained in this book and that explanation at such a level is way below the members of any agency. Some may feel that the comments are overly critical and that no one in law enforcement would ever make the basic mistakes alluded to here. Everything discussed in this book is based on what has been observed in researching and writing the book. If your agency has *everything* in place that is suggested, then the Chief and staff deserve commending for that. If you feel you have wasted your money—well, that is unfortunate, but maybe you can draw some comfort from the fact that the real cost of this book was paid for long before the pen hit the paper with lives that could have been saved. What was intended in writing the book has been to help law enforcement officers do a better job in managing intelligence. It is about adding to knowledge and generating discussion. If the author knew it all, and had all the solutions then…but that's a different story.

References

Bayer, M. (2007) *Can't We All Just Get Along? Improving the Law Enforcement-Intelligence Community Relationship.* National Defense Intelligence College. Washington, DC: NDIC Press.

Brown, E. (2010) *Snitch: Informants, Cooperators, and the Corruption of Justice.* New York: Public Affairs.

Goan, T., Fujioka, E., Knaneshiro, R., and Gasch, L. (2006) Identifying information provenance in support of intelligence analysis, sharing and protection. In: *Intelligence and Security Informatics. Proceedings of the 4th IEEE International Conference on Intelligence and Security Informatics.* San Diego, California, pp. 692–693.

Greene, J. and Allard, P. (2011) *Numbers Game: The Vicious Cycle of Incarceration in Mississippi's Criminal Justice System. A Justice Strategies Report.* Available at: http://www.aclu.org/files/assets/DLRP_MississipppiReport_sm.pdf (accessed July 2012).

Jones-Brown, D. and Shane, J.M. (2011) *An Exploratory Study of the Use of Confidential Informants in New Jersey: A Report Commissioned by the American Civil Liberties Union (ACLU) of New Jersey in Partnership with the Criminal Law Reform Project of the American Civil Liberties Union*. John Jay College of Criminal Justice. City University of New York. Available at: http://www.aclu-nj.org/files/1113/1540/4573/0611ACLUCIReportBW.pdf (accessed December 2012).

Klien, G. (2001) *Sources of Power: How People Make Decisions*. Cambridge, USA: MIT Press.

Martens, F.T. (2011) Uses, abuses and misuses of intelligence. In: Wright, R., Morehouse, B., Peterson, M.B. and Palmieri, L. Eds. *Criminal Intelligence for the 21st Century: A Guide for Intelligence Professionals*, pp. 192–203. Sacramento, CA; Richmond, VA: Law Enforcement Intelligence Units (LEIU) ; International Association of Law Enforcement Intelligence Analysts (IALEIA).

Natapoff, A. (2009) *Snitching: Criminal Informants and the Erosion of American Justice*. New York: New York University Press.

Osborne, D. (2006) *Out of Bounds: Innovation and Change in Law Enforcement Intelligence Analysis*. Washington, DC: Joint Military Intelligence College.

United States Senate—Committee on Homeland Security and Governmental Affairs—Permanent Sub-committee on Investigations. Carl Levin, Chairman. (2012) *Federal Support for and Involvement in State and Local Fusion Centers*. Available at: http://www.hsgac.senate.gov/download/report_federal-support-for-and-involvement- in-state-and-local-fusions-centers (accessed October 2012).

Walsh, P.F. (2011) *Intelligence and Intelligence Analysis*. New York; London, UK: Routledge.

White, J. (2004) *Defending the Homeland: Domestic Intelligence, Law Enforcement, and Security*. Belmont, CA: Thomson/Wadsworth.

Author's Note

I genuinely hope this book has been of use to you. Any faults you find in it are mine and mine alone. Though we may strive for perfection, we rarely get there and sometimes we have to be satisfied with what we have achieved, albeit far from what we wanted. Writing this book has taught me a lot about how little I really know about managing intelligence compared with what I thought I knew. I do not know why this should surprise me because I spent most of my life thinking I was intelligent only to find one afternoon that I was not even half as smart as I thought I was. Stay safe out there and do not forget—the really important things are at home.

Index

A

Abilene paradox, 133
Academic papers, non-IT related open source, 385
Access-level repositing, 204–206
Accountability, case law principle, 89
Actionable intelligence, 72
Agency records, 375–377
Agency's intelligence management systems, 229–233
Air India Inquiry, 14
American Psychiatric Association, 118
Analysis
    adding value, 303
    association, 332
    briefing products, 346–347
    communication, 332–334
    covert operations, 348–349
    crime, 303–304
    crime pattern, 321–322
    criminal business profiles, 324
    definition, 310
    demographic, 338–339
    drawing conclusions, 313
    event flow charts, 335–336
    facilitating integrated, 308–309
    factors for reporting, 312
    financial, 334–335
    geographic, 336–338
    integrated, 303–308
    intelligence, 303
    market profile, 331
    network, 324–326
    problem profiles, 317–321
    qualitative, 312
    quantitative, 311–312
    results, 331–332
    risk, 340–341
    risk assessment, 342–345
    risk-related products, 339–341
    social network, 326–329
    social trend, 338–339
    spatial vulnerability, 329–331
    strategic assessment, 347–348
    tactical assessment, 348
    target profile, 322–323
    technology on, 349
    threat assessment, 341–342
    victim profile, 323–324
    vulnerability assessment, 342–343
Analysts
    vs. collector, 301
    experienced, 310
    intelligence gaps, 317
    law enforcement, 304
    limitations, 299
    misconceptions, 299–301
    reporting, 314–315, 349
    statistical data, 305
    visualization, 301–302
Analytical products
    creation of, 315–316
    vs. intelligence products, 306
Anonymity, Human Rights, 89–90
Article entity, 261–262
Association analysis, 332
Association of Chief Police Officers, 34
Attractiveness, 343
Attribution bias, 132–133
Attribution theory, 121
Audit, 294
Australian version of intelligence cycle, 150
Automated vehicle plate readers, 395–397

B

Ballistic history, forensic information, 380
Being wrong, 142–143
Betweenness centrality, 327
Blackmail, ethical dilemmas, 115
Bounded rationality, 132
Briefing products, 346–347
Briefings, 438–439
Business continuity planning, 293